WHAT REMAINS

SPEKTRUM: Publications of the German Studies Association
Series editor: David M. Luebke, University of Oregon

Published under the auspices of the German Studies Association, Spektrum offers current perspectives on culture, society, and political life in the German-speaking lands of central Europe—Austria, Switzerland, and the Federal Republic—from the late Middle Ages to the present day. Its titles and themes reflect the composition of the GSA and the work of its members within and across the disciplines to which they belong—literary criticism, history, cultural studies, political science, and anthropology.

Recent volumes:

Volume 24
What Remains: Responses to the Legacy of Christa Wolf
Edited by Gerald A. Fetz and Patricia Herminghouse

Volume 23
Minority Discourses in Germany since 1990
Edited by Ela Gezen, Priscilla Layne, and Jonathan Skolnik

Volume 22
Beyond Posthumanism
The German Humanist Tradition and the Future of the Humanities
Alexander Mathäs

Volume 21
Feelings Materialized
Emotions, Bodies, and Things in Germany, 1500–1950
Edited by Derek Hillard, Heikki Lempa, and Russell Spinney

Volume 20
Names and Naming in Early Modern Germany
Edited by Marjorie Elizabeth Plummer and Joel F. Harrington

Volume 19
Views of Violence
Representing the Second World War in German and European Museums and Memorials
Edited by Jörg Echternkamp and Stephan Jaeger

Volume 18
Dreams of Germany
Musical Imaginaries from the Concert Hall to the Dance Floor
Edited by Neil Gregor and Thomas Irvine

Volume 17
Money in the German-speaking Lands
Edited by Mary Lindemann and Jared Poley

Volume 16
Archaeologies of Confession
Writing the German Reformation, 1517–2017
Edited by Carina L. Johnson, David M. Luebke, Marjorie Elizabeth Plummer, and Jesse Spohnholz

Volume 15
Ruptures in the Everyday
Views of Modern Germany from the Ground
Andrew Bergerson, Leonard Schmieding, et al.

For a full volume listing, please see the series page on our website:
http://berghahnbooks.com/series/spektrum

What Remains

Responses to the Legacy of Christa Wolf

Edited by Gerald A. Fetz and Patricia Herminghouse

berghahn
NEW YORK · OXFORD
www.berghahnbooks.com

First published in 2022 by
Berghahn Books
www.berghahnbooks.com

© 2022, 2026 Gerald A. Fetz and Patricia Herminghouse
First paperback edition published in 2026

All rights reserved. Except for the quotation of short passages
for the purposes of criticism and review, no part of this book
may be reproduced in any form or by any means, electronic or
mechanical, including photocopying, recording, or any information
storage and retrieval system now known or to be invented,
without written permission of the publisher.

Library of Congress Cataloging-in-Publication Data
Names: Fetz, Gerald Alan, 1944- editor. | Herminghouse, Patricia, editor.
Title: What remains : responses to the legacy of Christa Wolf / edited by
  Gerald A. Fetz and Patricia Herminghouse.
Description: New York : Berghahn Books, 2022. | Series: Spektrum:
  publications of the German Studies Association ; 24 | Includes
  bibliographical references and index.
Identifiers: LCCN 2022004590 (print) | LCCN 2022004591 (ebook) | ISBN
  9781800734968 (hardback) | ISBN 9781800734975 (ebook)
Subjects: LCSH: Wolf, Christa--Criticism and interpretation. | Memory in
  literature. | LCGFT: Literary criticism. | Essays.
Classification: LCC PT2685.O36 Z964 2022 (print) | LCC PT2685.O36 (ebook)
  | DDC 833/.914--dc23/eng/20220204
LC record available at https://lccn.loc.gov/2022004590
LC ebook record available at https://lccn.loc.gov/2022004591

British Library Cataloguing in Publication Data
A catalogue record for this book is available from the British Library

EU GPSR Authorized Representative
LOGOS EUROPE, 9 rue Nicolas Poussin, 17000, LA ROCHELLE, France
Email: Contact@logoseurope.eu

ISBN 978-1-80073-496-8 hardback
ISBN 978-1-83695-367-8 paperback
ISBN 978-1-83695-366-1 epub
ISBN 978-1-80073-497-5 web pdf

https://doi.org/10.3167/9781800734968

Dedicated to the memory of David Bathrick

~: CONTENTS :~

List of Illustrations	ix
Introduction Gerald A. Fetz and Patricia Herminghouse	1

Part I. Patterns of Memory: The Trauma of the Forgotten

Chapter 1. "Faraway So Close": Transcultural Memory as Christa Wolf's "Last Word" Silke von der Emde	21
Chapter 2. Who's Afraid of Christa Wolf or The Overcoat of Dr. Freud: Memory and Its Discontents Martina Kolb	34
Chapter 3. Fetishism or Working Through? Concerning the Role of Dr. Freud in *City of Angels or, The Overcoat of Dr. Freud* David Bathrick	62

Part II. Christa Wolf as a Writer of Time and Her Times

Chapter 4. The Notion of *Heimat* in Christa Wolf's *Patterns of Childhood* Marijke Mulder	73
Chapter 5. Writing the Self: Literary *Vergegenwärtigung* in Christa Wolf's *Patterns of Childhood* and *City of Angels or, The Overcoat of Dr. Freud* Mark Lauer	85
Chapter 6. The Heterochronic Narrative of Christa Wolf Heike Polster	99
Chapter 7. Subjective Authenticity as Realism: Christa Wolf and Georg Lukács Robert Blankenship	110

Part III. Christa Wolf in the Public Sphere

Chapter 8. To Be Recognized Again: Memory, Amnesia, and Sincerity in Christa Wolf 125
Christine Kanz

Chapter 9. "Was bleibt aber, stiften die Dichter": Christa Wolf's Contested Role as Spokesperson for Generations of Readers and Women Writers 136
Janine Ludwig

Chapter 10. "This Is No Longer My World": The Multiple Alienations of Christa Wolf 157
Daniela Colombo

Part IV. Illness, Anxiety, and Trauma

Chapter 11. "To Follow the Trail of Pain": Coming to Terms with the Past in Christa Wolf's *In the Flesh* 171
Deborah Janson

Chapter 12. Deliberating the "ängstliche Margarete": Coping with Anxiety in Christa Wolf's *City of Angels or, the Overcoat of Dr. Freud* 188
Ivett Rita Guntersdorfer

Chapter 13. Coming Full Circle: Trauma, Empathy, and Writing in "Change of Perspective" ("Blickwechsel," 1970) and "August" (2011) 201
Friederike Eigler

Part V. Christa Wolf and the Visual Arts

Chapter 14. A Woman's Voice on Screen: Christa Wolf and the Cinema 217
Barton Byg

Chapter 15. Women at the Edge of a Nervous Breakdown: The Berlin Wall and the Collapse of Female Consciousness in *Divided Heaven* and *Good Bye, Lenin!* 232
Susanne Rinner

Chapter 16. The Impact of Christa Wolf's *Cassandra* on Women Artists in East Germany 244
April A. Eisman

Index 265

ILLUSTRATIONS

Figure 2.1. Sigmund Freud's Loden Overcoat (on the door to his study, near the couch). Photograph by Martina Kolb (April 2014). Courtesy of the Freud Museum London.   44

Figure 16.1. Heidrun Hegewald, *Cassandra Sees a Serpent's Egg* (*Kassandra sieht ein Schlangenei*), 1981, acrylic on canvas, 134 × 154 cm. Photo: Kunstarchiv Beeskow © 2021 Artists Rights Society (ARS), New York / VG Bild-Kunst, Bonn.   247

Figure 16.2. Nuria Quevedo, Study for *Cassandra* (*Kassandra*) by Christa Wolf, 1982, charcoal, 87.6 × 60.3 cm. Photo: Paetzold 1986/Deutsche Fotothek © 2021 Artists Rights Society (ARS), New York / VG Bild-Kunst, Bonn.   248

Figure 16.3. Nuria Quevedo, Study for *Cassandra* (*Kassandra*) by Christa Wolf, 1982, charcoal, 87.6 × 60.3 cm. Photo: Paetzold 1986/Deutsche Fotothek © 2021 Artists Rights Society (ARS), New York / VG Bild-Kunst, Bonn.   249

Figure 16.4. Nuria Quevedo, Study for *Cassandra* (*Kassandra*) by Christa Wolf, 1982, charcoal, 87.6 × 60 cm. Photo: Paetzold 1986/Deutsche Fotothek © 2021 Artists Rights Society (ARS), New York / VG Bild-Kunst, Bonn.   250

Figure 16.5. Angela Hampel, print from the series on *Cassandra* (*Kassandra*) by Christa Wolf, 1984–85, gouache and acrylic on paper, 110.5 × 85 cm. Kulturstiftung Sachsen-Anhalt, Kunstmuseum Moritzburg Halle (Saale). Photo: Punctum/Bertram Kober © 2021 Artists Rights Society (ARS), New York / VG Bild-Kunst, Bonn.   252

Figure 16.6. Angela Hampel, *Come, Cassandra …* (*Komm, Kassandra …*), from the seven-print series *Kassandra*, 1984, lithograph, 52 × 70 cm. Kulturstiftung Sachsen-Anhalt, Kunstmuseum Moritzburg Halle (Saale). Photo: Kulturstiftung Sachsen-Anhalt © 2021 Artists Rights Society (ARS), New York / VG Bild-Kunst, Bonn.   253

Figure 16.7. Angela Hampel, from the series *Cassandra (Kassandra)/Penthesilea*, 1984/85, lithograph, 52 × 60 cm. Kunstfonds Dresden © 2021 Artists Rights Society (ARS), New York / VG Bild-Kunst, Bonn. 254

Figure 16.8. Angela Hampel, *And us? (Und wir?)*, from the seven-print series *Cassandra (Kassandra)*, 1984, lithograph, 47.7 × 75.8 cm. Kulturstiftung Sachsen-Anhalt, Kunstmuseum Moritzburg Halle (Saale). Photo: Kulturstiftung Sachsen-Anhalt © 2021 Artists Rights Society (ARS), New York / VG Bild-Kunst, Bonn. 255

Figure 16.9. Angela Hampel, painting on the cover of Christa Wolf's novel *Cassandra (Kassandra)*, dtv series © 2021 Artists Rights Society (ARS), New York / VG Bild-Kunst, Bonn. 259

Figure 16.10. Angela Hampel, *Hope Dies Last (Die Hoffnung stirbt zuletzt)*, 2012, mixed media, 100 × 70 cm. Photo: Angela Hampel. © 2021 Artists Rights Society (ARS), New York / VG Bild-Kunst, Bonn. 260

INTRODUCTION

GERALD A. FETZ AND PATRICIA HERMINGHOUSE

In the course of a literary career that spanned over fifty years, Christa Wolf was awarded many of the most prestigious literary prizes available to writers in the two German states, as well as prizes and honors bestowed by other countries in Europe and abroad. She was also mentioned repeatedly as a likely nominee for the Nobel Prize in Literature. With her literary works now translated into over thirty languages around the world, some of them in new translations, Wolf's works are read, taught, discussed, and debated extensively, beginning with her first publication *Moskauer Novelle* (1961; Moscow Novella) and continuing into the present, more than ten years after the publication of her final novel, *Stadt der Engel oder The Overcoat of Dr. Freud* (2010; *City of Angels or, The Overcoat of Dr. Freud*, 2013). However, as recent studies of Wolf suggest, many aspects of her work still invite further exploration.

The scholars whose essays comprise this collection pursue such new lines of inquiry into Wolf's oeuvre. As their essays attest, Wolf was an experimental writer who employed shifting poetological forms, which themselves often became themes in her works. The essays presented here were selected for their unique approaches, which offer new ways of reading and understanding Wolf's topics, issues, and texts. They also explore the relevance of these works for contemporary readers and provide evidence for the claim that Wolf's legacy as an exceptional writer of fiction and non-fiction endures.

Patterns of Memory

A major focus of the volume is Wolf's understanding of and engagement with memory in its positive (remembering) and negative (forgetting) manifestations. Attention to patterns of memory is evident in virtually all of her literary works, where memory functions as both a versatile narrative strategy and, not infrequently, as a complex and multifaceted theme itself. Together with personal experience, memory forms a major component of Wolf's approach to writing, which she termed "subjective authenticity."[1]

Dwelling on the past, however, was discouraged by East German political and cultural authorities, who were almost singularly focused on building a socialist future. Their future-oriented ideology espoused the false notion that the past, especially the Nazi era, was no longer of interest or relevance for postwar East Germans, asserting that, as an avowed anti-fascist state, the GDR (in contrast to the Federal Republic) did not bear any responsibility for remembering and working through that dark period of German history.

Initially, Christa Wolf appeared to accept these rationalizations. She repressed much about her life and that of her parents between Hitler's ascent to power in early 1933 to the end of World War II in 1945. That perspective shifted, however, when Wolf, her husband, and one of their daughters traveled to the town (now in Poland) where she had spent her first fifteen years, before the family fled westward as the Red Army approached. This 1971 trip and the surprising memories she recovered in her birthplace showed Wolf the consequences of such forgetting. She subsequently sought to work through her newly gained insights, including embarrassment and shame for having supported the Nazis as an enthusiastic member of the *Bund deutscher Mädel* (League of German Girls). By articulating a willingness to reflect on her past, she began to understand that she had not allowed herself to know who she was as a girl and how this still affected her identity twenty-five years later. Wolf's experiences in coming to terms with these repressed memories play a key role in her second novel, *Kindheitsmuster* (1976; *Patterns of Childhood*, 1980).

As she illustrates clearly in many of her subsequent novels and stories, this experience led Wolf to reject completely the claim that, unlike West Germans, East Germans had no reason to confront the Nazi past and engage in *Vergangenheitsbewältigung*. Indeed, that life-changing trip led Wolf not only to embark upon the long, arduous, and important process of remembering and working through the Nazi period, but also to develop an increasingly complicated and ambivalent relationship to the GDR. She gradually became skeptical of its promise to create a humane form of socialism, as the country increasingly pursued an inhumane and authoritarian reality. The trip to Poland and the subsequent process of writing *Patterns of Childhood* laid the groundwork for Wolf's profound recognition of the central role of memory as the focus of her creative work.

Last Words: The Trauma of the Forgotten

In the essay that opens this volume, "'Faraway So Close': Transcultural Memory as Christa Wolf's 'Last Word,'" Silke von der Emde traces the evolution of Wolf's concept of memory in her major works over almost fifty years, from the early *Moskauer Novelle* to *City of Angels or, The Overcoat of Dr. Freud*. Von der Emde points out how Wolf's concept and practice of remembering became more complex, dialogic, and feminist throughout her writing career until, in that last major novel, memory discourse ultimately moves beyond personal experiences and national concerns to global and international experiences that involve, extend, and deepen the concept of memory itself. "By displacing her memory work to Los Angeles," von der Emde asserts, "Wolf deterritorializ[es] German memory by bringing it into dialogue with non-GDR and even non-German perspectives." Not least among these are the community of diasporic German-Jewish refugees in Los Angeles; the Black housekeeping staff of Wolf's hotel (especially the migrant Ugandan Angelina); and even an extinct Native American tribe of Anasazi desert inhabitants. Drawing upon recent theoretical insights in the memory research of Daniel Levy, Natan Sznaider, Michael Rothberg, and Andreas Huyssen, among others, von der Emde demonstrates the possibilities that inhere in such a multi-vocal, transnational approach to memory discourses.

In his essay, "Fetishism or Working Through? Concerning the Role of Dr. Freud in *City of Angels or, The Overcoat of Dr. Freud*," David Bathrick expresses surprise at another neglected aspect of the novel: the last five words of its title. Addressing the psychoanalytical implications of a narrative voice that explains its epistemological focus, Bathrick cites the famous lines of the narrator: "It's about memories, about how we remember ... And somehow I could have forgotten *that*." Bathrick interrogates the trauma of the forgotten that was unleashed when, after gaining access to her Stasi file in 1992, Wolf was compelled to remember her collaboration with the East German secret police, who enlisted her as an informant (*inoffizieller Mitarbeiter* or IM) in the years 1959–62, just as she embarked upon her writing career. Citing the narrator's assertion at the end of *Patterns of Childhood* that memory functions to make it "impossible to avoid the mortal sin of our time: the desire not to come to terms with oneself," Bathrick calls attention to the numerous instances in Wolf's final novel that reference the moral and religious dimensions of remembrance. Amid the crisis caused by the narrator's attempt to understand how she could have forgotten her brief, youthful phase as a Stasi informer, her friend Sally challenges her wishful attribution of the fetish-like power of the overcoat to protect and comfort her: "On the contrary, said Sally. It's there to take your self-defense mechanisms away from you." At this juncture, Bathrick—referencing Eric Santner's work on "narrative fetishism"—juxtaposes the prescribed narrative of anti-fascism in the GDR, which functioned to absolve people from reflecting on their own complicity in beliefs and practices that were the legacy of Stalinism, with the situation in postwar West Germany, where the well-known paradigm of the "inability to mourn" described the difficulty in commencing a process of *Trauerarbeit* and "coming to terms" with the legacy of National Socialism. In the strikingly different environment of the Los Angeles Getty Institute, however, Wolf's narrator finally attains the strength to open herself to new experiences and different perspectives, enabling a form of historical witnessing that does not depend on the protection of a fetishistic raincoat.

In her essay, "Who's Afraid of Christa Wolf or The Overcoat of Dr. Freud: Memory and Its Discontents," Martina Kolb also remarks on how little detailed attention critics have expended on interpretations of that eponymous "Overcoat of Dr. Freud." She points out that Wolf had indeed seen this coat in a 1992 exhibition at the London Freud Museum shortly before she departed for California. In the novel, Wolf's narrator reports hearing a Getty colleague's account of how he had lost a coat of Freud's given to him by the widow of the architect Richard Neutra, a story from which she derives a title for the novel she began to write in Los Angeles. Grounding her analysis in Freudian theory, Kolb examines the function of this phantasmic coat described as "an imaginative fabrication rather than a material presence" in the realm between remembrance and repression. Like Bathrick, Kolb reads the coat as the narrator's fetish. Materially absent but verbally present, the coat functions as the narrator's interlocutor in what suddenly emerges as the all-consuming struggle in her life to understand her forgotten collusion with the Stasi. In addition to fetishism, Kolb draws on other Freudian concepts including the uncanny, transference, and repetition, to trace what she terms "the phantasmagoric scope of Freud's coat." Ultimately, her analysis demonstrates the ways in which Wolf dismantles the complex fabric of memory and oblivion in her final novel.

Subjective Authenticity: Christa Wolf Writes of Her Times

Memory plays a critical role not only in Wolf's plots and storylines, but also in the aesthetic form and narrative style of her texts. This style was criticized initially by GDR officials, making the process of publication approval for her work in the late 1960s and 1970s tedious and protracted. The officials condemned her modernist form as decadent and antithetical to the official doctrine of socialist realism, which insisted on simple, chronological storylines and didactic themes. Wolf accepted some features of socialist realism in her first literary work *Moskauer Novelle*, but she clearly rejected its precepts in *Der geteilte Himmel* (1963; *Divided Heaven*, 1965), moving even further from the doctrine in her subsequent novel, *Nachdenken über Christa T.* (1968; *The Quest for Christa T.*, 1971).

By 1965 Wolf had already grown genuinely skeptical with regard to the notion of socialist realism, and she spoke out as a "candidate member" of the Central Committee of the SED at its 11th Plenary Session that year, advocating for more open and experimental forms of writing. Wolf asserted that "art is not possible without taking chances, that means, art must ask questions that are new, that the artist believes to see, even those for which he cannot yet find an answer, a solution."² Perhaps unsurprisingly, her assertions and suggestions were completely rejected. In response, Wolf doubled down in the pursuit of her own alternative vision, which she termed "subjective authenticity," an approach that aims to give literary expression to social reality by intertwining personal experience with historical developments. In addition to memory work, Wolf's subjective authenticity also entails a deep engagement with time. Wolf challenges her readers to cease conceiving of time as a chronological and natural truth. That challenge forces us to think critically about how her complex notion of time also affects our reading and understanding of the content and meaning of her works.

Intertwined with Wolf's challenge to time is her critical focus on space, including the displacement that was a facet of her early life. In "The Notion of *Heimat* in Christa Wolf's *Patterns of Childhood*," Marijke Mulder addresses the important but neglected concept of *Heimat*, which she sees as constitutive of self-understanding in Wolf's work. Mulder begins her essay by reading *Heimat* as a highly ambivalent concept that offers security while also posing a threat to the individual and proceeds to examine the complicated experience of Nelly, the protagonist of *Patterns of Childhood*, when she travels to her original *Heimat*, Landsberg an der Warthe, in the part of Germany that was ceded to Poland after World War II. Despite the significant time lapse since she was last there, the city—now the Polish Gorzów—still seems in some strange way to be her real *Heimat*. As Mulder argues, this encounter with her original *Heimat* affects and changes Nelly, altering her sense of time. Mulder identifies three phases of memory work in the protagonist/narrator's attempts to revisit her relationship to *Heimat*, beginning with the "breakdown of her resistance" to undertaking an actual journey to the locus of her childhood. During her sojourn there, which comprises the second stage of the memory project, her emotional sense of connectedness to that place is reawakened as she encounters the sights, sounds, and smells of her childhood and re-experiences the sense of belonging that Mulder identifies as the basic experience of *Heimat*. For the adult narrator, however, displacement from the place that she can never again refer to as her real *Heimat*, due to the "ideological corruption" of the word by Nazi propaganda, creates an ambivalence with which, in a third stage, the narrator struggles as she undertakes to write an account of the journey. In the process, as Mulder notes, Wolf "shifts the objective from an account of a simple visit to her hometown to a more honest self-examination that no longer denies the complexity of the *Heimat* sentiment or its positive qualities. ... For her the novel appears to serve as a vehicle for exploring the question, 'How did we become what we are today?'"

In "Writing the Self: Literary *Vergegenwärtigung* in Christa Wolf's *Patterns of Childhood* and *City of Angels or, The Overcoat of Dr. Freud*," Mark Lauer works through the lens of recent memory research to investigate how Wolf uses her own lived experiences repeatedly in her writing. He explores Wolf's difficulty in addressing her own past in the first person and her changing point of view on what constitutes the present time. Lauer introduces a new perspective on Wolf's writing through the term *Vergegenwärtigung* (bringing into the present) to understand Wolf's literary technique of (re)creating the self through texts. For Lauer, the question of how we became the way we are leads to a somewhat different understanding of the dynamics of memory discourse. He traces Wolf's desire to find a new way of writing that "takes into account the changing ways of an individual's being in the world ... the desire to find the right voice to adequately address the different layers of reality." Lauer refers back to Wolf's early essay "The Reader and the Writer" (1968) and to her 1974 interview with Hans Kaufmann, in which she insists on a "fourth dimension" of modern prose, the dimension of the author ("Subjective Authenticity"). Even in *City of Angels*, one still encounters reflections on how memories are derived from layers of time, reality, and experience. As the protagonist puts it:

> Sometimes I wish I knew how the layers of time through which I have traveled, that I penetrate so easily in my thoughts, are actually arranged inside me: as actual layers, each one stacked carefully on top of the other? Or as a chaotic mass of neurons from which a power we do not understand can draw out whichever thread we want? (267)

This concept of the stacked layers of reality is already evident in Wolf's entry for the year 1970 in her collection of autobiographical writings *Ein Tag im Jahr, 1960–2000* (2003; *One Day a Year*, 2007), when Wolf mulls over the "technical problem that arises again and again when I write prose: how do I bring the stacked layers of time of which 'reality' consists safely over into my linear writing style?" (146). Lauer concludes that *Vergegenwärtigung* is a particularly apt way of describing this process of recalling past memories from the perspective of an ever-changing present.

In "The Heterochronic Narrative of Christa Wolf," Heike Polster also delves into *Patterns of Childhood*, but she approaches that work in a further innovative way by engaging the term heterochronic to analyze Wolf's multi-leveled narrative style with regard to time. Polster interrogates how heterochronicity operates as both a narrative and a temporal model for understanding Wolf's *Zeitgenossenschaft* (contemporaneity). Exploring the three time levels of narrative in *Patterns* as well as in several of the poetological writings, Polster posits contemporaneity as the paramount contention of Wolf's literary texts; she highlights the fluid ways in which Wolf couples the question of temporality (What *is* this thing called time?) with an aesthetic practice of portraying it (How does one *tell about* time?). Describing Wolf as "a writer of time itself, a teller, indeed, about time," Polster challenges readers to consider the significance and complexity of time as a significant feature of Wolf's works.

In "Subjective Authenticity as Realism: Christa Wolf and Georg Lukács," Robert Blankenship asks whether Wolf's notion of subjective authenticity really does reflect a complete rejection of socialist realism, as most scholars have claimed. By comparing several features of both narrative formulas, he suggests that Wolf's realism focuses largely on the mediation of experience and on engagement with literary history, elements that Lukács also emphasized. Blankenship poses the question: should it be surprising that Wolf's subjective authenticity did not reject all aspects of Lukács's version of socialist realism? After all, Wolf studied Lukács's writings on socialist realism "obsessively" while at the university and wrote in that vein in her earliest work, especially *Moskauer Novelle*. To be sure, Blankenship does not claim that Wolf's narrative style and topics aligned with socialist realism, and he explores her rejection of Lukács's more dogmatic demands for realism as well as her non-Lukácsian subjective, personal, feminist, and critical approaches to writing literature. At the same time, Blankenship offers an important reminder of the influence of Anna Seghers, and of other less dogmatic forms of socialist realism as they were espoused by Benjamin Bloch and Theodor Adorno, on Wolf's style and oeuvre.

Christa Wolf in the Public Sphere

In several of her most autobiographical works, Wolf alludes to how she lived in the world outside of her fiction writing, describing how she thought about, engaged in, and often struggled in the public sphere as an activist, a voice of truth, and a defender of individuals and groups she regarded as victims of the GDR government. Gradually, because she participated in several cultural and social organizations, she gained a reputation as an important intellectual and trustworthy moral voice.

Wolf addressed her concerns and worries about the extensive damage to the natural environment in the GDR and around the world, as well as the danger of potential wars, violence, nuclear weapons, and nuclear power of every kind. Following the nuclear explosions in Chernobyl, Wolf wrote a semi-fictional, but realistic and personal book about the local and global dangers of nuclear power, *Störfall: Nachrichten eines Tages* (1987; *Accident:*

A Day's News, 1989). Wolf was an accessible writer for interested fans of her literary works, she often gave readings and lectures, and her ideas about culture, society, and politics made her a sought-after speaker, the GDR equivalent of a public intellectual, who offered East Germans insights and information that were not made public in the official press. Just as Wolf did not shy away from controversial and even forbidden topics in her fictional works, she often made such topics the subject of her many essays, articles, speeches, and participation in both private and public events. While Wolf's fictional oeuvre consists of a large number of individual works, her non-fiction writings added up to some dozen collections that became popular with her followers.

In her essay "To Be Recognized Again: Memory, Amnesia, and Sincerity in Christa Wolf," Christine Kanz offers an insightful overview of the controversies surrounding Wolf in the last decades of her life. Issues of memory are central to Kanz's account of Wolf's lifelong pursuit of self-understanding, the relentless process of self-examination through which she—often through a fictionalized narrator—struggles "to understand who the person was that she had been ... and what the reasons were for her selective amnesia." While the insistent self-questioning and attempts to recuperate repressed memory in *City of Angels* most often elicit comparison with *Patterns of Childhood*, Kanz reminds us that the search for integrity was already central in *The Quest for Christa T.* The epigraph to that novel poses the decisive question, "This coming-to-oneself—what is it?" For the narrator, as for her deceased friend Christa T., Kanz points out, "it becomes obvious that ... language and writing are the only means available to them to counter confusion and fear," to resist and speak with a "true voice." In the immediate post-Wall period, however, Wolf's long-standing reputation as a writer who stood for truthfulness and personal integrity suffered attacks, especially in the overwhelmingly negative reviews of her 1990 work, *Was bleibt* (*What Remains*, 1993), in which a well-known writer, again a stand-in for the author herself, describes the frightening experience of being under constant observation by the Stasi. At issue was the fact that, although Wolf had written the text in 1979, she did not publish it until 1990, which led some conservative critics in West Germany to accuse her of opportunism and attempting to cast herself as a victim of the bygone regime.

Two years later, during Wolf's research stay at the Getty Research Institute in Los Angeles, an even worse scandal broke with revelations that from 1959 to 1962 she had occasionally cooperated with the Stasi as an informer. The fact that she had not provided any useful information to the Stasi and that her "services" were terminated after only a few encounters was not enough to protect her from another round of media defamation, made worse by her avowal of having absolutely no memory of a cooperation with the Stasi. Having forgotten, as Kanz points out, is the trauma at the heart of Wolf's challenging final novel.

Daniela Colombo begins her essay "'This Is No Longer My World': The Multiple Alienations of Christa Wolf" by asserting that Wolf's oeuvre was shaped significantly by her own biography and reflects a constant re-examination of her own history and her failures to remember. Colombo notes Wolf's personal conflict between her desire to conform and her frequent need to oppose and resist. Wolf was forced to address serious questions about her complicity with the Stasi and personal responsibility vis-à-vis the failures and corruption of the GDR government. Colombo investigates how and to what extent those conflicts led to Wolf's various forms of alienation, and how she often became a stranger to herself and to the societies in which she lived before and after the demise of the GDR. Colombo delves into those contradictory needs and actions as Wolf initially remembered them during the visit to Poland in 1971. Colombo also addresses Wolf's ambivalence toward the GDR regime. Although Wolf became and for many years remained a member of the SED, she was simultaneously quite critical of the fact that the GDR leaders were taking the country in the direction of increasingly brutal authoritarianism. As Colombo notes, by becoming more aware of her various ambivalences, Wolf also became cognizant of how alienated she often felt, toward herself and the GDR. Colombo leads her readers through Wolf's writing about alienation from *Patterns of Childhood* through *What Remains* up to *City of Angels*. The essay contributes to our understanding of Wolf's development over time, aided by memory and her willingness to confront her past, an understanding that invites readers of her work to be alert to the various ways in which Wolf writes about her own ambivalences and alienations.

In "'Was bleibet aber, stiften die Dichter': Christa Wolf's Contested Role as Spokesperson for Generations of Readers and Women Writers," Janine Ludwig explores the ways in which Wolf earned the status of "perhaps the most influential 'voice' of her times."[3] Ludwig traces the important influence Wolf exerted in the GDR, noting that she was regarded by many as a "public intellectual" and "moral instance" in a "surrogate public sphere," and that her fiction often reflected her public concerns. Ludwig discusses Wolf's strong commitment to women's rights and issues of gender, as well as how she introduced to the GDR a feminist form of modernism that is visible in many of her novels and stories. Ludwig also delves into Wolf's interest in long-neglected women writers from the German Romantic era and the fact that virtually all of her protagonists are women. Ludwig also points out how Wolf's public speaking and writing, as well as her fiction works, influenced many other writers in the GDR, especially women.

Christa Wolf in Dark Times: Illness, Anxiety, and Trauma

Throughout her adult life, Christa Wolf was plagued by a number of illnesses, some of which required surgery and hospitalization. Frequently, when she was under significant stress from having been harshly criticized or when she internalized political developments in the GDR, she also suffered physically and became ill. Unsurprisingly, illness, anxiety, and trauma became frequent themes in her works. Novels including *The Quest for Christa T.*, *Leibhaftig* (2002; *In the Flesh*, 2005), and *City of Angels* portray dark times when the autobiographical protagonists face, suffer, and attempt to work through their trauma in order to regain emotional and physical health. Although the stories in each of these novels were personal for Wolf, they are also sufficiently universal as to be relevant for readers of widely varying backgrounds.

In "'To Follow the Trail of Pain': Coming to Terms with the Past in Christa Wolf's *In the Flesh*," Deborah Janson examines the pain experienced by the protagonist, a stand-in for Wolf, as she lies ill in an East Berlin hospital just before the GDR collapses. As the protagonist dreams, she re-enacts "scenes that reflect the disillusionment, guilt, embarrassment, and despair she suffered as a result of her involvement in party politics." Janson analyzes how this embodied memory process helps the protagonist heal and articulates the new way that Wolf uses "literary analogies, dream images, and memory scenes to follow the trail of pain that was part of her intellectually rich and socially engaged life." During her illness and hospitalization, the protagonist is able to work through her "pain, confront the failures of the GDR government, her own stubborn reluctance to criticize it more boldly, and her decades-long naïve hope that somehow the GDR would transform itself into a kind of socialist utopia." Finally, Janson points to a change in Wolf's attitude about the relationship between author and protagonist. Wolf had previously asserted that the author and the protagonist in her works should not be regarded as one, but in a piece she wrote in 1993, she admitted that they had perhaps sometimes been just that. She wrote: "When will I— or will I ever again—be able to write a book about a distant, invented character? I myself am the protagonist, there is no other way, I am exposed, have exposed myself" ("Berlin" 244).

In "Deliberating the 'ängstliche Margarete': Coping with Anxiety in Christa Wolf's *City of Angels or, The Overcoat of Dr. Freud*," Ivett Guntersdorfer offers yet another interpretive approach that goes beyond the prevailing Freudian model to gain an insightful reading of that novel. The orthodox psychoanalytic approach to the narrator's anxiety is well represented in conversations with the psychologist Peter Gutman, the protagonist's closest friend at the Getty Research Institute. Guntersdorfer, however, identifies a little-noticed turning point at the center of the novel, just after the narrator's exchange with her friend Sally, who warns her against using Freud's coat as a defense mechanism. Their conversation is followed by a dream in which the narrator pictures herself unloading freight from the top of a moving, dilapidated freight truck, only to find that the truck bed itself is totally empty. Awakening, she poses the self-critical question, "What am I doing here?" (153). Referring to insights developed in the field of cognitive psychology, which focuses on mental processes—such as *angst*, anger, escape—that people employ to cope with or master stressful situations, Guntersdorfer identifies this moment as the cognitive turn after which the narrator finally settles down to the writing of her story and commences the process of moving beyond the *angst* that had marked her stay at the Getty Institute. As the protagonist grows calmer, Guntersdorfer identifies a final coping strategy, escape, in the narrator's mental progression toward emotional understanding: a kind of magical thinking, or what one of the real-life pioneers of cognitive psychology, David L. Gutmann, calls "magical mastery." While the protagonist's friend, David Gutman, does not appear to be a stand-in for the real Dr. Gutmann, the sequence of mysterious and seemingly irrational events that Wolf depicts in the last half of the book validates Guntersdorfer's use of cognitive psychology as an interpretive approach to understanding the novel.

In her essay "Coming Full Circle: Trauma, Empathy, and Writing in 'Change of Perspective' ('Blickwechsel,' 1970) and 'August' (2011)," Friederike Eigler compares these two stories written forty years apart in order to explore how they complement but also differ from one another. She challenges several reviewers who claimed that "August" was basically a sweet gift to Wolf's husband and places this work in the context of Wolf's overall oeuvre, pointing out that the title character, August, also appears in an often-overlooked passage from *Patterns of Childhood*, and in the early short story "Blickwechsel" ("Change of Perspective"), where he plays a significant role. Eigler asserts that for Wolf, who had experienced "fleeing from her home into the unknown at the end of World War II, the sudden loss of home remained 'unbeschreibbar' (indescribable)" until she returned to those events in "August," a short, final book written just before her death in 2011. Eigler concludes that both "Change of Perspective" and "August" can be read as meta-fictional commentaries on the role of creative writing and memory in the shadow of World War II and its aftermath.

Christa Wolf and the Visual Arts

The final cluster of essays collected here addresses Wolf's active participation in the creation of films, her strong personal connection to non-literary forms of art, and her impact on both GDR film and other visual arts. The authors of these three essays explore themes and issues that are addressed elsewhere in the volume—including memory, subjective authenticity, illness, trauma, and alienation—but they address them through the different lenses of other artistic genres.

In his essay "A Woman's Voice on Screen: Christa Wolf and the Cinema," Barton Byg discusses Wolf's participation in the creation of perhaps the best-known film for which she provided the script, *Der geteilte Himmel* (*Divided Heaven*, 1963). The film was based on her novel of the same name and directed by the famous GDR filmmaker Konrad Wolf (no relation). Byg probes how Christa Wolf's experiences with film—including three other films on which she collaborated—contributed to increased cinematic qualities in her own prose. At the same time, Byg argues that Wolf's "'melancholy modernist' critique of the ideology of socialist progress" influenced changes in GDR cinema more broadly. Another instructive aspect of Byg's essay is his discussion of non-German films that influenced those in which Wolf was involved, particularly the famous French film, *Hiroshima mon amour* (1959), written by Marguerite Duras and directed by Alain Resnais.

In her essay "Women at the Edge of a Nervous Breakdown: The Berlin Wall and the Collapse of Female Consciousness in *Divided Heaven* and *Good Bye, Lenin!*," Susanne Rinner explores ways in which the Berlin Wall, by separating East Berlin from West Berlin for twenty-eight years, affected the women protagonists' lives in these two works: one a novel (that was, however, made into a film shortly after its publication in 1963), the other a film created by Wolfgang Becker in 2004. By "crossmapping" these works that both represent women collapsing and spending time unconscious in hospitals (Rita when the Wall is built, and Christiane when it is torn down), Rinner provides "a critical framework for understanding the importance of the image of the unconscious woman in the continuing debates that shape the cultural memory of the GDR and the Cold War." Rinner notes that women's illnesses and the ensuing unconsciousness, which appears to be necessary for their recovery, become a common trope in Wolf's later works as well. Indeed, Rinner's analysis of *Divided Heaven* demonstrates that several key tropes and themes were first employed by Wolf in this novel, including the connection between the protagonist's physical breakdown and political, social, or historical upheavals; and the importance of how memory, replacing forgetting during the "down time" of an illness, allows for self-reflection and working through conflicts and traumas. An important contribution of Rinner's chapter is her focus on Wolf's complex commitment to thinking deeply and writing about the challenges that women face in gaining agency in a patriarchal society.

In her essay "The Impact of Christa Wolf's *Kassandra* on Women Artists in East Germany," April Eisman articulates the significant influence of Wolf's novel *Kassandra* (1983; *Cassandra*, 1988) on two quite different women artists, Nuria Quevedo (born in 1938) and Angela Hampel (born in 1956). Eisman considers how Wolf's novel provided these exceptional visual artists with an updated version of the Cassandra myth that emphasizes her fate as a woman in a patriarchal world, where women tend not to be listened to or believed by men. Wolf's *Cassandra* influenced these women's artworks, but it also helped awaken a "feminist" consciousness that moved them to confront the patriarchal treatment they are still subject to in their own time and place. Just as Wolf shifted the narrative focus onto the character Cassandra, who is a minor character in most versions of the mythical stories of the Trojan War, Quevedo and Hampel make her the center of their artworks. Eisman explores the major differences between those early recountings of the Trojan War in which Achilles "is not a hero but simply a beast" and Wolf's version, arguing that its alignment of "patriarchy with war and brutality, and the concomitant praise of matriarchal inclusiveness and pacifism, made [Wolf's] *Cassandra* at once controversial for the East German government and inspirational for many women on both sides of the Berlin Wall." As an art historian, Eisman places the works of Quevedo and Hampel in a broader visual context, emphasizing how the former's style in her mostly black-and-white drawings is reminiscent of the works of Käthe Kollwitz, while Hampel's prints and paintings that reinterpret the same story include "punk-inspired images of Cassandra and her 'crew.'" Eisman emphasizes the many ways in which Wolf's *Cassandra* awakened a "feminist" consciousness in women in East Germany and beyond.

The Legacy of Christa Wolf

In the title of her essay included here, Janine Ludwig cites a line from a Hölderlin poem: "Was bleibet aber, stiften die Dichter" (What remains, however, the poets provide). *Was bleibt* is also the title of Christa Wolf's 1990 autobiographical novel that set in motion the German *Literaturstreit* (Literature Dispute). At the conclusion of her essay, Ludwig posits an answer to the question of what remains: "the literature itself." Writing in 2010, Wolf's literary colleague and friend Günter Grass responded to that same question:

> What remains, above all, are her many books. At a time when East and West, bristling with weapons, faced off in rigid ideological confrontation, she wrote books that crossed and overcame this divide, books that have lasted: the great allegorical novels, the personal of illness and pain…

Certainly, the novels and stories themselves are the most tangible and accessible items in a writer's legacy. It was due to the exceptional quality, undeniable impact, and considerable enthusiasm for her novels and stories that Wolf received an exceptionally large number of major awards and prizes for her works during her lifetime. The continuing significance and international interest in her books today indicate that she is still one of the most admired and widely read German-language writers of the past sixty years.

Yet, as Ludwig asserts in her essay, there is a great deal more to say about what lends such vibrancy to Wolf's legacy today. It is not only the bold vision of her novels and stories, but as the scholar Margit Resch claimed in 1997, her legacy was also shaped by how she wrote and what she stood for as a person:

> Wolf's legacy is rich and powerful. Her literary reviews, essays, and fiction chronicle the writer's journey from passionate commitment to democratic socialism, on which the German Democratic Republic was constitutionally founded, to courageous yet judicious resistance to an authoritarian regime that increasingly violated these principles. Her work as a whole reflects self-realization under challenging social and personal circumstances, the central pursuit of every protagonist in her novels and stories. … Her recent work describes the varied situations and sentiments of East Germans after the Wall. Because what remains of the GDR and what is worthy of remaining are so powerfully recorded in her writings. Christa Wolf's literary achievement is one of her former country's most stubborn and enduring treasures. (169; 171)

By rejecting the staid and limiting requirements of the GDR's form of socialist realism, Wolf had a far-reaching influence on many East German writers. They felt liberated to experiment and write more openly, subjectively, truthfully, and in ways that took risks, both with form and content: modernist on the one hand, and feminist and critical on the other. Her works after the 1980s, which reflected her feminist, pro-environment, anti-war, and anti-nuclear concerns, spoke to and inspired readers far beyond the GDR. Her willingness to take risks, oppose publicly the increasingly authoritarian government in the GDR, as well as her friendships with and her mentoring of writers young and old, especially women writers, must also be cited as an important part of her legacy.

Most of the dozens of eulogies printed in newspapers, magazines, and other publications across Europe and North America following Wolf's death contained lofty praise of her life and works, even though some did mention the criticisms that tarnished her reputation in the early 1990s. Yet even the negative assertions and charges of those years had ultimately softened and were in some cases even retracted. Grass spoke about that "softening" in his eulogy for Wolf in 2012.[4] Nonetheless, some critics and readers still regard her stubborn but unrealistic hope that the GDR's authoritarian socialism could somehow turn into a humane and democratic socialism as a fatal blemish on her reputation.

In an obituary published in the *New Yorker* a few days after Wolf's death, Sally McGrane asserted:

> [Wolf's] death, at eighty-two, marks the end of an era in divided, then reunified Germany—an era in which literature played an existential role. As long as there was an East Germany, Wolf was an East German writer. But she wasn't just an East German writer. In the days since her death, one hears over and

over the lament that never again will a German authoress capture the attention of so many. Her impact was the result of a confluence of politics—only in an authoritarian state are writers so important—and an ear for the issues and concerns of the day, be it the building of the wall, the pain of the Nazi past, the search for a new and better society, women's rights, or environmental problems.

Karen Leeder, writing in the London *Independent*, stated the following in her obituary:

> Wolf has been called a "loyal dissident," whose work reveals and enacts the fraught negotiations between power and creativity in a dictatorship—and the inability to move on. But more than that, hers is a scrupulous and humane work that explores what it is to be an individual in a uniquely turbulent century. Moreover, it rests on the unfashionable, but potent belief that literature is important; and that writing is the best means to know oneself and to be more intensively in the world.

Günter Grass describes in his eulogy what he thought about Wolf's blind spots, but emphasized her deserved and positive reputation:

> Christa Wolf belonged to the generation in which I also count myself. We were stamped by National Socialism and the late—too late—realization of all the crimes committed by Germans in the span of just twelve years. Ever since, the act of writing has demanded interpreting the traces of that. One of Christa Wolf's books, *Patterns of Childhood*, responds to that imperative, exposing her successive immersions in brown-shirted dictatorship and the doctrines of Stalinism. False paths credulously followed, stirrings of doubt and resistance to authoritarian constraints and beyond that, the recognition of one's own participation in a system that was crushing the utopian ideals of Socialism—those are the hallmarks of the five-decades of writing that established Wolf's reputation… and the books remain.

The "lessons" that Wolf tried to live by were not always within her reach and became that much more important to her because she had not attained them. She chastised herself to the point of illness about not remembering her collaboration with the Stasi. She remained a member of the SED long after she knew that it had become an authoritarian and brutal government. She realized to some extent after the Wolf Biermann Affair in 1976, and the resulting flight of a number of her writer and artist friends to the West, that her hopes were not in fact realistic. Once Wolf openly admitted her failure to recognize that her idealistic vision of a utopian socialist government would not replace the one in power, she spoke up frequently and wrote about it extensively. This ultimate willingness to admit mistakes is also an important part of her legacy.

It is worth mentioning a few concrete indications that the interest in Wolf's life and works continues to grow and expand, adding positively to her legacy. Interest in her novels and stories remains high, as do their sales, and scholarship on them shows no sign of abating, as this volume demonstrates.

Attention to her non-fiction works, including several recently published ones—diary collections, letters, and essays that had not yet appeared at the time of her death—has also risen in tandem with the continuing scholarship on her fiction works. Twelve volumes in the *Werkausgabe* (Collected Works) are in print and more are being added. Among the most important recent book-length scholarly publications are the *Christa Wolf Handbuch: Leben—Werk—Wirkung*, edited by Carola Hilmes and Ilse Nagelschmidt (2016) and a collection of essays titled *Christa Wolf: A Companion*, edited by Sonja E. Klocke and Jennifer R. Hosek (2018). Additional signs of the continuing importance of Wolf and her writings are evident in the ongoing work of the *Christa Wolf Gesellschaft* (Society) that mounts exhibits and sponsors numerous programs. That same institution, located at the Humboldt University in Berlin, also hosts the *Arbeits- und Forschungsstelle Privatbibliothek Christa and Gerhard Wolf*, founded in 2016, which is dedicated to the literary, artistic, and publishing work of both authors, and encourages and supports the continuation of scholarship focused on their writings and their many public activities. There is also an expanding archive of Christa Wolf's works and related materials at the *Stiftung Archiv der Akademie der Künste* in Berlin.

Such publications, institutions, and activities dedicated to Christa Wolf and her work should encourage us as well to read her anew. All of this provides ample evidence of the viability of the legacy of Christa Wolf, and the sixteen essays in this volume add to it in important and innovative ways. As they abundantly demonstrate, there is yet much to learn from Christa Wolf and her extensive, complex, inspiring, and, yes, controversial writings.

Gerald A. Fetz is Dean and Professor Emeritus, University of Montana. He currently serves on the Board of the German Studies Association and is the chief editor at the University of Montana Press.

Patricia Herminghouse is Fuchs Professor emerita of German Studies, University of Rochester. She has written widely on German Literature since the nineteenth century, including the social contexts of women's writing, GDR literature, and German émigré culture in nineteenth-century America.

Notes

1. Christa Wolf described her program in "Subjective Authenticity: A Conversation with Hans Kaufmann" in 1973. English translation is found in *The Fourth Dimension: Interviews with Christa Wolf*, 17–38. Robert Blankenship's essay in this volume deals with the concept extensively.
2. Cited from the *Diskussionsbeitrag: Zum 11. Plenum—Dezember 1965*. This excerpt is taken from *Christa Wolf: Eine Biographie in Bildern und Texten*, edited by Peter Böthig. Citation translated into English by Gerald Fetz.

3. The quote in the title of Ludwig's essay comes from Friedrich Hölderlin's poem "Andenken" (1803).
4. Grass's eulogy for Christa Wolf appeared in English, translated by David Dollenmayer, on 17 January 2012.

Bibliography

Anz, Thomas, editor. *Es geht nicht um Christa Wolf: Der Literaturstreit im vereinten Deutschland*. Berlin: Spangenberg, 1991.
Böthig, Peter, editor, with assistance from Sunhild Pflug, Gerhard Wolf, and Helene Wolf. *Christa Wolf: Eine Biographie in Bildern und Texten*. Munich: Luchterhand Verlag, 2004.
Finney, Gail. *Christa Wolf*. New York: Twayne's World Author Series, Twayne Publishers, 1999.
Grass, Günter. "On Christa Wolf," translated by David Dollenmayer. *New York Review of Books*, 17 January 2012, https://nybooks.com/daily/2012/01/17/gunter-grass-christa-wolf-what-remains/.
Hilmes, Carola, and Ilse Nagelschmidt, editors. *Christa Wolf Handbuch: Leben—Werk—Wirkung*. Stuttgart: J.B. Metzler, 2016.
Klocke, Sonja E., and Jennifer R. Hosek, editors. *Christa Wolf: A Companion*. Berlin: Walter de Gruyter, 2018.
Kuhn, Anna K. *Christa Wolf's Utopian Vision: From Marxism to Feminism*. Cambridge, UK: Cambridge University Press, 1988.
Leeder, Karen. "Christa Wolf: Writer Whose Hard-Won Reputation Suffered When Her Stasi Links Surfaced." *Independent* (London), 7 December 2011.
McGrane, Sally. "Remembering Christa Wolf." *The New Yorker*, 13 December 2011.
Mitscherlich, Alexander, and Margarete Mitscherlich. *Die Unfähigkeit zu Trauern*. Munich: Piper Verlag, 1967.
Resch, Margit. *Understanding Christa Wolf: Returning Home to a Foreign Land*. Columbia: University of South Carolina Press, 1997.
Richards-Wilson, Stefani. "Cry Wolf? Encounter Controversy: Christa Wolf's Legacy in Light of the Literature Debate." *The New German Review: A Journal for Germanic Studies*, vol. 24, no. 1, Fall 2009, pp. 63–79.
Von Günderrode, Karoline. *Der Schatten eines Traumes, Gedichte, Prosa, Briefe, Zeugnisse von Zeitgenossen*. Edited by Christa Wolf. Munich: dtv, 1997.
Wolf, Christa. *Ansprachen: Reden—Briefe—Reflexionen*. Berlin: Luchterhand Literaturverlag, 1988.
———. *August*. Berlin: Suhrkamp, 2012.
———. *The Author's Dimension: Selected Essays*. Introduction by Grace Paley. Translated by Jan van Heurck. New York: Farrar, Straus and Giroux, 1993.
———. "Berlin, Monday, September 27, 1993." *Parting from Phantoms: Selected Writings, 1990–1994*, translated by Jan van Heurck. Chicago: University of Chicago Press, 1997, pp. 231–45.

———.*Der geteilte Himmel.* Halle: Mitteldeutscher Verlag, 1963.
[*They Divided the Sky*. Translated by Louise von Flotow. Ottawa: University of Ottawa Press, 2013.]
———.*The Fourth Dimension: Interviews with Christa Wolf.* Introduction by Karin McPherson. Translated by Hilary Pilkington. London: Verso, 1988.
———.*Kassandra: Erzählung.* Darmstadt: Luchterhand, 1983.
[*Cassandra: A Novel and Four Essays*. Translated by Jan van Heurck. New York: Farrar, Straus and Giroux, 1984.]
———.*Kein Ort. Nirgends.* Ost-Berlin: Aufbau Verlag, 1979.
[*No Place on Earth*. Translated by Jan van Heurck. New York: Farrar, Straus and Giroux, 1982.]
———.*Kindheitsmuster.* Munich: Luchterhand, 1977.
[*Patterns of Childhood*. Translated by Ursula Molinaro and Hedwig Rappolt. New York: Farrar, Straus & Giroux, 1980.]
———.*Leibhaftig.* Munich: Luchterhand Verlag, 2002.
[*In the Flesh*. Translated by John S. Barrett. Boston: Verba Mundi, 2005.]
———.*Lesen und Schreiben: Aufsätze und Prosastücke.* Darmstadt: Luchterhand Verlag, 1972.
[*The Reader and the Writer: Essays, Sketches, Memories*. Translated by Joan Becker. New York: International Publishers, 1977.]
———.*Medea: Stimmen.* Munich: Luchterhand, 1996.
[*Medea: A Modern Retelling*. Translated by John Cullen. New York: Bantam Doubleday. 1998.]
———.*Moskauer Novelle.* Halle: Mitteldeutscher Verlag, 1961.
———.*Nachdenken über Christa T.* Neuwied: Luchterhand, 1969.
[*The Quest for Christa T*. Translated by Christopher Middleton. New York: Farrar, Straus & Giroux, 1970.]
———.*One Day a Year: 1960–2000.* Translated by Lowell A. Bangerter. New York: Europa Editions, 2007.
———.*Parting from Phantoms: Selected Writings, 1990–1994.* Translated by Jan van Heurck. Chicago: University of Chicago Press, 1997.
———.*Sommerstück.* Berlin: Aufbau, 1990.
———.*Stadt der Engel oder The Overcoat of Dr. Freud.* Berlin: Suhrkamp, 2010.
[*City of Angels or, The Overcoat of Dr. Freud*. Translated by Damion Searls. New York: Farrar, Straus & Giroux, 2013.]
———.*Störfall: Nachrichten eines Tages.* Berlin: Aufbau Verlag, 1987.
[*Accident: A Day's News*. New York: Farrar, Straus & Giroux, 1989.]
———.*Was bleibt: Erzählung.* Frankfurt a.M.: Luchterhand Literaturverlag, 1990.
[*What Remains and Other Stories*. New York: Farrar, Straus and Giroux, 1993.]
———,with Gerhard Wolf. *Unsere Freunde, die Maler: Bilder-Essays-Dokumente.* Edited by Peter Böthig. Berlin: Janus Verlag, 1996.

PART I

Patterns of Memory
The Trauma of the Forgotten

CHAPTER 1

"Faraway So Close"
Transcultural Memory as Christa Wolf's "Last Word"

SILKE VON DER EMDE

In Christa Wolf's final work, *City of Angels* (*Stadt der Engel*, 2010), the narrator says, "It's about memories, about how we remember: my topic for decades" (150). Indeed, memory was always of vital concern for Wolf, who never wavered in her insistence on *Vergangenheitsbewältigung*, coming to terms with both the history of the GDR and the Nazi past. Throughout her work, she advocates a way of remembering that is at once personal and political, feminist and inclusive, self-reflexive and complex. Employing an open-ended poetics, she asks questions, provides multiple perspectives, and enters into a dialogic relationship with the reader, whom she encourages to rethink preconceived notions and to actively imagine alternative ways of thinking. Wolf insists on the necessity of counter-memory to put into question superficial calls to normalcy in unified Germany.[1] Yet, despite the apparent consistency in the importance she attaches to memory in her oeuvre, it is nonetheless possible to trace the evolution of her memory work. In the course of her writing, remembering becomes deeper, richer, and increasingly feminist in *The Quest for Christa T.* (*Nachdenken über Christa T.*, 1968), *Patterns of Childhood* (*Kindheitsmuster*, 1976), and *No Place on Earth* (*Kein Ort. Nirgends*, 1979). Remembering then transfers beyond the real to include the mythical in *Kassandra* (1983) and *Medea: A Modern Retelling* (*Medea: Stimmen*, 1996). Finally, in *City of Angels*, it moves away from the national to the global and transnational.

The two books that had preceded *City of Angels*, *In the Flesh* (*Leibhaftig*, 2002) and *One Day a Year* (*Ein Tag im Jahr*, 2003), still dealt mostly with GDR memory and, in the case of *In the Flesh*, with the desperate attempt by means of a new feminist body memory to understand her own loyalty to a broken state and bastardized socialist ideology. *City of Angels*, however, not only "embodies new facets in her writing," such as "a new, (self-)ironic tenor," as Anna Kuhn has emphasized (164), it also extends her remembering to include an international perspective on the past. In Los Angeles, the exile experience of Jewish, socialist, and communist expatriates functions not only as the prehistory of the GDR but also as part of Wolf's own life history (Magenau). Remembering is transformed into a new type of global and multi-directional memory through dialogue with a wide variety of people in Santa Monica, from her fellow artists at the Getty Center to Perma, the Buddhist nun. It moves from being grounded in the local collective memory of the nation (albeit a divided nation) to a new kind of transnational memory that now includes multiple perspectives from her host country. This transnational memory does not neglect the local or forget the specificity of particular experiences, but instead enters into dialogue with other local memories and international concerns. Carsten Gansel, who also has emphasized the importance of memory in Wolf's writing, likewise detects a development. He shows two parallel movements in Wolf's work: an increasingly deeper involvement with remembering caused by what Gansel calls "Störungen" (disturbances), such as conflicts or flashbacks of traumatic events, and at the same time, the creation of a network structure ("Netzwerkstruktur") that turns the text into a fabric of narrative strands and voices (16). To this important analysis, I want to add the international aspect that permeates Wolf's last texts, especially *City of Angels*.

From *Moskauer Novelle* (1961) on, Wolf has remembered and analyzed the important turning points in her life, with 1945 marking the most important caesura. While still rather rigid and formulaic in *Moskauer Novelle*, her memory discourse reflects the experiences of a whole cohort, the infamous generation of *Flakhelfer* (anti-aircraft brigades), who had been children during the Third Reich, old enough to see what was happening but too young to bear responsibility for the atrocities committed. These recollections are Wolf's legacy to her children and grandchildren, the "Nachgeborenen," as Brecht calls them in his famous poem "An die Nachgeborenen" ("To Posterity"). By looking to the future and seeking to prevent a repetition of past mistakes, Wolf's invocations of memory are highly political, envisioning the utopian goal of a peaceful and just society, while taking seriously Horkheimer's claim that the dead have a right to remembrance.

In seeking to prevent forgetting, her writing lets buried memories resurface as repressed remnants that hinder a full understanding of contemporary life. Already in *They Divided the Sky* (*Der geteilte Himmel*, 1963), for example, Wolf takes up taboo topics, such as the Berlin Wall, economic failings in the GDR, and the dogmatism that drives away the brightest young minds. The novel traces the protagonist's process of remembering and reflecting on the traumatic events that led to her breakdown in order to understand her role in the present. Her fiancé Manfred, and even more so his parents, refuse to take responsibility for the past and thus serve as a negative example in the novel.

Only by admitting to failings and working through the past can one make good decisions in the present, on both a personal and a collective level.

While Wolf's process of remembering in *They Divided the Sky* is increasingly multi-perspectival and dialogic, in *The Quest for Christa T.*, her writing becomes even more multi-vocal, always reflecting on the process of memory itself. The increasing intertextuality of her works involves a special form of remembering that works with quotations, allusions, and paraphrases of other texts. *Christa T.*, for instance, incorporates the diaries, letters, poems, and manuscripts of Wolf's friend Christa Tabbert, who is dying of leukemia. The text is marked by the exploration of successive layers of individual and collective memory, whereby each layer opens up yet another, even more submerged one (see Köhler). In *Sommerstück* (Summer Scenes) (1989), which especially recalls Sarah Kirsch, who had left the GDR, and Maxie Wander, who died of cancer at the time she was writing the novel, Christa Wolf repeats her technique of using the voices of absent friends as intertexts.

In its multi-perspectival and dialogic form, memory in Christa Wolf's texts functions as a counter-memory that deconstructs official discourses on history and the past. This is most apparent in *Patterns of Childhood*, where she probes the foundational narrative of the GDR as the antifascist state that made a clean break with Nazi Germany. Lacking a proper opening and haunted by the specter of the unmastered and perhaps unmasterable past of a "model childhood" during the Third Reich, the text begins by questioning the very possibility of a clean break and a fresh start that posited the GDR as the new model, antifascist state. Wolf's insistence on her memories and reflections puts into question various official "memories" that had become master narratives in the GDR.

In addition to developing her aesthetic approach to memory, Wolf expands the project of remembrance to include not only the recent German past—most importantly the Third Reich and the Shoah—but also other historical reference points, such as the emergence of bourgeois society in *No Place on Earth*, and even mythology in *Kassandra* and *Medea*. History becomes a thought-model and reference point for contemporary conflicts. Wolf's rewriting of myth in *Kassandra* and *Medea*, for example, not only deconstructs patriarchal misrepresentations of the female but also points to the GDR as a police state. Both novels interrogate collective memory processes that go back to the beginnings of mythology. In this way, Wolf explores ancient myths as foundational memories, a process that Jan Assmann demonstrates in his important work *Cultural Memory and Early Civilization* (*Das kulturelle Gedächtnis*, 2005). The importance of this type of memory work becomes immediately apparent, not only in light of women's subordinate position in history but also in light of the Shoah, for Horkheimer/Adorno the culmination of *The Dialectic of Enlightenment*.[2] Analyzing memory then becomes a deeply political process that offers a guiding principle for the future. Wolf's writing demands more and more insistently that literature recognize its responsibility toward the past in order to warn against instrumentalizing it for political purposes (Catani 325).

After the *Wende*, Christa Wolf insists with even greater urgency on the importance of memory work with her controversial texts *What Remains* (*Was Bleibt*, 1990), which triggered the *Literaturstreit* (literary critics' dispute) in 1990, *Medea* (1996), *In the Flesh* (2002), *One Day a Year* (2003), and *City of Angels* (2010). At a time of major paradigm shifts in a younger generation of authors, for whom literature is no longer necessarily committed to politically motivated memory work, as Gerstenberger and Herminghouse point out, Wolf insists on continuing to remember, while at the same time representing the breaks and discontinuities in dominant memory discourses. Against the ethos of *Spaßkultur* (a new turn to a hedonistic playfulness in German culture in the 1990s) and calls for a normalization of history in unified Germany, Wolf not only insists on the importance of memory, but also actively works to cultivate it as a flexible and open-ended process by contributing to theoretical discussions about the workings of memory itself.[3] Wolf's oeuvre is characterized by insistence on the importance of memory as a reference point for contemporary life after the reunification of the two German states, when global concerns, such as continuing discrimination against women, climate change, and global conflict and peace, have become such pressing issues. In *What Remains*, for example, the author insists bravely on precise remembering and contextualization when discussing the former GDR. Analyzing the devastating effects of censorship and surveillance on society, Wolf shows that easy and stable distinctions between victims and perpetrators, dissidents and *Staatsdichter* (state poets, a term that some of Wolf's attackers used in an attempt to discredit her), are superficial and unproductive. In this sense Wolf offers a type of counter-memory that can work against the dangers of ritualization, decontextualization, and dehistoricization that Friederike Eigler sees as trends in memory discourses in unified Germany.

In the Flesh, with its return to illness as metaphor (a structural motif in much of Wolf's oeuvre), reflects the author's expanded understanding of memory as feminist body memory that inscribes female ways of remembering onto the sick body. *In the Flesh* is one of Wolf's most open texts, playing with allusions, dichotomies, borders, intertextual connections, leitmotifs, and multilayered references that range from the Bible to history, mythology, songs, fairy tales, and literature. With its complex structure, *In the Flesh* most radically questions different kinds of GDR memories and mythologies by using the body to construct a new female and feminist memory discourse. Its double function of being simultaneously inside and outside of history, as Leslie Adelson emphasizes, makes the body especially suited for such an examination of history and memory (34). The narrator of *In the Flesh* comes close to the brink of death before she can fight back the unresolved conflicts that have been poisoning her body. Her fever fantasies are like archaeological digs, excavating more and more memory layers. The quick changes of perspective suggest the difficulties of such memory work, as well as the chaotic and unreliable nature of memory itself. But as Sigrid Weigel has shown, the body functions not only as the "Leidtragender der Geschichte" (the victim of history or, more literally, the bearer of suffering) in Wolf's work; it also possesses a means of expression that can lead to a new type of body language, "Körpersprache."

Against the loss of language that accompanies the collapse of a bankrupt society, Wolf proposes a new kind of language that can counteract the breakdown of communication in the end phases of the GDR. In fact, she begins her story with

> Hurting. Something's complaining, wordlessly. Words breaking against the muteness that's spreading persistently, along with faintness. Consciousness bobbing up and down in a primordial tide. Her memories like islands. Wherever it's carrying her now, words don't reach—that would be one of her last clear thoughts. (*In the Flesh* 3)

Aside from pain and failure, the extreme situation in the novel also allows for experiences that the healthy and integrated body cannot reach. The unavoidable rest that the sick body requires is exactly the gateway to new insights as well as to resistance to the dominant ideology. In fact, the loss of control in this situation of extreme powerlessness even leads to a grotesque sense of mischief, or "gräßlicher Übermut" (*Leibhaftig* 82),[4] and a sense of freedom because, as she writes, "It feels good, malicious thought that it is, but it feels good to have been tossed out of time's net, because on this earth, there's no other way to avoid being indebted to someone for something" (*In the Flesh* 57). In fact, Wolf's narrator asks: "What sort of inscription is being written upon my body? Will I ever be able to read it?" (90). To learn a new language and to speak without ambiguity seems to be the task that Christa Wolf sees confronting us after the *Wende*.

City of Angels or, The Overcoat of Dr. Freud (2010), Wolf's last novel, continues this memory work, resituating remembering outside the confines of the GDR or even of unified Germany into the broader context of the United States. Set in Los Angeles, the book not only reflects on her early faith in the antifascist new beginning after 1945 and subsequent growing disillusionment with "real existing socialism" in the GDR, marked by the turning points of 1965, 1976, and 1989,[5] it also weaves in reflections on U.S. turning points, such as racial tensions in Los Angeles after the Rodney King beatings in 1991, discussions about the Iraq War, the election of Bill Clinton as President of the

United States, modern day immigration into the United States, the history of Native Americans in the U.S., and the memories of the German exiles in Santa Monica. *City of Angels* thus presents a fascinating tapestry, densely woven from shifting narrative perspectives, temporal planes, and themes. It is Wolf's desperate attempt to recover her own repressed memories at a time when she is being viciously attacked by the German feuilletonists because of her short involvement with the Stasi more than forty years earlier. The research stay in the Getty Center allows her the necessary distance to recover her own peace of mind after an agonizing process of self-searching that culminates in a desperate night when, close to a total breakdown, the narrator recovers her own senses by singing out loud all the songs she knows. With her singing she not only chases away the tempting thought of ending her life but also invokes the whole course of German cultural history from the Middle Ages to the Romantic period, the Third Reich, and the reconstruction period in the GDR. All of these many songs with their different ideologies and sentiments are part of her cultural memory, one that is not fixed and constant, but is rethought and renegotiated with each added experience. Only the recognition that memory moves in unexpected and uncontrollable ways, that following the "traces of pain and suffering" (*City of Angels* 7) is a lifelong and extremely arduous undertaking, allows the narrator to accept that the goal of remembering is the process itself.

By displacing her memory work to Los Angeles, *City of Angels* takes Wolf's reflections on memory one step further, deterritorializing German memory by bringing it into dialogue with non-GDR and even non-German perspectives. Through conversations with a great variety of different people, such as the Jewish philosopher Peter Gutman, other scholars at the Getty Center, a group of adult children of survivors, a psychoanalyst, the Chinese acupuncturist Dr. Kim, the Buddhist nun Perma (through her book), the Feldenkreis teacher Rachel, and the Ugandan cleaner Angelina, the narrator gains a new transnational perspective by connecting her own memories and existential struggles with the traumatic events of a different nation and its people. With its multicultural, heterogeneous, and often contradictory cultural phenomena, Los Angeles as the "City of Angels" seems "faraway so close" to the Berlin that Wolf knows and that Wim Wenders celebrates in his film *Der Himmel über Berlin* (*Wings of Desire*, 1987). In all its complexity and contradictoriness, it is the perfect setting for Wolf's attempts to create a new type of transnational memory work in her writing.[6]

With this move to deterritorialize her own memory and bring it into exchange with international memories, the narrator/author performs a first step toward what Levy and Sznaider have called the formation of a new "cosmopolitan memory." The notion of collective memory, mostly understood as national memory, might have to be bracketed for a while, as Andreas Huyssen argues, since a homogeneous national memory is increasingly challenged by "group memories at the subnational or regional level, as well as by diasporic memory mixings encountered with the increasing flows of migration" (615). It is exactly this move, I argue, that Wolf makes with *City of Angels*. Santa Monica, the place of exile for so many German-Jewish emigrants, becomes the place where memory can be brought into flux. It is a place where the narrator can analyze the nature of her memories and their importance in her life. *City of Angels* does what Walter Benjamin called for in his "Excavation and Memory" ("Ausgraben und Erinnern"), which serves as the epigraph of the book: "So, for authentic memories, it is far less important that the investigator report on them than that he mark, quite precisely, the site where he gained possession of them." Santa Monica, Los Angeles, and Death Valley are places where many different strands of memory can come together to gain a new lighter sense, a "Leichtsinn," as Wolf emphasizes in *City of Angels*.[7] Anna Kuhn makes a related point about travel in the novel, noting that "travel figures both literally and figuratively in *City of Angels*: literally by placing the narrator outside of the socio-political order of her homeland, thereby affording her critical distance to reassess that order, and figuratively, by facilitating the narrator's fanciful explorations of different epistemological orders" (181–82). In addition to allowing the narrator to explore different epistemological orders, travel in *City of Angels* is also a means to re-examine and create a new approach to memory work that incorporates transnational and transcultural perspectives.

The study of transnational or cosmopolitan memory is a promising new approach that has been explored in memory studies in recent years. As Levy and Sznaider explain, global or cosmopolitan memory transcends "ethnic and national boundaries and its memories evolve from the encounter of global interpretations and local sensibilities" and "through the fiery interaction between the local and the global" (92–93). With regard to Holocaust memory, they argue that the dual processes of particularization and universalization have produced a symbol of transnational solidarity, one that does not replace national collective memories but exists as their horizon. To Levy and Sznaider this is an important development because a global collective memory could become the cultural foundation for global human rights policies. In connection with the need for such policies, Huyssen writes, the task would be to "recognize the universal dimension in systemic oppression and human suffering rather than pitting one kind of memory against another. Both memory and rights discourse need to nurture a universalizing dimension that recognizes particularity without reifying it" (621). Or as Michael Rothberg's concept of multidirectional memory suggests, this type of memory should be considered "subject to ongoing negotiation, cross-referencing, and borrowing; as productive and not privative" (3).

In *City of Angels*, such transnational and multidirectional memory functions in three important ways. Firstly, the discussions in Los Angeles open up new layers of the narrator's own memory, some of which had been forgotten and deeply buried in her psyche. For example, a TV film about Charlie Chaplin and his persecution by FBI director Edgar J. Hoover and the many miles of files Hoover left behind triggers memories of a district attorney in the GDR who had been removed from office when he refused to bring charges against Walter Janka, editor-in-chief of the Aufbau Verlag, and journalist Wolfgang Harich, who had been accused of conspiring against the socialist state. Janka's words to "stand by the flag of humanity" echo in her ear as she struggles to come to terms with her own confrontation with her "file" (*City of Angels* 201–3).

Secondly, conversations with friends and colleagues who offer help and their own experiences relativize the narrator's own traumatic memories and make her feel less alone. In these conversations, the balance between insistence on the uniqueness of her own memories and the need to compare is striking. When the narrator tries to explain to her friend Sally how incomprehensible it is to her that she could have forgotten that she collaborated with the secret police, Sally tries to console her by saying that she also had been just as certain that she would never find a letter from her husband's mistress in his pocket, adding quickly, "not that she wanted to compare the two cases, only our false certainties" (152). An important aspect in this exchange is the fact that Sally does not speak any German and all of these experiences must be translated into a foreign language, a step that affords additional negotiations and approximations. In fact, these instances of comparison and analysis of different memories from very different contexts in *City of Angels* echo the debates about the appropriateness of comparing other genocides to the Holocaust. In the context of the Holocaust, the claims of uniqueness versus comparability have triggered heated debates that reached a highpoint in the 1980s in the so-called *Historikerstreit* (historians' dispute). Against these longstanding debates, Rothberg argues that it is precisely the comparative approach of multidirectional memory that can provide new creative dimensions to memory.

Thirdly, aside from allowing the narrator to think through her own memories in dialogue with her friends, this practice of multidirectional and transnational memory gives the narrator completely new insights into her own situation and the predicament of the "small country from which I come" (314). While Wolf has always brought her own memories into conversation with contemporary national and international political concerns (in *Kindheitsmuster*, for example, the Vietnam War plays an important role), in *City of Angels* this dialogue is elevated to a new level, as the incorporation of and empathy for others' memories help her to heal. After all, it is Angelina from Uganda, part of the cleaning crew at the hotel Ms. Victoria, who helps her to emerge from the darkest moments of her memory work when she reappears to her as an angel. At the end of her trip, the narrator claims, "A task had been finished, Angelina, but why don't I feel a sense of accomplishment? A word came to me that I had been unconsciously seeking for weeks: preliminary. A preliminary work has reached a preliminary end. Angelina laughed: But isn't that always the case?" (314). Only in Death Valley, when she learns to incorporate her new U.S. experiences and integrate with her earlier ones in Germany, can she gain the necessary "carefreeness" (315), which allows her to see the journey as the goal. Thus the novel ends with the words: "she [Angelina] seemed satisfied and flew on in silence, keeping me at her side. Where are we going? I don't know" (315).

The story of Angelina, the new migrant worker in Los Angeles, who works two jobs and has not seen her children in three years and who accompanies the narrator on her trip through the Southwest, helps her to think through the universal aspects of human oppression and suffering, as well as her own complicity in it. After all, it is the insurmountable distance between the affluent white hotel guest and the black cleaning woman that prevents any kind of communication between the two in the real world. All of the narrator's attempts to reach out to the cleaning crew by offering them drinks and alleviating their workload are in vain and, later on, the narrator has to endure the sarcastic comments of the angel Angelina, which make her understand how utterly inadequate her feeble attempts have been. The capitalist system puts both women in their respective places, from which neither one of them can escape. Paradoxically, however, it is Angelina's story that helps to explain why the author Christa Wolf held on to the socialist utopia of an egalitarian society for so long. Just as the fate of the Anasazi that she experiences on her trip through the Southwest puts the struggles of the "little country I came from" (314) into a surprising and completely new context, so does the encounter with Angelina provide new connections that help her to understand her own struggles and transgressions. Through Angelina she understands, for example, that having been immersed in the antifascist ideology of the GDR, which prohibited her thinking about German suffering after the war as other than a just punishment, she has become guilty of never mourning the death by starvation of her grandmother on the trek west (308–9). Empathy with others and their memories of trauma and abuse create possibilities for a fresh understanding of one's own past. Just as Rothberg rejects memory as a zero-sum game and instead insists on a multidirectional memory that includes moments of appropriation as well as complex acts of solidarity, Wolf seems to contemplate memory as "a journey to the other side of reality" (293), one that includes hubris as well as moments of clear understanding, doubts as well as great insights in the turn to other people's suffering. Angelina's last act is to transfer her own *Leichtsinn* to the author:

> She wanted to make me as carefree as she was. She wanted me to enjoy our flight, to look down and, saying goodbye, etch into my mind forever the magnificent line of the bay, the white edge of foam that the ocean spilled onto the shore, the strip of sand between the water and the coastal road, the row of palm trees, and the darker mountain range in the background. (315)

Angelina's is an appeal to start at the beginning, if necessary, and to take seriously the "state of one's soul," because "every other catastrophe comes out of that" (315). Through Angelina, the narrator realizes that the stories of others, such as Angelina's story of economic oppression, the mysterious vanishing of the ancient Anasazi in the Southwest, and the news of xenophobia in unified Germany, are the real "traces of pain and suffering" that one needs to follow and connect. When the narrator is joined by Angelina at the end of her trip (she is conspicuously absent in Los Alamos and in Las Vegas), she knows that she has finally succeeded in arriving "at the other side of reality" (293). "It happened at some point during this tour of the canyon," she says,

> with its intense red and ocher tones that blazed back to life almost painfully against the bright green of the trees shortly before sunset (the sky had cleared up toward evening)—it was then that something fundamental changed within me. ... I stood there and looked at it and felt a message reach me, or an insight, I don't know what to call it. I took a deep breath. I was free. ... Maybe this was why I had come to America? (292)

The narrator knows at the end of her journey that memory needs to be dialogic, an "echo chamber," as Rothberg claims. The novel ends with memories of Los Angeles merging with those from her own country, allowing her to construct a new kind of memory that is, at once, specific and local, as well as multidirectional and transnational. Such a memory in *City of Angels*, which she knew would be her last major book,[8] is Christa Wolf's legacy; it reaches out to others and takes moral responsibility for caring about the suffering of others, even if they seem "faraway and so close" at the same time.

Silke von der Emde is Associate Professor of German Studies at Vassar College. She is the author of *Entering History: Feminist Dialogues in Irmtraud Morgner's Prose* (2004), as well as articles on GDR literature, feminist theory, memory, and German film. In addition to her scholarship on contemporary German literature, film, and culture, she regularly teaches courses on Holocaust and Memory Studies. She has also co-published several articles on foreign language pedagogy. She is currently writing a book with the working title *Women, Memory, and Archives*.

Notes

1. With the reunification of the two German states came calls for Germany to focus less on the past and to develop a more positive self-image. One example was Martin Walser's 1998 acceptance speech for the Peace Prize of the German Booksellers Association, in which he decried the pervasiveness of Auschwitz in societal discourse and challenged Germans to accept their own normalcy.
2. In *Dialektik der Aufklärung*, Adorno and Horkheimer argued that the final logic of Enlightenment was the development of an "instrumental reason," under which the domination of mankind over nature was later transformed into human beings dominating other human beings (e.g., the Nazi oppression of the Jews). Because the full horrors of the Holocaust were not yet uncovered at the time of the publication of the book, Adorno and Horkheimer did not specifically address the Shoah in *Dialectic of Enlightenment*. Yet their warnings about the legacy of Enlightenment were justified in light of the hyper-rationalist, ultra-bureaucratic planning behind the Holocaust that was discovered after the war. In his *Negative Dialektik*, published two decades later, Adorno articulates the true extent of the fall of humanity outside the bounds of the Enlightenment.
3. The term *Spaßkultur* originated in the 1996 cover story of *Der Spiegel*, as Stephen Brockmann explains in "The Politics of German Comedy." Katharina Gerstenberger and Patricia Herminghouse compare the generation of *Spaßkultur* to the me-generation in the U.S.
4. Barrett translates "mich ergreift ein gräßlicher Übermut" as "I'm getting horribly worked up" but "Übermut" also connotes the complete inappropriateness of the feeling in this life-threatening situation. This is repeated a little further in the text with "someone's grinning within me" (*In the Flesh* 55).
5. As a result of the 11th Plenum of the SED in 1965, functionaries decided to stage a crackdown on GDR cinema and the arts; Christa Wolf, then thirty-four years old, spoke in defense of the artists at the meeting, but was repeatedly interrupted and baited. 1976 was marked by the expatriation of Wolf Biermann; Wolf was one of the authors of the protest letter published in the West German magazine *Der Spiegel* ("Wir protestieren"). On 9 November 1989, as the result of a series of peaceful protests, in which she had participated, the Berlin Wall came down.
6. *In weiter Ferne so nah* (*Faraway so Close*, 1993) is Wim Wender's sequel to *Der Himmel über Berlin* (*Wings of Desire*, 1987). The film was remade and set in Los Angeles in 1998.
7. "Leichtsinn" is rendered as "carefreeness" in Damion Searls's translation. In German, *Leichtsinn* carries connotations of flippancy and thoughtlessness, as well as a more literal meaning as a light and easy sense/mind. Wolf is clearly playing with the double meaning of the term, going back to the literal meaning of the word.
8. In *Sei dennoch unverzagt: Gespräche mit meinen Großeltern Christa und Gerhard Wolf*, edited by her granddaughter Jana Simon, Christa Wolf states that *Stadt der Engel* will be her last book (141).

Bibliography

Adelson, Leslie. *Making Bodies, Making History: Feminism and German Identity.* Lincoln: University of Nebraska Press, 1993.

Adorno, Theodor W. *Negative Dialektik.* Frankfurt am Main: Suhrkamp, 1966.

Assmann, Jan. *Das kulturelle Gedächtnis: Schrift, Erinnerung und politische Identität in den frühen Hochkulturen.* Munich: C.H. Beck, 2005.

Benjamin, Walter. "Excavation and Memory." *Selected Writings: Volume 2 1927–1934,* edited by Michael W. Jennings, Howard Eiland, and Gary Smith; translated by Rodney Livingstone. Cambridge, MA: Harvard University Press, 1999.

Brecht, Bertolt. "An die Nachgeborenen." *Ausgewählte Werke in 6 Bänden.* Frankfurt a.M.: Suhrkamp Verlag, 1997.

Brockmann, Stephen. "The Politics of German Comedy." *German Studies Review,* vol. 23, no. 1, February 2000, pp. 33–51.

Catani, Stefanie. "Vom Anfang und Ende des Mythos: 'Medea' bei Christa Wolf und Dea Loher." *Monatshefte,* vol. 99, no. 3, Fall 2007, pp. 316–32.

Eigler Friederike. *Gedächtnis und Geschichte in Generationenromanen seit der Wende.* Berlin: Erich Schmidt Verlag, 2005.

Gerstenberger, Katharina, and Patricia Herminghouse, editors. *German Literature in a New Century: Trends, Traditions, Transitions, and Transformations.* New York: Berghahn Books, 2008.

Gansel, Carsten. "Erinnerung, Aufstörung und 'blinde Flecken' im Werk von Christa Wolf." *Christa Wolf: Im Strom Der Erinnerung,* edited by Carsten Gansel. Göttingen: V&R Unipress, 2014, pp. 15–41.

Der Himmel über Berlin (Wings of Desire). Directed by Wim Wenders, ufa, 1987.

Horkheimer, Max, and Theodor W. Adorno. *Dialektik Der Aufklärung: Philosophische Fragmente.* Amsterdam: Querido, 1947.

Huyssen, Andreas. "International Human Rights and the Politics of Memory: Limits and Challenges." *Criticism,* vol. 53, no. 4, Fall 2011, pp. 607–24.

Köhler, Astrid. *Brückenschläge: DDR-Autoren vor und nach der Wiedervereinigung.* Göttingen: Vandenhoeck & Ruprecht, 2007.

Kuhn, Anna K. "Of Angels, Trauma and Healing: Christa Wolf's *Stadt der Engel oder The Overcoat of Dr. Freud.*" *Gegenwartsliteratur: A German Studies Yearbook,* vol. 10, 2011, pp. 164–85.

Levy, Daniel, and Natan Sznaider. "Memory Unbound: The Holocaust and the Formation of Cosmopolitan Memory." *European Journal of Social Theory,* vol. 5, no. 1, February 2002, pp. 87–106.

Magenau, Jörg. "Ans Selbstgespräch gefesselt." *TAZ.de,* 26 June 2010, http://www.taz.de/1/archiv/digitaz/artikel/?ressort=ku&dig=2010 percent2F06 percent2F26 percent2Fa0028.

Rothberg, Michael. *Multidirectional Memory: Remembering the Holocaust in the Age of Decolonization.* Stanford, CA: Stanford University Press, 2009.

Simon, Jana. *Sei dennoch unverzagt: Gespräche mit meinen Groäeltern Christa und Gerhard Wolf.* Berlin: Ullstein Verlag, 2013.

Walser, Martin. "Rede in der Paulskirche am 11. Oktober 1998." http://www.friedenspreis-des-deutschen-buchhandels.de/sixcms/media.php/1290/1998_walser.pdf.
Weigel, Sigrid. *Bilder des kulturellen Gedächtnisses: Beiträge zur Gegenwartsliteratur.* Dülmen-Hiddengsel: tende, 1994.
"'Wir protestieren': Offener Brief der Berliner Künstler mit der Bitte um die Rücknahme der Ausbürgerung Wolf Biermanns vom 17. November 1976." http://www.1000dokumente.de/index.html?c=dokument_de&dokument=0213_bie&object=translation&st=&l=de.
Wolf, Christa. *City of Angels or, The Overcoat of Dr. Freud.* Translated by Damion Searls. New York: Farrar, Straus and Giroux, 2014.
——— . *Der geteilte Himmel.* 13th ed. Munich: DTV, 1981.
——— . *In the Flesh: A Novel by Christa Wolf.* Translated by John S. Barrett. Boston: David R. Godine, 2005.
——— . *Kassandra.* Darmstadt: Luchterhand Verlag, 1983.
——— . *Kein Ort. Nirgends.* Darmstadt: Luchterhand Verlag, 1979.
——— . *Kindheitsmuster.* Darmstadt: Luchterhand Verlag, 1976.
——— . *Leibhaftig. Erzählung.* Munich: Luchterhand Literaturverlag, 2002.
——— . *Medea: Stimmen.* Darmstadt: Luchterhand Literaturverlag, 1996.
——— . *Moskauer Novelle.* Halle: Mitteldeutscher Verlag, 1961.
——— . *Nachdenken über Christa T.* Neuwied: Luchterhand, 1968.
——— . *Sommerstück.* Frankfurt a.M.: Luchterhand Literaturverlag, 1989.
——— . *Stadt der Engel oder The Overcoat of Dr. Freud.* Berlin: Suhrkamp Verlag, 2010.
——— . *Ein Tag im Jahr.* Munich: Luchterhand Literaturverlag, 2003.
——— . *Was bleibt.* Frankfurt a.M.: Luchterhand Literaturverlag, 1990.

CHAPTER 2

Who's Afraid of Christa Wolf or The Overcoat of Dr. Freud
Memory and Its Discontents

MARTINA KOLB

> It didn't surprise me that an overcoat was talking to me.
> —*City of Angels* 188

> What lingers is the smell of her father's grey overcoat.
> —*Patterns of Childhood* 33

Christa Wolf was painfully aware of the vicissitudes of place and history, memory and anxiety. With her final novel,[1] she memorialized this acute sensitivity one last time in a complex mnemonic intertexture, beginning with the conspicuous bilingual conjunction of its German title: *Stadt der Engel oder The Overcoat of Dr. Freud* (2010).[2] While the first element has enjoyed significant attention, Freud's overcoat has not been considered in a detailed way to date.[3] Through the interdisciplinary lens of psychoanalysis and its primary interest in how and when memory can become language (how and when the unconscious is translated into the conscious), this essay sets out to remedy this neglect, and, in doing so, does not focus on angels, Los Angeles, Walter Benjamin's Angel of History, guardian angel Angelina, or Wolf's controversially debated retreat from the public during her Getty Residency.[4]

Rather, it has been my intention to look at Wolf's late novel as an experiential and linguistically adventurous quest that candidly reveals its narrator's vulnerability, and to explore intertextually the identity, scope, and fabric, as it were, of the overcoat in an argument anchored in Freudian thought, the therapeutic value of storytelling, and Freud's actual exile. Given Wolf's intriguing choice of Dr. Freud's coat, her frequent use of the noun "Gewebe" to qualify fiction is of heightened significance, that is: "fabric," "weaving," or "texture" figuratively deployed to visualize her nonlinear narrative method, particularly but not exclusively with regard to her last novel (see for example Wolf in Gansel 354 and 363). Further, it is not only critical in an analytic but also in a historical sense that Wolf explicitly summons Freud, whose mature work came to the fore right at the time of Germany's decline into collective totalitarian terror—which precisely coincides with the period of exilic experience ranging from Freud's (1938–1939) and Wolf's (1945–) own to that of the numerous first- and second-generation German-Jewish exiles whom she and her narrator meet in Los Angeles.

Unlike Bertolt Brecht, Thomas Mann, and many other exiles mentioned in *City of Angels, or, The Overcoat of Dr. Freud*, Freud never set foot in "Weimar under Palms" (*City of Angels* 155, 257), as Wolf repeats the nickname for the California colony of German speakers who fled there during Nazi rule.[5] Freud did, however, spend his last fourteen months in London and died there about three weeks after the German invasion of Poland. Wolf refers to Freud's coat with a definite article, although Freud surely owned more than one coat. In the narrative context of a multilayered story within the story where Wolf's reader learns that her narrator's friend Bob Rice was allegedly gifted with this coat of Freud's by the widow of Richard Neutra, the famous architect who had known Freud in Vienna (*City of Angels* 115–16),[6] the focus on a specific garment seems hardly farfetched: his last coat, worn in June 1938 on his flight from Vienna, via Paris, to London—the exilic overcoat of Dr. Freud.[7]

There are two conspicuous manifestations of imaginative proto-dialogue in the novel where the narrator's inner life reigns supreme. One when she addresses herself from the vantage point of the first person as a second person (with the effect of a soliloquy); the other when she conjures verbal interactions with the overcoat (in the third person rather than apostrophically), which presents a turn inward that is immediately followed by verbal externalization.[8] These two articulate manifestations are intertwined, when she occasionally addresses herself in the second person while talking about the coat, and when the critical voice in her soliloquies comes across as a parental representation typical for a transpersonal, internalized authority that once began in an actual relationship with the father.

Wolf's narrator cultivates an impassioned, if ambiguous relationship with the overcoat of Dr. Freud, a seemingly ordinary object that becomes an extraordinary subject in Bob's intriguing story, and ultimately, as an intermediate phenomenon between fictional fabrication and material presence, serves as an uncanny, fetishistic object and therapeutic interlocutor.[9] Through this coat, the narrator's desire to remember, write, and find deceased L(ily) seeks satisfaction. She invests the coat with psychic energy and stands in awe of it (her reverence is tinged with fear), as if tacitly undermining idiomatic meanings that coats have assumed in German. *Sein Mäntelchen nach dem Wind hängen* comes to mind, which signifies opportunism, or *etwas / sich ein Mäntelchen umhängen*, which intends sugarcoating—as well as the symbolic "heavy overcoat" on which Freud himself elaborated.[10] With the coat, Wolf, while "[c]loth[ing] the [absent] doctor with authority" (Freud, "Transference," 445), dismantles, as it were, by way of world literature and an anticipated end of life's journey, the complex texture of memory that Freud, too, painstakingly tried to reveal in analysis, relying on archaeological representations of spatialized time as a disciplinary point of comparison.[11]

The narrative method and literary intent of *City of Angels* are reminiscent of the early Wolf's autobiographically infused fictional technique, particularly as she employed it in *Patterns of Childhood* (*Kindheitsmuster*, [1976] 2007).[12] Counting on the author's commemoration of (dis)place(ment), both novels portray the fragmentary character of memory and present narrators affected by the exigencies of a past that lingers and burdens the present and repeats itself in literary reenactments. *Patterns of Childhood* recalls and fictionalizes Wolf's childhood and adolescence marked by the family's 1945 expulsion from their home in the formerly German province of Brandenburg, now western Poland, which she visited as an adult in 1971, when "Reiseziel G." (travel destination G./Gorzów) geographically coincided for her with "Geburtsort L." (birthplace L./Landsberg). And in *City of Angels*, where the "fateful cipher L." (38) encrypts the exiled psychoanalyst Lily and "G." (44) implies Peter Gutman, the narrator's closest colleague and principal partner in conversation at the Getty Research Institute, she pays tribute to her California sojourn (1992–1993) late in life.[13] In other words, the trauma-ridden toponym "G." returns in *City of Angels* as an exilic eponym. This repetition of initials strikes the inclined reader as noteworthy—in analysis, repetition is never considered arbitrary—even if beyond the chronology of L. preceding G., a precise significance seems difficult to determine.

Patterns of Childhood and *City of Angels* perform a plethora of Freudian concerns and concepts: memory, amnesia, denial, defense, repression, libido, sublimation, dissociation, the latent, the manifest, the uncanny, trauma, hypnosis, hysteria, parapraxis, psychosis, neurosis, transference, acting out, censorship, fetishism, screen memories, dreams, repetitions, translations, shame, fear, and pain. And the following formulations illustrate the pervasive presence of central Freudian notions in Wolf's two novels: "What is past is not dead; it is not even past." (*Patterns of Childhood* 3);[14] "How did we become what we are today?" (209); "to follow the traces of pain and suffering" (*City of Angels* 7); or "telling the story from the end" (17). No less important is the reappearance of a certain object that is the ambiguously charged father (figure)'s coat, which at once recalls, haunts, scares, affects, and protects. In *Patterns of Childhood*, "the smell" (33) and even the "odor of the coat" (177) is mentioned, as the girl is wrapped and buries her face in it. Linked to war and expulsion, the lingering, haunting characteristics of the father's coat have an affinity with the qualities of another exilic outer garment: Freud's overcoat.

And there is no surprise in *City of Angels* when this coat addresses the narrator, since there has been an authorial awareness over decades of the father's overcoat as one that had come to stay.

Along with Wolf's steadfast turn to Freudian garb and mnemonic texture in *City of Angels*, her related commitment to émigré etymology, multilingualism, translation, and world literature could not be stronger in a work whose title speaks exilic volumes (with the intermediate space between originals and translations resembling that between the unconscious and the conscious). If book and film titles tend to be descriptive headings or distinctive homages (such as *Stadt der Engel/City of Angels*), subtitles are generally conceived as explanatory additions or translations. In subtitled movies, they are simultaneous renderings in a different language (including a defamiliarizing shift from spoken dialogue to written word), provisions of a wider access via translation. At first glance, *The Overcoat of Dr. Freud* seems to be a subtitle since it appears second and in English. However, this curiously obsolete phrase is no secondary title; no punctuation separates the two portions of the full title and the article is capitalized, so that *The Overcoat of Dr. Freud* is syntactically coordinated with, rather than subordinated to *City of Angels*. Further, it refers to Bob's story of loss as it coincides with the narrator's incipient writing and hence marks the book's climax (meaning well for her, Gutman—'good man'—, too, encourages her "writ[ing] up" *City of Angels* 270). Conversely, although placed first, *Stadt der Engel* shares features with a subtitle, for it is an evocative translation of the novel's setting, the City of Los Angeles, nicknamed City of Angels.

Los Angeles is the Americanized Spanish toponym that Wolf translated into her native tongue to title her last novel, thus rendering the place at once literal and "secretly familiar" (Freud, "Uncanny," 245). Freud defined the uncanny in a way that foreshadows Wolf's narrator's sense of gloom, doom, haunting, and alienation. That *The Overcoat of Dr. Freud* should reflect the language in which she presumably listened to the story about this coat in Bob's memorable storytelling, further complicates the challenges of translation and estrangement. The book needs both titles, not only to announce its transferential, transitional, fetishistic, uncanny, and altogether repetitive qualities, but also to distinguish itself from other works set in Los Angeles and titled accordingly, such as Robert Rosenberg's *Stadt der Engel*, Tracie Peterson and James Scott Bell's, Cy Coleman, Larry Gelbart and David Zippel's, and Brad Silberling's *City of Angels* (a remake of Wim Wenders's *Wings of Desire*, the latter resonates with Wolf's outlook on lost angels).

Damion Searls's uppercase CITY OF ANGELS OR, THE OVERCOAT OF DR. FREUD introduces a strangely placed comma and does not convey the subtleties of Wolf's intricate original. Alain Lance's and Renate Lance-Otterbein's French translation, *Ville des anges: Ou The Overcoat of Dr. Freud*, by contrast, keeps the capitalized *The* and underscores Wolf's challenging coordination, as does Anita Raja's Italian translation, *La città degli angeli ovvero The Overcoat of Dr. Freud*. "Ovvero" translates as "or rather" (the simple "o" would be "or"), placing emphasis on Freud's coat as the more precise of the book's two titles—a welcome nuance for the present discussion, which features Freud's unexpected concreteness in opposition to the relative elusiveness of Los Angeles, while drawing attention to Wolf's strong reliance on psychoanalytic and exilic paradigms through which she tackles her position as novelist. Carmen Gauger's Spanish translation, *La ciudad de Los Ángeles o El abrigo del Dr. Freud*, albeit, along with the Italian rendering, most faithful to the original (no punctuation, lower-case *o*, and capitalized *El*), curiously presents both Wolf's German and Bob's English in Spanish.

In accord with the original, some variations render the toponymic implications of the setting more mysterious by translating the city's Spanish name into English, French, or Italian. This is most evident in French and Italian (lower-case *anges*, *angeli*), whereas in Spanish the task is challenging, since Los Angeles *is* Spanish (the translator capitalizes the name, leaving *ciudad* in lower case). The title of the English translation is monolingual and hence less intriguing than the bilingual original, but for an English translator to revert to a language other than English for *The Overcoat of Dr. Freud* would make little sense, since Bob presumably tells his story in English, which was Freud's exilic language as well. Indeed, the last mention of the coat in the German text reads: "*What about my overcoat?*" (*City of Angels* 284).[15] In sum, the exilic dimension of experience is marked in no uncertain terms by the book's bilingual title and the copresence of German and English throughout. Its macaronic and exilic qualities hovering between the familiar and the strange, floating between self and other, cannot be overestimated in any deep reading of Wolf's last work.[16]

Although proverbially warned not to indulge in such prejudicial practice, we often do judge books by their covers. The jackets of *City of Angels* either feature the Pacific location and climate or the Getty Museum (inaugurated after Wolf's departure from the Getty Center)—with the exception of the Spanish translation, whose cover portrays a coat.[17] When regarded on the basis of the publishers' visual preference for the city rather than the coat, Wolf's novel becomes a California book. Despite her narrator's fascination with Wilshire Boulevard and "the rough poetry of the freeways" (*City of Angels* 20) however, her places transcend the implication of mere literary settings, continuing, in Freudian manner, as what they have been for her since her expulsion experience in 1945: "mnemotopes" (Assmann 59).

After the title, Freud is first mentioned in one of the narrator's conversations with Gutman, who faces severe obstacles in completing his study on an unnamed philosopher (likely Walter Benjamin, see Smale 183–184). In the midst of this crisis, he asks rhetorically: "do we really need much familiarity with Herr Freud to find it neurotic, this unquenchable need to express [one]self through another, to take refuge behind another person?" (*City of Angels* 91). Gutman's diagnostic statement about neurotic replacement is intriguing, since both *Patterns of Childhood* and *City of Angels* begin with the words of others: the former with Wolf's translated appropriation of "the past is never dead; it's not even past," silently borrowed from *Requiem for a Nun*, William Faulkner's trans-generic experiment with dramatic technique and narrative perspective, in which the protagonist faces her violent past (73).[18] While Faulkner's narrative is composed in dramatic form, its storyline, like Wolf's, frequently interrupts itself, for instance by insertions of prose segments to reveal a seemingly actual history of an allegedly fictional place: *Yoknapatawpha*. This Chickasaw toponym signifies "split land" and accords with Wolf's narrators' affective, proto-schizophrenic experiences of places (re)named and borders (un)done, ranging from the wartime Oder-Neisse to the post-Wende Pacific Ocean half a century later, where her narrator "was sitting among refugees" (*City of Angels* 74), feeling the challenges of identity and identification in exilic experience.[19]

In *Patterns of Childhood*, Faulkner's words in translation are preceded by three other texts: Pablo Neruda's "Book of Questions," a poem that poses existential questions about childhood, identity, and death; then by Wolf's dedication to her daughters; and finally, by a paragraph (repeated in contraction in *City of Angels*), stating that her characters are fictional and, as such, not identical with actual people; the same, she states, applies to events. That this critical passage is frequently taken too lightly and various translations leave it out entirely, is highly problematic, in that a reader's generic lens—novel versus autobiography—significantly codetermines her interpretive vantage point. It is conspicuously in line with literary tradition that neither places nor times are included in Wolf's plea for fiction, so that the narrative situation presents fictional characters in real settings, such as Los Angeles in the 1990s or Landsberg/Gorzów in the 1930s, 1940s, and 1970s—an ongoing fictional convention at least as ancient than Attic tragedy (think Oedipus in Thebes, Hamlet in Denmark, Hanold in Pompeii—in *Gradiva*, see endnote 1). Further, Freud's intermediate status in *City of Angels* between historiography/biography on the one hand, and fiction/literary fabrication on the other, provides another avenue of access to Wolf's arrangement. A real person, Freud is not Wolf's invention. However, rather than being an actual character, Freud is, through a coat that was allegedly his, an absent presence in the text, reminiscent of Nikolai Gogol's *post-mortem* Akaky in the Russian novella of the eponymous overcoat.

City of Angels includes no dedication but starts with words by others that question what was previously characterized as fictional ("inventions of the novelist," *City of Angels* n. p.). Beyond the title, which is an intra-textual borrowing of Bob's story ("Take everything you can use," says Bob to the narrator, 155), there is Benjamin's passage about memory's intertwinement with place ("mark quite precisely the site," *City of Angels* n. p.), reminiscent of Freud's archaeological metaphors and followed by Edgar Lawrence Doctorow's claim that a writer cannot render the actual fabric of "lived life."[20] Wolf shares these considerations with her readers before her novel properly begins, and throughout it, there is a noticeable tension between Benjamin's relative optimism about mnemotopia and Doctorow's relative realism about art—as well as between Faulkner's apocryphal country and Wolf's experience of places as mnemonic loci of traumatic dimension.

In Freud's late life, Vienna and London became places of such traumatic scope. The German annexation of Austria in 1938 signaled the necessity of escape from Berggasse 19, so that Freud "was to spend the last year of his life in … exile … He knew that he was living on borrowed time" (Molnar, 227). In light of these facts, Wolf's fictional overcoat plays a significant role in her novel's altogether psychoanalytic scenario. After all, her narrator's stated reason for coming to Los Angeles in the first place is to learn the identity of L., the exiled Jewish psychoanalyst whose letters to Emma she carries with her (*City of Angels* 11).[21]

With its retrospective composition, *City of Angels* comes across as an assembly of fragments, a work in progress.[22] As such, it strongly resembles Freudian analysis as vertical endeavor, that is, as a nonlinear, unpolished process of increased awareness and distressing self-discovery, permeated by moments and mechanisms of defense, denial, and repression, as well as by those of transference projection. Written in the search mode, *City of Angels* stakes no claim to an accomplished confession or commemorative mission—and ends as openly as it begins (Smale writes of "an equivocal note," 199). Its narrator is intensely aware of "the blind spot" (32) but tries to recuperate and understand mnemonic and repressive processes psychoanalytically. Rife with personal and literary reminiscence and intertextual remembrance, the winding and frequently disjointed narrative reverts to oneiric contemporaneity and the dilemma of soliloquies—words by a self to itself as another: "to look into [one's] own otherness" (88)—reflecting memory and its discontents through the condensed and displaced entity that is (the narrative effigy of) Freud's exilic overcoat.

City of Angels invites comparisons with two other existential overcoats: indirectly (intertextually) with Gogol's bespoke *Overcoat*, the most famous literary text to honor such apparel; and explicitly (intra-textually) with Freud's outermost garment (introduced by Bob's captivating confabulation), which, as a transitional object of desire that anchors her narrator's intentions in times of upheaval, affects her, increases her capacity for suffering, offers a glimpse of hope, and helps her pave her way toward transference and inchoate articulation—on fictional grounds.

One day, the narrator, with Bob and a few others, drives around Los Angeles to see some Neutra houses. Upon their arrival in his apartment, Bob tells stories, offers wine, and displays his "knack for symbolic gestures" (113). "[A]lways attuned to what was going on around him" (115), Bob eventually tells

> the story of how he acquired Freud's overcoat and lost it again. It was Richard Neutra's widow who had given him, her husband's faithful chronicler, Neutra's overcoat as a memento after Neutra's death. Originally, she assured him, it had been *the overcoat of* Dr. Freud—they were both Austrians, both from Vienna, and had known each other well. The coat was old by that point but not shabby: good prewar manufacture. Bob was certain that he would be able to handle any situation in life in this coat … Bob said he had not worn it but had hung it on the door of his *office* at the university so that he could always see it. Then he had had to go away for a few days, and he had locked his door … He could swear to that. When he came back, he couldn't believe his eyes. The coat was gone … He was and remained inconsolable. All he had was the thought that … the coat had ended up on … one of the *homeless people* and was keeping him warm …
>
> *What do you think of my story*, Bob asked me later.
>
> Listen, I said, tomorrow I am going to start writing a book that will be called: THE CITY OF ANGELS, OR, THE OVERCOAT OF DR. FREUD. Do it, Bob said, and then came his generous offer: Take everything you can use. Everything? I said.
>
> Everything, he said.
>
> That will be a book, I said, I can never publish.
>
> It's a working hypothesis you use to get closer to things, Bob said.
>
> That won't be enough this time, I said. I'm scared, of course.
>
> I know, Bob said. Take care of yourself.
>
> He brought a book of poems to the table, bilingual … for me to pick one and recite it in German. (115–16)[23]

Bob's story reaches the reader in the narrator's reported speech. In German grammar, such indirect speech requires the subjunctive mode, which places an even greater emphasis on the story's conjectural qualities than is the case in English. Another remove from directness results from the assumption that if Wolf in California heard any such coat story at all, she most probably did so in English, so that what she presents to her reader, if not pure invention, is her memory of another's story in her German translation, sprinkled with Bob's original English—Wolf mentions the effect of English on her as a "fremde Sprache" ("foreign language"; Wolf in Gansel 362) and emphasizes how her understanding of her native German was fine-tuned by the presence of English as she was conceiving her last book. But then who *is* Bob anyway, storyteller, university professor and Neutra's alleged chronicler, since Wolf emphatically calls her characters fictional (with Bob possibly based on Neutra expert Thomas Hines, whom Wolf met in Los Angeles; see Blankenship 59 note 3)? Bob, in any case, invites her narrator to "take care of [her]self," which beyond the colloquial scope of a well-intended "so long" also implies his appeal to her for self-analysis (which is where Freud began his analytic career)—"to get closer to things" through writing, against the odds of wavering between care and scare ("I'm going to start writing … I'm scared, of course").

What exactly *is* this verbally conjured overcoat, whose specter accompanies the narrator, assisting her (and Bob) in coping with loss through storytelling, while advising them not to forget the mnemonic mandate—almost as Hamlet's father's ghost with his insistent words "Remember me" reminds his procrastinating son of the onerous task he has bestowed upon him (Shakespeare 30)? Simply claiming the coat's material absence without complicating its presence in the novel, seems specious at best, since the narrator's ongoing interaction with the coat is the precise transitional venue for her to actively experience a narrative breakthrough rather than passively suffering a nervous breakdown.

Bob's story about Freud's coat is an intra-text known through Wolf, whereas Gogol's novella independently tells of Akaky Akakyevich, a copier of documents whose life changes radically when he affords the replacement of his threadbare overcoat. It is evident that this coat is not only of great practical but also of enormous sentimental value to its owner. When a stranger attacks Akaky and steals the coat, and Akaky fails to recuperate it, his death approaches suddenly. For an understanding of Gogol's implicit uncanny presence in Wolf—from Bob's story on, Freud's coat is explicitly mentioned an additional fifteen times, whereas no direct reference is made to Gogol's *Overcoat*[24]—Akaky's death is decisive, for Gogol's story ends not with the protagonist's death, but with his *post-mortem* appropriation of the coat of the very officer who had refused to assist him in bringing it back. Here is where Gogol's spooky fantasy properly begins, as the deceased creature's specter haunts the scene, trying to purloin the coats of others.

The somber play with, and the ill-fated aura of the coat's presence and absence, have a phenomenological affinity not only with Bob's story of Freud's vanished overcoat, but also with *City of Angels'* narrator's experience of her own death in a dream (*City of Angels* 188)—an oneiric variant indicative of inner change and self-scrutiny. Further, above and beyond the superficial discrepancies between St. Petersburg's "northern frost" or Akaky's "cabbage soup" (*Overcoat* 240; 238) and *City of Angels'* palm trees or the narrator's enjoyment of *Star Trek*, cocktails, and international fare, lies Gogol's featuring of another theme that makes for an interesting comparison with Wolf's novel. Both stories are concerned with writing, although Akaky "saw nothing but his own neat lines" (Gogol 237), while *City of Angels'* narrator, rather than a copying enthusiast is, like Gutman, a writer in crisis who could not be more aware of the hardship that writing can bring. Incidentally, this difference is spelled out in *Patterns of Childhood*: "separate the process of copying from the process of writing" (240).

Gogol's/Akaky's and Wolf's/Bob's/Freud's coat-stories are fabrications by others. At her typewriter, *City of Angels'* narrator struggles with pain, fear, shame, guilt, oblivion, and an attendant writer's block—and turns to another: Bob's Freud. To recall Gutman's comment cited earlier, Wolf's narrator "take[s] refuge behind [other] person[s]" who provide a last chance to confront the past, to recognize life's "borrowed time" (in Molnar's sense of Freud's late life, cited earlier), and to articulate their last words in "late style."[25] Significantly, this rediscovery, in Wolf's case, takes place out of place and time—not in clock-time Berlin, but at her own mental tempo in California.

The London Freud Museum in Freud's final residence at 20 Maresfield Gardens, Hampstead, has repeatedly displayed Freud's coat[26]—in 2010 for *Freud in England 1938–39*, in 1999 for Sophie Calle's *Appointment*, in 1996 for Paul Coldwell's *Freud's Coat*, and in 1992 for the *Freud in His Time* exhibition, based on Michael Molnar's *Diary of Sigmund Freud*.[27] On 15 May 1992, Wolf was invited to London by the Richmond German School to read from *What Remains* (*Was bleibt*, 1990), the topic for the school's translation competition that year.[28] In London, Wolf's attraction to Freud's overcoat seems to have been awakened. Wolf may have anticipated Bob's story shortly before her journey to California, as it is highly conceivable that she saw Freud's coat in London about four months prior to her departure for Los Angeles. That her narrator then follows the "traces of émigrés" (*City of Angels* 258), visits the Villa Aurora, and "love[s] places like that" (259) supports the hypothesis about Wolf's earlier visit to Freud's house in Hampstead (the museum does not keep an official record of visitors).

The strong possibility rather than certainty of Wolf's visit to the Freud Museum only adds to the haunting aspects of her uncanny, paradoxical play with Freud's absent presence in *City of Angels*—through the coat (fetish).[29] Beyond fetishism's close relationship with the castration complex since Freud, the fetishist's ambiguous stance toward absence is essential for an assessment of the overcoat's role in Wolf's book. An object of condensed force that crystallizes desire, the fetish is a metonymic, and with Freud's coat perhaps even a synecdochic compromise that enables a simultaneity of "disavowal" and "affirmation" (Freud, "Fetishism," 153 and 156).[30] The coat that Freud wore during his escape from Nazism may be considered a fetishistic part of the Freud Wolf cares about most: the aged, ailing, vulnerable, dying man in exile, whose late pain is now, more than half a century later, intimately interwoven

"Bob ... started to tell us a story ... of how he acquired Freud's overcoat and lost it again ... the overcoat of Dr. Freud ... good prewar manufacture ..." (*City of Angels* 115)

"... misery and grief were the lining of Dr. Freud's overcoat ..." (117)

"The overcoat of Dr. Freud ... what in the world might be hidden in its inner lining, working its way out only bit by bit?" (132)

"The overcoat of Dr. Freud can also be abused to protect vulnerable sore spots ..." (144)

"The overcoat of Dr. Freud came to mind. I wished it could protect me." (152)

"The overcoat of Dr. Freud. But what if I turned the coat backward? Inside out?" (171–72)

"There was not a single corner of Dr. Freud's overcoat I could cling to." (178)

"I still remember the feeling I had that the overcoat of Dr. Freud was hovering above me ... that it would protect me." (188)

"Your resistance is giving way. The overcoat of Dr. Freud ... the coat that keeps you warm but also hidden, that you have to turn inside out. To make the inside visible." (197)

"By the way, you have now crawled your way rather deeply into the overcoat of Dr. Freud." (199)

"The overcoat of Dr. Freud ... wouldn't that be a good title?" (204)

"...what about my overcoat of Dr. Freud? My fetish?" (235)

"Now I knew that I had to die ... The overcoat of Dr. Freud had gotten torn ..." (255)

"To cut up the inner lining of the overcoat of Dr. Freud into all its component parts, you know what I mean?" (271)

"Hey, [Bob] said when we were saying goodbye. What about my overcoat? Oh Bob, I said. That overcoat is indestructible. It has served me well. I believe I have given it back to you already." (284)

"... I realized that this overcoat of Dr. Freud's had been sent to me for no other reason than to remove my doubts about this spirit [of offerings and reverence]" (303)

Figure 2.1 Sigmund Freud's Loden Overcoat (on the door to his study, near the couch). Photograph by Martina Kolb (April 2014). Courtesy of the Freud Museum London. "Bit by bit," "backward," and "inside out" capture, *in nuce*, a desired mentalization and gradual mnemonic verbalization of a complex retrospective fabric that Freud's exilic coat holds—be it in London as material garment bearing the traces of its former owner, or in California as a storyteller's phantom presence.

with hers. Moreover, her narrator's coat fetish is also an object of uncanny scope (and, as such, ends a clear discernment of animate versus inanimate, and of father versus Freud), linked to the sense of smell ("the smell of her father's grey overcoat").[31] It resembles a screen memory, where the traumatic experience of expulsion is mnemonically condensed in a detail (the father's coat's smell mingled with that of grandma's bosom) which in *Patterns of Childhood* stands for emotional complexity. This early attachment is later reedited in *City of Angels*, displaced from the father's coat to Freud's in a rapport that enables an estranged element to return in its uncanny capacity—now to be recognized and placed into a related but new historical, geographical, mental, and fictional context.

In *City of Angels*, with few exceptions—most prominently Gutman's first reference to Freud (91) and the biographically accurate mention of Freud's wish "for an assisted suicide at the end of his life" (280)—Freud always appears in conjunction with his coat. The novel's verbal register regarding the coat is laconic at times, while at others it is wistful or inquisitive. The instances in which the coat is mentioned range from Bob's story about receiving, losing, and mourning the loss of the coat, to considerations of what the coat's lining may harbor; from the desire to cover up vulnerable spots by its comforting warmth (reminiscent of the "protection from the abysses of memory" in *Patterns of Childhood*[32]), to the temptation to turn the coat inside out and the related difficulty in fully embracing it; from a partial success in lowering resistance, to the anachronistic question of whether *The Overcoat of Dr. Freud* would make a good title for the book that the narrator struggles to write—and that we, paradoxically, are already reading;[33] from the coat as fetishistic token, to its impeccable prewar quality on the one hand, and its wear and tear (recalling Gogol) on the other; from how material traces of life relate to aging, dying, and the coat's corporeal and sentimental legacies, to the desire to lay bare the components of the coat's lining; and from Bob's question about "his" coat and the narrator's recompense for the gift of Bob's wistful story (and the related Fleming poem), to her assurance that the overcoat was given to her as a reminder of the spirit of reverence and sacrifice.

Wolf is not only reluctant to deliver decisive beginnings; she also has trouble ending, "coming to terms." That the German *fertig werden* captures the semantic spectrum of both "dealing with" and "ending" (it means "to finish up" and "to cope with") felicitously points to the posited endpoint from which Wolf's narrations tend to begin. Such points of departure retrospectively commit themselves to tracking fear and pain back into the past. The many tell-tale starts and stops in the book point to a psychoanalytically informed effort to restart, continue, understand, and struggle to complete her story—to become conscious and to come to *terms*, that is: her final words in late style. Even though the narrative process is oftentimes blocked as a result of the narrator's guilt, fright, and anticipation of life's end, in many moments her dialogue with her traumatized self is merely interrupted and then continues somehow, while she dramatically casts herself in different pronouns. She talks to herself and, in doing so, positions herself anew in soliloquies fashioned as proto-dialogues. A sincere proto-analytic conversation about the past is thus staged in the present, in which a first-person observer (in lieu of an actual interpreting analyst) speaks to a second-person observed (the verbalizing patient as agent). The narrator, then, is not only the writer in residency disguised and yet exposed as the text's traumatized protagonist in crisis, but also a patient-therapist who is analysand and analyst at once, attempting a self-analysis in which symptom, diagnosis, and treatment are intricately intertwined and threaten to become one—and although he looked upon self-analysis ambivalently, it did hold a crucial status in the early Freud's attempts to grasp his own anxiety.

For Freud, transference implies the replication of an original, and in Wolf's text, the coat emerges as this replicated original. Freud addresses the intermediate realm of transference as a potential third space that is at first discovered and imaginatively construed to then be gradually dismantled through the dynamics of projection, repetition, and becoming conscious (working through). Transference is observational and shows a "tolerance for the state of being ill" (Freud, "Remembering" 152). Part and parcel of repetition (151), it creates "an intermediate region between illness and real life" (154). When patients move into transference, analysts spontaneously respond by their respective moves into countertransference, finding themselves, in the act of assisted repetition, temporarily transported into their patients' lives.

In *City of Angels*, Wolf presents her readers with Freud's coat as a concrete, personified placeholder for an actual analyst, thereby facilitating the transference that Freud characterized as a necessary condition for any curative process—as the patient's "tendency to react to another person as if she were an emotionally important but unconscious part of oneself" (Frattaroli 70)."[T]ransference and countertransference reactions [are] in one sense resistances against feelings of closeness and dependency, but in another sense they [are] therapeutic progress" (264). While in Wolf's novel the analyst's absence is ingeniously circumvented by the narrator's insistence on an overcoat that stands in for the therapist-absentee, countertransference as "the spontaneous inner reaction elicited in the therapist by the patient's transference" (Frattaroli 219) is necessarily excluded from this scenario, for the inanimate coat, even though she claims it "was talking to [her]" (see second epigraph above), is ultimately incapable of offering a subjective response to the narrator's positive and negative transference.[34] The interaction between observer and observed in the book is reduced to one person, so that the narrator's transference projection necessarily stops short at first, for her internal conflict becomes transpersonal only in delay, that is: after the completion of her fiction—through her readership (which may or may not offer a response that may or may not arrive in time to be heard).

It is crucial for an understanding of the psychoanalytic dynamic in Wolf that the experience of transference is defined as fictional. Phrased differently, its structure is that of an *as if*. Hans Vaihinger situated the *as if* (*als ob*) between actual analogy and rhetorical device (less than the former, more than the latter), defining it as *the* linguistic formula for fiction. Vaihinger's grammatically informed philosophical take on fiction seems in part analogous to Freud's provisional analytic realm of transference and hence valuable for a reading of Wolf. While the conditional *if* gestures toward non-reality, the comparative *as* evokes presence and encourages a perception of Freud's overcoat as real. In other words, the narrator paves the way toward herself via another, so that a split persona is fictionally posited as a potential relation between that which is and that which was or might have been.

However autobiographical/historical Wolf's novel may (or may not) be, it cannot, as fiction, transcend the stage of transference and thus forecloses analytic termination. Instead, it remains and ends in the realm of literature. The text's fictionality by definition lacks analytic progress beyond transference and can therefore not fully reach that which "fill[s mnemonic] gaps" and allows for a move beyond repetition into "memory" (Freud, "Transference" 435). Nevertheless, there is a writer's successful analytic scenario in absence of an actual therapist in the fiction, as a result of which she becomes the conscious author of her externalized story. Assisted by the overcoat as a transitional object "retained … in the intense experiencing that belongs to the arts" (Winnicott 97), *City of Angels* emerges as a "unified expression of the soul" through the sublimation that leads to the fabric of Wolf's novel as a "work of art" (Frattaroli 297). Wolf's fiction, then, is not only the story of *City of Angels*; it is also the commemorative inscription of her late life as a literary author. *City of Angels*' fiction includes a combination of lay-analysis and self-analysis to which Wolf has herself and her narrator commit—as lay practitioners without medical training but a keen sense for clinical work on language nonetheless, and by assuming, within the realm of the novel's fiction, two roles at once.

According to the precise Aristotelian distinction of fiction's instructive, universal qualities versus historiography's mere particularity, Wolf's novel is fictional and universal. As such, it is entitled to poetic license. And in an assessment of fiction, veridiction cannot be defined on the grounds of historical verification alone, also because the line between fact and fiction in (hi)storytelling is elusive at best. Further, while her novel is, by generic definition, free beyond the limits of autobiographical specifics, its therapeutic process dwells in the realm of fiction, with the analytically idealized transience of transference solidified—and memorialized—instead in her last book.

It is critical to recall that the narrator's process of noteworthy inward attention starts with her clear articulation of anxiety ("I'm scared, of course"). Anxiety is "consciousness trying to happen" (Frattaroli 407), and when it happens, it at once destabilizes and humanizes (422). She is scared, but not sufficiently scared anymore not to seriously sound the depths of her inner voice, let the coat facilitate her awareness of inner conflict, and bring the creative potential of this conflict to a verbal surface. And it is in reference to literature's tasks that Wolf uses the participle "bohrend" (Wolf in Gansel 366), which intends the literal "drilling" as well as the metaphorical "boring" or "brooding"—in their deep dimension, both relate to the vertical axis of spatialized time in analysis. Similarly, Wolf writes of "abtauchen" into the "Untiefen" of memory ("plunging" into the "unmeasured depths of memory"; "Nachdenken über den blinden Fleck" 79). And it is in these precise ways that her narrator pays attention to her symptoms, honors them as part of an active therapeutic process, and, as a result, gains further access to herself—also to herself as a writer. Although she is at once drawn to and afraid of the overcoat of Dr. Freud and, by the same token, of herself, unlike Bob (who first never wears and then loses the coat) she quickly intuits after his tell-tale encouragement that she must secure this object for her narrative intentions (marked by ongoing tensions between resistance and transference) by granting it a strong place in her life as a writer—until the coat is torn beyond darning and she closer to having written up her story toward life's end end—the overcoat as *memento mori*.

City of Angels maximally intertwines language and consciousness by writing up anxiety—with writing as a reflexive act where language transcends communication and becomes action. In its very fragmentation, *City of Angels* establishes its own analytic logic. It challenges writing by writing about the challenges of writing, questioning with extreme self-consciousness the propriety of a writer's presumed authority toward articulate self-scrutiny. The narrator constantly steps back and interrupts herself, which leads to a text that stammers eloquently and ends openly ("there is no end of things in the heart," wrote Ezra Pound memorably in "Exile's Letter"). She keeps beginning, inserting paper into that typewriter, searching for the right moment to turn to L.'s letters and to Freud's coat, combining numerous attempts at remembering with just as many doubts about memory. Her writing is self-reflexive and forces that *you* to listen to a self that continually threatens to leave. This *you* mediates the conversation in the present, but as soon as the narrator's grammar falls back into the first person, she defensively resists, relocating time and again to other times and places.

The argument in this chapter has refrained from presenting compunctions, assigning culpabilities, or offering exculpations. Rather than concentrating primarily on the book's content, I have placed emphasis instead on the process, and progress, of Wolf's narrator who fears most what she secretly desires, that is: reaching the unattainable father (the father's law-giving words are a

Freudian commonplace) and granting authority to memory. She keeps trying to break through her resistance, ultimately confronting both her fear of pain and her fear of death—in a dream of her own death as a message from the unconscious where she is creator and interpreter at once. "The simple act of paying attention to [her] inner world ... becomes a dawning recognition that each moment of experiencing crystallizes the core meanings of [her] life as an individual. This recognition involves a mysterious shift from content to process, from the perspective of distance ... to that of immediacy" (Frattaroli 350).

Wolf's principal narrative *modus operandi* is explorative, introspective, querying. Her text's composition is located between the act of writing and a concomitant Kafkaesque "inability to write" (*City of Angels* 19). Illustrating this felt inability articulately is reminiscent of Hofmannsthal's *Chandos Letter* and just as paradoxical as the narrator's alleged oblivion by which she always remembers *some*thing. This "memory work" is a "never-ending process" (Kuhn 170). Wolf was engaged in this process at least as heavily as in the actual content of memories, as is obvious also in her lifelong interest in brain chemistry and electric stimulation, addressed already in *Patterns of Childhood*. Her speech "Nachdenken über den blinden Fleck" at the Psychoanalytic Congress in Berlin points into this direction as well when she addresses neurobiology and psychology in the context of memory (77–79) and suggests that what she calls the "blind spot" is close to what Freud called the Id (84). That said, although she never referred to herself as an expert in memory, she has been dealt with as such by certain critics who manipulate her fiction into the realm of autobiography and then attack her for an alleged memory failure regarding her early Stasi involvement as *IM Margarete*.[35]

Wolf has always been painfully aware of memory and its discontents — memory and the ways in which it does (not) function. The carefully staged "computer crash" presents the risk of involuntary memory loss *in nuce* (*City of Angels* 125), whereas the temptation of choosing "delete" over "save" in light of the "disk capacity exhausted" alert (212) gives rise to ethical questions about conscious erasure. In any case, rather than expertise, Wolf's was an ongoing battle with and for memory. She was just as overwhelmed by the discontents of memory (and by the related porous line that separates reality from fiction), as Freud himself had been on the Acropolis—he addressed his "Disturbance of Memory" only decades later in his "Open Letter to Romain Rolland (see Kolb 340–43), shedding some retrospective light on his previous guilt trip.

Wolf, as it were, cloaked her last novel in Freudian garb. Her composition of it took place in a Freudian spirit. By way of Freud's exilic overcoat as a transitional and/or fetishistic object, she mentally staged a *Freud redivivus* as her narrator's proto-analyst. *City of Angels* unequivocally pays homage to the putative father of psychoanalysis, time and again reminding the reader not only of psychoanalytic diagnostics and mnemonic successes, but also of defensive memory failures. Wolf's late style confronts the paradoxes of her life, as her narrator commits herself to creative contradictions and irreconcilable experiences. She keeps coping, and at l(e)ast partially comes to terms—reminiscent, in part, of that earlier "desire not to [fully] come to terms with oneself" (*Patterns of Childhood* 404)—but to confirm her place as a novelist.

Even when the touristic highlights of the American Southwest have been covered in the embedded travelogue toward the end of the book—Grand Canyon, Canyon de Chelly, Mesa Verde, Monument Valley, Death Valley, and the Four Corners, among others—the journey is not quite over yet. True, the overcoat has now been returned, and a "preliminary work has reached its preliminary end" (314). And yet the reader has another page to cover before reaching the novel's last line: "That I don't know" (the narrator's reply to "Where are we going?," which confirms one more time the immense emotional investment in the anticipation of death and its specter accompanying her many attempts at mentalization).[36] We end then where we began, literally up in the air, above that California "playground," as Freud suggestively called the transitional space of transference ("Remembering" 154).

Unlike Wolf, who arrived in Los Angeles and returned to Berlin nine months later, her retrospectively composed fiction based on her experience and notes written as Getty Resident begins and ends in transit, hovering back there somewhere in the Western air. This is due to a lack of countertransference and of analytic termination (the resolution of transference). The novel's open ending could not be more suitable for the analytic process that is at its core. As a matter of ongoing introspection and empathy, analysis is never complete, so long as there is more life to be lived and hence more working through to be done. "[T]he task of reality-acceptance is never completed," writes Winnicott, "no human being is free from the strain of relating inner and outer reality [... and] relief from this strain is provided by an intermediate area of experience which is not challenged" on the grounds of its transitional objects' internal, external, or combined origins (96).

It is generally the abstract nature of absence that causes the pain of loss and conjures a concrete presence. Even if such actual presence (Freud's, his coat's) cannot be materially achieved, the fetishistic/screen/metonymic character of the verbalized overcoat expresses the narrator's wish for therapeutic presence—in the sense of the proverbs *man muß den Mantel suchen, wo man ihn verloren hat* (one must look for the coat where one has lost it) and to wear it on both shoulders (*den Mantel auf beiden Schultern tragen*) that is, to face what comes one's way. Once the story is completed, the coat has served its purpose and as a transitional object can be "allowed to be decathected" (Winnicott 91), divested, that is, of the psychic energy previously invested in it (cathexis).

As metanarrative or story within (and about) the story, Bob's anecdotally related confabulation about Freud's overcoat shares qualities with the play within the play in Shakespeare's *Hamlet* (titled *The Murder of Gonzago* and as a result of its driving the plot, better known as "The Mousetrap")—not only in that it is a literary device installed to reveal something allegedly hidden and to mnemonically drive the action in a very specific direction, but also in that it is meant to verify and further necessitate the ultimately unavoidable confrontation with the past (be it his father's murder by the uncle as told to Hamlet by the ghost, or Wolf's narrator's peripety regarding self-analysis, facing specters, and beginning her writing up). Further, the play's spectators and novel's readers are not the primary audiences here; rather, what matters is the respective work's internal audience (such as Claudius in Shakespeare and the protagonist in Wolf). Metafictional elements such as these are strongly reminiscent of the psychoanalytic transference present in Wolf's novel, where the process of writing and the devices used to approach verbalization gain primary importance. Bob's "The overcoat of Dr. Freud," if you will, is Wolf's *The Murder of Gonzago*, a story she stages by way of Bob and with the intention to push her narrator into what she deemed the right analytic direction.

The coat's spectral nature as phantom presence and transitional object fulfills the therapeutic wish. Searls translated "zurückerstattet" as "given back" (284), in the narrator's reply to Bob's enquiry about "his" overcoat. Wolf's *zurückerstatten*, however, is a subtler word choice, in that it not only means "give back" or "return," but also implies "compensation" or "refund." Providing Bob and herself with the promised text, the narrator may have assisted him, too, in overcoming the loss that triggered his story, which, in turn, laid the foundation for the articulation of hers. "Zurückerstattet" further entails a suggestion that she paid her dues by experiencing herself in intimate connections and mutual influence of analytic transference and literary prose, by becoming conscious and to many terms, as it were, when writing her one-person self-therapy-fiction. Wolf's novel accomplished this task by way of Freud's overcoat and Bob's intermittent ownership of and fanciful story about it.

Martina Kolb holds a Ph.D. in Comparative Literature from Yale University and is Associate Professor of German Studies and Winifred and Gustave Weber Professor in the Humanities at Susquehanna University of Pennsylvania. She is the recipient of various competitive awards, including a Miller Fellowship in Exile Studies at the University of London and Academic Fellowships with the American Psychoanalytic Association in New York and the Psychoanalytic Center of Philadelphia. She specializes in European art and literature of the long twentieth century, has taught internationally across the humanities, and has researched and published widely at the interdisciplinary intersections of modernist poetics, aesthetics and the inter-arts, translation and world literature, and psychoanalysis and the medical humanities—currently with a focus on pain. Published in 2013 by the University of Toronto Press, her monograph *Nietzsche, Freud, Benn, and the Azure Spell of Liguria* comes highly recommended by reviewers. She has authored numerous articles, most recently "Daughter Courage and Her Mother: Affect,

Gesture, Voice" (*The Brecht Yearbook* 46), as well as two essays on Edith Jacobson's expressionist prison writing (*Journal of the American Psychoanalytic Association* 68[5]and 68[6]).

Notes

1. All unattributed translations in this essay are my own (© Martina Kolb). In both *Patterns of Childhood* and *City of Angels*, Wolf indicates in no uncertain terms the fictionality of all her characters and events. Rather than referring to the author's, she writes of "the narrator's inventions" ("Erfindungen der Erzählerin" n. p.), which Searls translates as "inventions of the novelist." Hein and Pormeister (94), among others, oppose a classification of *City of Angels* as a novel, with Hein offering categories such as "Selbstbefragung" (self-inquiry) and "Lebensbeichte" (life confession). True, Wolf did not explicitly add "novel" to her titles—most novels do not claim to be but are novels, and any "long fictional prose narrative … typically representing character and action with some degree of realism and complexity" does count as such (*OED*). Regarding her book's genre, Wolf does say that the label "Roman" ("novel") was the publisher's rather than hers, which various critics have referred to when establishing their doubts about the genre. It seems crucial to note how Wolf carries on, a passage that has repeatedly been omitted in such argumentation: "Aber ich hätte den Text auch 'Roman' nennen können. Denn: Das Fiktive ist sehr stark und dies viel stärker als man annimmt, wenn man die Ich-Figur mit mir gleichsetzt." ("I could also have called the text a 'novel,' for the fictional is very strong and indeed much stronger than one would assume, if one takes the first-person character to be me"; Wolf in Gansel, 353). In the same conversation, Wolf refers to Freud (355) and self-analysis (360). Unlike Hein and Pormeister (but similar to Haase's and Kuhn's tolerance regarding fictional tension), I suggest that in line with Wolf's own assessment, a tolerance for a potential generic unease and a concomitant insistence on the fictionality of her last book are imperative, as it is the very fiction (with its etymological root of Latin *fictilis*: "worked by hand" and/or "invented in the mind" rather than its later meanings surrounding falsehood) that enables her actual memory work as an author and a person—through her fictional narrator who determines the psychoanalytic dynamics throughout the novel. It is, in other words, the fictional realm of analytic transference that opens up a third space where trauma can be negotiated and the past reencountered. Wolf could not have accomplished comparable memory work in an autobiography. I suggest to take Wolf's fictional narrator as seriously as we would take the author of an autobiography, in line with Freud himself, who took his analysis of fictional protagonists just as seriously as that of actual patients (for example with Oedipus and Hamlet, or Norbert Hanold in Jensen's novella *Gradiva: A Pompeiian Fantasy*). For additional approaches to the work's genre(s), see, among others, Michelis ("novel-cum-memoir," 75); Kuhn ("Wenderoman," 164); Klocke ("Autofiktion," 471); Smale ("loosely autobigraphical novel," 182); and Sousa ("autobiography," "autofiction," "metafiction," and "literature," essay title). Summers goes so far as to claim Wolf's "exploit[ing] the boundary between fact and fiction" (232), a statement that runs counter to a psychoanalytic reading of the text.
2. Hereafter, references are to Searls.

3. In "Fetishism or Working Through," the English version of his equally brief "Fetisch oder Aufarbeitung?" (2015), Bathrick claims "the last five words" of Wolf's title (*The Overcoat of Dr. Freud*) as his focus, pointing to the "psychoanalytic implications" of the story. However, he then proceeds historically, presenting the psychoanalytic lens only through Eric Santner's concept of "narrative fetishism." Without any reference to Freud's writing, Bathrick calls the coat a "key metaphor" and points to the narrator's "misuse of Freud's overcoat as a fetish," concluding that "Freud's overcoat … does not actually exist." In his article on "Neutra's bridging of Freud and L.A." (57), Blankenship acknowledges Bathrick's "relevant questions" (56), realizing a lack of analysis of the coat on Bathrick's part. It is curious that despite her rejection of *City of Angels* as a novel, like Bathrick, Pormeister denies the overcoat's actual existence and simply calls it "fictive" ("fiktiver Mantel," 98). In contrast to Bathrick and Pormeister, I propose a complication of the coat's status in the novel through the lens of fiction and/as transference—minding Winnicott who, letting perception and conception intersect, writes that the "question" whether the "transitional object" originates internally or externally "is not to be formulated" (95). See Michelis (63), who without elaboration on the coat introduces Freud's "overcoat" by quoting his essay on the "Uncanny" in English (the German original, however, says "Kleider" rather than the free English rendering "overcoat"); and see Klocke, who, without reference to Freud, mentions the protagonist's "Selbsttherapie" (478), a word Wolf herself repeatedly used, but with a pronounced interest in Freud's talking cure on her part. The dated noun Wolf uses for the coat-object in the original *Kindheitsmuster* is "Überzieher" (57), which best translates into the equally dated English noun "overcoat" that she inscribed, in English, in *City of Angels*. This word choice accentuates historical atmosphere and linguistic usage at the time of World War II—the time of Freud's exile and Wolf's expulsion.
4. Wolf's California sojourn was marked by withdrawal and illness. Her return from Los Angeles in 1993 followed the publication earlier that year of "Eine Auskunft" in the *Berliner Zeitung*, acknowledging her stint as Stasi informer. Also in 1993, her victim and perpetrator files were published as *Akteneinsicht Christa Wolf: Zerrspiegel und Dialog*, edited by Hermann Vinke. *City of Angels* (2010) was published seventeen years later. It is neither a documentary, nor an autobiographical confession, nor a willful deceit in the absence of total testimony. Rather, Wolf's fictional narrator is tormented by the reemergence of the past and, through her, Wolf strikingly demonstrates her profound psychoanalytic interest in the intriguing processes of memory, repression, dissociation, denial, and amnesia—an interest that is clearly present, too, in "Nachdenken über den blinden Fleck", where on 12 pages she refers to 18 international literary writers in the context of memory, and stresses "Literatur … als Gedächtnisspeicher" ("literature as memory storage" 72), while addressing the "psychoanalytische[n] Prozeß" ("psychoanalytic process" 72), her reliance on "Assoziationen" ("associations" 74), and Freud's "Redekur" as "Erinnerung durch Erzählen" ("talking cure" as "memory by way of narration," 78).
5. Wolf weaves the names of many exiled artists and writers into the work (see for example 156). See also her "Nachdenken über den blinden Fleck" 72 and 85. See also Bahr, Hampton, and especially Lentz (374–84), who, in ways comparable to Wolf, reconstructs, through literary memory, the improvised lives of exiles on the Pacific—albeit, unlike Wolf, without having lived through Nazism or being on location.
6. Bob's story in the novel is staged by way of Neutra, who in real life was born in Vienna and moved to Los Angeles in 1923. His connection was with Freud's son

Ernst Ludwig rather than with Freud himself. It is conceivable that Neutra received a coat of Freud's before leaving Vienna. Or Sousa's erroneous claim that Freud was an exile in California rather than London turns into a *felix culpa* here. In any case, Neutra died in Germany in 1970, at about the time his wife purportedly passed on her husband's (Freud's former) coat to Bob Rice. More likely perhaps, Bob loves storytelling and passes on his story of the coat, which is Wolf's way of assuring concrete connections between Freud's exile and her own creativity, memory, and late style.

7. On 6 June 1938, the *Daily Herald* reported Freud's arrival in London, printing a photo of him wearing the Loden overcoat when reaching his first address, 39 Elsworthy Road.
8. In *Patterns of Childhood*, Wolf already practiced this play with pronominal perspective. In the first chapter, she addressed living in the third person and presented a "you" that an "I" engages in conversation, so as to avoid silence. The sixth chapter of *Patterns of Childhood* claims that the second person is only seemingly closer to the first person than to the third. And the novel's last page reverts to all three persons before ending with deliberations on the oneiric realm.
9. Despite Winnicott's focus on infants, Wolf's overcoat's actuality in defense against anxiety may be regarded as a "transitional object," an "intermediate area of *experiencing*, to which inner reality and external life both contribute" (Winnicott 90). Winnicott writes of the "nature" and the "place of the object," the mind's capacity to "produce an object," and the "initiation of an affectionate ... object relationship" (89), stressing that the child's teddy, for instance, "give[s] warmth ... ha[s] texture ... has a vitality or reality of its own" (91). Wolf's transitional overcoat-object is first present during an early experience (the expulsion narrated in *Patterns of Childhood*) and "reappear[s ...] later when deprivation threatens" (Winnicott 91)—in *City of Angels*. Winnicott enters the realm of "artistic creativity ... and of fetishism" (91), with transitional objects representing a "first relationship" and "eventually develop[ing] into a fetish" and "becom[ing] smelly" (93). He emphasizes the difference between fetishism as pathological and transitional objects as healthy for the "illusion which is at the basis of initiation of experience" (97). See also Kuhn 176 and 184 note 18.
10. Haase calls the coat a "geräumige Metapher" as well as a "Sinnbild" ("spacious metaphor," "symbol," 228); Michelis anything from "metaphor" and "signifier" to "anecdotal reference," "figurative site" and "trope" (75); and Blankenship a "symbol" (55) and "metaphorical" (61). Kuhn relies on Freud's concept of the "pleasure principle" (and its "fort-da") and writes of the "symbolic overcoat" (165) and its "metaphorical use" (177), considering it a "motif" and "symbolic" (164), an "idea," "imaginary," and a "totem" but "not a material object" or "fetish" (176). Freud once deployed the metaphor of the "heavy overcoat woven of a tissue of lies," worn to hide sexuality. Patients initially conceal desire, but eventually "discard this veil of lies" ("Five Lectures" 41). His own metaphor could have underscored Kuhn's argument. Relying on Freud's elaborations on transference, fetishism, and the uncanny as manifestations of repetition, I interpret the coat not as a symbol or a metaphor, but as metonymic and transitional (and possibly synecdochic and fetishistic).
11. Wolf uses the same noun ("Sog") when referring to the magnetism of life's end (and of writing as a warding off of the death that it conjures), and to the attraction of books ("I feel a pull for the end" and "those books sucked me in" [234; 262]). The pull in the original comes "vom Ende her," which means from the end rather than for the end. In other words, the end is imminent, death pulls her closer, with no such agency on the narrator's part.

12. See Michael Minden for a reading of *City of Angels* as a continuation of *Patterns of Childhood*. Hereafter, references are to Molinaro and Rappolt. *Kindheitsmuster* is translated as *Patterns of Childhood*. Their first translation was titled *A Model Childhood*. The original *Kindheitsmuster* is suggestive of the repetitions prominent in the narrative. "Pattern" is only one possible meaning of *Muster*, which also signifies "sample," or, less commonly, "model." *Sample(s) of Childhood* would point to the selective dynamics of memory and the metonymic qualities of Wolf's narrative. In the original, Wolf quotes the etymology: Latin "monstrum": "showpiece" (36), or sample. Wolf's preference was for the singular rather than the plural *Muster* (though in German this difference in number is not grammatically marked). She did not consider *Patterns of Childhood* an account of a "model childhood." Rather, her word choice *Muster* intends "sample," stressing metonymy as at once fragmentary and representative (in the sense of *pars pro toto*).
13. "L." stands for Landsberg/Warthe, German during Wolf's childhood, but Polish "G.," Gorzów Wielkopolski, at the end of World War II. *Patterns of Childhood* refers to all toponyms bilingually, including Posen/Poznán and Küstrin/Kostrzyn.
14. Curiously, the back translation of Wolf's rendering of Faulkner's line is not the same as Faulkner's original, quoted and discussed later. The translators do not acknowledge Wolf's unsourced quotation from *Requiem for a Nun*.
15. Searls italicizes words that appear in English in the German original, a graphic reminder of the book's implicit bilingualism ("Translator's Note," n. p.).
16. For my comparative approach to the two novels, it is noteworthy that already in *Kindheitsmuster* Wolf inserted English snippets, including ones on slavery, freedom, and hypnosis. Further, in *City of Angels*, there is a chapter in the *irrealis*, with the narrator imagining what her life might have been like had the family's flight in 1945 ended in the American rather than the Russian occupation zone.
17. While this cover shows a trench that neither reflects Freud's time nor the haunting factor of his coat, Barnaby Hall's photograph of a fading coat on the cover of Gogol's book would perfectly convey the ghostly quality of the coat in Wolf's text. Freud's library held an edition of Gogol's oeuvre.
18. Wolf frequently practiced unsourced borrowings from literature and philosophy: *Patterns of Childhood* 148: "Something's rotten in the State of Denmark" (Shakespeare 27); 178: "One must eventually break the silence about difficult things"—her play, in the original, with Ludwig Wittgenstein's final lines of the *Tractatus* about speech and silence is misinterpreted in this translation: "Wovon man nicht sprechen kann, darüber muß man schweigen" (Wittgenstein 128), which does not imply the burial of difficult truths that eventually resurface, but suggests that what enables speech and thought cannot at the same time be the object of speech and thought; *Patterns of Childhood* 187: "The most beautiful thing about being under the sun is being under the sun." (Ingeborg Bachmann, "An die Sonne"). On other occasions, Wolf at least partially cites her sources, such as in *Patterns of Childhood* 449: "I have done much writing, in order to lay the foundation for memory (Johann Wolfgang Goethe)"—from *Italian Journey*; or 344, regarding Gottfried Benn's Landsberg.
19. "I was sitting among refugees" is preceded by "I was almost the only non-Jew" (*City of Angels* 74), which points to the narrator's status as the sole German in a group of primarily second-generation Jewish émigrés from Nazism. The situation is delicate and complex, as Wolf, albeit not Jewish, is a surviving refugee herself: "You were there. You survived" (*City of Angels* 161). "To come to the West. In May 1945. To cross the

Elbe. Our caravan of refugees was trying to get there" (182). In *City of Angels*, she also introduces a first-person narrator who passes US immigration with "the still-valid passport of a no-longer extant country" (4): her post-GDR GDR document triggers difficult memories and eerie aspects of identity and identification.
20. Searls translated "gelebtes Leben" with the present rather than the past participle: "living life" (3), which renders Doctorow's line less mnemonic, less experiential.
21. While at work on *City of Angels*, Wolf spoke, on 25 July 2002, at the opening ceremony of the 45[th]International Psychoanalytic Association's Congress in Berlin (25-28 July 2007). Her presentation was titled "Nachdenken über den blinden Fleck" ("Thinking about the Blind Spot"), and the congress theme was: "Remembering, Repeating, and Working Through in Psychoanalysis and Culture Today," (see *Rede, daß ich dich sehe* pp. 72–95 and p. 205), which not only stages the title of one of Freud's writings on technique, but also the theme of collective guilt, *Aufarbeitung der Vergangenheit* ('working through the past') and *Vergangenheitsbewältigung* ('overcoming the past'). Beyond Freud, therapy plays a powerful role in *City of Angels*, including Feldenkrais, Dr. Kim, Sally's therapy, Angelina's spiritualism, and Perma's (*sic*) therapeutic philosophy. Wolf's daughter Annette Simon is a psychotherapist.
22. Wolf's canonized precursor in the genre of the retrospective travelogue is the *Italian Journey*. Goethe, too, had left Germany in a state of crisis and based his writing in a diaristic poetics of (dis)place(ment). Unlike Wolf's, however, his sojourn abroad was not a guilt trip. Wolf spent under two decades (1992–2010) from the conception to the completion of her last book, while Goethe's travelogue appeared in 1816/17, about three decades after the actual Italian sojourn (1786–1788). Given Wolf's immense interest in world literary intertexts and the fact that she refers to Los Angeles as Weimar under the Palms trigger another Goethe connection—via Freud, who quoted from *Wahlverwandtschaften* on a postcard from Italy: "Es wandelt niemand ungestraft unter Palmen" (see Tögel pp. 157 and 206), that is, one might have to expect a lenient penalty for relishing clement weathers in far-away places that provide a time-space to begin an often painful self-analysis.
23. She chooses Paul Fleming's "An sich"/"To oneself" (Searls rendered it as "To himself" *City of Angels* [116]), which recommends being "undismayed." Her recitation is followed by a discussion that concentrates on the repercussions of repression and eventually leads to the "lining" of Freud's coat (117). In the original, the question Bob asks is: "What do you think about my story," not "of my story" (he has no discernable interest in her assessment of the formal qualities of his story, but is curious about her thoughts on its content). Bob felt that *in* the coat he could have faced anything in life. Rather than wearing the coat though, he hung it up vertically as a trace of Freud's living past (in contrast to recumbent funeral effigies). Emphasis in original.
24. Wolf refers to "*Gogol*" as the ship's name that once took her narrator on the Moskva to Nizhni Novgorod (*City of Angels* 277). Gogol's name, but not his *Overcoat*, is embedded in a series of water memories presented in the narrator's stream of consciousness.
25. Said writes on the late style of others in his own late style (*mise-an abîme*), meditating on creative contradictions, while facing age, illness, and death (*late* also means "deceased" and hence encapsulates the proximity of age, lateness, and death). Said died before completing his book, whereas Wolf saw the publication of *Stadt der Engel* in 2010. Regarding their autobiographically infused creativity vis-à-vis a strong sense of mortality, a comparison of Wolf's and Said's final works is worthy of further investigation, particularly with respect to their confrontation with previous late, exiled

writers and artists and their recapitulation of prominent irreconcilable experiences. In their inconclusiveness, Said and Wolf similarly thwart the expectations of readers who desire a neat farewell, complete memory, and final wisdom from established senior authors. See Magenau (249–66). See Smale.

26. In *Behind the Scenes at the Freud Museum*, caretaker Alex Bento is shown finding the coat hidden in a closet, which is misleading, for Freud's coat had already been on exhibit repeatedly before the film came out.
27. Calle actually wore Freud's coat, but presents other empty garments in ways reminiscent of the overcoat in Wolf. Calle gestures toward the continuous presence of what is absent. I saw Freud's coat in 2013 and again in 2014 at the Freud Museum, where the caption read: "The overcoat Freud wore on his journey from Vienna to London in 1938." I thank Ivan Ward for informing me that Freud's coat was most likely displayed for *Freud in His Time*, and that photographs of Freud wearing the coat were definitely shown during this exhibit at the time of Wolf's 1992 London visit (see Molnar 237, 249, 254, 257 and 260 for photographs of Freud wearing the coat).
28. I am grateful to Georgina Paul, who was present at this event, for sharing this piece of information with me. Also in May 1992, Wolf visited the Gauck-Behörde where she was confronted with her Stasi victim and perpetrator files.
29. Visiting Faulkner's home in Mississippi in the late 1990s, I was struck by an empty hanger, arguably a more appropriate visualization of Bob's story than an image of an actual coat (not to mention Freud's actual coat). A deserted hook on Bob's office door and the empty hanger in Rowan Oak drive home Freud's, Faulkner's, and Wolf's psychoanalytic truth that "the past is never dead." And yet, the alleged former presence of a coat that Bob never wore implies Freud's absence and illustrates Wolf's involvement with Freud's presence through her narrator's simultaneous attraction to, and repulsion by its (and his) phantasmagoric presence. That the museum visitor to Freud's pre-exilic residence in Berggasse 19 in Vienna should not only see a hat, a cane, a flask, a travel case, and a travel blanket of Freud's in the display case, but also an empty hanger (the coat is in London, so is the couch), further illustrates the insistence, the facets, and the vicissitudes of the phantasmagoria here discussed.
30. Synecdoche and metonymy refer to a whole by mentioning a part. Flesh and blood can be a synecdoche for the human body (as parts of the whole they stand for that whole), whereas the crown as a replacement for the king would be a metonymy (in that it is not a physical, integral part of the king). Strictly speaking, Freud's overcoat would be metonymic; however, Freud's coat worn during his escape from Nazism may be considered existentially, corporeally, as a part of the exiled Freud himself to whom Wolf grants her undivided attention.
31. Freud connects fetishism to smell, referring to the case study of the "rat man" ("Fetishism" 149). Regarding the father's overcoat and its lasting smell, "identification with the father" (157) is crucial, as the child blames the father for having castrated the mother, while the fetish remains "a token of triumph over the threat of castration and a protection against it" (154). Like fiction in Vaihinger's analysis, Freud's fetish is a present absence and an auxiliary, a compromise that unites "denial" and "affirmation" ("Leugnung" and "Behauptung," Vaihinger 95 and 99). It is similar to a Freudian screen memory but is also a "quasi-thing" ("Quasiding" 100) with subjective validity ("subjektive Gültigkeit" 99).
32. "Schutz vor den Abgründen der Erinnerung" (*Kindheitsmuster* 114). The English rendering is my own, as *Patterns of Childhood* skips this passage at the very beginning of chapter four.

33. This recalls Gutman's take on neurosis and the need to express oneself through the words of another. It is unlike what he calls the narrator's "unnecessary psychosis" (*City of Angels* 179). Psychosis amounts to the loss of the sense of reality and Freud's treatments remained ineffective with it.
34. Kuhn, who astutely writes of Magenau's "distrust of psychoanalysis" (170), classifies Gutman as the narrator's analyst (174). While both Rice and Gutman facilitate her access to Freud and to articulation at certain points (with both men imaginable as her friendly mentor-therapists), I cannot see the classical analyst in either Rice or Gutman, who in his conversations with the narrator is thoroughly relational (Gutman likes talking). I propose to read Freud's silent yet insistent overcoat as Wolf's metonymy for an analyst, an auxiliary or "observer" instructed to "avoid the role of a mentor" ("Transference" 433–34). As it is paramount for patients on the couch to pay attention to themselves in the presence of but without facing another (rather than vis-à-vis, the analyst sits behind the recumbent patient's head) onto whom transferential stories are projected, so is it paramount for Wolf's narrator to pay attention to herself in the presence of an overcoat that does not sit across from her. Her transference is intensified by increased visitations of the coat following Bob's tale. It appears fifteen times on pages 117 to 303 and constitutes the book's climax (including moments of anagnorisis and peripety).
35. When in 1933 the Berlin Psychoanalytic Institute began its alignment with Nazi policies, Freud sanctioned this step. One prominent result was the exclusion of Jews by Jews. While Wolf's short-term work as an informer is certainly not directly comparable to this situation, it shares with it the lowest common denominator of painful paradox (she was surveilled/a long-time victim and herself an informer/a short-term perpetrator).
36. Searls translates "I don't know" (315), whereas the original says: "Das weiß ich nicht." (415), emphasizing the ultimate unknown: death. Not knowing (ignorance or innocence?) is also a part of the final sentences in *Patterns of Childhood*—in response to the omnipresent question of voices and pronouns in which a person may speak to, of, or about herself. The Getty Residency was a hiatus which, despite the media terror and the billow of fax messages inundating her at the Victoria (in Germany, the world would have been too much with her) offered a therapeutic time-space to Wolf in which real life was at least somewhat distant, clearly suspended.

Bibliography

Aristotle. *Poetics*. Translated by Anthony Kenny. Oxford: Oxford University Press, 2013.

Assmann, Jan. *Das kulturelle Gedächtnis: Schrift, Erinnerung und politische Identität in frühen Hochkulturen*. Munich: Beck, 2007.

Bachmann, Ingeborg. *Sämtliche Gedichte*. Munich: Piper, 2010.

Bahr, Ehrhard. *Weimar on the Pacific: German Exile Culture in Los Angeles and the Crisis of Modernism*. Berkeley: University of California Press, 2007.

Bathrick, David. "Fetisch oder Aufarbeitung? Zur Rolle des Dr. Freud in *Stadt der Engel oder The Overcoat of Dr. Freud*." *Zwischen Moskauer Novelle und Stadt* der Engel: Neue Perspektiven auf das Lebenswerk von Christa Wolf. Ed. Therese Hörnigk and Carsten Gansel. Verlag für Berlin-Brandenburg, 2015, pp. 107–16.

Blankenship, Robert. "Christa Wolf's Richard Neutra: Architecture, Psychoanalysis, and Southern California in *Stadt der Engel oder The Overcoat of Dr. Freud*." *The Germanic Review: Literature, Culture, Theory*. Special Issue: German Exiles in Los Angeles 95(1) (2020), pp. 55–64.

Calle, Sophie. *Appointment with Sigmund Freud*. London: Thames and Hudson, 2005.

Coleman, Cy, Larry Gelbart, and David Zippel. *City of Angels*. Milwaukee: Hal Leonard/Applause, 2000.

Faulkner, William. *Requiem for a Nun*. New York: Vintage, 1994.

Frattaroli, Elio. *Healing the Soul in the Age of the Brain*. New York and London: Viking Penguin, 2001.

Freud, Sigmund. *The Standard Edition of the Complete Psychological Works of Sigmund Freud*. Translated and edited by James Strachey. 24 vols. London: The Hogarth Press and the Institute of Psychoanalysis, 1953–1974. (Hereafter cited as *Standard Edition*.)

———. "A Disturbance of Memory on the Acropolis: Open Letter to Romain Rolland" (1936). *Standard Edition* XXII (1964), pp. 237–48.

———. "Delusions and Dreams in Jensen's *Gradiva*" (1907). *Standard Edition* IX (1959), pp. 1–95.

———. "The Dynamics of Transference" (1912). *Standard Edition* XII (1958), pp. 97–108.

———. "Fetishism" (1927). *Standard Edition* XXI (1961), pp. 147–57.

———. "Five Lectures on Psycho-Analysis" (1910). *Standard Edition* XI (1957), pp. 1–55.

———. *The Interpretation of Dreams* (1900). *Standard Edition* IV (1953).

———. "Remembering, Repeating, and Working Through (Further Recommendations on the Technique of Psycho-Analysis II)" (1914). *Standard Edition* XII (1958), pp. 145–56.

———. "Transference" (1917). *Standard Edition* XVI (1963), pp. 431–47.

———. "The Uncanny" (1919). *Standard Edition* XVII (1957), pp. 217–56.

Gansel, Carsten, and Christa Wolf. "'Zum Schreiben haben mich Konflikte getrieben'—ein Gespräch," in *Christa Wolf—Im Strom der Erinnerung*. Edited by Carsten Gansel. Göttingen: V & R unipress, 2014, pp. 353–66.

Goethe, Johann Wolfgang. *Italian Journey*. Translated by W. H. Auden and Elizabeth Mayer. London: Penguin, 1970.

Gogol, Nikolai Vasilievich. *The Overcoat and Other Tales of Good and Evil*. Translated by David Magarshack. New York: W.W. Norton & Company, 1965.

Haase, Michael. "Christa Wolfs letzter 'Selbstversuch'—Zum Konzept der subjektiven Authentizität in 'Stadt der Engel oder The Overcoat of Freud.'" *Christa Wolf — Im Strom der Erinnerung*. Edited by Carsten Gansel. Göttingen V & R unipress: 2014, pp. 215–30.

Hampton, Christopher. *Tales from Hollywood*. London: Faber & Faber, 2002.

Hein, Christoph. "Stadt der Engel: Laudatio auf Christa Wolf." *Der Freitag* 2 October 2010. Retrieved 16 September 2019 from www.freitag.de/autoren/der-freitag/201estad-der-engel201c.

Hofmansthal, Hugo von. *Der Brief des Lord Chandos*. Ed. Fred Lönker. Stuttgart: Reclam, 2019.

Klocke, Sonja. "Patientin unter Palmen: Symptomatische Körper, Leiden und Heilung in Christa Wolfs Stadt der Engel oder The Overcoat of Dr.Freud." *Triangulum: Germanistisches Jahrbuch für Estland, Lettland und Litauen*, 2016, pp. 469–79.

Kolb, Martina. "Guilt Trips on Royal Roads: Freud's Mediterranean Affinities." *Quaderni di Studi Indo-Mediterranei*, vol. II, 2009, pp. 329–46.

Kuhn, Anna. "Of Trauma, Angels, and Healing: Christa Wolf's *Stadt der Engel oder The Overcoat of Dr. Freud*." *Gegenwartsliteratur*, vol. 10, 2011, pp. 165–85.

Lentz, Michael. *Pazifik Exil*. Frankfurt a.M.: Fischer, 2007.

Magenau, Jörg. *Christa Wolf: Eine Biografie*. Berlin: Kindler, 2002.

Michelis, Angelica. "'To Learn to Live without Alternatives': Forgetting as Remembering in Christa Wolf's *The City of Angels; or, The Overcoat of Dr. Freud*' , *Journal of Literature and Trauma Studies* 3(1) (Spring 2014), pp. 63–80.

Minden, Michael. "Social Hope and the Nightmare of History: Christa Wolf's *Kindheitsmuster* and *Stadt der Engel*." *Publications of the English Goethe Society*, vol. LXXX, no. 2–3, 2011, pp. 196–203.

Molnar, Michael. *The Diary of Sigmund Freud 1929–1939: A Record of the Final Decade*. London: The Freud Museum Publications, 1992.

OED Online, Oxford University Press. www.oed.com. "Novel, n." Retrieved 25 June 2020.

Peterson, Tracie, and James Scott Bell. *City of Angels*. London: Compendium 2012.

Pormeister, Eve. "Vom Nachdenken über das Vergessen zur 'schonungslose[n] Selbsterkenntnis': *Stadt der Engel oder The Overcoat of Dr. Freud* von Christa Wolf." *Zwischen Moskauer Novelle und Stadt der Engel: Neue Perspektiven auf das Lebenswerk von Christa Wolf*. Edited by Therese Hörnigk and Carsten Gansel. Verlag für Berlin-Brandenburg, 2015, pp. 94–106.

Pound, Ezra. "Exile's Letter." *New and Selected Poems and Translations*. Edited by Richard Sieburth, New York: New Directions, 2010, p. 62.

Rosenberg, Robert. *Stadt der Engel*. Berlin: List, 2000.

Said, Edward. *On Late Style: Music and Literature against the Grain*. New York: Vintage, 2007.

Shakespeare, William. *Hamlet*. Edited by Robert S. Miola. New York: Norton, 2011.

Silberling, Brad. *City of Angels* (film, 1989).

Smale, Catherine. "Towards a Late Style? Christa Wolf on Old Age, Death and Creativity in *Stadt der Engel oder The Overcoat of Dr. Freud*." *Christa Wolf: A Companion*. Edited by Sonja Klocke and Jennifer Hosek. Berlin: de Gruyter, 2018, pp. 181–99.

Sousa, Celeste Ribeiro de. "Autobiography, Autofiction, Metafiction and Literature: The Case of *Stadt der Engel* by Christa Wolf." *Pandaemonium* (São Paolo) 17(23) (June 2014), pp. 119–37.

Stobart, Craig (ed.) and Richard Macer (dir.). *Behind the Scenes at the Freud Museum*. London: BBC, 2009.

Summers, Caroline. "Translating Subjective Authenticity from *Christa T.* to *Stadt der Engel* and *August*: Re-presenting Christa Wolf's Subaltern Voice." *Christa Wolf: A Companion*. Edited by Sonja Klocke and Jennifer Hosek. Berlin: de Gruyter, 2018, pp. 219–41.

Tögel, Christfried, ed. *Sigmund Freud: Unser Herz zeigt nach dem Süden: Reisebriefe 1895–1923*. Berlin: Aufbau-Verlag, 2002.

Vaihinger, Hans. *Die Philosophie des Als Ob: System der theoretischen, praktischen und religiösen Fiktionen der Menschheit auf Grund eines idealistischen Positivismus. Mit einem Anhang über Kant und Nietzsche*. Edited by Raymund Schmidt. Leipzig: Felix Meiner, 1924.

Vinke, Hermann, ed. *Akteneinsicht Christa Wolf: Zerrspiegel und Dialog*. Munich: Luchterhand, 1993.

Wenders, Wim. *Der Himmel über Berlin* (film, 1987).

Winnicott, Donald W. "Transitional Objects and Transitional Phenomena." *The International Journal of Psycho-Analysis* 34(2) (1953), pp. 89–97.

Wittgenstein, Ludwig. *Tractatus Logico-Philosophicus: Logisch-philosophische Abhandlung*. Edited by Joachim Fest and Wolf Jobst Siedler. Frankfurt a.M.: Suhrkamp, 1988.

Wolf, Christa. "Eine Auskunft." *Berliner Zeitung*, 21 January 1993.

———. *City of Angels or, The Overcoat of Dr. Freud*. Translated by Damion Searls. New York: Farrar, Straus and Giroux, 2013.

———. "'Die Dimension des Autors,' Gespräch mit Hans Kaufmann." *Fortgesetzter Versuch: Aufsätze, Gespräche, Essays*. Leipzig: Reclam, 1982, pp. 7–9.

———. *Kindheitsmuster*. Frankfurt a.M.: Suhrkamp, 2007.

———. *La città degli angeli ovvero the overcoat of Dr. Freud*. Translated and edited by Anita Raja. Rome: Edizioni Eo, 2011.

———. *La ciudad de Los Ángeles o El abrigo del Dr. Freud*. Translated by Carmen Gauger. Madrid: Alianza Edición General, 2011.

———. "Nachdenken über den blinden Fleck." *Rede, daß ich dich sehe*. Berlin: Suhrkamp, 2012, pp. 72–95.

———. *Patterns of Childhood* (formerly *A Model Childhood*). Translated by Ursule Molinaro and Hedwig Rappolt. New York: Farrar, Straus and Giroux, 1980.

———. *Stadt der Engel oder The Overcoat of Dr. Freud*. Berlin: Suhrkamp, 2010.

———. *Ville des anges: Ou The Overcoat of Dr. Freud*. Translated by Alain Lance and Renate Lance-Otterbein. Paris: Éditions du Seuil, 2011.

———. *Was bleibt*. Berlin: Suhrkamp, 2007.

———. *What Remains and Other Stories*. Translated by Heike Schwarzbauer and Rick Takvorian. New York: Farrar, Straus and Giroux, 1993.

CHAPTER 3

Fetishism or Working Through?
Concerning the Role of Dr. Freud in City of Angels or, The Overcoat of Dr. Freud

DAVID BATHRICK

My reading of Christa Wolf's *City of Angels or, The Overcoat of Dr. Freud* will focus primarily on the last five words of its title. What struck me as significant in many of the sometimes scathing reviews of this work in the German press was their failure to account for or even address the psychoanalytical implications of a narrative voice that quite explicitly, if not pleadingly, explains its epistemological focus as follows: "It's about memories, about how we remember: my topic for decades you understand. And somehow I could have forgotten *that*" (*City of Angels* 202). The trauma of the forgotten, unleashed by the discovery of her Stasi file with the code name (Deckname) "Margarete," gives birth to a new voice that, while less controlling, is perhaps more revealing of its inner workings than its more canonical narrative predecessors in the oeuvre of Christa Wolf.

Generically labeled an autobiographical novel and a "fabric (ein Gewebe) into which components of experienced reality are interwoven" (Grombacher), Wolf's *City of Angels* delivers a diary of her nine-month stay at the Getty Research Center near Los Angeles between September 1992 and July 1993, introduced by the following clumsy disclaimer in the front matter: "All characters in this book, with the exception of historical figures mentioned by name, are the invention of the novelist. None of them is identical with anyone living or dead. Just as little do the episodes described coincide with actual events" (6). Ostensibly narrated by a visiting scholar in residence in search of information regarding a female German Jewish exile named L., the text conveys from the start the lurking presence of larger concerns; issues of loss, defiance, and even mourning that have accompanied her to this far away land.

Upon her arrival at the Los Angeles airport, for example, we are informed by the narrator that after she handed the seemingly suspicious customs official a still valid GDR passport, the following exchange ensued: "'Are you sure that country exists?' 'Yes, I am,' I said curtly ... That was one of the acts of defiance that I was still capable of then, acts which, it occurs to me now, become fewer and fewer with time" (10). Here a moment of playful, yet not so playful denial that will be re-enacted with increasing intensity—at first indeed with defiance, and then with growing self-doubt and fear as the narrator permits herself to confront the traumatic events that occurred during the three years prior to her nine-month stay on the palisades of the Pacific.

Three areas of historical, if not also fantastical source material were seminal to the narrator's obsessive reworking of her recent and not so recent past. First, the virtual implosion of the GDR in November 1989, experienced initially as a non-violent uprising that stirred in the narrator utopian hopes for a reformation of GDR socialism "where nobody runs away" (Dolzauer), only then to dissolve gradually into the shock that such was not forthcoming—shock, for instance, at the post-Wall sight of drunken East Germans carrying home their paper bags full of goodies purchased at department stores in West Berlin. In the words of the narrator: "That was what really mattered at the core. But what did I know back then?" (84). And following shock, her mood gives way to a growing sense of loss. In responding to questions by colleagues at the Getty Center about the recent "wondrous" events in Germany, the narrator refuses to employ codified phrases like "the turning point" (*die Wende*, 54), or "reunification," but speaks instead, with echoes of 1945, of herself as a person who comes "from a country that has ceased to exist" (7) ("aus einem untergegangen Staat," 15). At one point, speaking to herself—and speaking to herself becomes the dominant discourse of this search for the self—she asserts: "We loved this country. An impossible sentence that would have earned you nothing but mocking jeers if you had spoken it out loud. But you didn't. You kept it to yourself, the way you were keeping so much to yourself now" (51). What she also kept to herself were the ideological underpinnings for her cathected relationship to "my tiny country": namely her belief that socialism was ontologically the absolute negation of and therefore the only possible antidote to the rise of fascism.

A second source of trauma derives from her early post-Wall interactions with the German media. The so-called "literary controversy" (*Literaturstreit*) or, as it was also labeled, "The Christa Wolf Debate," focused in very large part on the publication of Wolf's *What Remains* (*Was bleibt*, 1990), where she portrays a day in the life of a female author being observed by the Stasi: three uniformed men sit in a car in front of her house ostensibly watching and waiting. In the highly condemnatory post-Wall atmosphere in which it appeared, this work was either ridiculed for its supposed self-serving glorification of the author herself as a victim in a situation where she enjoyed the highest privileges, or the author was taken to task for not having published the book ten years earlier, either in the East or in the West, when it would have challenged the still "real existing socialism." While the narrator did not respond publicly to the retributions aimed at her and other dissidents in the GDR, she more than once let it be known that it felt like a "witch hunt" (203).

The third, and by far most devastating bit of source material was the narrator's discovery and reading of her Stasi files in May 1992, when she learned from the Gauck Behörde (office for Stasi files) that she had in fact two sets of files, one a victim file consisting of forty-two volumes, the other a perpetrator or IM (Stasi Informer) file with the code name "Margarete." Her meetings with the Stasi occurred from 1959 to 1962, when, as a committed young member of the Party, she was making a name for herself within the literary public sphere. Although the voice to emerge from the file clearly adheres to some of the sectarian rhetoric of the GDR cultural politics of the 1950s— Wolf herself spoke publicly of her "ideological dogmatism" during those early days (Kopka)—the information given to the Stasi did not differ in tone or content from the views she was expressing publicly as a literary critic writing in the mainstream press; nor did she denounce anyone. Moreover, Wolf appears to have written only one or two reports, and early on she insisted that their conversations take place at her home, with her husband present, rather than in a "conspiratorial apartment," as was the usual practice. While the latter fact does not excuse her of anything, it might well explain why she claimed to have no memory about working as an IM. It is also clear from written comments by her interrogators, complaining about her excessive "caution" and "discretions," that she was not giving them much that they needed, which is why they decided to close the file.

Returning to our "narrative" of everyday life in West Los Angeles, it certainly is significant that in this 315-page book of memorial recuperation, locked as it is in a repetition compulsion of the pains and traumas of a recent history, it is not until page 139 that we first get the full story of Margarete. Having decided to go public about her perpetrator file in January 1993, with an article in the *Berliner Zeitung*, (Wolf) the narrator is soon faced with yet another level of public approbation within a political environment in which the words IM and Stasi had taken on enormous meaning in the realm of categorical evil. Panic and horror seize her. What is spewing forth in the German press and pouring out of her fax machine at the Getty on a daily basis appears once again to be a full-scale witch hunt. The accusations and denunciations, she tells us, throw her back to what she experienced in 1969 in the GDR following the publication of her canonical book, *The Quest for Christa T.* (*Nachdenken über Christa T.*, 1968). In those days it was the Party, today it is the class enemy.

At one level, as she herself knows, and as many of her colleagues at the Getty seek to reassure her, the question as to why thirty-five years prior she would talk with the Stasi and write a few reports is not difficult to answer: because she was young and inexperienced, because the Stasi was not yet the "Stasi," and because her own life as an author, that is as a self-reflexive intellectual, had just begun to flower. She simply wasn't the same person. But for the narrator, and this was her neurosis, she was the same person, which is why the much more difficult question is not how she could have done such a thing, but how she could have possibly obliterated the memory of it. "Looking into these files completely undermined and defiled the past, you know, and poisoned the present along with it" (136). In short, the narrator's forgetting about her Stasi file "Margarete" has thrown into question the validity of her entire work as one unending struggle against displacement. At the end of Wolf's book *Patterns of Childhood* (*Kindheitsmuster*, 1976) we read the following: "Has memory done its duty? Or has it proven—by the act of misleading—that it's impossible to avoid the mortal sin of our time: the desire not to come to terms with oneself?" (404).

The moral and religious dimensions of this remembrance are legion throughout *City of Angels*: the Marxist narrator speaks often of her Prussian Protestantism. Also significant is that with the central figure in sudden crisis seemingly headed for a breakdown, this heretofore scattered collection of diary notations suddenly assumes the shape of a novel. And what more intriguing trope to appear at the narrative turning point of our novel of trauma than the figure of Sigmund Freud? Freud's overcoat, which supposedly came from the estate of the Viennese émigré architect Richard Neutra living in Los Angeles, does not actually exist. It was lost somehow by Neutra, we are told, and in turn retrieved by the author as a key metaphor for her book. It continuously and reliably pops up whenever the narrator appears in need of solace and comfort. Regardless of what its interior fur may have traditionally contained in the way of "very painful secrets," its function in *City of Angels* is that of a protective shield for the beleaguered narrator—which is why a number of reviewers have read it as an antidote to her Stasi files, embodying, if nothing else, the utopia of a liberating memory that refuses fruition.

The narrator's efforts to enlist the services of Freud in her struggle against the forces of amnesia are met with two gentle rejoinders that reveal to the reader, if not to the narrator, the extent to which Freud's overcoat is serving as a fetish and not a facilitating source for working through. In the middle of a seemingly never-ending conversation with her "Jewish" friend Sally, we suddenly come across the following exchange: "The Overcoat of Dr. Freud came to my mind. I wished it could protect me. On the contrary, said Sally. It's there to take your self-defence mechanisms away from you" (152). Two pages later the narrator telephones a psychiatrist friend in Zürich to ask for his thoughts: "Can someone forget something like that? That they gave me a code name? That I wrote a report?" The predictable answer: "Don't you know the line from Freud: We cannot live without forgetting?" The narrator's reply: "So what do you think I should do? Go into therapy?" "That would be the best thing," he replied, and the conversation was ended. "But that's out of the question," the narrator says to herself, "I don't need help, I am not allowed to need help, I must deal with this alone … and it was only much later, perhaps just today, that I have come to understand that this overbearing persistence was not so very far from my older ways of thinking that got me 'into this mess' in the first place" (154).

And what was the narrator referring to with the phrase "my older ways of thinking"? I referred above to her use, or rather misuse, of Freud's overcoat as a fetish and would like now to draw on Eric Santner's Freudian-based theory of "narrative fetishism." In his essay entitled "History beyond the Pleasure Principle: Some Thoughts on the Representation of Trauma," Santner focuses on a number of differing narrative strategies of trauma in the Federal Republic of Germany in the 1970 and 1980s. Here he uses the notion of "narrative fetishism" to describe a phenomenon in which dominant and literary constructions focusing on the past are able to mutually support one another. In lieu of a serious and critical analysis of the consequences of the Holocaust or National Socialism, Santner argues, what one finds in West Germany instead is a fixation on narratives that brush clean and eradicate any disorderly elements in favor of absolutely coherent and teleological structures of meaning and matter. Here Santner is thinking of public controversies such as "Bitburg" (1985), the "Historians' Debate" (1986–87), and the "Fall of the Wall" (1989). Thus, narrative fetishism is a development which he defines as:

> the construction and deployment of a narrative consciously or unconsciously designed to expunge the traces of the trauma or loss that called that narrative into being in the first place. The use of narrative as fetish may be contrasted with that very different mode of symbolic behaviour that Freud called *Trauerarbeit* or the "work of mourning." Both narrative fetishism and mourning are responses to loss, to a past that refuses to go away due to its traumatic impact. The work of mourning is a process of elaborating and integrating the reality of loss or traumatic shock by remembering and repeating it in symbolically and dialogically mediated doses. Narrative fetishism, by contrast, is the way an inability or refusal to mourn emplots traumatic events; it is a strategy of undoing in fantasy, the need for mourning by simulating a condition of intactness, typically by situating the site and origin of loss elsewhere. (144)

Santner's theory of psychoanalytical narrative is relevant to my interpretation of *City of Angels* precisely because we are dealing with a novel that generically is much more than just a novel. For what we find here is a narrative voice that is capable of articulating more explicitly than ever perhaps the extent to which the underlying tensions of a crisis are at once subjective and historical. Thus, I now propose to analyze what I regard as a narrative cluster system in *City of Angels* where the narrator would seem to be struggling within a paradigm that could be mapped according to notions of narrative fetishism and the work of mourning.

At the broadest level of ideological articulation as well as at the deepest level of emotional attachment was the role played by the narrative of anti-fascism, particularly among the second generation of dissident writers in the GDR. Asked in a radio interview of the *Deutschlandfunk* whether in the years following the founding of the GDR in 1949 he had experienced anti-fascism as something "prescribed" rather than "consciously lived" ("bewusst gelebt"), the dissident writer Günter Kunert spoke for an entire generation when he replied:

> This prescribed anti-fascism: well yes, I lived through all that and for me it wasn't at all prescribed. This is a very vital point that is too often misunderstood. The late emergence of any kind of oppositional stand by people in the GDR is related to the fact that this socialism, unlike the ones in other socialist countries, came directly out of fascism. (208)

Kunert's words reveal clearly how the discourse of anti-fascism was from the very beginning doubly coded. In 1989, Christa Wolf states it even more clearly: "We felt a strong reluctance to organize resistance against people who had been in concentration camps during the Nazi period. We did resist them intellectually, that was clear to me starting in the 1960s. But any massive or even political opposition worth mentioning was not formed" ("Schreiben im Zeitbezug" 136).

In *City of Angels* the ever-present memorial trace of the anti-fascist heritage continues to assert itself on the narrator in contradictory ways due in part to the fact that West Los Angeles was home to so many German exiles and refugees who fled Nazi aggression in the 1940s: Jews, writers, artists, intellectuals like Bertolt Brecht, Erich Weinert, Lion Feuchtwanger, Thomas Mann and Heinrich Mann, Franz Werfel, Alfred Döblin and Theodor W. Adorno, to name a few. "In this new Germany," writes the narrator, speaking of the post-1989 era, "they will be consigned to oblivion. But that was exactly the point, that was why I had clung to the smaller Germany. I saw it as the legitimate successor to this Other Germany, the one that, in all the prisons and concentration camps, in Spain, in the various countries of emigration—persecuted, tortured, horribly decimated—nevertheless resisted" (264).

This is indeed a very affirmative and, as the narrator says, "legitimate" dimension of the anti-fascist exile legend, one that was to remain absolutely vital for the development and career of Christa Wolf. It appears in many of her writings and plays a vital role in *City of Angels*. However, we also are confronted in this very same book, for example, with a report by the narrator about a trip she took to Moscow in the 1960s, where the older-generation GDR writer Willi Bredel took her on a tour of the Moscow of his years in emigration: "That's the Hotel Lux, we all lived there," Bredel says, during the bad times, during the terrible purges ("Säuberungen") we would call each other up at night to hear if the other person was still there ... and some comrades weren't "there" anymore. ... And here's the Lubjanka, the NKWD headquarters with the bars on the windows, from here they were sent to the camps, and we never heard from some of them again. And when Ribbentrop and Molotov signed the non-aggression pact between Hitler Germany and the Soviet Union, we émigrés had to stop our public anti-Fascist propaganda. (62)

This memory of her tour with Bredel closes with the following very blunt statement by the narrator to her younger self:

That wouldn't happen to you and your generation. You were young back then and you sat around together, hour after hour, night after night. Your task, you thought, would be to exorcise the demon of Stalin from social life, to get through the conflicts, which were more severe than you predicted, and to not give up. A naive agenda. (62)

What we find in *City of Angels* thematically and aesthetically under the rubric of anti-fascism are the various disparate, even conflicting pieces of an assiduously woven cloth. Or returning to Freud, its narrative concerns a process of "elaborating and integrating the reality of loss or traumatic shock by remembering it and repeating it in symbolically and dialogically mediated doses" (Santner 144).

Anna Chiarloni has quite rightly written that Christa Wolf's *City of Angels* is a "mass of narrative" ("eine Masse von Erzähltem") that dissolves itself only to come together in consciousness" (197). I would only add to that: in order to dissolve itself once more and then to come together again and again. These repetitions, which refuse to be exact replications, are in Therese Hörnigk's words the driving force of

self-analysis as the presupposition for constructing one's own past and in so doing gaining a future. In a narrative web made up of reflections and dreams, descriptions and documentations of historical events that follow the lines of one's own memory, she (Wolf) confronts subjective powers of remembering and mechanisms of displacement with historical witnessing. (27)

In closing I would like briefly to mention another memorable quality in this process of working through that I found notable and particularly moving—namely the willingness and indeed courage on the part of the narrator to open herself up in this foreign locale of West Los Angeles to new experiences, perspectives, habits, customs, yes, narratives. Not uncritically to be sure, and sometimes with defiance as well, but always with a driving curiosity that productively calls everything into question in a manner that for passages on end has absolutely nothing in common with fetishization.

David Bathrick was the Jacob Gould Schurman Emeritus Professor of Theatre, Film & Dance and Professor of German and Jewish Studies at Cornell University. Publications include *The Powers of Speech: The Politics of Culture in the GDR*, which was awarded the 1996 DAAD/GSA Book of the Year Prize. In addition, he has published books and articles on twentieth- and twenty-first-century German culture and Holocaust studies. He was also a co-founder of the journal *New German Critique*. David passed away in 2020.

Note

This chapter is a slightly revised version of David Bathrick, "Fetisch oder Aufarbeitung? Zur Rolle des Dr. Freud," in *Stadt der Engel oder The Overcoat of Dr. Freud*, edited by Therese Hörnigk and Carsten Gansel, Berlin, Verlag für Berlin-Brandenburg, 2015, pp. 107–16.

Bibliography

Chiarloni, Anna. "Für eine Anamnese der Gegenwart: Zu Christa Wolfs *Stadt der Engel.*" *Text und Kritik*, vol. 46 (Neue Fassung): *Christa Wolf*, 2012, pp. 191–99.
Dolzauer, Gregor. "Irrtum als Weg." *Der Tagesspiegel*, 1 December 2011.
Grombacher, Wolf. "Christa Wolfs neuer Roman *Stadt der Engel.*" *Thüringer Allgemeine*, 17 June 2010.
Hörnigk, Therese. "Nachdenken über Christa Wolf." *Text und Kritik*, vol. 46 (Neue Fassung): *Christa Wolf*, 2012, pp. 27–37.
Kopka, Fritz Jochen. "Christa Wolf Interview mit Fritz-Jochen Kopka." *Die Wochenpost*, 24 January 1993.
Kunert, Günter. "Der ausgeträumte DDR-Traum von Antifaschismus und Solidarität." Kunert Interview mit Heinz Klunkert. *Deutschland Archiv*, vol. 23, no. 2, 1990, pp. 207–11.
Santner, Eric. "History beyond the Pleasure Principle: Some Thoughts on the Representation of Trauma." *Probing the Limits of Representation: Nazism and the "Final Solution"*, edited by Saul Friedlander. Cambridge, MA: Harvard University Press, 1992, pp. 143–54.
Wolf, Christa. *City of Angels or, The Overcoat of Dr. Freud*. Translated by Damion Searles. New York: Farrar, Straus & Giroux, 2013.
———. *Kindheitsmuster*. Berlin: Aufbau-Verlag, 1976.
———. *Patterns of Childhood*. Translated by Ursule Molinaro and Hedwig Rappolt. New York: Farrar, Straus & Giroux, 1984.

———. "Schreiben im Zeitbezug: Gespräch mit Aafke Steenhaus." *Im Dialog*. Frankfurt a.M.: Luchterhand Verlag, 1990, pp. 131–57.

———. *Stadt der Engel oder The Overcoat of Dr. Freud*. Berlin: Suhrkamp Verlag, 2010.

PART II

Christa Wolf as a Writer of Time and Her Times

CHAPTER 4

The Notion of *Heimat* in Christa Wolf's *Patterns of Childhood*

MARIJKE MULDER

Despite the somewhat meager attention paid to the themes of *Heimat* and *Heimweh* (homesickness) in critical studies of Wolf's work, the longing to belong to a certain place and community is so prominent in her writing that, as Jutta Birmele suggests, her entire oeuvre can be summed up as one "continual search for 'Heimat'" (71).[1] Starting with Rita in *They Divided the Skies* (*Der geteilte Himmel*, 1963) asking herself whether to join her fiancé in the West or to remain in her country (East Germany), nearly all of Wolf's major characters struggle in some way with the question of where they belong and with the underlying fundamental sense of "not belonging."

For Christa Wolf herself, the importance of the topic is undeniable. Her approach to the effects of growing up during the National Socialist regime is closely connected to her thinking about the significance of *Heimat*. During a question-and-answer session following a reading from the manuscript in 1975, she emphasizes *Heimweh*, the nostalgic longing for her native city, as a major motivation behind the novel ("A Model of Experience" 42). In a conversation with the Polish journalist Adam Krzemiński, she also points out the importance for her well-being of a specific landscape: "I was born in Landsberg an der Warthe, which is now Gorzów. After that I lived in Saxony, Thuringia, and Mecklenburg, but I still feel most at home amongst sand and pine forest" ("Sand and Pines" 70).

Christa Wolf is not alone in considering her childhood *Heimat* as a defining and enduring influence on her entire life. Whether it is Max Frisch developing a questionnaire on the topic, culminating in the question of whether one could imagine oneself without any *Heimat* at all ("Tagebuch" 357f.), Heinrich Böll experiencing *Heimat* whenever he notices a vending machine dispensing chocolate from the Cologne chocolate company Stollwerck ("Heimat und Keine" 113), or Martin Walser noticing that you can never really leave your *Heimat* behind ("Heimatkunde" 41), there is hardly a German-speaking writer in the last two centuries who was not in some way concerned with the notion of *Heimat*.² Although it implies a place of familiarity and safety, the concept has never been without complications. Not only does *Heimat* refer to a lost safe haven that is impossible to re-enter, the longing for *Heimat* has frequently been accompanied by a simultaneous aversion to how the demands of belonging to a *Heimat* also restrict the individual. In many texts one encounters both a sense of relief over having escaped from the narrow confines of *Heimat* and the feeling of loss of a stable point of reference.

Since World War II, however, discussion of the topic has taken a more critical turn, since the notion of *Heimat* was tainted by the National Socialists' deployment of the term in the service of their ideology, both to construct a *German* community, as opposed to a local or regional one, which had been predominant, and as an argument for their *Heim-ins-Reich* offensives toward neighboring countries where large numbers of ethnic Germans lived. The aura of innocence surrounding *Heimat* was ultimately lost in the face of the deadly aggression executed in its name. Additionally, after the war, the grievances of German expellees longing for their *Heimat* in the former German east were regarded by many as an unwelcome form of revanchism that complicated any engagement with the *Heimat* in a positive vein, especially for young writers on both sides of the Iron Curtain.

East German authors faced still further complications since nostalgic *Heimat* sentiments stood in stark contrast to the officially declared function of literature to support and strengthen the new socialist state. Furthermore, the self-portrayal of the GDR as a nation of antifascists could neither accommodate the punishment of its citizens for the German crimes of the Third Reich nor assign any guilt to the Soviet Union. For this reason, German expellees from these regions were referred to as "re-settlers" (Ther 91f.), as opposed to "refugees," for instance. Longing for one's *Heimat* was considered a revanchist and, therefore, politically suspect sentiment. *Patterns of Childhood* is one of the few novels published in the GDR to deal with this displacement at all.

Aside from the political context, *Heimat* signifies a space of "knowing oneself, being known by others, and receiving recognition from them" (Greverus 18), offering the individual security and an uncomplicated relationship to the self. While "man as a species is a mobile being, … he also needs a place, a territory, that he belongs to and that affords him identity" (12). *Heimat* provides a foundation for identity by representing a space that is immune to change, for example by significant industrial progress or social and political change. It is this static quality of *Heimat* that underlies both the rise of the concept to a key word in German culture (Ecker 8), as well as the suggestion of backwardness that resonates in it.

Originally a term referring either to the medieval *Heimatrecht*, the judicial right of residence, or to the place of origin, as it is still used in the classification of plants and animals, *Heimat* gained its emotional charge during German Romanticism. In the face of the Industrial Revolution, *Heimat* was discovered as a "haven without irony" (Blickle 41) for those who felt estranged by developments of the modern age. Like an archaic idyll, *Heimat* served as a contrast to the alienating modern city and promised the individual a stability that reality lacked (Bausinger 19).

Accordingly, *Heimat* was "never a word about real social forces or real political situations" (Applegate 19), but an idealized fiction of a more authentic life deemed lost, its imagery offering a simplified vision of the rural German hometown. Its fundamentally conservative ideology of the "good old days" and the attendant presumption of innocence (Blickle 130ff.) render it immune to social and technical progress. In its denial of change and its idealization of the past, the *Heimat* sentiment reflects the nostalgic longing of the adult for the (assumed) innocence of childhood: "In Heimat a naïve state of mind is not only promoted: it is a precondition" (136), leaving the adult no chance for genuine individuation.

Thus, *Heimat* was never an entirely beneficent realm, since its authority depends upon its complete and unchallenged acceptance by its inhabitants. Alterity, both in custom and in person, poses a challenge and a threat to the restricted world view that is at the heart of *Heimat*, since it offers an alternative to such a confined world. The naive state of mind on which it depends implies that no critical assessment of *Heimat* is possible without sacrificing its implicitness. This intrinsically dangerous potential becomes evident only indirectly, as when someone experiences the personal or social limitations of *Heimat*.

The same principle, however, also enabled the National Socialists to deploy *Heimat* as a device to prepare the German people for their wars. Within Nazi ideology *Heimat* has both a metaphysical and concrete connotation. On the one hand, the status of belonging to the German *Heimat* is an inborn quality that proclaims a higher unity of all Germans, while, on the other, *Heimat* also refers to a concrete space that needs to be defended or, sometimes, reconquered. Both concepts coincide in the doctrine of "blood and soil," the central element of the Nazi ideology that proclaims a metaphysical connection between the Germans and the land, by asserting that the dead forefathers' blood functions as "Krume des Ackers für das Korn der Enkel" (soil of the fields for the grandchildren's grain) (Schwierin 37th minute).

This proclaimed connection functioned as a justification for reconquering regions that Germany had been forced to give up after World War I and at the end of World War II. Instead of the local space, that is, the hometown and its surroundings, the Nazi *Heimat* refers to Germany as a whole. Likewise, the social group within this concept includes the whole of the German people (*Volk*), understood to be only those who were considered part of a purported

German race. *Heimat* thereby became a highly exclusionary device that barred everybody who was not considered Aryan. Although the National Socialists present an extreme example of such misuse, this discriminatory quality is inherent in the *Heimat* concept, combining, as it does, "territorial claims with a fundamental ethical reassurance of innocence" (Blickle 1).

Christa Wolf, like numerous other writers of her generation, is aware of these conflicting implications of the *Heimat* concept. Her 1976 novel *Patterns of Childhood* constitutes an attempt to work out her personal stance on the issue. Both the ideological implications of the *Heimat* concept during the war—namely, the political claim to and glorification of the idea and its ensuing misuse, as well as its complication by events after the war—greatly influenced Wolf's approach. She does not concentrate, however, on the displacement of Germans, like herself, from the east or utter any accusations related to the experience, but focuses, rather, on the consequences the era had for the individual and on the personal significance of *Heimat*, this "childhood abode, so deeply anchored in German poetry and the German soul" (*Patterns* 284).

Published without any genre specification, *Patterns of Childhood* is both a fictional work and an autobiographical account, one that deals with the author's own youth, employing a fictional mask to discuss very personal issues. On the plot level, the book tells the story of Nelly Jordan's childhood and early adolescence (the "young Nelly") in "L., now called G." (4), that comes to a sudden halt in 1945 when her family is among the thousands that flee west ahead of the approaching Russian Army. Twenty-six years later, in the summer of 1971, the narrator takes a trip to the now Polish city with her family, revisiting the places of her childhood. As the adult Nelly, she approaches the child and therefore her own childhood as a stranger, reassessing her relationship to both her past and her native city. The narration employs a structure of three intertwined time layers that allows the narrator to tell both the stories of young Nelly and the journey back to her hometown twenty-six years later, as well as, on a third time level, to reflect back upon both of those plot and time lines and the continuing implications of *Heimat* into the present, that is, into the time of writing. In trying to understand the child she once was, she also gets closer to the emotional bond this child had to her living environment. As a result, the journey that the narrator and her family take to visit "L., now called G." constitutes a revisiting of her *Heimat* in more ways than one.

First, there is the actual trip the family undertakes, the literal journey into the geographical *Heimat*. The narrator's approach to her childhood hometown is presented rather "schauplatzorientiert" (focused on location, Wisniewski 161) and takes place in several stages, all of them based on her initial encounter with particular sites that trigger familiarity and remembrance.

The most poignant of these stages occurs right after crossing the Oder River, the East German-Polish border, just when the journey to her native city becomes a reality. The narrator's hesitation regarding the necessity of this trip crumbles when she recognizes elements of an eastern landscape she knows from long ago. "It is, by the way, remarkable how a single peasant woman with a white kerchief tied in a certain way and a rake over her shoulder can change a familiar landscape," she muses, and wonders how the summer heat of her childhood seems to have survived in this region (80). When noticing a certain cover of vegetation at the roadside, she insists that this variety could only grow east of the Oder, ignoring the observations of her daughter and husband that it is quite common elsewhere, too (56). In this first stage of her approach to *Heimat*, her inner defense against revisiting her native city and her denial of any kind of *Heimat* attachment break down. Her emotional connection to this geographical space is revived as images and sensations she knew as a child immediately take possession of her and diminish her capacity for critical evaluation.

Another significant stage in her approach to *Heimat* is occasioned by the "weeping willow behind Café Voley" that takes her by surprise because she has forgotten about the tree that she had "always considered the most beautiful tree in the world" (80f.). Unlike the general layout of the city, this special tree had not been preserved in her memory. Because she is unprepared for the encounter, it breaches the rational defense that she has constructed to shield her attachment to *Heimat*. Although the adult is unable to understand why the child Nelly considers this provincial town "den Ort …, der ihr ein für allemal zugewiesen war" (the place allocated to her once and for all, 187), she is likewise drawn in by "the old summer smell that hung over the ravine and the sand mountain and the Jordan's garden, where Nelly lies reading in the potato furrow" (129). The unique smell brings back the memory of "how much at home she felt here" (129) and her intention as a child to never leave this place. The gradual expansion of her childhood environment, caused by displacement, but also by simply growing up, has loosened the grip of the locus of childhood on the adult. Yet, at the same time, the familiar feeling of belonging, sparked by these sensory triggers, lets her comprehend the value the child had attached to her environment.

Heimat constitutes itself through an imaginary of the senses. Sensations, such as tastes, smells, and colors, do not need to be processed as narratives and can therefore enter the subconscious unhindered, producing an almost Pavlovian reflex. Whenever this taste or smell is re-experienced, it evokes the same sense of familiarity and belonging. Consequently, spatial separation from sensations innate to *Heimat* can lead to the individual feeling abandoned and lost outside its familiar environment. The recurrence of those same sensations, however, can temporarily re-establish the child's feeling of belonging to and in that place.

While the journey to her native city lends a concrete and sensual dimension to the retrieval of memory, it also reveals the power of *Heimat* over the individual. Within moments after re-entering the *Heimat*, the narrator depicts it as different from any other place, whereby rational arguments for its comparability are easily dismissed, as the minor disagreement about the roadside vegetation demonstrates. Just as during her youth, she is absorbed again by her environment without being able to reflect on the conditions of her belonging.

Memories as such are never mere playbacks of the past, but "present time constructions of combined data provided by constantly evolving cognitive schemata" (Henke 80). In other words, the present exerts a huge influence on the way the past is remembered. Hence the adult Nelly's experience of *Heimat* during the trip must be understood as a result of both the emotional, almost physical, remembrance triggered by her senses, as well as by the perspective of the adult in its own particular social and political context. The struggle between the adult's emotional longing for *Heimat* and the politically motivated denial of this longing is not the least a struggle between "the individual and the collective or, more precisely, the level of the cognitive on the one hand, and the levels of the social and the medial on the other" (Erll 5), as when her personal memory finds itself in opposition to the official version of history.

By addressing this conflict, the novel not only tells the story of the actual journey to "L., now called G.," it also focuses on the personal stance of the narrator toward her sense of *Heimat*. While writing the novel, in the years after the journey, she reflects on the child's sense of belonging; her own vague feeling of attachment to her native city now, three decades later; and "what it is like to arrive in a town which is now Polish but which was also one's home town ("A Model of Experience" 42). The disparity between the child's and the adult's feeling toward *Heimat* is not only motivated by the displacement, but also by the ideological corruption of the term during the Third Reich. The young Nelly began to lose her feeling of belonging long before her family had to flee the town; now for the adult narrator, questions of responsibility and guilt are inextricably connected to the term.

As long as she is a child, Nelly's sense of belonging is unchallenged and unproblematic. "She is happy that her environment (the place where the Jordans are going to live for eight and a half years) seems to be consolidating into a firm, stable foundation. Nelly, conscientious and steady, was attached to her environment"[3] (*Patterns* 141f.). The girl's positive associations with her living environment let her experience her surroundings as unique. Verbally, this idealization finds its expression in the use of superlatives and pronounced distinctions: Nelly elevates the "dry continental summer that crackled with heat" (80) to a norm against which every other summer had to be measured: "You've always had a profound feeling for it and have unconsciously compared all subsequent summers to it" (80). She is convinced that a certain ice cream is only produced in the local Italian confectionery and "nowhere else in the world" (202), and that the vacation setting "Plau am See" is, "if not the most beautiful, then at least the most wondrous town in the world" (60). Seeing herself as a part of this particular environment provides a sense of security and identity to the child.

For the adult, however, *Heimat* carries more complex implications. Not only does she suffer from the taboo on using the word *Heimweh* for the regions that are now Polish, since it was feared that nostalgia could support revanchist sentiments. Even more importantly, for the narrator, *Heimat* is closely connected to National Socialism and her own ideological involvement with it. Just as the young girl Christa Ihlenfeld (Wolf) herself did, young Nelly becomes a member of the Bund Deutscher Mädel (BDM, League of German Girls) and an enthusiastic follower of the Nazi regime. In this enthusiasm, the child in *Patterns of Childhood* finds herself in opposition to her family's values (189). After several years of indoctrination Nelly is so steeped in Nazi ideology that even the flight from the advancing Soviet army does not shake her confidence in Germany's supremacy (304). For the adult, *Heimat* immediately recalls the unifying feeling of excitement about Hitler's visit among the population of Landsberg (45), the unquestioned obedience to the BDM (191), and the songs young people were taught to sing (129, 169). Even though it uses comparable imagery, such as birds singing and the praise of nature, the National Socialist concept of *Heimat* constitutes a perversion of the child's non-judgmental experience of *Heimat* as an innocent space of security and well-being.

As previously mentioned, the National Socialists had turned *Heimat* into a propaganda term that was invoked to mobilize the populace to defend what was considered German territory, both on the battlefield and at home. In this understanding, the geographic aspect is conjoined with the second key element of *Heimat*: the social group. Belonging to a certain social group or community promises the individual support and recognition, offering an "individualization that is based on disindividualization" (Blickle 6). During the Third Reich, *Heimat* was not just one element of social propaganda; it was the very foundation of the Nazi concept of a "Volksgemeinschaft." The emphasis on *Heimat* and one's affiliation to it as a measure of a person's worth and superiority could therefore be seen as a justification for deportation and even extermination of those excluded from it. At the same time, a strong social body and an un-reflected sense of identity were fabricated.

While this concept of *Heimat* and her entanglement with it enables the adult to deny herself any kind of *Heimat* attachment, for young Nelly the strict division into friend or foe creates a feeling of belonging to a group that recreates the security she experienced during her childhood. In growing up, however, she loses the uncomplicated *Heimat* attachment of her early years, and school does not give her the approval to which she is accustomed (100). The price for belonging to this larger ideological *Heimat* is a surrender of one's individuality and a growing distrust of one's own emotions and thoughts, as young Nelly recognizes when she learns to define compassion as "an improper emotion" (160) and "to turn compassion for the weak and the losers into hate and fear" (161). Later, after leaving "L., now called G.," she will turn the same cold heartedness against herself.

Yet, the flight from her hometown is traumatic for the adolescent Nelly because it undermines the foundation of her life, geographically as well as ideologically. This double loss of *Heimat* shatters her self-perception. Eventually, the complete breakdown of her belief system gives way to a new ideological outlook, beginning in the early postwar years, but initially the flight and the gradual realization of the barbarity of National Socialist ideology leave her without any sense of self.

However, young Nelly's loss of *Heimat* does not start suddenly with leaving her hometown. Throughout her childhood, she experiences moments of fear and loneliness. As a very young girl she finds herself wondering whether love "doesn't get smaller when it is divided among a number of people" (13), not really trusting her mother's reassurance that she has enough love for both Nelly and her baby brother. Later, when a fellow BDM girl commits a theft and is suspended for three months as punishment, young Nelly does not react with disgust toward her, but rather with fear of the BDM leader who enforces the suspension; she actually becomes ill. "In her feverish state, Nelly ... admitted to herself, to her own bewilderment, that she didn't want to go on serving in the unit until kerchief and knot had been returned to Gerda Link" (193), whose facial features rather unmistakably fit the Nazi stereotype of a Jewish person. This psychosomatic reaction of the generally loyal child marks the first and, for a long time, only act in contradiction to official Nazi ideology. Becoming ill as the only way out indicates the power of the BDM system over Nelly: subconsciously recognizing the unjust harshness of the verdict, she does not know how to take a stand against it.

Thus, even before the flight toward the west, Nelly's sense of belonging is temporarily weakened. Neither during her childhood nor her years in the BDM was *Heimat* an entirely secure state of being; her fear of not being normal, "the worst thing by far" (57), was the sign of unconscious knowledge about the workings of *Heimat*. From her perspective in the 1970s, long after overcoming and rejecting Nazi ideology, the narrator recognizes the "intellectual ghetto" (Wisniewski 176) that her younger self had lived in and the "horrible wish for self-surrender [that] doesn't allow the self to emerge" (*Patterns* 231). The political distortion of the concept by the National Socialists had contaminated her sense of *Heimat*. Since the ideology and the space meet in the concept of *Heimat*, the adult narrator feels the need to distance herself from both in order to be sure that no suspicion of alliance between her and the Nazi ideology can arise. Such self-censorship at first prohibits her from feeling excited about the journey to her native city, although she does acknowledge her reservation as a mechanism of self-protection. "Is that reason enough for putting off the journey to the once jubilant hometown you have lost? For you shouldn't feign disinterest. Perhaps you have as little desire as anyone else to cross borders behind which all innocence stops" (55).

Preceding the visit to "L., now called G.," the narrator does not "claim that you'd never been homesick … But it has been years since the streets of your hometown have appeared in your dreams" (56). Consequently, she only agrees to the journey in order to accommodate her family's wishes. She herself initially denies any real interest in the place, gibes that "the tourist business to hometowns was booming" (4), and points out that the perfect conservation of the city in her mind makes a visit redundant, even unnecessary. Her adamant denial of any attachment to her native city dissipates, however, when she confronts her childhood environment and is forced to acknowledge the self-deception in her assertion that she has no attachment to it.

Patterns of Childhood demonstrates how the notion of *Heimat* can produce feelings of ambivalence, especially when looking back on its unquestioned nature during childhood. In the context of early childhood, *Heimat* conveys a sense of warmth and security, of belonging; growing up, however, the narrator dismisses her attachment on a rational level because of the negative political implications of the Nazi ideology that turned one group of people against the other and excluded all critical voices. Eventually, the journey to her native city does not result in a reconciliation with her *Heimat* or a reduction of her feeling of homelessness, but rather in reconciliation between her longing for *Heimat* and a more honest view of self. This honesty prevents the narrator from reverting to her naive attachment to *Heimat*, but it also allows the comforting realization that not all elements of her sense of *Heimat* are ideologically contaminated, because there are individual and emotional qualities that do not carry any political implications. While in the past she "struggled against it [homesickness] ruthlessly at times" (56), the familiar sensations of the journey reconcile her to her emotional bond with her childhood environment. Not the changes of the city are noted, but the constancy with which "the foundation [der Grund] that had been laid decades earlier resurfaced and added depth to your perception" (215). In the process of writing down her personal journey, she shifts the objective from an account of a simple visit to her hometown to a more honest self-examination that no longer denies the complexity of the *Heimat* sentiment or its positive qualities.

Nonetheless, *Heimat* remains beyond reach. The novel depicts it as a utopian place that is located in the past, mirroring Ernst Bloch's description of

Heimat as "something which shines into the childhood of all and in which no one has yet been: home" (1376). The emotional *Heimat* of the narrator's childhood is preserved in singular moments that seem to be captured in time and can be experienced again, if only tentatively and briefly, but they cannot transcend their temporality. Yet, at the same time, insight into its ideological complexities also reveals the inherent danger of the concept.

Heimat can only exist on the basis of a surrender of much of one's individuality to one's surroundings, whether political or natural. With a growing sense of its own individuality, a child automatically loses the intact sense of harmony with the *Heimat*, gradually noticing its imperfections and limitations. Yet *Heimat* is immune to social change, since its quality of safety and security is strongly connected to its quality of stability. When it is approached by a person with any state of mind other than complete naiveté and a distinct willingness to accept it unquestioningly, *Heimat* loses much of its power over such a critical individual. Thus, the possibilities of scrutinizing one's *Heimat* and being a part of it are in tension with one another. Nelly's forced flight lends her loss of *Heimat* a more dramatic and tangible dimension, but even without leaving her hometown, her uncritical sense of *Heimat* likely would eventually have changed and lost some of its firm grip on her.

In a discussion about her novel in 1975, Christa Wolf mentions "a sense of a lacuna, this feeling that something is missing" in the biographies of people of her generation between the years of the National Socialist regime and the present ("A Model of Experience" 40). Distancing herself from stories of early resistance and sudden conversion that were often featured in GDR literature, she remarks that her experience was different, that "it was a very long time before I gained even the first limited insights, and only later did more profound changes become visible" (40), a development which she considers the more common experience among those in her generation. For her the novel appears to serve as a vehicle for exploring the question, "How did we become what we are today?" (*Patterns* 209).

The lost sense of *Heimat* and belonging is fundamental to the above-mentioned lacuna, the seemingly pervasive disconnect between the past and present of Wolf's own contemporaries. For the narrator, revisiting "L., now called G." becomes a way of acknowledging this and coming to a better understanding of her younger self. In *Patterns of Childhood*, *Heimat* is presented as the nagging ache that reminds the individual that something is missing and needs to be addressed. "We would suffer continuous estrangement from ourselves if it weren't for our memory of the things we have done, of the things that have happened to us" (4). For her generation, acknowledgment of the past includes the painful process of coming to terms with one's own entanglement with National Socialism and its heavily politicized invocation of the concept and word *Heimat*. Subsequently, however, by focusing on the emotional bond to a certain place and the attendant sense of familiarity, without denying the negative political and social implications of the term, the narrator gains new access to her personal experience of *Heimat*, one that is less taboo-ridden regarding the emotional importance one's place of origin can have.

Marijke Mulder completed a Research Master Literary and Cultural Studies: Literature and Performing Arts in Society as well as a Master in German Language and Culture at the Rijksuniversiteit Groningen, The Netherlands. She became a graduate student in the German-Italian Graduate School of the Institut fuer Germanistik, Vergleichende Literatur- und Kulturwissenschaft at the Rheinische Friedrich-Wilhelms-Universität in Bonn, Germany. Her research interests include the notion of Heimat and literary treatments of German terrorism. Curently she is working for the Human Richts Organisation FEMNET e.V.

Notes

1. Among the few articles addressing the role of *Heimat* in Wolf's oeuvre, Birmele's article is a noteworthy exception, focusing on the importance of the topic for the author's entire work. Other contributors tend to either neglect the complexity of the notion of *Heimat* or merely cite a list of *Heimat*-related quotes from the novel.
2. One could also mention the writings of Heinrich Heine, Heinrich von Kleist, Friedrich Nietzsche, Thomas Mann, Günter Grass, Siegfried Lenz, and numerous others up to the present day.
3. The German original is more explicit on Nelly's emotional bond with her environment, stating that she "hing an diesem Schauplatz, den sie nie zu verlassen wünschte" (*Kindheitsmuster* 187).

Bibliography

Applegate, Celia. *A Nation of Provincials: The German Idea of Heimat*. Berkeley: University of California Press, 1990.
Bausinger, Hermann. "Auf dem Weg zu einem neuen, aktiven Heimatverständnis: Begriffsgeschichte als Problemgeschichte." *Heimat heute*, edited by Hans-Georg Wehling. Stuttgart: Kohlhammer, 1984, pp. 11–27.
Birmele, Jutta. "Christa Wolf: A Quest for 'Heimat'." *Der Begriff "Heimat" in der deutschen Gegenwartsliteratur*, edited by H.W. Seliger. Munich: iudicium, 1987, pp. 71–80.
Blickle, Peter. *Heimat: A Critical Theory of the German Idea of Homeland*. New York: Camden House, 2002.
Bloch, Ernst. *The Principle of Hope*. Vol. 3. Translated by Neville Plaice, Stephen Plaice, and Paul Knight. Oxford: Basil Blackwell, 1986.

Böll, Heinrich. "Heimat und Keine." *Essayistische Schriften und Reden*, Vol. II, edited by Bernd Balzer. Cologne: Kiepenheuer and Witsch, 1979, pp. 113–16.

Ecker, Gisela. "Heimat: Das Elend der unterschlagenen Differenz." *Kein Land in Sicht: Heimat—weiblich?*, edited by Gisela Ecker. Munich: Fink, 1997, pp. 129–42.

Erll, Astrid. "Cultural Memory Studies: An Introduction." *Cultural Memory Studies: An International and Interdisciplinary Handbook*, edited by Astrid Erll and Ansgar Nünning. Berlin: Walter de Gruyter, 2008, pp. 1–15.

Frisch, Max. "Tagebuch 1966–1971." *Gesammelte Werke in zeitlicher Folge*, Vol. 2, edited by Hans Mayer. Frankfurt a.M.: Suhrkamp, 1976.

Greverus, Ina-Maria. "The Heimat Problem." *Der Begriff "Heimat" in der deutschen Gegenwartsliteratur*, edited by H.W. Seliger. Munich: iudicium, 1987, pp. 9–27.

Henke, Christoph. "Remembering Selves, Constructing Selves: Memory and Identity in Contemporary British Fiction." *Journal for the Study of British Cultures*, vol. 1, 2003, pp. 77–100.

Schwierin, Marcel, director. *Ewige Schönheit: Film und Todessehnsucht im Dritten Reich*. Berlin: Neue Visionen unabhängiger Filmverleih, 2003 (Documentary).

Ther, Philipp. *Deutsche und polnische Vertriebene, Gesellschaft und Vertriebenenpolitik in der SBZ / DDR und in Polen 1945–1956*. Göttingen: Vandenhoeck & Ruprecht, 1998.

Walser, Martin. "Heimatkunde." *Heimatkunde: Aufsätze und Reden*. Frankfurt a.M: Suhrkamp, 1968, pp. 40–50.

Wisniewski, Roswitha. "Einst jubelnde und jetzt verlorene Heimat: Zu Christa Wolfs *Kindheitsmuster*." *Vergessene Literatur: Ungenannte Themen deutscher Schriftstellerinnen*, edited by Petra Hörner. Frankfurt a.M.: Peter Lang, 2001, pp. 147–87.

Wolf, Christa. *Kindheitsmuster*. Berlin: Aufbau-Verlag, 1976.

———. "A Model of Experience: A Discussion on *A Model Childhood*." *The Fourth Dimension*, translated by Hilary Pilkington. London: Verso, 1988, pp. 39–63.

———. *Patterns of Childhood*. Translated by Ursule Molinaro and Hedwig Rappolt. New York: Farrar, Straus and Giroux, 1980.

———. "Sand and Pines of Brandenburg: A Conversation with Adam Krzemiński." *The Fourth Dimension*, translated by Hilary Pilkington. London: Verso, 1988, pp. 64–73.

CHAPTER 5

Writing the Self
Literary Vergegenwärtigung *in Christa Wolf's* Patterns of Childhood *and* City of Angels or, The Overcoat of Dr. Freud

MARK LAUER

Throughout her writing career, one of the major themes in the work of Christa Wolf was the (re)construction of the past through the process of writing. Wolf's investigation of the relationship of past to present entered into her writing in a variety of forms as her narrative voice incorporated, challenged, and transcended more traditional literary practices of personal story writing. Wolf's thematic trajectory and the variety of literary genres in her writing about the self from 1968 to 2003 is the focus of a 2011 study by Anna Nunan, who examines the "movement or progression from personal writing in *The Quest for Christa T.* (*Nachdenken über Christa T.*, 1968) to autobiographical enterprise in *Patterns of Childhood* (*Kindheitsmuster*, 1976) to journal writing in *One Day a Year* (*Ein Tag im Jahr*, 2003)." Through her engagement with memory and identity as fluid processes, however, Wolf's writings push beyond such discussions of autobiography. For this reason, in the context of memory research, focusing solely on the autobiographical nature of Wolf's texts or discussing autobiographical writing as a separate literary genre cannot do her approach full justice.[1] Her repeated turning to the same elements of lived experiences, her difficulty in addressing her own past in the first person, as well as her changing perspective on what constitutes the present time, all suggest the need for an interpretation that takes into account the process nature of her writing. By viewing it through the lens of memory research and particularly the theoretical framework provided by Aleida and Jan Assmann in their work on memory discourses, we may attain a new perspective on Wolf's writing.[2]

Christa Wolf's Writing in the Context of Autobiographical Theory

Because autobiographical theory serves as an important starting point for analyzing Wolf's literary approach, a brief survey of some of its central contributions to, and criticism of, literature in this field is necessary in order to situate her approach within the broader context of autobiographical writing. Such theoretical concepts are most relevant to Wolf's texts where they address her remarks on subjective authenticity ("Subjective Authenticity") as well as Nunan's concept of autobiographical writing as a "narrative ... rooted in experience while allowing an interplay between fictional self-representation and 'reality'" (5). When analyzing Wolf's writing about the self, merely situating it in the context of autobiographical theory can impede our attaining a textual understanding that goes beyond autobiographical discourse. It also carries the risk of creating a self-serving theoretical discussion that does not necessarily offer new or progressive responses to Wolf's oeuvre. In the broader context of autobiographical writing, Paul de Man points to this risk when he addresses "the difficulties of generic definition" as well as the "inherent instability that undoes the model as soon as it is established" (923).

Other often-cited theoretical frameworks for a literary analysis of autobiographical writing—and of Wolf's work—are Georges Gusdorf's essay on "Conditions and Limits of Autobiography" and Philippe Lejeune's remarks on "The Autobiographical Pact." Both Gusdorf's theory, with a one-sided focus that heavily privileges a masculine subject, and Lejeune's definition of autobiography, requiring an explicit identity between the author and a first-person narrator, have limited value for an interpretation of Wolf's work. With regard to her writing, which often addresses the difficulty of writing in the first person, neither theory fully explains, contradicts, or adds to the concepts of fact, fiction, authenticity, subjectivity, and truth, as they are reflected and addressed in her work. Still concerned with the difficulty of saying *I*, even in her final novel, Wolf asks:

> Who is this reporting "I" supposed to be? It's not just how much I've forgotten. What is maybe more troubling is that I'm not sure who's doing the remembering. One of the many I's who have taken shifts in me decide to take up residence in me, replacing one another in a sequence, slowly or quickly. From which one of the I's is the memory instrument extracting the memories? (*City of Angels* 161)

Aware of the complexity of "truthfully" identifying subjectivity and objectivity in literary texts, Wolf comments on the often unrealistic demands imposed on literature:

> We cannot deny the plain fact that the writer of "good" literature cannot depict "the world," or "reality" or anything so intangible. Writers are not natural scientists, and literature is not a branch of philosophy. As Anna Seghers said, "The writer is the curious crossing point where object becomes subject and turns back into object." ("Subjective Authenticity" 23)

Memory Patterns in Wolf's Writings about the Self

Aleida and Jan Assmann's framework for the analysis of private and public memory discourses helps us to understand Wolf's dilemma in writing about the self and to appreciate how her literary voice anticipates the theoretical discussion of memory that was mostly developed in the 1990s. Their theoretical concept builds on, but also distinguishes itself from the earlier memory research of French philosopher and sociologist Maurice Halbwachs in his posthumously published (1950) study, *La memoire collective* (*On Collective Memory*, 1992). The Assmanns view memory as defined by its constant changes and transformations, taking into account political systems, societies, and individual memories that shape a personal history and identity.

Looking beyond Halbwachs's focus on the social group and "expanding his theory of memory into the realm of a theory of culture," Jan Assmann argues that "memory ... works through reconstruction. The past itself cannot be preserved by it, and thus it is continually subject to the process of reorganization according to the changes taking place in the frame of reference of each successive present" (32). Wolf articulates this "process of reorganization" in her own words and in the context of writing, when she states that, "It's a question of finding a style of writing ... so that past and present can be seen not only to 'meet' on the paper, but as they constantly do in every one of us, to interact and be endlessly rubbing up against each other" ("Subjective Authenticity" 25).

Sidonie Smith's research in the context of women's autobiography helps us to contextualize this perception of the present and past as being endlessly interconnected, calling for a "realization" that existing models of traditional autobiographical concepts mostly ignore. For Smith,

> an effort of recovery and creation, an exploration into the possibilities of recapturing and restarting a past, autobiography simultaneously involves a realization that the adventure is informed by shifting considerations of the present moment. For example, the autobiographer has to rely on a trace of something from the past, a memory; yet memory is ultimately a story about, and thus a discourse on, original experience, so that recovering the past is not a hypostasizing of fixed grounds and origins but, rather, an interpretation of earlier experience that can never be divorced from the filterings of subject experience or articulated outside the structures of language and storytelling. As a result, autobiography becomes both the process and the product of assigning meaning to a series of experiences, after they have taken place, by means of emphasis, juxtaposition, commentary, omission. (45)

Smith's perspective on the genre *autobiography* as one that encompasses elements of interpretation, as well as a process assigning meaning to grounds that are not fixed, takes into account the nature of a changing present and, with it, a changing perspective that is central to memory research. Even though her contribution fits well with and lends support to the argument I make with regard to Wolf's writing, I believe that it is even more helpful to move the discussion away from the autobiographical discourse still inherent in Smith's concept. It is here that Jan and Aleida Assmann's work in the field of memory discourses provides a fruitful framework for a new approach to Wolf's writing about the self.

Layers of Time

In *Cultural Memory*, Jan Assmann explores the connection between "memory (or reference to the past), identity (or political imagination), and cultural continuity (or the formation of tradition)" (2), a problem that still concerns Wolf in her final novel, *City of Angels or, the Overcoat of Dr. Freud* (2010). Her narrator wonders:

> Sometimes I wish I knew how the layers of time through which I have traveled, that I penetrate so easily in my thoughts, are actually arranged inside me: as actual layers, each one stacked carefully on top of the other? Or as chaotic mass of neurons from which a power we do not understand can draw out whichever thread we want? Will neuroscientists ever find out? (267)

In *One Day a Year* (*Ein Tag im Jahr:1960–2000*, 2003), the task of exploring these "layers of time" can be traced as one of Wolf's main concerns throughout decades of writing about the self. Her journal entry from 1970 demonstrates her awareness of the difficulty of keeping hold of the different layers of time in a linear writing style: "Technical problem that arises again and again when I write prose: how do I bring the stacked layers of time of which 'reality' consists safely over into my linear writing style? (Obviously, by no means only a technical problem.)" (146).

The difficulty of untangling these layers of time goes hand in hand with Wolf's desire to create a new way of writing, as formulated in her 1968 essay "The Reader and the Writer" ("Lesen und Schreiben"). In a 1973 conversation with the East German literary scholar Hans Kaufmann she articulates her desire for a way of writing that takes into account the changing ways of an individual's being in the world. Wolf considers the desire to find the right voice to adequately address the different layers of reality a necessary challenge. In her view,

> This mode of writing is not "subjectivist," but "interventionist." It does require subjectivity, and a subject who is prepared to undergo unrelenting exposure—that is easy to say, of course, but I really do mean as unrelenting as

possible—to the material at hand, to accept the burden of the tensions that inexorably arise, and to be curious about the changes that both the material and the author undergo. ("Subjective Authenticity" 22)

The difference of *being* in the world manifests itself for Wolf in an individual's changing sensual perception throughout the course of time, which also affects memory patterns.[3] What Jan Assmann describes as "changes taking place in the frame of reference of each successive present" (30) can serve as the theoretical concept that helps to explain Wolf's much earlier observation of a changing sensual perception and, with it, changing memories.

Emphasizing the connection between memory, remembrance, and sensual perceptions in her final novel, Wolf implicitly refers to an individual's changing sensory perception when she acknowledges "sense memory" (*Gefühlsgedächtnis*) as "the most lasting and reliable" (*City of Angels* 28). The narrator again emphasizes the sensual component of memory, when she argues that "the landscape of memory spreads out far and wide, I think, and the beam of our thoughts scans across it" (107). This interconnection of memory and sensual perception to describe her "emotional state" (52) is a theme in Wolf's writing since *Patterns of Childhood*, where she addresses the discrepancy between historic events portrayed in films and personal experiences based on emotional perceptions: "A comparison of memories with films taken by the Soviet cameramen shows the expected result: the memories have been distorted by emotion (shame, humiliation, compassion)" (329). Wolf's insight into the connection between constantly changing emotional states and memory patterns helps to explain the development across time of changing perspectives on writing about the self.

Past and identity, and with them the portrayal of the self, are central to the concept of cultural memory. When analyzing Wolf's literary approach to the past, a brief look at her evolving understanding of the impact of the past on the present will help to situate my analysis in the context of her writing within the former GDR. This approach to her past from a changing present perspective that encompasses sensual perceptions, an articulation of the difficulty of finding the right pronouns when writing about the self, as well as her use of intertextual allusions and quotations comprise the technique I suggest calling *literary Vergegenwärtigung*. Wolf employs a similar terminology in *City of Angels*. Here, referring to the approaching farewell from her nine-month stay at the Getty Center in 1992–93, the narrator declares: "Die Abschiede. Ich versuch sie mir zu vergegenwärtigen—Welch passendes Wort!" (370) ("The goodbyes. I try to recall them— such an appropriate word in German for 'recall': *vergegenwärtigen*, 'bring them into present'!", 282). My choice of this terminology also builds on Aleida Assmann's concept of *presentifying* (*Zeit und Traditionen*), which she introduces to describe a strategy for accessing the past and making it available to the present. Whereas Assmann refers to horizons of meaning within cultures, I hope to show in what follows how my formulation captures the literary component in establishing the interchanging relationship between past and present in prose writing.

A Literary and Political Journey: Wolf's Evolving Approach to Writing about the Self and the Past

Christa Wolf's concept of *literary Vergegenwärtigung* developed over decades and was manifest in her prose writings, as well as in interviews and discussions with colleagues. Driven by questions about changes in the self across time, Wolf tried to uncover, and (re)discover, this self through the process of writing about the past in texts from the 1950s until her final novel in 2010. In so doing, she transcended and redefined the boundaries of a teleological approach to writing about the self. In analyzing her approach, it is important to consider the political circumstances surrounding the beginnings of her writing career, which had a demonstrable impact on her approach to subjectivity, the past, and the present.

At the second Socialist Unity Party of Germany (SED) Conference held in Berlin on 12 July 1952, Walter Ulbricht, the Communist Party Secretary General of the SED and official head of the East German state from 1950 to 1971, formulated his vision of a systematic implementation of socialism according to the Stalinist dictate that the life and work of artists be aligned with the socialist endeavor. For writers, this meant that authors were to focus on the present time and on utopian socialist ideas. Concern with the past was only to be addressed in the form of historic reviews that foregrounded the revolutionary fight of working people. Looking back at her memories of the spring of 1946, Wolf's narrator remembers being in full agreement with the tenets of literary Realism, which advocated what was shortly thereafter demanded by the Politbüro:

> You can still see yourself sitting with the others around the square table in the seminar room, surrounded by bookshelves, you can hear the young docent talk enthusiastically about George Lukàcs, whose theories made you see that what mattered was Realism, what else was there, and you and the class enthusiastically drank in his arguments and could not imagine how anyone could judge literature differently. (*City of Angels* 99)

At the fourth GDR Writers' Congress in 1956, authorities demanded that authors focus on the needs of the present in their writing (Schubbe 428). Literary texts were to reflect the concepts and values of socialism and to function as a means to educate the masses. This concept was elaborated during the Bitterfeld Conferences in 1959 and 1964, where the development of socialist culture in the GDR was discussed. Here, the party and members of the intelligentsia and the working class came together in an attempt to draw all citizens, including workers, into artistic activity. Such efforts to dictate literary developments culminated in the 11th Plenum of the SED in December 1965. Finally, one year after unification, film historian and critic Günter Agde introduced the term *Kahlschlag!* (clean sweep), as the title of a compendium of records from this period, documenting the ban of numerous films, plays, books, and music, as demanded and implemented by Erich Honecker.

In considering Christa Wolf's concept of the present and past during this specific period, it becomes clear that she agreed, at least up until the late 1950s, with these demands. Referring to the 1953 *Volksaufstand* (popular uprising) in East Germany, she saw no need to portray that past event in literary texts and suggested in 1958 that one should focus on the immediate present:

> Who benefits from it? That is what it all comes down to. It also comes down to this banal and, some would say, primitive question in the literature on contemporary topics. *It* is the standard, not the subjective intention of the authors ... Before an author, for example, needs lessons on "purely" aesthetic questions, he needs clarity about the fundamental problems of the social reality, which he needs to understand as the fundamental problems of aesthetics. ("Eine Lektion" 120–23, my translation)

Here Wolf draws a connection between social reality, literary aesthetics, objectivity, and contemporary topics that, according to the demands of the party, do not allow for a subjective view of past events. At this point, she still favored focusing on a present that excludes the significance of the past and, thereby, the interrelationship of past, present, and subjectivity.

In the years that followed, however, Wolf's perspective on subjectivity and the influence of the past on the present evolved. In her 1968 novel, *The Quest for Christa T. (Nachdenken über Christa T.)*, Wolf's approach to reality shifts in the direction of subjectivist experimentation, when the death of a friend becomes the motivation for her writing. Again in the interview with Hans Kaufmann, she articulates her new vision of writing and the "dialectic relationship" of time layers, citing Bertolt Brecht to support her argument:

> As Brecht wrote in 1953: "We have been all too keen to turn our backs on the immediate past and, hungry with curiosity, to look to the future. But the future will depend on whether we can come to terms with the past." Perhaps you will agree that Brecht's point about the dialectic relationship between the past and the future is equally valid today. ("Subjective Authenticity" 29)

In Wolf's case, a meta-level discussion of "how we became the way we are today"—a question she repeatedly raises in her 1976 novel *Patterns of Childhood*—entails a literary interrogation of the reliability of her own personal memories and her relation to the past. It also calls for a subjective approach to memory and writing. Her struggle to address an individual's past, which she would thematize in the years to come, is also a political one. The Office for Literature and Publishing (Amt für Literatur und Verlagswesen), founded in 1951, and the State Arts Commission (Staatliche Kommission für Kunstangelegenheiten) controlled most forms of publication through various modes of censorship. In her conversation with Kaufmann, Wolf touches both on officially imposed censorship, as well as the mechanisms of this even more dangerous self-censorship, specifically pointing to the risks and pressure that arise when one "internalize[s] the kinds of demands that can prevent literature from being created" (28).

In 1975, Wolf introduced her new novel *Patterns of Childhood* (*Kindheitsmuster*) during two readings at the Academy of Arts, Berlin ("A Model of Experience"; "Erfahrungsmuster"). Here, she addresses her view of the present, which differs markedly from what she had asserted in her previously cited 1958 statement. Now, shortly before the 1976 publication of the novel, she emphasizes that the present is much more than what is happening today.

Patterns of Childhood and *City of Angels*: The Continuing Struggle to Articulate Memory through Writing

Rather than pursuing a teleological approach to her personal history, which would situate her in a traditionally linear and male-dominated autobiographical discourse, Wolf (re)constructs the notion of self as a pattern of identity that is—in the present and the past—constantly subject to change. In this context, the first sentence of *Patterns of Childhood*, referencing Faulkner, reads like a complete rejection of the doctrinaire cultural policies in effect since the 1950s when she writes: "What is past is not dead; it is not even past" (3).[4] This literary journey toward her own past begins with a claim that implicitly points to the limits of Lejeune's definition of the "autobiographical pact" when she claims in an epigraph to the novel:

> All characters in this book are the invention of the narrator. None is identical with any person living or dead. Neither do any of the described episodes coincide with actual events. Anyone believing that he detects a similarity between a character in the narrative and either himself or anyone else should consider the strange lack of individuality in the behavior of many contemporaries. Generally recognizable behavior patterns should be blamed on circumstances.

Despite this claim, critics generally—and rightfully—read the 1976 novel as an autobiographical one. Only separated through layers of time, author and narrator become one in *Patterns of Childhood*. Once again, addressing this complex relationship between author and narrator, it is no coincidence that Wolf makes a similar disclaimer at the very beginning of *City of Angels*:

> All the characters in this book, with the exception of historical figures mentioned by name, are inventions of the novelist. None of them is identical with anyone living or dead. Just as little do the episodes described coincide with actual events.

Rather than reading these statements in an autobiographical framework, I suggest approaching them in the context of memory discourses, interpreting Wolf's remarks as an articulation of the process character of memory, as embodied in the concept of *literary Vergegenwärtigung*, which is bound to the point in time when the creation of the text takes place and which, as such, invokes the past from a constantly changing perspective. The person remembering the past and articulating it in writing is different from how she once was or ever will be.

No doubt the childhood Wolf describes in *Patterns of Childhood* could have been similar to that of many of her contemporaries, and it probably was. But the important point for Wolf is that the *lived* experience is subjective, unique, and deeply personal. Consequently, it lives on and continues to change as it is remembered. The difficulty of finding the appropriate voice and personal pronoun to describe her lived experiences is met by the narrator recalling memory patterns through self-imposed repetition, culminating in repeating the first-person pronoun five times:

> Yours is an authentic memory, even if it's slightly worn at the edges, because it is more than improbable that an outsider had watched the child and had later told her how she had sat on the doorstep of her father's store. Trying the new word out in her mind: I…I…I…I…I… each time with a thrilled shock which had kept a secret, that much she knew right away. (*Patterns of Childhood* 5)

Here, she records her efforts to recall the past and the person she once was. At the end of *Patterns of Childhood*, she is still struggling with the idea of saying "I" when looking back:

> The child who was hidden in me—has she come forth? Or has she been scared into looking for a deeper, more inaccessible hiding place? Has memory done its duty? Or has it proven—by the act of misleading—that it's impossible to escape the mortal sin of our time: the desire not to come to grips with oneself? (406)

It is through repetition as a strategy to recall memory patterns that Wolf's narrator seeks to invoke and access her past, hoping to find the appropriate voice to articulate the process of identity formation and subjectivity. She also employs and portrays this strategy in *City of Angels* when writing about her difficulties in trying to cope with accusations of having been an IM (Stasi informer) for the East German Ministry for State Security. In the chapter, "Then I Started Singing," the narrator describes how she "sang the whole night through, every song I knew—and I know a lot of songs, with a lot of verses" (188). In fact, the first two pages of this chapter consist of a list of more than eighty songs by title, which she sang throughout the night until the next morning. Remembering and singing the songs she learned throughout her life functions as a means to access her sensual memory, to reappraise the past, and to remember long-forgotten events that are relevant to the immediate present of Wolf's 1992–93 stay as a fellow at the Getty Research Institute.

The process character of memory and the need for repetition to reconstruct past events also explain why Wolf retells stories she had shared with readers on earlier occasions. In *City of Angels*, the narrator tells the story of her childhood encounter with a Communist, a recently liberated concentration camp inmate, at a campfire in Schwerin, Mecklenburg, in May 1945. The narrator admits to having "told this story many times" (238). In fact, Wolf had first introduced the story in "Exchanging Glances" ("Blickwechsel," 1970) and again in 1976 (*Patterns of Childhood* 39). In both instances, she uses the retelling of her "stream of memories" (*City of Angels* 238) not only to access the past, but also to make sense of the present time, in which she reflects on the impact that this past encounter has had on contemporary personal exchanges with her daughter Lenka (*Patterns of Childhood*) and, later, with her friend Ruth (*City of Angels*). Here, it becomes clear that memories fulfill different purposes at different points in time. Any answer as to how we have become the way we are today cannot be final: it is always a temporal one, focusing on a snapshot of one specific point in time that has already passed, by the time it is articulated in writing.

Conclusion

In her final novel, the protagonist engages in a discussion with her friend Sally about her attempt to remember the circumstances of her 1959 collaboration with the East German Ministry for State Security. Sally's remark that she "was a different person then!" (151) implicitly supports Wolf's efforts to understand and evaluate how writing about the self needs to take into account the constant process of changing memories. The protagonist's response illustrates the connection between past, present, and memory that we have been examining against the background of political developments, interviews with the author, and her essays, as well as the novels *Patterns of Childhood* and *City of Angels or, The Overcoat of Dr. Freud*: "Never mind that, Sally. It's not about that. It's about memories, about how we remember: my topic for decades, you understand?" (151).

The subject of memory discourses and remembering is indeed the focus through which Wolf developed her literary voice in writing about the self. Just as memories change over time, her perspective on the interconnection of past and present evolved significantly from the 1950s to the 1960s and beyond. The importance of subjectivity and, concomitantly, the process of reorganizing and reconstructing the past become central to Wolf's writing about the self, continuing through her final writing project. Experimentation with layers of storytelling and analysis of the narrative voice on a meta-level within her texts become increasingly fundamental to her writing about the self. That her personal past and attendant questions of identity are constantly in flux is effectively articulated by the author on an allegorical level in *City of Angels*. In the chapter "Washed with All Waters," for instance, she lists rivers and lakes she encountered throughout her lifetime, tying her memories to the flow of time and the names of the streams (274).

Through *literary Vergegenwärtigung*, Wolf tries to uncover the process character of memories by writing about past experiences from ever-changing present perspectives. This concept is evident in textual features, such as repeated references to a single past experience in different texts, articulations of her sensual perceptions, repeated questioning of the suitability of personal pronouns to address the self, and the citing of songs and poems to invoke past memories and experiences that might be attached to learning them. A final answer to the question of how we have become the way we are is not possible; it can be, at best, only a tentative and time-bound one. In the context of memory research, Jan Assmann points to the legitimacy of such a changing perspective in the literary realm, when he states that "writing, however, need not necessarily fix things permanently" (44). Implicitly emphasizing the importance of the process character of memory patterns for her writing, Wolf's final sentences in *City of Angels* can be read as a statement on the impossibility of final answers and as a call for continuing analysis of memory patterns: "Where are we going? I don't know" (315).

Mark Lauer is a faculty member in the humanities at the Webb Schools in Claremont, CA. With a Ph.D. in German literature from Georgetown University, his research interests include (auto)biographical literature, memory research, contemporary fiction, and travel literature.

Notes

1. For a genre discussion of autobiographical writing, see also William Spengemann's *The Forms of Autobiography: Episodes in the History of a Literary Genre*. Spengemann argues that "we need to understand the conditions that have led different autobiographers at different times to write about themselves in different ways" (xiii).
2. Here, I will refer primarily both to Jan Assmann's concept of cultural memory, as presented in *Cultural Memory and Early Civilization: Writing, Remembrance, and Political Imagination*, and to Aleida Assmann's theory of Erinnerungsräume, articulated in her publications *Erinnerungsräume: Formen und Wandlungen des kulturellen Gedächtnisses* and "Memory, Individual and Collective."
3. See also "The Reader and the Writer": "The need to write in a new way follows a new way of living in the world, although there may be a time-lag. 'One' hears, sees, smells, tastes in a different way at different times, at intervals that seem to get shorter. A change has occurred in one's perception of the world that even casts doubts on the unimpeachable memory; we see 'the world' once more—but what do we mean by the world?—in a different light; even feelings seem less permanent nowadays than in former times; there is a deal [sic] of confusion" (177).
4. William Faulkner writes: "The past is never dead. It's not even past" (*Requiem for a Nun*, Act I, Scene 3).

Bibliography

Agde, Günther, editor. *Kahlschlag: Das 11. Plenum des ZK der SED 1965. Studien und Dokumente*. Berlin: Aufbau, 1991.

Assmann, Aleida, *Erinnerungsräume: Formen und Wandlungen des kulturellen Gedächtnisses*. Munich: Beck, 1999.

———. "Memory, Individual and Collective." *The Oxford Handbook of Contextual Political Analysis*, edited by R.E. Goodin and C. Tilly. Oxford: Oxford University Press, 2006, pp. 210–24.

———. *Zeit und Tradition: Kulturelle Strategien der Dauer*. Cologne: Böhlau, 1999.

Assmann, Jan. *Cultural Memory and Early Civilization: Writing, Remembrance, and Political Imagination*. New York: Cambridge University Press, 2011.

Faulkner, William. *Requiem for a Nun*. New York: Random House, 1951.

Frieden, Sandra. "Falls es strafbar ist, die Grenzen zu verwischen: Autobiographie, Biografie und Christa Wolf." *Vom Anderen und vom Selbst: Beiträge zu Fragen der Biographie und Autobiographie*, edited by R. Grimm and J. Hermand. Königstein: Athenäum, 1982, pp. 153–67.

Goodin, R.E., and C. Tilly, editors. *The Oxford Handbook of Contextual Political Analysis*. Oxford: Oxford University Press, 2006.

Gusdorf, Georges. "Conditions and Limits in Autobiography." *Autobiography: Essays Theoretical and Critical*, edited by James Olney. Princeton, NJ: Princeton University Press, 1980, pp. 28–48.

Halbwachs, Maurice. *On Collective Memory/La memoire collective*. Chicago: University of Chicago Press, 1992 (first published 1950).
Lejeune, Phillippe. "Der autobiographische Pakt" (first published 1973). *Die Autobiographie: Zu Form und Geschichte einer literarischen Gattung*, edited by Günter Niggl. Darmstadt: Wissenschaftliche Buchgesellschaft, 1989, pp. 214–57.
de Man, Paul. "Autobiography as Defacement." *Modern Language Notes*, vol. 94, 1979, pp. 919–30.
Nunan, Anna. *Autobiographical Progression in the Writings of Christa Wolf: Nachdenken über Christa T. (1968), Kindheitsmuster (1976), and Ein Tag im Jahr (2003)*. Lewiston, NY: Edwin Mellen Press, 2011.
Schubbe, Elimar, editor. *Dokumente zur Kunst-, Literatur- und Kulturpolitik der SED*. Stuttgart: Seewald, 1972.
Smith, Sidonie. *A Poetics of Women's Autobiography: Marginality and the Fiction of Self-Representation*. Bloomington: Indiana University Press, 1987.
Spengemann, William. *The Forms of Autobiography: Episodes in the History of a Literary Genre*. New Haven, CT: Yale University Press, 1980.
Ulbricht, Walter. *Geschichte der deutschen Arbeiterbewegung*. Berlin: Dietz Verlag, 1969.
Wolf, Christa. "Blickwechsel." *Lesen und Schreiben: Aufsätze und Prosastücke*. Darmstadt: Luchterhand Verlag, 1972.
——— . *City of Angels or, The Overcoat of Dr. Freud*. Translated by Damion Searls. New York: Farrar, Straus and Giroux, 2013.
——— . "Erfahrungsmuster: Diskussion zu Kindheitsmuster." *Die Dimension des Autors: Essays und Aufsätze, Reden und Gespräche 1959–1985*. Darmstadt: Luchterhand, 1987, pp. 806–43.
——— . "Exchanging Glances." *Ingeborg Bachmann and Christa Wolf: Selected Prose and Drama*, edited by Patricia Herminghouse. The German Library, Vol. 94. New York: Continuum, 1998, pp. 152–64.
——— . "Eine Lektion über Wahrheit und Objektivität." *Neue Deutsche Literatur*, vol. 2, no. 7, 1958, pp. 120–23.
——— . "A Model of Experience: A Discussion on *A Model Childhood*." *The Fourth Dimension: Interviews with Christa Wolf*, translated by Hilary Pilkington. New York: Verso, 1988, pp. 39–63.
——— . *One Day a Year: 1960–2000*. Translated by Lowell A. Bangerter. New York: Europa Editions, 2007.
——— . *Patterns of Childhood*. Translated by Ursule Molinaro and Hedwig Rappolt. New York: Farrar, Straus and Giroux, 1980.
——— . *The Quest for Christa T*. Translated by Christopher Middleton. New York: Farrar, Straus and Giroux, 1968.
——— . *The Reader and the Writer: Essays, Sketches, and Memories*. Translated by Joan Becker. New York: International Publishers, 1972.
——— . *Stadt der Engel oder The Overcoat of Dr. Freud*. Berlin: Suhrkamp, 2010.

———. "Subjective Authenticity: A Conversation with Hans Kaufmann." *The Fourth Dimension: Interviews with Christa Wolf*, translated by Hilary Pilkington. New York: Verso, 1988, pp. 17–38.

———. *Ein Tag im Jahr: 1960–2000*. Darmstadt: Luchterhand Literaturverlag, 2003.

———. *What Remains and Other Stories*. Translated by Heike Schwarzbauer and Rick Takvorian. New York: Farrar, Straus and Giroux, 1993.

CHAPTER 6

The Heterochronic Narrative of Christa Wolf

HEIKE POLSTER

Behind the doubts of prose writers concerning the future prospects of their genre, lies nothing but self-suspicion: that of being anachronistic.[1]
—Christa Wolf, "The Reader and the Writer," 181

The title of Christa Wolf's *Was bleibt* (*What Remains*) has always resonated with my interest in time and its expression in literature. What drew me in was the present tense of "bleibt," a word of hesitance, endurance, or even resistance that performs its own meaning. We feel the pull of the past, tugging at the present to let go. Wolf shortened Hölderlin's quotation, "was bleibet aber stiften die Dichter" ("what remains, the poets bestow"), eliminating what must have seemed redundant. It speaks for itself. The insistence on poetic writing as memory, history, or legacy is expressed ever more strongly by omitting "die Dichter." From a semantic perspective, speaking of the present is simply the act of positioning deictic points of reference as they relate to their respective current section in the temporal window between past and future (Röhnert 13). The scope and duration of "the present moment," and the very conditions under which it is possible to recognize, define, or even observe it, depend on the observers' perceptions, conscious or unconscious attitudes, as well as their cultural and linguistic conditioning. The manner in which we perceive, conceptualize, and experience the present and the manner in which we express our relationship to it have long been the object of literary texts and, by extension, literary criticism. A given age and literary period will contain a meta-discursive debate about the literary aesthetics of its own time from the perspective of immediate participation, the position of *Zeitgenossenschaft/contemporaneity* (12). In short, "the present" has always talked about, with, and of itself.

Given the hermeneutic difficulties of speaking about the present in the present, however, there cannot be any agreement on the criteria for

Gegenwartsliteratur (contemporary literature) if they are of a normative temporal nature, that is, derived during a particular *period*[2] or based on what Wolf calls the "spirit of an epoch" ("Siebte Kreuz" 188). Within the pages of literary criticism from the late twentieth and early twenty-first centuries, *Gegenwartsliteratur* is at last being approached from a theoretical perspective.[3] It offers another avenue of interpretation through an exploration into what *Zeitgenossenschaft*/contemporaneity can entail. As I will argue, Christa Wolf's *Zeitgenossenschaft* is a deliberate narrative approach in which an author and/or narrator can attempt to relate to their present, describe it, and express the difficult work of articulating this process from a poetic standpoint. It relies on the narrative strategy of heterochronicity, of letting or making the past, present, and future coexist and interact within the same moment of observation (see also Polster, 2012). As I will demonstrate, an analysis of Wolf's heterochronic narrative will shed light on her literary aesthetics and ethics of *Gegenwart*. Although a systematic examination of historiography was never the goal or driving force behind the crafting of her narratives, Wolf's understanding of what it means to be a "contemporary," as well as a "contemporary writer," points to a deep preoccupation with history, so much so that it is not inappropriate to refer to her as a writer of time itself, a teller, indeed, *about* time.[4] *Zeitgenossenschaft*, or contemporaneity, is a pivotal concern in her work, where she couples the ontological question of temporality ("What *is* this thing called time?") with the aesthetic practice of its portrayal ("How does one *tell about* time?"). The effect is a dramatic expansion of the present that challenges routine definitions of the passage of time. As we shall see, Wolf's contemporaneity is a quality independent of, but nevertheless related to, temporality, a quality that is revealed by what I term *heterochronic narration*.

Heterochronicity, as I have argued elsewhere (*The Poetics of Passage* 58ff.), denotes the arrangement or design of different levels of time, including both arbitrary time constructs (the century, the period, the era; the ubiquitous "pre-" and "post-"), as well as normative, perhaps even innate, ideas of temporality (past, present, future), within the same perceptual and epistemological field or "frame." In visual imagery of a non-heterochronic nature, "frame" is understood as a relatively uncomplicated "picture," a representation limned by color and shape, by objects and characters, by juxtapositions and logical orders. Resulting in a kind of tripartite intermingling of overturned notions of chronology, linearity, or continuity, the heterochronic artwork, however, offers us a unique and multifaceted representation of temporality by incorporating the three temporal phases within the *same* "frame." Likewise, in literary texts of a heterochronic nature, the "frame" delineates a narrative field that contains the three phases of time within one train of thought, one textual episode, or one formal unit of text (a passage, a verse, a chapter).

As its distinct and essential feature, the heterochronic artwork comprises a strong self-awareness that arrives as a critical commentary upon its own practices of representing character, dialogue, event, or attitude (or any combination of these). Since heterochronic artworks deepen the experience of time on the levels of both content (what is being represented) and form (how this is being done), heterochronicity operates as both a narrative model and a temporal model for understanding "contemporaneity."[5] Starting from this conception of heterochronicity, I shall attempt, in the course of this inquiry, to uncover the subtler implications of that "most uninteresting question of all": Does a critical self-awareness, created through constant interrogation of what time is and how it is told, allow Wolf, in the end, to achieve her contemporaneity?

The thematic complex of "time and narrative"—the "what and how"—has enjoyed a long critical tradition focusing on its aesthetic constitution, especially in autobiography and trauma studies, as well as its philosophical implications, studied by phenomenology and hermeneutics. For this reason, even the most systematic historian of philosophy (or, for that matter, philosopher of history) is confronted with more than a few difficulties in trying to offer a comprehensive overview of "time and narrative" in light of the historical intricacies of the discussion and its broad spectrum of methodological approaches. One of the more notable aesthetic-philosophical takes on this complex, Gerard Genette's *Narrative Discourse* outlines the anachronistic methods of prolepsis and analepsis, or, in the language of the moving image, the "flash forward" and the "flashback." Genette's project offers some useful tools for demonstrating how seemingly anachronistic strategies aid in creating a sense of immediacy, of authentic temporal experience in the reader. Additionally, Paul Ricoeur's *Time and Narrative* has provided many of the critical approaches through which later phenomenological and narratological studies have come to view time and its discursive representations. One such approach is Ricoeur's differentiation between tales *about* time and tales *of* time.[6] Such differentiation creates a nomenclature of narrative representations designed to evoke an awareness of temporality in the reader so that she may experience time with a heightened mindfulness of its makeup and passage.[7] Even though Genette's and Ricoeur's contributions have significantly informed my conception of heterochronicity, they ultimately rely, however, on a reductive definition of time-space that does not allow for assigning any narrative properties to space, a disallowance which—to my mind—results in seeing only half the picture. As I shall later demonstrate, heterochronicity owes a great debt to British geographer Doreen Massey's definition of space as a contemporaneous plurality, that is, a sphere in which differing temporalities can be included in order to form a "coexisting heterogeneity"

(9). Space, I would hence suggest, is a fluid construction of heterochronic elements, a *contemporaneity* of outcomes, ideas, and possibilities.

Within Wolf's insistent distinction between "official History" (or Historiography) and "personal" narrative, there exists an equally compelling distinction between the remembering "I" (who tells) and the past (that which is told). The "I" and the past are not situated, in the form of subject and object, as *oppositional entities*; such a configuration would evince a pre-Modern and simplistic perception of the world. Rather—and the term "contemporaneity" points to this—the "I" and the past are situated as entirely mutually *dependent entities*.[8] The attainment of "contemporaneity"[9] thus always points to the attempt to claim a stake in one's own historical reality, a creative and critical engagement with one's own social, political, and even economic surroundings. A "contemporary writer," Wolf explains, can be evaluated on "the *depth* of the questions he asks" as well as his "productive relationship to his times" ("The Reader and the Writer" 209; emphasis added). The dimension of this *depth* can be sounded out by cultivating an awareness of the interplay of narrative (i.e., fictional)[10] enterprise and memory activation. As Wolf points out, depth is not some kind of free-floating particle which attaches itself to the things around one, but rather is the experience of becoming aware of these very things. It is an experience that is neither "particularly rare nor particularly complicated" because it is commonplace (209). The experience of depth comes from an active engagement with history and with culture; consequently, it overcomes superficiality and boredom, two detriments to the quality of life that result, for example, from constraints in mobility and limitations in material growth. "Depth," as Wolf explains, "is not a property that sticks to things. The experience of it is linked up with human awareness" (209). She calls it "an everyday state" of the human psyche that amounts to "a relativizing and temporary removal of objective time" (209). Depth is the ordinary experience that may become the extraordinary, an experience which "can be stretched out almost to infinity, [which] has within it a vast quantity and many layers of possibilities of experience" (180). Removing the notion of objective time (with its presuppositions of continuity and "progress") from the components of depth, Wolf situates the extraordinary at the moment when a rift—dissatisfaction, disappointment, disillusionment—occurs, forcing the self to contend with "the present."

Wolf looks past "objective" reality to the point of dismissing it, insisting instead on an "extended reality," a term which she uses synonymously with "depth" to indicate an awareness of the self as a historical subject ("The Fourth Dimension" 12). This extension of (present) "reality" is composed of memory ("unsatisfied needs," as she refers to them, as well as "inconsistencies") and imagination (the "tremendous efforts people make to grow beyond themselves").[11] This capacity to infinitely extend, and the role it must play in a humane society, gives rise, of course, to ethical concerns, for as she warns us, if "society does not know how to take advantage of the oft-recurring ability to do this, we are bored" (12). Wolf views ethics as deeply involved with boredom, for it reveals the coterminous boundaries of self-awareness and world-awareness in an experiential moment of lack: lack of challenge, lack of motivation to transcend the obvious, lack of critical engagement, lack, indeed, of autonomy. The "superficiality" which results from any or all of these lacks applies equally to society, which is not an autonomous institution, but rather a collective that "depends on whether people create the conditions that enable them to discover themselves, whether they can find an active interest ... in their own lives." It is only when people "regard themselves as sufficiently important, exciting, and valuable that they will do everything possible to save themselves" (12). Literature's humanistic role lies in engendering opportunities to spark the reader's interest in herself, or to rekindle it, in a moment of sheer self-discovery.

Within Wolf's creative enterprise, self-discovery hinges on this ability to extend the present (or, if you will, intensify depth), and, crucially, to view oneself as a historical subject, suffused with agency and significance. The present, by definition, is already a historical space because it always contains the "I" who tells about history. Such is the nature of a personal history or narrative: it cannot help confronting the larger world whenever it speaks of the self, even if that self harks from long ago, from a country no longer one's own. Since the publication of *Patterns of Childhood*, Wolf has suggested that her fluid conception of the "present"—the site for one's process of self-discovery, which is always directed at becoming a viable participant in history—depends for its intelligibility on its relationship to the larger historical backdrop, such as the postwar German/East German narrative and the enduring tensions and artifacts of National Socialism. The narrator recounts her experiences as a child living not just under the Third Reich, but indeed during the earlier prewar period, and, in a further layering, as a young woman during the postwar period. It is important to note that any of these three temporal realms or "periods" is *not* suggested within the text as a temporally finite sequence of historical or personal events, although certainly they all may have arrived to Wolf/the narrator as such. The only means by which we could accord any of these periods a finite nature would depend on the reader's ability to parse any one from the others. By doing so, however, the heterochronic interweave or frame would disappear, and time itself would become a mere marker of dates and events, arranged chronologically—not to mention *teleologically*—rather than remain a narrative of significance, of "depth" (which occurs when the "I" is confronted with rich, discontinuous memories).[12]

A holistic image of the creative process occurs in *One Day a Year*, in which Wolf describes her methodology of compiling notes for the eighth chapter of *Patterns of Childhood*. Here, we can look over her shoulder as the narrator discloses her routine of laying out four pieces of paper, each one for a different narrative: "travel level, level of the past, manuscript level, level of the present" (176). While these narratives are at first separate and sequential, they later merge. The grown-up "I" who revisits her childhood home, the child "I" living at that time long ago, the "I" who has begun to flicker on the page, and the "I" who reads that page—all come to occupy the same frame at the chapter, section, even sentence levels, in what Wolf describes as "that moment of melting together (in an artistic idea)." Such a "moment of melting together" demonstrates the decidedly heterochronic underpinning of Wolf's valorization of writing as a tool of becoming "present." After all, it is her awareness that calls attention to "all the real and dreamt-of experiences connected with" a particular object within her surroundings and designs them according to "chain[s] of associations" of not just past situations and episodes but also of past thoughts (176).

In her own way, Wolf comes to the same conclusion as do many theorists of time (particularly Husserl), namely, that the kernel of the temporal structure of experience lies in its narrative design or, better still, its *redesigning*. Especially as it pertains to long-term sequences of actions, experiences, and human events, Wolf's approach draws out the complex nature of narrative experience as it necessarily involves more than a mere temporal organization of events. Narrating more temporally complex experiences requires what David Carr refers to as a "different subjective role" on the part of the narrator (51). The subject is no longer immersed in the larger-scale phenomenon "through a retentive-protentive awareness," that is, a mind at work that remembers and anticipates. When a multiplicity of actions and experiences are related, Carr argues, they must "be held together by a grasp which attends not only to the object, or objective, but also to the disparate and temporally discrete parts of my [the reader's] experience or activity that render the object present or constitute my engagement in the action" (55). Drawing on Husserlian imagery, we might call this grasp "reflective" or "reflexive."

Patterns of Childhood demonstrates this reflexive grasp through its use of heterochronic storytelling: describing the journey back to her childhood home, the narrator encounters "one of those rare moments when you think you know what to say and what not to say, and how to go about it" (48). Thematizing the difficulty of addressing her memories, she finds it "impossible to create the high temperatures it would require to melt down the years." She continues to relate her anxious experience regarding the distance she feels toward her younger self. Since "the child refuses to talk, [l]et's hope that whoever gets hold of her will not exploit her helplessness, as so easily happens." The landscape gliding by as she travels takes on metaphoric significance: "Beyond the mountains, the chasms, the deserts of the years … Your heart is pounding." These observations are immediately followed by her recognition of the extent to which "your century has revived the old invention of torture, in order to make human beings talk." Faced with this recognition of the historical continuity of violence and oppression, she musters up a simple conviction: "You're going to talk" (48). In one short passage, she has managed to create a relationship between her own past and present with the brutal and inhuman practices of political powers (the vagueness of which allows us to speculate whether she is criticizing the GDR, the Stasi, etc.). The "reflexive grasp" tying it all together is the topic of language and talking. First, empathy with the silent child, then the forceful information-seeking of torture, and, finally, her own refusal to remain silent. In this latter, she includes an aspect of futurity within the grammatical construction, thereby finally achieving a *connection* among all three temporal phases that, paradoxically, *dissolves* all sense of "phase" itself.

Wolf's method of self-consciously breaching the very notion of "temporal linearity" continuously broadens the present into a discursive space through which the heterochronic frame arises. It appears in her literary writing as early as *Patterns of Childhood*, and, since Wolf adheres to this writing strategy through her final novel, *City of Angels or, The Overcoat of Dr. Freud*, I think it appropriate to generalize the unique conception of time that lies at the heart of her work.

Linear/chronological time can end or be overcome by continually turning every present moment into a past moment: the process we call, often unmindfully, the "passage of time." Wolf's "time," however, enables, indeed insists upon, a kind of memory that catches up to the present and identifies, therefore, any "present" as a historical "space." Time has become transformed from the linear, chronological idea of "History" into a narrative in which past, present, and future do not simply supplant each other but rather exist simultaneously, or more precisely, heterochronically. In the heterochronic framework, not only linearity is rendered obsolete but also singularity, since the plurality of stories and histories present within this discursive frame are not a mere montage of discrete temporal phases. The heterochronic frame operates not unlike the kind of space that Massey opposes to our traditional understanding of space, which, we unconsciously believe, is never temporal, always exterior, forever static. Wolf's conception of the present as an "extended reality" also bears a strong resemblance to Massey's reconceptualized "space," which contains "the dimension of multiple trajectories, a simultaneity of stories-so-far" (24). In accord with this definition, the "extended present" is not just a temporal model; it is the locus of contemporaneity, an interactional space where connections are waiting to be made.

It is unnecessarily complex to ask if Christa Wolf can still be considered a "contemporary writer." If, however, the question is posed to her work so as to ask what *she* understood "contemporaneity" to mean, we then may forge a useful tool for understanding the temporal dimensions of her writing. Wolf consistently renders the intricate relationship between time and narrative into both the form and content of her art. This is especially evident in her conception of *Zeitgenossenschaft*, "contemporaneity," which is not simply a temporal but also a narrative approach. In constructing an "extended present" and an "extended narrative 'I,'" fiction and memory come together to deliver a story with the significant narrative depth that Wolf regarded as the marker of "timely" literature.

I have argued that Wolf's work evinces a strong perceptual and experiential affinity to heterochronic practices in its generation of a critical and productive self-awareness. We have seen that by extending the reach of the present, we may attain a level of depth that staves off the ethical and social dangers of superficiality. The question remains, then, of her legacy. Perhaps it would help to remind ourselves that, ultimately, Wolf's narrative model insists on the genuine openness of history and relies on her conviction that "a writer's work is a precious and lasting phenomenon in which the time sees itself and later sees us" ("Faith in the Terrestrial" 137). Literary writing, when engaged with the sort of contemporaneity Wolf so cherished in the texts of Anna Seghers, for example, forms a critical perspective on ongoing historical change and bears witness to historical events and their significance, to which many contemporaries may turn a blind eye. "It is just what many living at the time do not want or cannot bear to know that will remain alive, because the future takes it up," she asserts (137). What remains is the trajectory of our "stories-so-far," and authors' and readers' willingness to continue reading and writing them.

Heike Polster is Associate Professor of German at the University of Memphis. Her research focuses on temporal concepts in philosophy, visual arts, literary texts, and their intersection. She received her Ph.D. from Washington University in St. Louis, where she also taught Women's Studies. She is the author of *The Aesthetics of Passage: The Imag(in)ed Experience of Time in Thomas Lehr, W.G. Sebald and Peter Handke* (2009) and *The Poetics of Passage: Christa Wolf, Time, and Narrative* (2012). Her current projects include *Heterochronic Visions: Framing the Present*, a study of the aesthetics of the contemporary.

Notes

1. My translation differs slightly from Joan Becker's version: "At the back of the prose writer's doubts about the future of his genre, there lies simply a doubt of himself: that he is an anachronism" (Wolf, "The Reader and the Writer" 181).
2. "'Period': a term, in fact, that would itself seem as vague as *Gegenwart* (the present) and *Gegenwartsliteratur* (contemporary literature) themselves. We have inherited from culture in general, and traditional literary history and newer historicisms alike, a reliance on understanding 'period' as a meaningful, self-evident, stable unit of time … Our notion of 'period,' however, is also dependent on our sense that "temporal parameters shift, that zeitgeist and material conditions are mutable" (Trumpener 349–50).
3. An excellent study on "Gegenwart" as a poetic construction in contemporary literature is Jan Röhnert and Valentina Di Rosa's *Im Hier und Jetzt: Konstellationen der Gegenwart in der deutschsprachigen Literatur seit 2000.*
4. Examples of Wolf's titles—*What Remains, One Day a Year, August, Sommerstück* (Summer Scenes), *Accident: A Day's News, Wir, Unsere Zeit*—attest to this fact.
5. Heterochronicity differs from simultaneity in that the latter describes processes which occur at the same time but in different places, whereas the former concerns itself with distinct temporal phases which appear within the same frame.
6. A tale *about* time takes as its content the nature and passage of time. A tale *of* time is simply a story set in time, its form uncomplicated by nonlinear chronologies or anachronisms, its characters going about their business as though the points on the time continuum were tidy, terminal, and intuitive. Although this dichotomy rather simplifies the subject, it is nevertheless important to note that Wolf's texts are consistently both *about* and *of*.
7. Ricoeur falls short in one important regard: while he does show how information in texts is organized and transmitted as narrative, and while this may help the reader to draw a mental picture of the chronologically organized world on the page, he cannot adequately explain the underlying idea of time-consciousness. Even though these shortcomings will figure in subsequent deliberations, I cannot here provide a discussion of time itself as the present inquiry serves solely a narratological—not a philosophical—purpose.
8. See also Lutz Koepnick, "Rettung und Destruktion: Erinnerungsverfahren und Geschichtsbewußtsein in Christa Wolf's *Kindheitsmuster* und Walter Benjamins Spätwerk" and Ortrud Gutjahr, "Erinnerte Zukunft: Gedächtnisrekonstruktion und Subjektkonstitution im Werk Christa Wolfs."
9. In a discussion of Georg Büchner's works, Wolf points out his discovery of the fourth, "real" dimension of the narrator: "This is the coordinate of depth, of contemporaneousness, of inevitable involvement" ("The Reader and the Writer" 198). Instead of "contemporaneousness," I use the term "contemporaneity" because much that has been published on the narratological concerns of temporality since the publication of Wolf's essay employs the latter term.
10. Often, Wolf's texts are grouped under the category of "autobiographical writing." While her published correspondence, essays, and interviews would certainly affirm this classification, we must not forget that her narrating voice persistently and methodically follows the rules of fiction. Take the disclaimer at the beginning of *Patterns of Childhood*, for instance, in which we are informed that all characters in

the novel are fictional. Moreover, the narrator, who has been identified as an alter ego of Wolf, goes by a different name.

11. Christa Wolf, as has been widely noted, grappled with ways of expressing "subjective authenticity," as her 1970s catchphrase characterized her pursuit of a kind of writing that, in the formulation of Hans-Dieter Weber, would allow complex individual experience to "pass into literature and still remain socially significant. In German one can put the issue more clearly by asking, can *Erlebnis* contribute to *Erfahrung*, and what part might literature play in this process?" (Weber 93; my translation).

12. The fictionalized novel is entitled "patterns" and not, for example, "scenes," or just "a childhood," for neither of these would have foregrounded the nonlinear nature of memory.

Bibliography

Carr, David. *Time, Narrative, and History.* Bloomington: Indiana University, 1986.

Genette, Gerard. *Narrative Discourse: An Essay in Method.* Translated by Jane E. Lewin. Ithaca, NY: Cornell University Press, 1983.

Gutjahr, Ortrud. "Erinnerte Zukunft: Gedächtnisrekonstruktion und Subjektkonstitution im Werk Christa Wolfs." *Erinnerte Zukunft: Elf Studien zum Werk Christa Wolfs*, edited by Wolfram Mauser. Würzburg: Königshausen und Neumann, 1985, pp. 53–80.

Harweg, Roland. "Story-Time and Fact-Sequence-Time." *Time: From Concept to Narrative Construct. A Reader*, edited by Jan Christoph Meister and Wilhelm Schernus. Berlin: Walter de Gruyter, 2011, pp. 143–70.

Koepnick, Lutz. "Rettung und Destruktion: Erinnerungsverfahren und Geschichtsbewußtsein in Christa Wolf's *Kindheitsmuster* und Walter Benjamins Spätwerk." *Monatshefte*, vol. 84, no. 1, 1992, pp. 74–90.

Massey, Doreen. *For Space.* London: Sage, 2005.

Meister, Jan Christoph. "The Temporality Effect: Towards a Process Model of Narrative Time Construction." *Time: From Concept to Narrative Construct. A Reader*, edited by Jan Christoph Meister and Wilhelm Schernus. Berlin: Walter de Gruyter, 2011, pp. 171–216.

Müller, Günther. "Erzählzeit und erzählte Zeit." *Morphologische Poetik: Gesammelte Aufsätze*, edited by Günther Müller. Darmstadt: Wissenschaftliche Buchgesellschaft, 1968, pp. 269–86.

Polster, Heike. *The Poetics of Passage: Christa Wolf, Time, and Narrative.* Newcastle-upon-Tyne: Cambridge Scholars, 2012.

Ricoeur, Paul. *Time and Narrative.* Translated by Kathleen McLaughlin and David Pellauer. Chicago: University of Chicago Press, 1984–88.

Röhnert, Jan, and Valentina Di Rosa. *Im Hier und Jetzt: Konstellationen der Gegenwart in der deutschsprachigen Literatur seit 2000.* Cologne: Böhlau, 2019.

Trumpener, Katie. "In the Grid: Period and Experience." *PMLA*, vol. 127, no. 2, 2012, pp. 349–55.

Weber, Hans-Dieter. "Phantastische Genauigkeit: Der historische Sinn der Schreibart Christa Wolfs." *Erinnerte Zukunft: Elf Studien zum Werk Christa Wolfs*, edited by Wolfram Mauser. Würzburg: Königshausen und Neumann, 1985, pp. 81–105.

Wolf, Christa. *Accident. A Day's News: A Novel*. Translated by Heike Schwarzbauer and Rick Takvorian. Chicago: University of Chicago Press, 2001.

———. *August*. Translated by Katy Derbyshire. London: Seagull Books, 2019.

———. *City of Angels, or The Overcoat of Dr. Freud*. Translated by Damion Searls. New York: Farrar, Straus, Giroux, 2013.

———. "Das Siebte Kreuz." *Fortgesetzter Versuch: Aufsätze, Gespräche, Essays*. Leipzig: Reclam, 1979, pp. 181–93.

———. "Faith in the Terrestrial." *The Reader and the Writer*, translated by Joan Becker. New York: International Publishers, 1977, pp. 111–37.

———. *One Day a Year: 1960–2000*. Translated by Lowell A. Bangerter. New York: Europa Editions, 2007.

———. *Patterns of Childhood* (formerly: *A Model Childhood*). Translated by Ursule Molinaro and Hedwig Rappolt. New York: The Noonday Press, 1980.

———. *Sommerstück*. München: Luchterhand Literaturverlag, 2002.

———. "The Fourth Dimension: A Conversation with Joachim Walther." *The Fourth Dimension: Interviews with Christa Wolf*, translated Hilary Pilkington. London: Verso, 1988, pp. 1–16.

———. "The Reader and the Writer." *The Reader and the Writer*, translated by Joan Becker. New York: International Publishers, 1977, pp. 181–212.

———. *What Remains and Other Stories*. Translated by Heike Schwarzbauer and Rick Takvorian. New York: Farrar, Straus, Giroux, 1993.

———. *Wir, Unsere Zeit*. Ed. Gerhard Wolf. Berlin: Aufbau Verlag, 1959.

CHAPTER 7

Subjective Authenticity as Realism
Christa Wolf and Georg Lukács

ROBERT BLANKENSHIP

> Every major realist fashions the material given in his own experience, and in doing so makes use of techniques of abstraction, among others. But his goal is to penetrate the laws governing objective reality and to uncover the deeper, hidden, mediated, not immediately perceptible network of relationships that go to make up society.
> —Georg Lukács, "Realism in the Balance," 38 ("Es geht um den Realismus," 1938)

> It is still, and always will be, a question of realism and the fight for it. ... [What] the reservoir writers draw on in their writing is experience, which mediates between objective reality and the authorial subject. And it is highly desirable that this should be socially meaningful experience.
> —Christa Wolf, "Subjective Authenticity," 61 ("Subjektive Authentizität," 1974)

The death of Christa Wolf in 2011 became the occasion for renewed attempts to examine the nature of her aesthetic project, to evaluate her remarkable body of work as a whole, and to ask difficult questions of it. These are not the kinds of questions that led to personal attacks on Wolf, instigated first by the scandal surrounding the publication of *What Remains* (*Was bleibt*, 1990), which some critics condemned as conveniently belated, and subsequently by the scandal that ensued when news broke that Wolf had been a Stasi informant in the years 1959–62. The time has passed for such sensationalism. Instead, it is time to ask literary and philosophical questions of Wolf's work, to reappraise it with diverse literary methodologies, and to ask what influences are at work in her writings, without the necessity of either defending or attacking Wolf herself. Her work is varied and rich enough to withstand such methodological exploration. One move in such re-examination involves re-evaluating the influence of the Hungarian, Hegelian-Marxist literary theoretician Georg Lukács on her overall literary project. Indeed, as I intend to show in this chapter, the extent to which Wolf's project is antithetical to that of Lukács has been vastly overstated.

In highlighting the influence of Lukács on Wolf, my intention is not necessarily to rehabilitate him for the twenty-first century, or to value realism over expressionism, modernism, postmodernism, or other literary movements. Instead, a focus on the relationship between Lukács and Wolf will aid in understanding the complex mechanisms at work in Wolf's project. While she created her own innovative aesthetic and epistemology, an understanding of what influenced her and the ways in which she interacted with other thinkers should help us to assess these innovations. Wolf's realism, like that of Lukács, focuses largely on the mediation of experience and on dynamic engagement with literary history. Whatever we may think of Lukács—and, indeed, whatever Wolf may have thought of Lukács—understanding his influence on her in terms of mediation and literary history helps to complete the larger picture of Wolf's rich aesthetic and epistemological project.

Although Wolf's aesthetic can be located somewhere between modernism and realism—assuming that those two -isms create a useful dichotomy, which may not be the case—its modernist leanings are highlighted in scholarly criticism much more frequently than its realist tendency. Anne Dwyer, in setting Wolf in contradistinction to Iurii Trifonov, goes so far as to declare that "Wolf is a child of European modernism" (622). While Wolf pioneered a new and inspiring aesthetic, one that may be placed under the rubric of modernism—among other possible categories—her relationship to realism has been understated. In this vein, scholars of Christa Wolf have often made the point that Wolf's project operates in stark opposition to the critical realist theories of Georg Lukács. Margit Resch, for example, asserts that "Wolf rejects both past and present literary norms and practices, including the widely accepted theories of the genre 'novel' of the Marxist literary historian and theoretician Georg Lukács" (69). Such claims are not surprising, given the way that Wolf incorporated subjectivity, illness, dreams, and allusions to Romanticism into her works—all of which, on the surface, run counter to Lukács's central tenets. For all her resistance to Lukácsian realism, however, Wolf was not opposed to realism *per se*. That is, her "subjective authenticity" is, in fact, a type of realism that was influenced to a considerable extent by Lukács. My contention, then, is that Wolf's apparent turn away from Lukács may, in part, be better understood as an act of taking Lukács more seriously, of attempting to answer some of the questions he posed, and of developing critical realism even further. In order to address the nature of Lukács's influence on Wolf, it may be helpful to situate Wolf within a larger field of Marxist thinkers.

Christa Wolf and Marxist Aesthetics

In seeking answers to questions about reality, realism, epistemology, and aesthetics, Christa Wolf adopted a wide variety of Marxist theories. Early on, however, she was especially enthusiastic about the writings of Georg Lukács. As a student in Jena, she studied his works under Edith Braemer (Magenau 47). She even wrote her thesis (*Diplomarbeit*) on "Problems of Realism in the Works of Hans Fallada" under the direction of Hans Mayer (who was himself greatly influenced by Lukács).[1] The thesis was written, according to Christa Wolf, "in the spirit of Lukács's concept of realism" ("im Geiste der Realismusauffassung von Lukács") ("Die Dauerspannung beim Schreiben"). As Gerhard Wolf confirmed in a conversation with Henry Schmidt and colleagues at The Ohio State University, he and his future wife Christa Ihlenfeld read and studied Lukács thoroughly. "Wir haben diese Lukácsschen Theorien sehr verinnerlicht" ("We internalized these theories of Lukács very intensively"), he declared ("Ein Gespräch" 97). In Wolf's final novel, *City of Angels or, The Overcoat of Dr. Freud* (*Stadt der Engel oder The Overcoat of Dr. Freud*, 2010), the unnamed narrator, who bears a clear resemblance to Wolf, recalls being a student at Jena, listening to young instructors speaking excitedly about Georg Lukács and his theories of realism and sharing their enthusiasm:

> You can still see yourself sitting with the others around the square table in the seminar room, surrounded by bookshelves, you can hear the young docent talk enthusiastically about Georg Lukács, whose theories made you see that what mattered was Realism, what else was there, and you and the class enthusiastically drank in his arguments and could not imagine how anyone could judge literature differently. (99–100)

In a conversation with her granddaughter, Jana Simon, Wolf described studying Lukács in terms similar to those of her narrator: "Georg Lukács was the teacher. The young docents were completely steeped in his intellect, and they passed that on to us. We adopted Lukács's concept of realism and argued with bourgeois students about the ideas" (*Sei dennoch unverzagt* 92; my translation). While the young Wolf clearly studied Lukács, her biographer, Jörg Magenau, implies that she later broke from his influence: "For the students Ihlenfeld and Wolf, Lukács was the *non plus ultra*. They studied his works word-for-word and adopted his judgments—pertaining, for instance, to Expressionism and Romanticism—which they then later had to correct" (47, trans. ed.). Such "corrections," as Magenau calls them, include Wolf's subsequent focus on subjective experience and the appreciation of Romanticism that she acquired in part through Anna Seghers and which is particularly evident in her novel *No Place on Earth* (*Kein Ort. Nirgends*, 1979) and her short story "New Life and Opinions of a Tomcat" ("Neue Lebensansichten eines Katers," 1970), as well as in several essays. But how are these "corrections" best understood? Does Wolf's interest in subjective experience and her development of an appreciation for Romanticism represent a complete break with Lukácsian critical realism?

Wolf no doubt did break with Lukács in several key ways, but her project remains focused largely on realism. If, as Paul Fry proposes, there are four possibilities for Marxist aesthetics (222)[2]—Lukács's realism, Benjamin's participatory aesthetic, Bloch's utopianism, and Adorno's high Modernist aesthetic—then the question arises: which of these modes best describes Wolf's aesthetic? Scholars have offered varying answers to this question, often describing Wolf in terms of either Benjamin or Bloch. Lutz Koepnick, for example, locates Benjaminian memory in Wolf's *Patterns of Childhood* (*Kindheitsmuster*, 1976) and Helen Fehervary notes Wolf's similarity to Benjamin in her focus on authorial subjectivity in the construction of history ("Christa Wolf's Prose" 165–67). Both Andreas Huyssen ("Traces of Ernst Bloch") and Fehervary ("Christa Wolf's Prose" 163–65) have identified connections between Wolf and Bloch in their thinking about synchronicity and utopia, for example, adding to evidence that Wolf was influenced by both Benjamin and Bloch. She may, in fact, have had direct contact with Bloch, as she did with Mayer, as both Bloch and Mayer were on the faculty at the University of Leipzig in the 1950s. In addition to the allusion to Lukács, Wolf's final novel, *City of Angels or, The Overcoat of Dr. Freud* (2010), contains multiple allusions to both Benjamin and Bloch, including a quotation from Benjamin as an epigraph to the novel. However, the similarity that also exists between the respective projects of Wolf and Lukács may be illustrated with a quotation from Fredric Jameson: this "work may be seen as a continuous and lifelong meditation on narrative, on its basic structures, and its relationship to the reality it expresses, and its epistemological value…" (163). While this quotation would be an entirely accurate description of Wolf's oeuvre, it is, in fact, Jameson's description of Lukács's work.

The Expressionism Debate that began in the 1930s provides another framework for organizing a taxonomy of Marxist aesthetics. The rich constellation of voices in the Expressionism Debate allows for mention of Anna Seghers, who perhaps had a greater influence on Wolf than any of the thinkers whom Fry lists, and to whom I must necessarily return. However, if the debate is reduced to Brecht vs. Lukács, as it often is (Mittenzwei; Kiralyfalvi), the evidence for Brecht's influence on Wolf is particularly thin. Wolf knew the works of Brecht and, to some degree, respected them. She describes her experience attending a production of Brecht's adaptation

(1950) of Lenz's *The Tutor or, The Advantages of a Private Education* (*Der Hofmeister oder die Vorteile der Privaterziehung*, 1774) and simultaneously watching both the play on stage and Brecht himself, who was sitting in the front row laughing uncontrollably, and she was frustrated and confused by his lack of respect for tragedy ("Brecht and Others"). Although she learned to admire his project from a distance, Wolf was never a Brechtian. She is quite clear about this later in her Frankfurt Poetics Lectures: "I have never felt the raging desire for confrontation with the poetics, or the model, of a great writer (in parentheses, Brecht)" ("Ein Gespräch" 141; my translation). Further, Wolf insisted in the interview with the Ohio State colleagues "that Brecht had absolutely no influence on me as an author, ... I never was really concerned with him in a positive or negative way, which, of course, is also an indictment" ("Ein Gespräch" 102; trans. ed.). To my mind, the voice from the debates about realism and modernism that influenced Wolf at least as much as those of Benjamin, Bloch, and Lukács—and much more than that of Brecht—is that of Anna Seghers. Of importance here is both the nature of Seghers's seeming opposition to Lukács and the influence that she exerted on Wolf. Seghers's interventions in the complex, polyphonic, and decades-long debates with Lukács are unique in that they largely lack the *ad hominem* tone characteristic of others who opposed Lukács (to be sure, much of that harsh tone was instigated by Lukács's own propensity toward such attacks) and in the fact that her interventions do not oppose realism *per se*. Indeed, Seghers did not so much oppose the positions of Lukács, as much as she opposed the dogmatic way he defended them. Seghers, like Lukács, admired the works of the great French and Russian realists. However, unlike Lukács, Seghers wished to broaden the concept of realism and free it from Lukács's narrow formula. She wanted him to see that writers such as Kleist, whom Lukács generally dismissed, could offer an epistemology that leads to a deeper understanding of reality, and that a flexible realism could offer a more dialectical understanding of the world than could Lukács's sclerotic realism. However, even as Seghers tried to convince Lukács to soften his stance, she remained influenced by him, especially by his earlier works, such as *Soul and Form* (*Die Seele und die Formen*, 1911), "Aesthetic Culture" (1910), and *The Theory of the Novel* (*Die Theorie des Romans*, 1920). Indeed, as Helen Fehervary correctly states: "Anna Seghers's prose, even as late as the 1960s and 1970s, remained indebted to the aesthetics of the young Lukács" (*Anna Seghers* 103). Much of what Wolf derived from Seghers seems to be at odds with basic tenets of Lukács's middle period, where he creates a dichotomous view of literary history, but Wolf also derived from Seghers an indirect, implicit acceptance of some of his earlier ideas.[3]

Wolf and Lukács on the Mediation of Experience and Literary History

Wolf's "subjective authenticity" seems, on the surface, to be the theoretical focal point of her opposition to Lukács. However, this concept also reflects much of Wolf's Lukácsian inheritance. It offers a realism that allows for, indeed requires, subjective experience. In her 1974 interview with Hans Kaufmann, she defines "subjective authenticity" in terms of reality and in a way that is not altogether opposed to Lukács: "I would like to give the provisional name 'subjective authenticity' to the search for a new method of writing which does justice to this reality. I can only hope I have made it clear that this method not only does not dispute the existence of objective reality, but is precisely an attempt to engage with 'objective reality' in a productive manner" ("Subjective Authenticity" 60). Wolf's will to such engagement with objective reality suggests that she considered Lukács's ideal of realism to be valid to some extent, but that she came to consider the methods of achieving realism championed by Lukács to be outdated or inadequate. Wolf adds to realism her notion of experience, which she explains as follows: "experience of 'life,' by which I mean experience of the tangible reality of a particular time in a particular society; experience of myself" (56). This recalls Wolf's earlier statement in her 1968 essay "The Reader and the Writer" that, while there is a such thing as reality, it is impossible to narrate it objectively and at best a narrator can "tell, that is invent, truthfully on the foundation of her own experience" (193). This notion of experience is similar to the one described by Benjamin, but Wolf invoked it for the sake of realism. Even as she incorporates profound emotion, fantasy, and dreams into her fiction, they function to propel realism. Kaufmann fortifies this interpretation in his essay "On Christa Wolf's Principle of Poetics": "The fantastic and the utopian, when made artistically recognizable for what they are, can intensify the sense of reality; they can also permit a clearer representation of the really existent and possible" (83).

Although such intensification of a sense of reality through subjective experience is at the center of Wolf's aesthetic, her methods intend to mark a break with the so-called reflection theory (*Widerspiegelungstheorie*) often associated with Lukács (although Lenin used the term before Lukács did). She cleverly attacked reflection theory in "The Reader and the Writer," asserting that "literature and reality do not stand face to face like a mirror and what it reflects" (206). Although this statement may seem to signal a sharp break with Lukács, two problems emerge here that cast this assumption into question. First of all, Wolf does not claim that literature has nothing to do with reality. Rather, she indicates that literature's connection to reality is a complicated one. Her approach to prose, as she explains in that same essay, is to portray reality in such a way as to reveal its complexity. "Prose" is, indeed, an important concept for Wolf. It is not to be understood simply as writing that is free of meter and rhyme scheme; rather, it is a force that makes us who we are: "Prose makes people. ... It helps mankind to become conscious subjects. It is revolutionary and realistic; it entices and encourages people to achieve the impossible" (212). For Wolf, then, "prose" constructs a representation of reality that counters oversimplified notions of reality. Her realism struggles to know reality even while admitting the impossibility of the task: "Writing can only begin for those to whom reality is no longer a matter-of-course" (202). Such an approach to prose certainly differs from that of, say, Walter Scott, whom Lukács so strongly championed, but it remains a realistic approach, one concerned with understanding reality.

The second problem with using Wolf's condemnation of reflection theory to separate her from Lukács centers around the importance that Lukács attaches to mediation in his concept of realism. As Sara Nadal-Melsió—in reconciling Lukács's notion of realism with his other, more philosophical ideas—correctly explains, "Lukácsean [sic] realism is not a question of objective representation, that is, a reflection theory, but rather a matter of subjective referentiality and mediation" (78). While reflection theory is often credited to him, Lukács later differentiates this notion: his problem with Naturalism had been its focus on the documentation of external data. He compares the works of Émile Zola, for example, to "the scientific monograph" ("Critical Realism and Socialist Realism" 100). Wolf expressed similar disdain for positivist approaches to reality, declaring, for example: "There is a truth outside the important world of facts" ("The Reader and the Writer" 203). For Lukács, critical realism, as opposed to both Naturalism and Zhdanovian Socialist Realism,[4] was not to record external reality, but rather to narrate dynamic reality, that is, to mediate reality. In other words, Lukács was not so much opposed to subjectivity as he was to immediacy, whether subjective or objective. Seen in this light, Wolf's and Lukács's respective approaches to reality have much in common.

Literary history is another arena in which Wolf's relationship to Lukács is more complex than it seems on the surface. Wolf's approach to literary history entails, in part, wresting it away from the Lukácsian paradigm of literary heritage.[5] His rather dogmatic view of literary history can be seen in the dichotomy he established between realism and Romanticism, whereas Wolf came to champion certain aspects of Romanticism, an appreciation she had at least partially inherited from Anna Seghers. Wolf and Lukács also had different views of Greek literature. By questioning multiple layers of the sanctioned understanding of literary heritage ("Erbe")—from Lukács's dichotomy of the healthy versus the sick, through Goethe and the Weimar classicists versus Kleist and Günderrode, for instance, through to the ancient Greeks—Wolf is able to reveal that literary history cannot be readily shaped according to a static mold. Further, whereas Lukács looks to ancient Greece as a great, healthy, rationalist society, for example,[6] Wolf indicates that the Greeks might just as easily be viewed as irrational and self-destructive. Although she went on to construct an approach to literary history somewhat antithetical to that of Lukács, they shared the view that contemporary aesthetic battles are often best fought on the battleground of literary history. Given that the young Wolf so thoroughly internalized Lukács, the question emerges whether she also acquired her appreciation of the power of literary history, in part, from him. In a section of "The Reader and the Writer" titled "Tabula Rasa," Wolf laments having read many of the texts available to her as a girl in the Third Reich and wishes she had read other books at that age, claiming that the "prose" that human beings read makes them who they are. She thus constructs her own view of literary history, which is not altogether unlike that of Lukács. Although Wolf's literary history was less dogmatic than Lukács's, and although it evolved substantially over her career, Wolf's "subjective authenticity," like Lukács's realism, depended, in large part, upon the assessment of earlier works of literature. Further, for both Lukács and Wolf, engagement with literary history, like their engagement with reality, centers on mediation. That is, the mediation of earlier works of literature, just like the mediation of subjective experience, is vitally important to both thinkers.

Lest we think that Wolf's Lukácsian inheritance applies only to her early works,[7] a brief look at her final novel is in order. *City of Angels or, The Overcoat of Dr. Freud* constructs a more or less portrayal of reality complicated by the mediation of subjective experience. Mindful of the problems of realism, Wolf cites at the outset two quotations about authenticity and reality. First, as the epigraph to the entire work she cites Benjamin's statement from "Excavation and Memory": "So, for authentic memories, it is far less important that the investigator report on them than that he mark, quite precisely, the site where he gained possession of them." Then, in an echo of her 1968 criticism of reflection theory, Wolf quotes E.L. Doctorow in the epigraph to her first chapter: "No writer can reproduce the actual texture of living life." This quotation, however, does not indicate opposition to realism *per se*, as the novel proceeds both to construct a more or less realistic depiction of the narrator's stay in Los Angeles in the early 1990s and to investigate the nature of realism. The narrator's friend Peter Gutman, who is writing a book on Walter Benjamin, asks her, "What does 'real' mean anyway?" (35). Although she can offer no easy answer to that question, she continues to strive toward an understanding of reality. Later, as Gutman reminds her that there must always be a blind spot in our perception of reality, she declares, "But one day it will all collapse if we don't face reality" (78). This blind spot and its epistemological ramifications continue to trouble the narrator for much of the novel. Her implicit answer—seemingly informed by conversations with Gutman, a book by a Buddhist nun, and frequent visits from an angel—echoes Wolf's conception of subjective authenticity, namely, that there is such a thing as objective reality, but in order to portray it, one must rely on subjective experience. Yet, the narrator's notion of reality, like Wolf's, is also evocative of Lukács's. As she attempts to describe her experience of living in the GDR to American acquaintances, explaining that there is more to a lived life than what can be read in American newspapers, she sounds almost like Lukács lambasting Naturalism: "Facts lined up one after the other don't give you reality, you know. Facts are not enough. There are many layers and facets to reality and the naked facts are only its surface" (194). Furthermore, the narrator's realism, like that of Wolf and Lukács, relies heavily on literary history. *City of Angels or, The Overcoat of Dr. Freud* is replete with allusions to earlier writers. It mentions Goethe, Kleist, Chekov, Brecht, Thomas Mann, Anna Seghers, Luther, the ancient Greeks, and Agatha Christie, among others. The narrator, like Wolf and Lukács, also seems to conclude that reading helps to shape human subjects. Like Wolf in "The Reader and the Writer," the narrator reflects on what she read before 1945 and what she read after 1945. She finds a used bookstore in Los Angeles full of books by German exile writers and books by writers they had read and realizes that she had not known any of those books before 1945 (258). This unnamed narrator, in her struggle to understand the inner workings of reality and realism, also has much in common with several of the main characters in Wolf's previous works. Like the narrator who is on a quest for Christa T., like Wolf's Kleist and Günderrode (*No Place on Earth*), like Nelly (*Patterns of Childhood*), even like Rita Seidel (*They Divided the Sky*), she struggles to understand and to depict reality, but does so by refracting reality through subjective experience, which also includes reading.

In conclusion, I contend that Wolf's "subjective authenticity," which has long been thought to be the antithesis of Lukácsian realism, bears the mark of Lukács's influence, at least insofar as it explores the nature of reality through its insistence on mediation. Indeed, Wolf took questions of realism very seriously and strove to create a realism that represented her experience of the world. Her "corrections" of Lukács, as Magenau calls them, are indeed that: they are corrections (that is, improvements) to concepts of critical realism. They push realism away from simplification. Wolf's criticism of Lukács, in other words, can be compared to Heiner Müller's 1984 criticism of Brecht. Responding to accusations[8] that he had killed Brecht, Müller declared his murder of Brecht to be patricide ("Vatermord") ("Interview"). Two years earlier Müller had foreshadowed such sentiment when he warned "To use Brecht without criticizing him is betrayal" (*Rotwelsch* 149). Likewise, Wolf, in her criticism of Lukács, constructively appropriated critical realism for her time and place. Indeed, her realism of "subjective authenticity" moves beyond Lukács's critical realism. However, it also remains deeply indebted to Lukács, perhaps more than even Christa Wolf acknowledged.

Robert Blankenship is Associate Professor of German at California State University, Long Beach. He is author of the monograph *Suicide in East German Literature: Fiction, Rhetoric, and the Self-Destruction of Literary Heritage* (Camden House, 2017) as well as articles and book chapters such as "'Erzählt ist erzählt': The Ethics of Narration in Christa Wolf's *Stadt der Engel oder The Overcoat of Dr. Freud*," in *Envisioning Social Justice in Contemporary German Culture* (Camden House, 2015) and "Christa Wolf's Richard Neutra: Architecture, Psychoanalysis, and Southern California in *Stadt der Engel oder The Overcoat of Dr. Freud*" (*Germanic Review*, 95[1], 2020).

Notes

1. In a 1987 interview with Beate Pinkerneil, Mayer reveals that he found Marx through Lukács, not the other way around. (See "Hans Mayer im Gespräch mit Beate Pinkerneil.")
2. Fry's rubric is certainly an oversimplification, but his broad coordinates, nonetheless, remain useful.
3. In a conversation at the German Studies Association conference in Milwaukee (2012), where the original, shorter version of this chapter was presented, Fehervary told me that she doubts that Wolf ever read Lukács's earlier works.
4. Andrei Zhdanov directed cultural policy under Stalin and propagated a strict, oversimplified, and anti-Western doctrine of Socialist Realism in all forms of the arts.
5. The notion of "Erbe" or literary and cultural heritage was important in the GDR, as the country sought to create a heritage antithetical to that of fascism. Wolf's conflict with Lukács over literary history is situated in the context of "Erbe."
6. See, for example, Lukács's work, *The Destruction of Reason* (*Die Zerstörung der Vernunft*, 1954).
7. There seems to be consensus in much of the secondary literature that Wolf gradually moved from Socialist Realism in her early works toward modernism in her later works. This argument is made most explicitly by George Buehler in *The Death of Socialist Realism in the Novels of Christa Wolf*, 1984.
8. In a 1978 article in *Der Spiegel*, Hellmut Karasek declared: "Brecht ist tot." In 1984, a caption in *Theater heute* calls Müller a "Brecht-Killer" (61). David Bathrick recounts this development in *The Powers of Speech*, 151–64.

Bibliography

Bathrick, David. *The Powers of Speech: The Politics of Culture in the GDR.* Lincoln: University of Nebraska Press, 1995.

Brecht, Bertolt. *The Tutor.* New York: Hal Leonard, 1988.

Buehler, George. *The Death of Socialist Realism in the Novels of Christa Wolf.* New York: Peter Lang, 1984.

Dwyer, Anne. "Runaway Texts: The Many Life Stories of Iurii Trifonov and Christa Wolf." *Russian Review,* vol. 64, no. 4, October 2005, pp. 605–27.

Fehervary, Helen. *Anna Seghers: The Mythic Dimension.* Ann Arbor: University of Michigan Press, 2001.

———. "Christa Wolf's Prose: A Landscape of Masks." *Responses to Christa Wolf: Critical Essays,* edited by Marilyn Sibley Fries. Detroit, MI: Wayne State University Press, 1989, pp. 162–85.

Fries, Marilyn Sibley, editor. *Responses to Christa Wolf: Critical Essays.* Detroit, MI: Wayne State University Press, 1989.

Fry, Paul H. *Theory of Literature.* New Haven, CT: Yale University Press, 2012.

Huyssen, Andreas. "Traces of Ernst Bloch: Reflections on Christa Wolf." *Responses to Christa Wolf: Critical Essays,* edited by Marilyn Sibley Fries. Detroit, MI: Wayne State University Press, 1989, pp. 233–47.

Jameson, Fredric. *Marxism and Form: Twentieth-Century Dialectical Theories of Literature.* Princeton, NJ: Princeton University Press, 1971.

Karasek, Hellmut. "Brecht ist tot." *Der Spiegel,* no. 9, 27 February 1978, pp. 216–17.

Kaufmann, Hans. "On Christa Wolf's Principle of Poetics." *Responses to Christa Wolf: Critical Essays,* edited by Marilyn Sibley Fries. Detroit, MI: Wayne State University Press, 1989, pp. 76–90.

Kiralyfalvi, Bela. "Georg Lukács or Bertolt Brecht?" *British Journal of Aesthetics,* vol. 25, no. 4, Autumn 1985, pp. 340–48.

Koepnick, Lutz. "Rettung und Destruktion: Erinnerungsverfahren und Geschichtsbewußtsein in Christa Wolfs *Kindheitsmuster* und Walter Benjamins Spätwerk." *Monatshefte,* vol. 84, no. 1, 1992, pp. 74–90.

Lenz, Jakob Michael Reinhold. *The Tutor and the Soldiers.* Translated by William E. Yuill. Chicago: University of Chicago Press, 1980.

Lukács, Georg. "Aesthetic Culture." *The Lukács Reader,* translated by John and Necke Maunder, edited by Arpad Kadarkay. Oxford: Blackwell, 1995, pp. 146–59.

———. "Critical Realism and Socialist Realism." *The Meaning of Contemporary Realism,* translated by John and Necke Maunder. London: Merlin, 1963, pp. 93–135.

———. *The Destruction of Reason.* Translated by Peter Palmer. London: Merlin, 1980.

———. "Realism in the Balance," translated by Rodney Livingston. *Aesthetics and Politics,* by T.W. Adorno et. al., edited by Fredric Jameson. London: Verso, 2007, pp. 28–59.

———. *Soul and Form*. Translated by Anna Bostock. London: Merlin, 1991.
———. *The Theory of the Novel*. Translated by Anna Bostock. Cambridge, MA: MIT Press, 1974.
Magenau, Jörg. *Christa Wolf: Eine Biographie*. Berlin: Kindler, 2002.
Mayer, Hans. "Hans Mayer im Gespräch mit Beate Pinkerneil." *Zeugen des Jahrhunderts*. Mainz: ZDF, 1987 (now available on YouTube: http://www.youtube.com/watch?v=pA2ziHzWZcY).
Mittenzwei, Werner. "Die Brecht-Lukács-Debatte." *Sinn und Form*, vol. 19, no. 1, 1967, pp. 235–69.
Müller, Heiner. Interview. *Theater heute*, no. 1, January 1984, pp. 61–62.
———. *Rotwelsch*. Berlin: Merve, 1982.
Nadal-Melsió, Sara. "Georg Lukács: Magus Realismus?" *Diacritics*, vol. 34, no. 2, Summer 2004, pp. 62–84.
Resch, Margit. *Understanding Christa Wolf: Returning Home to a Foreign Land*. Columbia, SC: University of South Carolina Press, 1997.
Wolf, Christa. "Brecht and Others." *The Reader and the Writer: Essays, Sketches, Memories*, translated by Joan Becker. New York: Seven Seas, 1977, pp. 57–59.
———. *City of Angels or, The Overcoat of Dr. Freud*. Translated by Damion Searls. New York: Farrar, Straus and Giroux, 2013.
———. "Conditions of a Narrative: Cassandra." *Cassandra: A Novel and Four Essays*, translated by Jan van Heurck. New York: Farrar, Straus and Giroux, 1984.
———. "Die Dauerspannung beim Schreiben." Conversation with Helmut Böttinger. *Frankfurter Rundschau* (Supplement für Bücher), 22 March 2000.
———. "Ein Gespräch mit Christa und Gerhard Wolf." Henry Schmidt, Christa Wolf, Gerhard Wolf, Helen Fehervary, and Susanne Pongratz. *The German Quarterly*, vol. 57, no. 1, Winter 1984, pp. 95–105.
———. "New Life and Opinions of a Tomcat." *What Remains and Other Stories*, translated by Heike Schwarzbauer. Chicago: University of Chicago Press, 1995.
———. *No Place on Earth*. Translated by Jan van Heurck. New York: Farrar, Straus and Giroux, 1982.
———. *Patterns of Childhood*. Translated by Ursule Molinaro and Hedwig Rappolt. New York: Farrar, Straus and Giroux, 1980.
———. *The Quest for Christa T*. Translated by Christopher Middleton, New York: Farrar, Straus and Giroux, 1970.
———. "The Reader and the Writer." *The Reader and the Writer: Essays, Sketches, Memories*, translated by Joan Becker. New York: International/Berlin: Seven Seas, 1977, pp. 177–212.
———. "*Sei dennoch unverzagt*": *Gespräche mit meinen Großeltern Christa und Gerhard Wolf*. Edited by Jana Simon. Berlin: Ullstein, 2015.
———. "Subjective Authenticity: A Conversation with Hans Kaufmann," translated by Hilary Pilkington. *Responses to Christa Wolf: Critical Essays*, edited by Marilyn Sibley Fries. Detroit, MI: Wayne State University Press, 1989, pp. 55–75.

———. *They Divided the Sky*. Translated by Luise von Flotow. Ottawa: University of Ottawa Press, 2013.

———. *What Remains and Other Stories*. Translated by Helke Schwarzbauer and Rick Takvorian, New York: Farrar, Straus, and Giroux, 1993.

PART III

Christa Wolf in the Public Sphere

CHAPTER 8

To Be Recognized Again
Memory, Amnesia, and Sincerity in Christa Wolf

CHRISTINE KANZ

Ultimate proof came from the funeral and subsequent ceremony for Christa Wolf, who had died on 1 December 2011 in Berlin: the non-presence of many prominent intellectuals, politicians, and colleagues from the West—with the exception of Günter Grass—was striking. On this day it became more than obvious: the Wall between East and West Germany had not really fallen, at least not on an attitudinal or emotional level. Peter Schneider's 1982 formulation "die Mauer im Kopf" ("the Wall in our heads") still rang true.[1] After the fall of the Berlin Wall, most East Germans and West Germans continued to identify themselves as such. Seeking reasons, one encounters a whole array of what still seem to be rather different characteristic features of eastern and western German daily life, behavior, and writing practices. Even writers who decided to leave the GDR before 1989, such as Monika Maron, are sometimes talked about as GDR writers, and critics tend to look for a certain "Nähe" (spiritual closeness) among them, although their completely different biographies and political views are well known.[2] All in all, it is simply not true that since 1989–90 there is again just *one* German literature. That "Nähe" would seem to exist primarily as wishful thinking, constructed by media, performances, and public lectures, most of them shaped by a specifically western German perspective.

Especially after 1989, this perspective also shaped the image of Christa Wolf. During the last two decades of her life, the once internationally celebrated author (among other writers such as Stephan Hermlin) was accused of having written a sort of "autoritätsgläubige 'Stillhalteliteratur'" (Anz 8), a conformist, quiescent literature, under the GDR regime and then of having acted like a Stasi victim—or even a dissident—right after the collapse of the system, despite the fact that for a short time, very early in her career, she had cooperated with the Stasi as a so-called IM, an *informelle Mitarbeiterin*, an informer. This response was particularly true in the many negative reactions, especially from western critics, to her work *What Remains* (*Was bleibt*, 1990).

Given this background and the changed attitude toward Christa Wolf, both as a person and as a writer, in the wake of the so-called "Literaturstreit" (the literary controversy about the publication of *What Remains* in the early 1990s), and the subsequent defamation campaign against her as a former Stasi informer (IM), how do we read her texts today? How are her once recognized masterpieces, written and published before 1989, such as *The Quest for Christa T.* (*Nachdenken über Christa T.*, 1968) or *Cassandra* (1983) now received? And what of her more recent texts, written after the fall of the Wall, such as *In the Flesh* (*Leibhaftig*, 2002) and *City of Angels or, The Overcoat of Dr. Freud* (*Stadt der Engel oder The Overcoat of Dr. Freud*, 2010)? Did her death again affect attitudes toward her as a writer?

In what follows I would like to draw attention to representations of sincerity in Christa Wolf's texts, to her credibility as an author, and to the role attributed to her as a moral authority, for many readers and for many years. "Everything we express must be the truth because we feel it: there you have my confession of faith as a poet," Wolf's Günderrode says in *No Place on Earth* (*Kein Ort. Nirgends* 35). Much the same can be said of Wolf's own writing: language for her functioned as a marker of sincerity, that is, speaking and writing in a genuine, serious, and honest way. A "true" voice in Wolf's perspective is one which speaks primarily on the basis of personal experience, feelings, and convictions. In what follows, I want to examine the link between "sincerity" (in German: *Lauterkeit, Ernsthaftigkeit, Aufrichtigkeit*) and the "true" voice of the author's and narrator's own experience. In distinguishing between Wolf's texts written before 1989 and those written after the fall of the Berlin Wall and after the "Literaturstreit," such as *Medea* (1996) and *In the Flesh* (*Leibhaftig*, 2002), I want to focus on the historical context in order to define the parameters of the term "experience." In allowing her protagonists to speak critically with a "true" voice, Wolf did not shy away from representing affects that were viewed negatively (because of their critical or—in the eyes of the regime—even destructive potential). While offering some interpretations of the representation of fear and mourning in her texts, I will finally demonstrate how all this relates to the "fallen integrity" of former "IM Margarete," that is, Christa Wolf, which was proclaimed in the media in the early 1990s—and is still being invoked, even after her death (Krumbholz).

The Quest for Christa T. depicts a female character who dies of leukemia and whose sensitivity the narrator contrasts with the superficiality of the "Up-and-doing people," the "Factual People," the "people without imagination" (51), who cause confusion and fear in Christa T. Here it is the narrator who describes the protagonist's "inclination to write poems, to tighten the structures, make resistant the beautiful, bright, and firm world that should be for her" (20), since writing poems is "'dichten,' *condensare*, make dense, tighten; language helps" (16). In these reflections on Christa T., it becomes obvious that for both the first-person narrator and her late friend Christa T., language and writing are the only means available to them to counter confusion and fear. In *Cassandra* (1983), by contrast, it is the female protagonist herself whose memories and reflections address the contradictions within her daily life between individual desire and claims of the collective. "Liberation" from her fear also entails a struggle to become a subject with its own history. Instead of remaining silent like a "normal" woman, Cassandra prophesizes incidents that turn out to be true. She realizes: "It occurs to me that secretly I am tracking the story of my fear. Or more precisely, the story of its unbridling, more precisely still: of its setting free" (35). Cassandra's "Unkenrufe" (prophecies of doom) set her own story of *Angst* in motion: her dark words cause fear among the men around her. Consequently, she is punished for her words by being diagnosed as insane.[3]

In Cassandra's view, disease is caused by suppressed affects; she speaks, for example, of "what cunning compacts link illness to suppressed manifestation" (39). Thus, she seeks to express her emotions, including fear and rage. Her convulsed body becomes a sort of seismograph, performing truthfulness and sincerity, and conveying *Angst*, thereby producing her own history of *Angst*. This concept of the body as a medium of "authenticity" (Köhler) is connected to the "New Subjectivity"[4] that emerged in German literature of the 1970s and early 1980s. We need to remember that *Angst* in the eyes of the Enlightenment, but also under the GDR system, was seen as a counterproductive force, which was to be rejected, even suppressed. Hence, Cassandra's language of *Angst* becomes her expression of protest.

Because of such depictions, Wolf was long regarded as a writer who stood for truthfulness and personal integrity. The media uproar ("Literaturstreit") following the publication of her story *What Remains* in early June 1990 could only take on such enormous significance because she was—and for some readers and supporters *remains*—the embodiment of integrity and credibility. It is also true, however, that even many of her most devoted followers were disappointed when it came to seem possible that the belated publication of this story could have been a calculated attempt to stage herself as a victim of the GDR system.

Many readers may remember what happened: at the beginning of June 1990, the publication of *What Remains*, written in 1979 and slightly revised in 1989, caused one of the biggest German literary scandals of the second half of the twentieth century. It started in the West, where the feuilleton sections of newspapers and magazines, such as the *Frankfurter Allgemeine Zeitung*, *Die Zeit*, and *Der Spiegel*, published sharp attacks on Wolf, which were soon followed by attacks in the French media, other European journals, and even US papers such as the *New York Times* (Anz 7–9).⁵

Why did Christa Wolf's description of a day in the life of a woman writer living in the former GDR generate such negative reactions? The protagonist bears striking similarities to Christa Wolf herself. The text is constructed through self-interviews and monologues by the protagonist, who torments herself with self-critical questioning. The uncomfortable realization of being watched incessantly by three Stasi officers is part of her daily experience and gives rise to fear and anger, feelings that need to find some form of expression. They are sublimated in literature, which functions as a sort of shield against conditions that otherwise would be unbearable, but "Die Gedanken sind frei" (thoughts are free)—thus the title of one of the numerous folk and revolutionary songs revived by GDR civil rights groups. It is thus no coincidence that *What Remains* starts with the words "DON'T PANIC," and in what follows we learn about the numerous anxieties of the protagonist (7).

Once more, it becomes evident that for Wolf the literary articulation of *Angst* and mourning was a means to hold onto or, better, to maintain a sense of humanity. We can see a narratological pattern here: according to Wolf ("Conditions of a Narrative" 305), it is the writer's task to articulate such issues and to express grief, anger, and fear in order to bring about change. Of course, the public representation of "negative" feelings offended against the East German political imperative to be a merry and optimistic socialist. Instead of being seen as encouraging and supporting the new, ideal socialist society, such representations were regarded as "Schwarzmalerei" (doom-mongering). These more or less veiled, between-the-lines descriptions of contradictions, weaknesses, and injustice within the socialist system were, of course, a major reason why Wolf had so many followers in both East and West Germany, although few among those in power in the East.

Thomas Anz, together with several students, edited an anthology of documents that appeared following the publication of *What Remains*. According to him, the public furor in 1990 merely provided a welcome opening for some intellectuals to comment publicly on the political incidents preceding the fall of the Wall and their consequences for contemporary German literature; it was not, in Anz's estimation, about Christa Wolf herself. For this reason, the volume was entitled *Es geht nicht um Christa Wolf* (It's not about Christa Wolf).⁶ Wolf, however, refused to write a contribution, although she did later comment on it, on several occasions. She considered herself the victim of a "Hetzkampagne" (smear campaign; Anz 239), who suffered under accusations of engendering a "deutsche Gesinnungsästhetik" (aesthetics based on political convictions), a formulation used by Ulrich Greiner in *Die Zeit*. Wolf's famous speech in East Berlin's Erlöserkirche on 28 October 1989 ended as follows:

We need to examine our own "Difficulties with the Truth." We will see that we, too, have cause for shame and contrition. Let's not deceive ourselves: until the renewal (reform) of our society has penetrated to the depths of self-questioning and self-criticism in every individual it will remain merely responsive to external symptoms, capable of abuse, and endangered. ("Wider den Schlaf der Vernunft" 99)[7]

Anz, too, stresses Wolf's popular reputation for truthfulness and sincerity (25), as a writer whose literary aesthetic was linked to morality and integrity. She had been honored, not because she *represented* the GDR state, but in part because, after the 1970s, she was in constant inner *conflict* with this state, whose founding utopia—the creation of a humane socialist society—she had wholeheartedly supported as the political intellectual that she definitely was. This permanent inner conflict can be discerned between the lines in each of her major novels, from *The Quest for Christa T.* (1968) to *City of Angels*. Against this background, the accusations that were initially raised in June 1990 had a devastating effect on Christa Wolf. Long recognized as a moral authority, she was suddenly the center of a scandal.

Worse, however, was yet to come. Two years later, Wolf lost still more credibility with her critics when she published a brief notice disclosing her early activities as an IM in the *Berliner Zeitung*. The brief period of cooperation, she asserted, was something she had simply "forgotten" and was only reminded of when given the chance to see the slim entries regarding her activity as an "IM" in her so-called "perpetrator files" (Vinke 11).

Wolf's long pursuit of truth did not, apparently, preclude self-deception or amnesia. Her short time as a Stasi informer, when she was a thirty-year-old enthusiastic, but naive socialist, is reflected in a single note, written in her own hand, that contained innocuous information on a colleague, who subsequently accepted Wolf's belated apology and publicly defended her against the media defamation that once again ensued. The file also contained a few irrelevant reports on her meetings with other colleagues, reports which were not written by Wolf, but by Stasi agents. If one wishes to put the relationship between her and the Stasi into proper perspective, the modest scope of these reports must be contrasted with the vast number of spying reports that were maintained on Wolf and her husband, Gerhard Wolf. Even after her death, not everyone held her in positive regard, as demonstrated by the divided or simply absent media echo in the days that followed. After the posthumous publication of her short story "August" (2012) and the continuation of her autobiographical journal, *Ein Tag im Jahr im neuen Jahrhundert 2001–2011* (One Day a Year in the New Century, 2013), the tone regarding Wolf seems to have become more respectful again, especially in comparison with the treatment of her contemporaries Martin Walser and the late Günter Grass, who have endured criticism for superficiality, narcissism, and even worse "sins" in their writing (see Krause).

City of Angels or, The Overcoat of Dr. Freud describes that defamation and the hurt it caused during her "Exil auf Zeit," her temporary exile at the Getty Research Institute in Santa Monica, near Los Angeles, in 1992–93. Overwhelmed by feelings of shame and pain for having forgotten about her IM activities, she struggled to understand who the person was that she had been more than thirty years earlier and what the reasons were for her selective amnesia. The question of whether and why such amnesia *can* happen is central to this text. However, there is no easy answer, and the book is no easy read, despite some light-hearted and even humorous descriptions of daily life in Los Angeles.

Wolf had also revisited her past in *Medea* (1996), a novel which was noticeably devoid of any humor. Centered on a female outcast, the book could be read on one level as a reckoning with the media protagonists of the literary debate surrounding *What Remains* in 1990. As she had done in *Cassandra*, Wolf was here reinterpreting myth, transposing the story of the child-murderess Medea into that of a woman who is incapable of killing her own children, but who is seen by people around her as terrifying, uncivilized, and wild. In reading this book, it becomes clear that Medea's extraordinary integrity, her honesty, and her wisdom are what actually arouse suspicions in the people around her. Moreover, she knows the truth of Corinth, which had been founded on a crime. Many reviews listed the obvious parallels between Medea and the author herself, and Wolf was criticized for having written whiny, weepy, lachrymose *Sündenbock* (scapegoat) prose. While the aesthetic complexity of this polyvocal text has so far been widely overlooked, one central sentence likewise did not receive much public attention: Medea's insight "that we can't deal with the fragments of the past any way we like, piecing them together or ripping them apart to suit our convenience" (76). Clearly, this passage reads as one of the many self-accusations found throughout Wolf's work.

Wolf's 2002 novel *Leibhaftig* (*In the Flesh*) can be understood as a reflection on the downfall of the GDR system and the *Wende*—a word she actually refused to use without quotation marks, because she criticized this metaphor as misleading (in the sense of suggesting a complete turnaround), or as turning only to the western German perspective.[8] When the female protagonist of the novel falls seriously ill and almost dies, she thinks back on the important periods in her life. We learn about her dreams and participate in her feverish fantasies. This time, critics diagnosed a parallel between the dying protagonist and the slow decay of socialism.[9] The most striking passage, however, which actually makes this parallel obvious, perhaps too obvious, occurs when the patient urges her doctors to find the root of all that has befallen her. They should get to the "roots," she asserts, "to the very thing, the realm of roots." Again, we are confronted with the depiction of an intense urge for the truth, but this time a truth interwoven with deception or self-deception in a complex accretion, "the moment in which every mask, every disguise falls away and nothing remains but the naked truth, which, of course, is called suffering" (49).

This longing for truth, combined with relentless self-examination, is also discernable in Wolf's essays from the early 2000s, published in 2006 as *Der Worte Adernetz* (Arterial Net or Words). One of them describes a dinner conversation with her husband and friends. The narrator selects a few words that she finds most essential for imagining and describing a humane society. Today, she claims, such words have disappeared. The words are: honest, righteous, incorruptible, truthful, kind, loving, and vulnerable ("Kenntlich werden" 15, my translation).

Evidence for Wolf's relentless pursuit of truth and the humane is extensive. It is part of her self-representation to let us participate in this search by performing the longing for integrity and truthfulness in the form of insistent and permanent self-questioning. In reading her texts, it becomes clear that emotions, including negative affects, such as *Angst* and mourning, belong to the humane and indeed often stand in for truthfulness and sincerity (see Kanz 94). Wolf insists on every person's right to mourn. Mourning, however, was an implicitly forbidden emotion in the former GDR, and remained so in its "undead" afterlife during the unification process when one was supposed to be happy and enthusiastic about the dramatic changes at hand. In an essay on Nelly Sachs ("... der Worte Adernetz" 93), Wolf resentfully uses the word that most characterizes today's Germany: *Spaßkultur* (fun-loving culture). For her, the *Spaßgesellschaft* (hedonistic, good-time society), with Nazi symbols scrawled on walls, had lost its humane potential. In her above-mentioned biographical essay on the conversation with friends, Wolf and her friends ask themselves how to counter the irrational hatred of everything unknown and strange and how to keep or regain the humane. Is it possible at all? Wolf articulates her hope that it is possible, stating that, "As an antidote to crazy delusions to which I subjected my own body, I recall names of writers, titles of books, fates of literary figures" ("Kenntlich werden" 13).

As I suggested at the beginning of this chapter, the media uproar surrounding the publication of *What Remains* could only take on such enormous dimensions because Wolf was a writer who had always advocated the principle of integrity and who enjoyed high regard as a trustworthy moral voice. Thus, the publication of this story, especially its timing, led many critics to again call into question her reputation and credibility. The image of Christa Wolf as a moral authority began to crumble, even among many of her most loyal supporters, and it was further damaged when her IM activities were revealed.

However, and in this I agree with Thomas Anz, the larger context here is that this debate offered the very first possibility after 1989 to discuss important differences between East and West German writers. Moreover, there was a certain pressure to come to terms with a repressive regime, at least *this* time.

Thinking of Günter Grass's own revelations, made first in an interview on 11 August 2006 ("Ich war Mitglied"), and in his autobiographical work, *Peeling the Onion* (*Beim Häuten der Zwiebel*, 2006), one is confronted with a parallel case, this time not in the German Democratic Republic, but in the Federal Republic of Germany: the 1999 Nobel Prize winner divulged for the first time that he had been a member of the *Waffen-SS*, out of youthful naiveté ("aus jugendlicher Naivität") ("Ich war Mitglied"), while only seventeen years old in 1944. Had he forgotten about it, perhaps like Wolf suffering from some kind of amnesia? Or was it rather shame that had silenced him— he, who had always been one of the most outspoken advocates for morality, integrity, and humanism in the Federal Republic of Germany throughout the postwar period? In a *Spiegel* interview he stresses the burden ("die Last") of his silence and the sense of guilt ("Schuldgefühl") that had oppressed him over the years. But why then did he only make this disclosure so late, why wait for so long? Only Grass himself, if anyone, could attempt an answer to such difficult questions; indeed, he tried, asserting that he had dealt with it through his writing, but that this taint ("Makel") had always remained. Whatever remained—in his case, the final disclosure—promised a certain sense of relief. To Grass, the memoir seemed the best outlet for such a revelation, which, however, in the eyes of many, even further legitimized criticism of him as a fallen model of integrity.

Numerous intellectuals and writers in Germany, particularly those of the older generation, still must confront accusations, from others as well as from themselves, of never having really dealt with their Nazi past. This time, in the controversy concerning Christa Wolf, they found their opportunity to deal with that most burdensome past. In doing so, however, it was not Christa Wolf's past that mattered, but their own de- or reconstructions of truth.

Christine Kanz (M.A. 1994, Dr. phil. 1998; "venia legendi"/habilitation 2008) is Professor for Modern German Literature at the University of Education in Linz and a Visiting Professor for German Literature at Ghent University. She has taught modern German and European literature and culture at universities in the United States, Germany, Austria, Switzerland, and South Africa. In 2015 she was awarded the Klara Marie Faßbinder Guest Professorship for Women and Gender Studies of the universities in Rheinland-Palatinate. The holder of fellowships and stipends from the Alexander von Humboldt Foundation, the Swiss National Science Foundation, and the DAAD, she is the editor of several books and author of two monographs: *Angst und Geschlechterdifferenzen: Ingeborg Bachmanns "Todesarten-Projekt" in Kontexten der Gegenwartsliteratur* (1999) and *Maternale Moderne: Männliche Gebärphantasien zwischen Kultur und Wissenschaft, 1890–1933* (2009). Her research interests include European literature since the eighteenth century with an emphasis on European avant-gardes; postwar and contemporary literature, culture, and art; the history of knowledge formations; history and theory of emotions; gender and family studies; and ecocriticism.

Notes

This essay is a slightly revised and longer version of Christine Kanz: "To Be Recognized Again: Christa Wolf's Paradigm of Sincerity." *German Studies Review* 36.2 (2013), 373–379. It is based on a talk delivered at the German Studies Association Annual Conference in Milwaukee, Wisconsin, October 2012.

1. "It will take us longer to tear down the Wall in our heads than any wrecking company will need for the Wall we can see" (Schneider, *The Wall Jumper* 119).
2. See, for example, Hage, "Deutschland im Herbst."
3. Medea had known of three penalties awaiting her should she revolt against societal norms: "Priam the king had three devices against a disobedient daughter: He could declare her insane. He could lock her up. He could force her into an unwanted marriage" (Wolf, *Cassandra* 78–79).
4. This literary movement of the 1970s focused mainly on the writer's own inner life, including autobiographical details, such as dreams, relationships, diseases, or feelings. Peter Schneider's *Lenz* (1973) and Karin Struck's *Klassenliebe* (1973) are often cited as prototypical examples of this "Neue Subjektivität" (New Subjectivity). The term was coined by the literary critic Marcel Reich-Ranicki, who clearly regarded it as the opposite of the "New Objectivity" movement in literature of the 1920s.
5. Compare, for example, Binder, Graves, and Buruma.
6. The quotation comes from German dissident poet and songwriter Wolf Biermann, in his contribution to the debate.
7. Wolf's remarks regarding her own difficulties with the truth are an allusion to Walter Janka's memoir, published in October 1989, under the title *Schwierigkeiten mit der Wahrheit* (Difficulties with the Truth). Janka, a German Communist, political activist, and writer who became a publisher (Aufbau-Verlag), spent much of his life as a political prisoner, first during the Nazi regime and again in the GDR. His was one of the more prominently discussed cases after the fall of the Wall.
8. "The word 'turning point' (Wende) is one I have problems with. It makes me picture a sailboat when the wind turns. The captain calls out a warning and the crew duck down while the boom sweeps across the deck. Is this an accurate picture of what is happening? Does it apply to us, in this situation which every day moves on to something new? I would rather speak in terms of a 'revolutionary revival.' Revolutions start at the bottom" (Christa Wolf in her public speech at the demonstration on 4 November 1989, "The Language of the Turning Point" 316).
9. See, for instance, Hage, "Auf Leben und Tod" 199; or Maus.

Bibliography

Anz, Thomas, editor. *"Es geht nicht um Christa Wolf": Der Literaturstreit im vereinten Deutschland*. Munich: edition Spangenberg, 1991.
Biermann, Wolf. "Nur wer sich ändert, bleibt sich treu. Der Streit um Christa Wolf, das Ende der DDR, das Elend der Intellektuellen: Das alles ist auch komisch." *Die Zeit*, 24 August 1990.
Binder, David. "Despite All, German Literati Keep Jousting." *New York Times*, 24 August 1990.
Buruma, Ian. "There's No Place Like Heimat." *The New York Review of Books*, vol. 37, no. 20, 20 December 1990.
Grass, Günter. *Beim Häuten der Zwiebel*. Göttingen: Steidl Verlag, 2006.
———. "Ich war Mitglied der Waffen-SS." *Der Spiegel*, 11 August 2006.
Graves, Peter. "Not above Reproach." *Times Literary Supplement*, 24–30 August 1990.
Greiner, Ulrich. "Die deutsche Gesinnungsästhetik: Noch einmal: Christa Wolf und der deutsche Literaturstreit." *Die Zeit*, 2 November 1990, cited in Anz, *"Es geht nicht um Christa Wolf"* 208–16.
Hage, Volker. "Auf Leben und Tod." *Der Spiegel*, 18 February 2002, pp. 198–200.
———. "Deutschland im Herbst." *Der Spiegel*, 21September 2002. http://www.spiegel.de/spiegel/print/d-25211861.html.
Janka, Walter. *Schwierigkeiten mit der Wahrheit*. Berlin: Rowohlt, 1989.
Kanz, Christine. *Angst und Geschlechterdifferenzen: Ingeborg Bachmanns "Todesarten"-Projekt in Kontexten der Gegenwartsliteratur*. Stuttgart: Verlag J.B. Metzler, 1999.
Kaufmann, Walter. "Leserbrief an den Spiegel." *Akteneinsicht Christa Wolf: Zerrspiegel und Dialog. Eine Dokumentation*, edited by Hermann Vinke. Hamburg: Luchterhand Literaturverlag, 1993, p. 158.
Köhler, Andrea. "Reisender Schnee oder Realismus ohne Resignation. Die deutschsprachige Literatur und das 'Authentische'." *Neue Zürcher Zeitung*, 30 November/1 December 1996, pp. 49–50.
Krause, Tilman. "Christa Wolf dokumentiert ihr Verlöschen." *Die Welt*, 8 March 2013. http://www.welt.de/kultur/literarischewelt/article114252616.
Krumbholz, Martin. "'Wir müssen gross von uns denken': Zum Tod von Christa Wolf." *Neue Zürcher Zeitung*, 1 December 2011. http://www.nzz.ch/aktuell/feuilleton/literatur/wir-muessen-gross-von-uns-denken-1.13479995.
Maus, Stephan. "Kassandra im Kernspintomographen: Christa Wolfs Erzählung *Leibhaftig*." *Frankfurter Rundschau*, 20 March 2002.
Schneider, Peter. *Lenz*. Berlin: Rotbuch Verlag, 1973.
———. *The Wall Jumper: A Berlin Story*. Translated by Leigh Hafrey, 2nd edition. Chicago: University of Chicago Press, 1998.
Struck, Karin. *Klassenliebe*. Frankfurt a.M.: Suhrkamp Verlag, 1973.
Vinke, Hermann, editor. *Akteneinsicht Christa Wolf: Zerrspiegel und Dialog. Eine Dokumentation*. Hamburg: Luchterhand Literaturverlag, 1993.
Wolf, Christa. "August." *Erzählungen*. Berlin: Suhrkamp Verlag, 2014.
———. "Eine Auskunft." *Berliner Zeitung*, 21 January 1993.

———. "Cassandra." *Cassandra: A Novel and Four Essays*, translated by Jan van Heurck. New York: Farrar, Straus and Giroux, 1984, pp. 3–138.

———. *City of Angels*. Translated by Damion Searls. New York: Farrar, Straus and Giroux, 2013.

———. "Conditions of a Narrative: Cassandra." *Cassandra: A Novel and Four Essays*, translated by Jan van Heurck. New York: Farrar, Straus and Giroux, 1984, pp. 141–305.

———. *In the Flesh*. Translated by John S. Barrett. Boston: David R. Godine, 2005.

———. *Kassandra*. Darmstadt: Luchterhand Literaturverlag, 1983.

———. *Kein Ort. Nirgends*. 6th edition. Darmstadt: Luchterhand Literaturverlag, 1983.

———. "Kenntlich werden: Vorwort." *Der Worte Adernetz: Essays und Reden*. Frankfurt a.M.: Suhrkamp Verlag, 2006, pp. 9–24.

———. *Kindheitsmuster*. Halle: Mitteldeutscher Verlag, 1976.

———. "The Language of the Turning Point." Translated by Jan van Heurck. *The Author's Dimension: Selected Essays*, edited by Alexander Stephan. New York: Farrar, Straus and Giroux, 1993, pp. 316–18.

———. *Leibhaftig*. Munich: Luchterhand Literaturverlag, 2002.

———. *Medea: A Modern Retelling*. Translated by John Cullen. New York: Doubleday, 1998.

———. *Medea*: Stimmen. Munich: Luchterhand Literaturverlag, 1996.

———. *Nachdenken über Christa T*. Halle: Mitteldeutscher Verlag, 1968.

———. *The Quest for Christa T*. Translated by Christopher Middleton. New York: Farrar, Straus and Giroux, 1970.

———. "Sprache der Wende: Rede auf dem Alexanderplatz." *Christa Wolf im Dialog*. Munich: Luchterhand Literaturverlag, 1990, pp. 119–21.

———. *Stadt der Engel oder The Overcoat of Dr. Freud*. Berlin: Suhrkamp Verlag, 2010.

———. *Ein Tag im Jahr im neuen Jahrhundert 2001–2011*. Berlin: Suhrkamp Verlag, 2014.

———. *Voraussetzungen eines Romans: Kassandra*. Frankfurt a.M.: Suhrkamp Verlag, 2008.

———. *Was bleibt*. Berlin: Aufbau-Verlag, 1990.

———. "What Remains." *What Remains and Other Stories*, translated by Heike Schwarzbauer and Rick Takvorian. New York: Farrar, Straus and Giroux, 1993, pp. 231–95.

———. "Wider den Schlaf der Vernunft." *Reden im Herbst*. Berlin: Aufbau-Verlag, 1990, pp. 98–100.

———. *Der Worte Adernetz: Essays und Reden*. Frankfurt a.M.: Suhrkamp Verlag, 2006

———. "… der Worte Adernetz: Nelly Sachs heute lesen." *Der Worte Adernetz: Essays und Reden*. Frankfurt a.M.: Suhrkamp Verlag, 2006, pp. 83–94.

CHAPTER 9

"Was bleibet aber, stiften die Dichter"
Christa Wolf's Contested Role as Spokesperson for Generations of Readers and Women Writers

JANINE LUDWIG

The frequently acknowledged cultural and political influence of Christa Wolf—both as a person and with her works—in the GDR and beyond is difficult to describe or even assess with any precision. Yet it is important to recognize the different roles that she played as a widely recognized "voice" of her times, beginning with her influence on East German readers, that is, with status attributed to her as a "spokesperson," a public intellectual, and moral instance; then with her importance for the emergence of feminist thought in East Germany, particularly in literature by women writers; and finally, through her prominent role in the peaceful revolution of 1989. I propose to examine some of the challenges to Wolf's special role as a public intellectual that arose in the German-German literary controversy ("Literaturstreit") of 1990 and to offer some observations about her legacy.

Wolf as Moral Authority

Christa Wolf's prominence as a moral authority for readers in the GDR—and as a voice heard by audiences in Western countries as well—offers an almost prototypical example of the role of the writer/intellectual in the GDR. To a historically unique extent, the ruling elite of the GDR sought to incorporate artists, especially writers, into a political agenda for shaping a new, socialist society. To this end, they offered writers a prominent role as "educators" of the people and explicitly urged them to bring their art into the service of shaping new human beings ("den neuen Menschen") and the ideal socialist human community ("sozialistische Menschengemeinschaft"). In short, GDR cultural politics encouraged an *engaged literature* and, to this end, also promoted and nurtured selected, young, and talented writers.

This concept of intellect and power ("Geist und Macht") working hand-in-hand towards a common goal, a new and "better" German country, was even described in military terms, as when Walter Ulbricht demanded to mold literature and art "into a powerful weapon in our struggle for solutions to challenges we face as a nation" ("zu einer mächtigen Waffe unseres Volkes im Kampf um die Lösung unserer Lebensfragen zu gestalten," Ulbricht 239, trans. ed.).[1] We should recall that originally Christa Wolf and many other GDR writers were indeed willing to function as "brothers in arms" for the education of the people.

By the mid-1960s, however, it became evident how greatly understandings of this "cooperation" and of *engaged literature* diverged: while many writers were often under the false impression that their engagement was welcome as constructive criticism, the party (SED), in keeping with Lenin's *Party Organization and Party Literature* (*Parteiorganisation und Parteiliteratur*, 1905), viewed literature under the "primacy of politics" and demanded unconditional partisanship ("Parteilichkeit")—a concept later popularized by Georg Lukács before his fall from grace due to his involvement in the Hungarian uprising in 1956. At the infamous 11th Plenary Assembly of the party's Central Committee ("11. Plenum des ZK der SED," 16–18 December 1965), the divide between writers and politicians became blatantly obvious. From this point on, some writers' understanding of their role gradually shifted to that of critical educator and conscience of the nation, creating a surrogate public sphere ("Ersatzöffentlichkeit"). Wolf herself described her function as comparable to a "doctor" or "pastor" for the spiritual and mental well-being of the people.[2] Yet, at the same time, these (reform-socialist) writers remained part of the official discourse and cultivated that peculiar position of sitting on the fence, as both official and unofficial voices, a role that David Bathrick analyzes in "Die Intellektuellen und die Macht" (2000).

In this respect, Wolf was prototypical, yet her poetological concept of "subjective authenticity," as described in her essay "Reading and Writing" ("Lesen und Schreiben," 1968), was *sui generis* and highly influential in the development of GDR literature. Her poetology owed much to her role model Anna Seghers, who had reacted to the Soviet "Expressionism Debate" of the 1930s by defending the subjective element in literature, in pointed disagreement with Georg Lukács (the debate was reincarnated as the "Formalism Debate" in the GDR in the early 1950s). In her famous correspondence with Lukács (1938), Seghers defended writers of crisis, such as Kleist, Hölderlin, Lenz, and the Romantics in general—whom Lukács had criticized; he preferred the harmonious quality of German Classicism instead, following Goethe's characterization of the Classics as healthy vs. the Romantics as sick (Lukács/Seghers 345f.). She argued that crisis-driven writing was always a logical consequence of transition periods and that the GDR after World War II was itself in such a period.[3] In consequence, she was much more open to new approaches and formal experiments and less dogmatic than Lukács, especially in her understanding of realism. For instance, she turned Maxim Gorky's complaint about the writer no longer offering a complete mirroring of the world, but merely a splinter (Lukács/ Seghers 357f.), into a positive notion, valorizing the fragmented, subjective world view over the Classical aim of totality:

> Well, what kind of "mirrors" did we have during the War and afterwards when we grew up? ... We would much rather have splinters that just show some fragment of our own world authentically than all the pseudo-mirrors. (Lukács/Seghers 365, my translation)

In the same vein, Christa Wolf became a forerunner in the rediscovery and re-evaluation of the Romantic period, which was frowned upon in the official literary discourse of the GDR. Her famous book, *No Place on Earth* (*Kein Ort. Nirgends*, 1979) was read as a juxtaposition of Classicism and Romanticism, with its main characters Kleist and Günderrode standing for the latter in their emotionally tense situation as outsiders in society. At the same time, many GDR intellectuals, who as individuals and with their ideas of utopia (no-place) had come up against the walls of the GDR system after the Biermann expatriation, could find themselves in both figures. Wolf continued her examination of Romanticism in public, for example in an interview with Frauke Meyer-Gosau in 1982, which was then included in a larger 1985 collection entitled *Ins Ungebundene gehet eine Sehnsucht: Gesprächsraum [Projektionsraum] Romantik* (A Desire Goes into the Unbound: Projection Space Romanticism).

In "Reading and Writing," she not only *en passant* refutes Lukács' reflection theory ("Widerspiegelungstheorie"):

> Let's let mirrors do what they were made to do: to mirror. That's all they can do. Literature and reality do not stand to each other in the relation of mirror to what is mirrored. They are fused within the mind of the writer. The writer, you see, is an important person. ("Reading and Writing" 44)[4]

She also explicitly defends the "splintered" or "fragmentary" perspective as *the* adequate narrative position towards the modern world—in which subjective perceptions of crises can best be narrated through psychological and aesthetic self-reflection, laying bare internal aspects of cognition and consciousness—in sum, by interjecting the author-subject between the world and the text. All this meant nothing less than the reintroduction of modernism into GDR literature, in opposition to the narrow definitions of Socialist Realism which were founded on Lukács' theories. The impact of her fiercely contested book *The Quest for Christa T.* (*Nachdenken über Christa T.*, 1968) as her first example of such writing can hardly be overestimated.

Wolf's Importance for East German Feminism and Women's Literature

An unsurprising consequence of Wolf's subjective poetology was the emergence of a female perspective in her writings, which often featured female, mostly first-person narrators. Here I confine myself to some limited remarks, since Wolf's feminist perspective has been widely analyzed by prominent American scholars, such as Anna K. Kuhn, Sara Lennox, Patricia Herminghouse, Christiane Zehl-Romero, and Helen Fehervary. Christa Wolf was especially important for the rise of women's literature in the GDR in the 1970s, since she was the most theoretically informed author, producing not only fiction but also essays and other texts relating to the topic of women as writers. One has to remember that there was not the same kind of women's movement (or theoretical public debate) in the GDR as in the FRG—which was due not only to political suppression by the regime, but also to differing situations in each country. Since women in the GDR had already been granted certain rights that their West German sisters still had to fight for (integration into the workforce, juridical equality, a liberal divorce law, the right to abortion, state-guaranteed child care, among other measures), the "woman question" was officially considered "solved" (Kuhrig and Speigner 19). Thus, it was again left to literature to highlight cultural and psychological aspects that were not necessarily addressed by these political, legal, and economic measures: private, everyday life, especially the spheres of sexuality, love, and family—themes ideally suited for literary treatment.[5]

Christa Wolf not only identified, but also examined theoretically the fallout of the all-too-frequent reduction of emancipation to the aforementioned legal, political, and economic equality of socialist theory and practice. Her influence is readily evident in important books of the 1970s written by other women, often friends of hers: Gerti Tetzner, author of *Karen W.* (1974), was a protégée, who had contacted Wolf in 1965 and sent her manuscripts with a request for advice. Brigitte Reimann (*Franziska Linkerhand*, 1974) was both a dear friend and regular partner in discussion. Wolf's foreword, "In Touch" ("Berührung") for the West German edition (1978) of Maxie Wander's interview protocols *Guten Morgen, du Schöne* (Good Morning, My Pretty One) not only helped to sell the book there, but offered her own perceptive interpretation of the statements of the interviewees towards a conclusion that they had not yet formulated themselves:

> Our society made it possible for women to do what men do; to this they have, predictably, raised the question: What *do* men do? And is that what I really wanted? ... Should women even wish that greater numbers of them be admitted to ... hierarchically functional mechanisms? ("In Touch" 167)

Wolf pursues such questions further in her own writings, as in the story "Selbstversuch" ("Self-Experiment") in *Blitz aus heiterm Himmel* (Bolt from the Blue, 1975), an edited anthology of stories on gender switching. In a medical experiment, the female protagonist is being transformed into a man: "I had to prove my worth as a woman by consenting to become a man" (118). However, after analyzing the effect on her mind of the changes to her body, she decides to cancel the experiment and return to her female self, since the species "man," who cannot love, but merely seeks to organize his world rationally, hierarchically, instrumentally, and cynically, is the one who really needs a sex (or, rather, gender) transformation. In Wolf's subsequent texts, women regularly represent a corrective to men's world, suggesting a more sensitive, peaceful, and communal solidarity as an alternative to streamlined modern industrial societies with their unquestioning faith in technological and scientific progress (note here the influence of Horkheimer and Adorno's *Dialectic of Enlightenment*).

Thus, Christa Wolf extended issues of gender into issues of humankind, introducing a feminist modernism that found deep resonance not only in the GDR, but equally in West Germany, the United States, and elsewhere. However, criticism was not lacking. The question arose whether Wolf's all-too-positive views of female qualities, tending towards "cultural feminism," could be upheld. Did Wolf, in her juxtaposition of (good) female and (bad) male attributes, perpetuate a fatal dichotomy that for thousands of years has assigned opposite qualities to women and men, such as: emotion vs. rationality, sensitivity or instinct vs. reason, body vs. mind, and nature vs. culture? Since such dichotomies have served to stigmatize, pathologize, and repress women, it is doubtful whether it would suffice to just exchange the valences of positive and negative. In Wolf's defense, it should be noted, she considered destabilizing these oppositions by feminizing the male world (for example, Anchises in *Kassandra*). Yet it is never quite clear in her texts whether these purported gender differences are somehow assumed to be "natural," that is, inevitable or, rather, culturally constructed and interdependently recreated time and again. Nor is it certain that Wolf's utopian vision of a community united in sisterhood (which is, by the way, another version of the socialist utopia) is not overly idealistic.

Clearly, this topic deserves a much more differentiated examination than can be accomplished here (and it would need to include, among other works, Irmtraud Morgner's *Trobadora Beatriz*, 1974), as well as contextualization in terms of more recent feminist theory). Nonetheless, Wolf's general critique of present-day technological societies, which bears truth for former Eastern and current Western industrial states alike, remains as valid as her quest for a more peaceful world remains unresolved.

Wolf's Influence on Fellow Women Writers

Christa Wolf was known as an extraordinarily open and sympathetic person, praised for her ability to listen and thus allow for unusually intimate discussions.[6] With her personal integrity underlying the authenticity of her writing,[7] she became an important role model for other GDR women writers, both as a person and as an author. She was on friendly terms with many well-known writer colleagues, such as Sarah Kirsch, Maxie Wander, Gerti Tetzner, and especially Brigitte Reimann, who loved her like an older sister and admired her as a literary role model whose approval she sought.[8] Disillusioned after the expatriation of Wolf Biermann (1976) and the subsequent suppression of intellectuals and artists, Wolf and a few friends sought periodic refuge in the countryside where they lived in close proximity to one another and practiced an ideal of sisterhood somewhat reminiscent of the Skamander community in *Kassandra*. Wolf depicts one such shared summer in her story *Sommerstück* (Summer Scenes, 1989), in which many figures are modeled after these friends: Sarah Kirsch (Bella), Maxie and Fred Wander (Steffi and Josef), Helga Schubert[9] (Irene), and Wolf herself (Ellen, the narrator) with her family. Sarah Kirsch, in turn, later preserved that summer in her "chronicle" *Allerlei-Rauh* (Patchwork of Furs,[10] 1988), ending it with a surrender of those ideals. Such intertextual relations were frequent in the close-knit community of GDR literature.

Wolf, however, was not only a friend or sister to writers of her own age, but also became important for writers of the next generation, among them Gabriele Eckart and Daniela Dahn. Dahn was a schoolmate of Wolf's daughter Annette and a member of a literary circle for young readers that the Wolfs held privately, reading Proust, Kafka, and Seghers (Hörnigk 23). When the girls got into political trouble at school for making a wall newspaper during the Prague Spring, the Wolfs defended them, with the result that the headmaster was dismissed, rather than the pupils punished. Dahn remained a close friend of Christa Wolf's until the latter's death. In her touching funeral oration in December 2011, Dahn described how formative this solidarity had been for her future development and what she had learned in that literary circle: "Literature exists ... to give strength to the self" ("Literatur ist ... dazu da, das Ich zu stärken," Dahn 44). She also pointed out that the network "Weiberkreis," which had formed around

Wolf in 1985, had continued to bring women writers together once a month for more than a quarter of a century. Among its members have been Helga Schütz, Daniela Dahn, Gerti Tetzner, Renate Drescher, Helga Königsdorf, Rosemarie Zeplin, Brigitte Burmeister, and Sigrid Damm. Besides literature, the group also discussed GDR politics: they initiated a critical resolution to the GDR Writers Union in mid-September 1989, and on the eve of the event, discussed with Wolf her speech for the famous 4 November demonstration on the Alexanderplatz in Berlin.

Wolf in the Peaceful Revolution of 1989

Many have claimed that GDR intellectuals, with their easier access to the public sphere, helped to pave the way for the peaceful revolution in 1989. Günter de Bruyn, for instance, was "convinced that most notably the influence of Christa Wolf's books on the development of critical thinking in the GDR was massive. ... The reactions to her books that I witnessed were always along the same lines: Finally, someone says how we actually feel" (Pinkerneil and de Bruyn 9).[11] Throughout that autumn of 1989, Wolf played a significant role in the revolutionary process, tirelessly giving speeches and interviews, answering letters, attending meetings:

> People are always coming to me with one request or another or I am going to meetings. For weeks now, I haven't had a minute to myself, except maybe in the evening, but then we watch the news of the day on television. I haven't seen a single movie except documentary films. And for weeks I haven't read a single book, not even a line. It's just completely impossible for me to read literature: it's too painful and also too uninteresting just now. I can't recall that such a thing ever happened in my life up until now. (Wolf, "Schreiben im Zeitbezug," 205, trans. ed.)

Knowing that she could use her reputation to attract public attention, Wolf also co-organized events, such as a reading (together with Heiner Müller) of Walter Janka's autobiographical text *Schwierigkeiten mit der Wahrheit* (Problems with the Truth) at the Deutsches Theater Berlin on 28 October. Janka's report on his show trial in 1956 had not been widely known and thus served now to open people's eyes to the sheer extent of Stalinist repression in the earlier years of the GDR. How important this was is documented in an anthology of the solidarity letters Janka subsequently received from GDR citizens (Eichhorn and Reinhardt). Just one day later, at the artists' demonstration "Wider den Schlaf der Vernunft" (Against the Sleep of Reason) in the Erlöserkirche in Berlin, Wolf and colleagues such as Stefan Heym, Helga Königsdorf, and Christoph Hein all spoke and discussed with the audience their demand for commissions to investigate acts of violence committed by security personnel at the demonstrations of 7 and 8 October. Unsurprisingly, Christa Wolf—whose daughter was among those arrested—was the most prominent figure to take on that task, and she remained fully engaged in it for an entire year.

The leadership of writers and artists in the 1989 revolution or, in other words, the unity of the people and the intelligentsia, reached its zenith on 4 November on Alexanderplatz in Berlin when actors, dramatists, and writers, such as Wolf, Heym, Hein, Müller, and Ulrich Mühe, spoke to half a million people at the biggest free demonstration ever held in the GDR. Subsequently, critics have identified this as the moment at which the intellectuals began to lose touch with the general populace. While many writers saw themselves at the dawn of a renewed socialist experiment, in reality those weeks marked the beginning of the end of the GDR, since people were already heading unstoppably towards German reunification. Just a few weeks later, on 28 November, when Wolf, Braun, Heym, and others initiated the appeal *Für unser Land* (For Our Country; www.ddr89.de/ddr89/texte/land/html), it was already far too late to halt this momentum (even though 1.15 million GDR citizens had signed it).

Easy as it may be to retrospectively call Wolf and her fellow writers naive, the situation at the time was not particularly clear and the dynamics of the movement hardly predictable. Wolf's perspective may have been clouded by the number of letters and requests for support she had received from GDR citizens. Nor is it fair to say, as some critics insinuated, that the writers just *usurped* their role as speakers, ignoring that it was *given* to them by the people. Following Wolf's article "We Don't Know How" ("Das haben wir nicht gelernt") about failed educational policies, GDR readers wrote more than three hundred letters to her, many of which attest to their respect for the writers' moral authority and their hopes that they would continue to offer guidance and leadership:

> Dear Christa Wolf, as a reader of almost all of your books … I pay special attention whenever your voice is raised somewhere in this (or that) world … Because of all these questions and worries, I turn to you. For me, you are in a certain sense also a public sphere ("Sie sind gewissermaßen für mich auch Öffentlichkeit"), people pay attention to you, people hear you! (Gruner 60ff., my translation)
>
> You write: "In those days somebody said to me, we have to save the GDR!" … Then, you have me as your partner! (Gruner 41)
>
> I had actually felt inclined to write to you already in late summer when you were still silent about the wave of refugees in Hungary. I wanted to ask you to publish your opinion on this, since you were the one who came to mind when I

grew frightened by this mass hysteria. I could not have thought of anyone who could have said something about this more clearly, humanely, and convincingly than you. (Gruner 153)

Even high-ranking foreign politicians deemed Wolf important. The Soviet ambassador visited her in Pankow in November, thinking she was "in charge" of the citizen movement and could make sure they would not storm Soviet barracks (Magenau 397). When François Mitterand came to Berlin in December, he met with the Wolfs, Heiner Müller, and Stefan Heym in order to get information on the situation in the GDR (Magenau 399, from his interview protocols with Wolf). Shortly before the first free elections in March 1990, the soon-to-be transitional prime minister Lothar de Maizière told Wolf that the parliamentary group ("Fraktion") of his party (CDU) had decided to offer her the position of State President of the (dying) GDR, an offer that she, however, refused: "Sind Sie des Teufels? Machen Sie das rückgängig!" ("Are you crazy? Take it back!") (Magenau 393, from his interview protocols with Wolf).

What Remains—Relinquishing the Role of Spokesperson

In June 1990, Wolf published her story *What Remains* (*Was bleibt*), which dated back to the years 1976–79 and described the Stasi surveillance she and her husband, Gerhard Wolf, had endured in the aftermath of the Biermann expatriation. Some damning reviews of the book were the opening volleys in the so-called "Literaturstreit." Although this is not the place to rehearse the details of this rather sordid debate,[12] of special interest for our topic is the attack on *engaged literature* in general and on the aforementioned special role of GDR writers as moral instances in particular—the attack summed up by Karl Heinz Bohrer: "An enlightened society doesn't need any high-priest writers" (1016, my translation). In this regard, I want to call attention to just two important encounters of the first-person narrator in *What Remains*, which have been strikingly neglected in the controversy: the first with a young female writer only called "the girl," and the second with a rebellious young audience in her final public reading. In both instances, the narrator, a famous writer (obviously modeled on Wolf herself) openly questions her own role as a moral authority for the young, despite being seen by them in this role.

The girl, a writer who had been expelled from the university and put in prison for one year due to an unspecified political "affair," turns to the narrator in order to show her some of her recent texts. (This girl is modeled on Gabriele Stötzer-Kachold, who had actually sought out Christa Wolf for help and was sentenced to the infamous women's prison Hoheneck for distributing the Biermann petition.) The narrator is impressed with the girl's texts and even more so with her bravery and vitality. She seems relieved, inspired, and proud that young people can master the task that she has still failed to accomplish: "The time has come. The young people are writing it all down" (274). Comparing herself to this young writer reinforces her self-accusation of cowardice: "The girl had not asked small-mindedly: What remains? Nor had she asked how much she would remember when she was old someday" (276).

Jörg Magenau cites Wolf's own account of several readings she held after the Biermann expatriation, often for student groups. She admits that, even though she herself was rather fearful of these discussions, she tried to shield the students from trouble by being more radical than they, since she saw it as her duty to facilitate such conversations (Magenau 323f.). The narrator-writer in *Was bleibt* at first takes the same approach and tries to tone down the young audience's frank questions, but later criticizes her own paternalism (or, rather, maternalism): "They were putting themselves in danger. But what right did I have to think them more stupid than myself? What right did I have to protect them from themselves? … The terrible habit of speaking for others faded away and everyone spoke for themselves" (287, my translation).[13] Christa Wolf thus apparently thought about vacating her position as "spokesperson" for the people and leaving it up to the young to take the lead where she had failed—as early as 1979. Ironically, she was again in a difficult position: on the one hand, she wanted to encourage younger generations to assume leadership in bringing about change and, on the other, she knew that she had the name and reputation to play a leading role in that process—indeed, many people were still asking or expecting her to do so.

It is also important to note that Wolf had already read publicly from the manuscript of her yet unpublished book, *Was bleibt*, in the Berliner Ensemble on 25 and 26 November 1989, while she was still engaged in the process of revising and editing. Yet the West German feuilleton took no notice of it then, or later when a recording of that appearance was aired on GDR television on 4 March 1990.[14] This is peculiar, because Frank Schirrmacher, one of the main "antagonists" in the debate, was convinced that Wolf had manipulated her text in order to present herself as a victim: "Anyone can see that these sentences were written in 1989, not 1979" (87). Yet, as Roswitha Skare has shown in her dissertation, Wolf had made only marginal stylistic adjustments and cuts, while almost all of the text was already fixed in 1979, including the title[15]—which at the time could not have referred to the real dissolution of the GDR, but rather to the insight that the socialist utopia had failed. West German critics could have at least considered that possibility, had they bothered to take notice of this reading amidst the ongoing revolution.[16]

Another incident that was not taken into account took place a few months before the beginning of the so-called "Literaturstreit" at the extraordinary GDR writers congress in March, 1990, where Christa Wolf had publicly declared the "end of the era in which we were often expected to speak on behalf of others—because no other institution would address the contradictions that had torn this country apart and because others would often have paid more dearly than we, had they spoken up" (Wolf, "Heine, die Zensur und wir" 166, my translation). Here again, she indicates her willingness to vacate her position as spokesperson (which, one may speculate, might at times have been more a burden than a joy).

After this hurtful controversy,[17] Wolf went silent and eventually found refuge at the Getty Center in Santa Monica, where she was awarded a fellowship and worked on *Medea—A Modern Retelling* (*Medea. Stimmen*, 1996). In January 1993, when the news of her short-term collaboration with the Stasi (between 1959 and 1962) was about to break, she retreated even more from the public eye and, in a rather historically insensitive remark, claimed that she felt as if she were in "exile" in California.[18] Yet again, Wolf found herself in a conflicted position: while she shunned public appearances in those years, her readers missed her voice. In her eulogy for Wolf, Daniela Dahn claims that she implored her several times "to get involved again and to let her voice, as essential as ever, be heard once more" (Dahn 46, my translation). Indeed, in a German poll conducted by the Allensbach Institute on behalf of *Forbes Magazine* in September 1990, Wolf was still ranked twenty-fifth among the one hundred most influential women in Germany (Lukoschat). And, as it turned out, her (mostly East German) audience again deemed her voice indispensable, since in unified Germany so many felt demeaned as second-class citizens and still respected her as an important figure, whose views they wanted to hear. On 27 February 1994, at her first public appearance since November 1989, hundreds of people tried in vain to get a seat in the long sold-out Semper Opera House in Dresden, where Wolf spoke on the situation in Germany, leading the *Süddeutsche Zeitung* to proclaim "Christa Wolf as a symbol" (Magenau 435). At the Leipzig Book Fair one month later, on her sixty-fifth birthday, hundreds of people again fought for entrance into the venue, shouting the old slogan "Wir sind das Volk" ("We are the people"). Not inconsequentially, her role as a sort of Jeanne d'Arc for the humiliated East of Germany seemed to be her last public appearance as a socialist writer. It is not entirely clear whether it was still her writing or more her persona that seemed to perpetuate the older concepts of "Literatur als Lebenshilfe" (literature as a guide to living), according to a prediction she had made in 1990: "Literature will be called upon to perform the same task it must perform in all times and places: to investigate the blind spots in our past, and to accompany us into our changing future" ("Momentary interruption" 13).

Wolf's literary colleagues continued to stand by her as well, attesting their loyalty in books published upon her sixty-fifth and eightieth birthdays.[19] Many writers such as Annett Gröschner, Kerstin Hensel, Angela Krauß, Brigitte Struzyk, and Elke Erb sent letters and congratulations. Additionally, the young West German writer Tanja Dückers spoke about her first encounter with Wolf's works in school in the 1980s and how honored she felt when asked to give a double interview together with Wolf (Hörnigk 32–35). The Catalan poet Mirasol Alt reports her twenty-year-long admiration for Wolf, as well as that of her compatriots (Hörnigk 118). It is probably fair to say that Wolf is still the most admired woman writer the GDR ever produced. Scholars like Astrid Köhler can trace Wolf's poetic hand in the works of younger authors, such as Angela Krauß and Irina Liebmann, claiming: "This working with the fictive identity between author, narrator, and protagonist that we find in Wolf, is found all through the narratives of Krauß and Liebmann" (Köhler 223, my translation). Even Kerstin Hensel, she claims, still belongs to a tradition of writing à la Wolf, although she deals with her playfully and almost parodistically in her 1991 novel *Auditorium panopticum* (229). Köhler, who analyzed seven GDR writers' works before and after 1989, concludes: "It is impossible to miss seeing (and also unsurprising) that Christa Wolf is the most important person for many of the writers discussed here" (228, my translation).

One final question needs to be addressed: what remains of Christa Wolf and her works? Certainly, one positive indicator of her ongoing relevance is the fact that international scholars and readers, in places such as Greece, Italy, England, France, India, and the United States, which were themselves not directly involved in the politically and ideologically motivated German-German literary controversies of the early 1990s, have continued to view Wolf from their own critical, yet more even-handed perspectives. It may be noted here that Wolf received many other indications of solidarity from the West. In the autumn of 1990 she was awarded the prize "Officier des Arts et des Lettres" by the French minister of culture, as well as the Italian Mondell prize. In June 1993, 174 North American German Studies scholars expressed solidarity with her in a signed protest, "Das Kind mit dem Bade" (dumping the baby out with the bathwater), published in *Die Zeit*. Scholars in the United States have shown great interest in Wolf's works for almost fifty years, often from a feminist perspective. Stephen Brockman, in his presidential address at the 2012 German Studies Association Annual Conference, went so far as to attribute key importance to her works, not only for gender studies, but for German Studies in the USA in general.[20] In Germany, too, the controversies have long since died down. Just three evident examples of this are the Berlin-based Christa Wolf Society, founded in 2013, which initiates regular events, the associated Working and Research Center

Private Library Christa and Gerhard Wolf at Humboldt-Universität zu Berlin, which supports young researchers in particular, and the continuous publication of secondary literature, including two recent handbooks.

Thus, we return to the Hölderlin quote implicit in the title of Wolf's story: "Was bleibet aber, stiften die Dichter" ("Andenken") ("But poets establish what remains," "Remembrance"). I suggest we can go beyond continuing to defend Wolf against criticisms levied against her in the all-too-German literary debates and, instead, turn to her texts themselves, which, I would argue, speak to us in important ways today. While it is true that two "functions" which GDR literature *nolens volens* used to serve—that of "Ersatzöffentlichkeit" (substitute public sphere) and "Lebenshilfe"—are now outmoded, what remains is: the literature itself.

Concerning GDR literature, two opinions have been frequently voiced in the heated debates of the 1990s: either that its whole text corpus is outdated and to be disposed of in the dumping ground of history, or that it, as a closed chapter, can still be useful as historical documentation of a bygone society. While the first opinion is simply politically motivated and historically ignorant,[21] the second one neglects the aesthetic factor that distinguishes literature from documentaries and non-fictional texts. Although it is true that literature can be a bearer of knowledge (Klausnitzer), for example as one complementary factor in the preservation of historical experience besides other, more matter-of-fact types of documentation, at the same time, literature as a piece of *art* transcends the boundaries of the political and societal humus from which it grew. After all, to put it in simple terms, we are not staging Greek plays today in order to learn about the specific issues of Attic societies in the fourth century BC, nor do we read Schiller's *Kabale und Liebe* because we are interested in the problem of arranged marriages and pride of place in the eighteenth century—issues which, at first glance, seem to have no relevance to our modern (Western, that is) societies. Instead, we seek and find answers to, or at least explications of, questions about core issues of human nature and about us as individuals and societal beings at the same time.

Thus, I would insist on a third option which takes key literary texts seriously as "solitaires" that can be read and can affect readers in different situations or times and from different backgrounds because they address this *condition humaine*. While some of Wolf's texts (e.g., *Ein Tag im Jahr* or *Moskauer Novelle*) may well be used primarily to serve a historic interest in tracing societal developments in the former GDR, others, such as *Nachdenken über Christa T., Kein Ort. Nirgends,* or *Kassandra,* display an exceptional literary quality that enables them to stand on their own merits, as they engage with enduring questions, such as the individual's appropriate place in the world, the chances for free individual development despite the constraints of societal demands, the way in which great powers use ideology and pretexts in order to wage war, or the possibilities of creating united human communities. While the country in which she wrote is gone, many of the issues Wolf addressed remain unsolved, especially those which had resonated strongly in Western countries,[22] such as questions about hierarchic power structures and instrumentally rational thinking that exploits nature and humans alike—issues which seek to affect the core of our modern industrialized societies. Equally unresolved remain Wolf's questions about the role of women in these societies, in very practical and more general ways, such as questioning how far they want to or should use their increased influence to bring about changes to the system itself instead of just wanting to be an equal part in it (see Ludwig, "Utopie" 213ff.). Volker Braun believes that literary works, when liberated from their concrete situation of origin, may even gain in significance over time because "in larger fields the human content of a work can be perceived better and what has been thought from a deficit becomes important in a global perspective."[23]

Finally, besides those topics and contents, we should not overlook aesthetic qualities, that is, matters of *form*. Christa Wolf's writing offers a prime example of the congruence of form and content. Since she was always asking questions rather than giving answers, not only did her texts forgo dramatic impact in favor of fragmented, multi-perspectival structures; her narrators were also never all-knowing, omnipotent, auctorial authorities who would guide or patronize the reader, but, rather, characters who were always questioning and scrutinizing themselves. Consequently, her cautious, sensitive, grasping, questioning language often resembled feeling one's way in the dark, refraining from any absolute terms that would fix reality into a corset of determining terminology and easy truths. Thus, she developed a unique "sound" in her language that appealed to many readers (though not all critics). Her quest for truth was inextricably linked to her search for language, her own ("die eigene Sprache finden") as well as a new language that would offer new approaches to the world, as she so often emphasized in *Was bleibt*. In this way, all of Christa Wolf's writing is an offer to dialog or, as Heiner Müller once put it, "a universal discourse that leaves nothing out and excludes nobody" ("universaler Diskurs, der nichts ausläßt und niemanden ausschließt," Müller 211, my translation). It remains for readers to take up this discourse and engage in an ongoing dialog.

Janine Ludwig studied Contemporary German Literature, Philosophy, and Theater Studies/Cultural Communication in Göttingen, San Diego, and Berlin. She received her Ph.D. in 2008 from Humboldt-Universität zu Berlin and worked there as its Academic Representative in New York and as advisor to the Vice President for International Affairs and Public Relations. She is currently Academic Director of the Dickinson College Durden Bremen

Program at the University of Bremen, where she held a guest lectureship in 2013–14. She also serves as President of the Board of the International Heiner Müller Society and Vice Head of the Institut für kulturwissenschaftliche Deutschlandstudien (IfkuD) at the University of Bremen. Her publications include: *Heiner Müller, Ikone West: Das dramatische Werk Heiner Müllers in der Bundesrepublik—Rezeption und Wirkung* (2009), *Macht und Ohnmacht des Schreibens: Späte Texte Heiner Müllers* (2009), *Literatur ohne Land?* and *Schreibstrategien einer DDR-Literatur im vereinten Deutschland*, 2 vols, edited with Mirjam Meuser (2009, 2014).

Notes

"Was bleibet aber, stiften die Dichter.": "But poets establish what remains." (Friedrich Hölderlin, "Andenken"/"Remembrance")

1. With this phrase, Ulbricht directly cites an earlier formulation by the Central Committee (Zentralkomitee) of the SED, of which he was a part: the final proclamation in the programmatic pamphlet "The Fight Against Formalism in Arts and Literature, For a Progressive German Culture," a decisive paper that cemented certain aesthetic doctrines for decades—and written in a rather martial tone concerning the fight against the West (Zentralkomitee 186).
2. Wolf alluded to such a concept already in her early article "Achtung, Rauschgifthandel!" ("Attention, Drug Traffic!") in 1955 and mentioned it again—with a reference to Fühmann—as late as 1998: "Franz Fühmann hat Anfang der achtziger Jahre mal so eine Formel gefunden: Wenn möglich, sollten Pfarrer, Ärzte und Schriftsteller hierbleiben, also die Leute, die für das physische und seelisch geistige Wohl zuständig sind. Das hat mir irgendwie eingeleuchtet" ("Schreiben als Lebensäußerung" 596). ("At the beginning of the 1980s Franz Fühmann found such a formulation: Whenever possible, ministers, doctors, and writers should stay here, that is, the people who are responsible for spiritual and intellectual well-being. Somehow that made sense to me." My translation.)
3. "Diese Realität der Krisenzeit, der Kriege usw. muß also erstens ertragen, es muß ihr ins Auge gesehen und zweitens muß sie gestaltet werden ... Solche Krisenzeiten sind in der Kunstgeschichte von jeher gekennzeichnet durch jähe Stilbrüche, durch Experimente, durch sonderbare Mischformen ... Doch was Du als Zerfall ansiehst, kommt mir eher wie eine Bestandsaufnahme vor; was Du als Formexperiment ansiehst, wie ein heftiger Versuch eines neuen Inhalts, wie ein unvermeidlicher Versuch" (Lukács/ Seghers 348, 353). ("This reality of times of crises, of wars and so on must, first of all, be confronted, then shaped artistically ... Such times of crises have always been marked in art history by sudden breaks in style, by experiments, by peculiar hybrid forms ... But what you see as decay, appears to me rather as a taking of stock; what you see as formal experiment, [appears to me, J.L.] as a vigorous attempt at new content, an inevitable attempt." My translation.)
4. "Lassen wir Spiegel das ihre tun: spiegeln. Sie können nichts anderes. Erzähler und Wirklichkeit stehen sich nicht gegenüber wie Spiegel und das, was gespiegelt wird.

Sie sind ineinander verschmolzen im Bewußtsein des Autors. Der Autor nämlich ist ein wichtiger Mensch" (Wolf, "Lesen und Schreiben" 496).
5. For a more detailed description, see Ludwig, "Utopie."
6. Volker Braun, in a personal conversation with J.L., on 26 September 2012, also praised her persona, the way she always presented herself as a human being ("sich kenntlich machen als Mensch"), as well as her "immense achievement in developing a new world of thought in each of her books" ("mit jedem Buch ein neues Denkfeld erarbeiten").
7. However, exactly that intertwining of life and work would become her Achilles' heel in the literary dispute ("Literaturstreit"), in which little or no distinction was made between her and her book.
8. See Magenau 211, and the exchange of letters: Reimann and Wolf, *Sei gegrüßt und lebe*.
9. Schubert had earlier portrayed herself and Wolf in *Die Silberkrone* (1975). See Firsching 189ff.
10. The German title alludes to one of the Grimms' fairy tales, "Allerleirauh."
11. Volker Hage called Wolf eine "Mächtige unter Machtlosen" ("a powerful figure among the powerless," Hage).
12. I have enlarged upon this in *Heiner Müller, Ikone West* chapter 3. See also Deiritz and Krauss; and Anz.
13. For Wolf's own account of that specific reading in 1979, see also Wolf, *Ein Tag* 262–69.
14. Wolf distinctly stated that she was in the process of revising the 1979 manuscript. See Skare 59–68.
15. Skare 120. In the reading, the title was announced with a question mark: "Was bleibt?"
16. In his scathing review that, together with Schirrmacher's article, opened the controversy, Ulrich Greiner demands to know exactly when Wolf made her revisions: "A lot of things happened this fall, so the exact date really matters" (66).
17. For Wolf's account of her experiences in 1990, see, for example, her entry in *One Day a Year* 463f.
18. She first alluded to such a comparison in her journal *Ein Tag im Jahr* on 27 September 1992 (*Ein Tag* 491–507, esp. 492) and then made an even more specific remark in the TV format "Kulturreport" (ARD) on 24 January 1993: "These days, people in Germany think one could do without the culture that existed in the GDR. Back then, Germany got rid of the left, of the Jewish culture, this immense, great, humanistic culture that existed there. We know what this led to. Now, the ones whom Germany believes it can get rid of by casting such a shadow on them—Heiner Müller and myself, among others—only await being criminalized" (*Akteneinsicht* 170, my translation).
19. See Gerhard Wolf, *Ein Text für C.W.* (1994) and Therese Hörnigk, *Sich aussetzen* (2009).
20. Marilyn Sibley Fries's article, "Christa Wolfs 'Ort' in Amerika," offers a comprehensive survey of that development and Wolf's relevance in American academe, especially after 1990; Edith Waldstein, in an article on *Kein Ort. Nirgends* in American classrooms, also describes students' engaged reactions (in Brandes 169–82 and 113–18).
21. I also reject the idea of holding art hostage to the societies where it has been created and denouncing it because of the failures of this society, which happened, for

instance, in 2009 when the exhibition "60 Years, 60 Works" (60 Jahre, 60 Werke) in the Gropius-Bau Berlin displayed an overview on fine arts in Germany. The curators seriously argued that they exhibited no piece of art created in the former GDR because no real art could develop in unfree societies—an argument which led Christoph Hein to stay away from the celebrations of the sixtieth anniversary of the Basic Law of the Federal Republic of Germany (Hein).
22. This is not only true for Christa Wolf, but texts by Heiner Müller and Christoph Hein also found praise in many foreign countries. One critic, for example, remarked that Hein's *Der fremde Freund* could well be describing a life in New York.
23. "In großen anderen Räumen wird der Menschheitsgehalt eher wahrgenommen; das aus dem Mangel heraus Gedachte wird wichtig im globalen Maßstab." Volker Braun in a conversation with J.L. on 26 September 2012, my translation.

Bibliography

Anz, Thomas, editor. *"Es geht nicht um Christa Wolf": Der Literaturstreit im vereinten Deutschland*. Munich: Edition Spangenberg, 1991.

Bathrick, David. "Die Intellektuellen und die Macht: Die Repräsentanz des Schriftstellers in der DDR." *Schriftsteller als Intellektuelle: Politik und Literatur im Kalten Krieg*, edited by Sven Hanuschek et al. Tübingen: Niemeyer Verlag, 2000, pp. 235–248.

Bohrer, Karl Heinz. "Kulturschutzgebiet DDR?" *Merkur*, vol. 44, no. 10/11, 1990, pp. 1015–18.

Brandes, Ute. *Zwischen gestern und morgen: Schriftstellerinnen der DDR aus amerikanischer Sicht*. Berlin: Peter Lang, 1992.

Brockmann, Stephen. "Remembering What Remained: German Studies Association 2012 Presidential Address." *German Studies Review*, vol. 36, no. 2, May 2013, pp. 347–61.

Dahlke, Birgit. *Christa Wolf (1929–2011): Antifaschistin – Humanistin – Sozialistin*. Würzburg: Königshausen & Neumann, 2019.

Dahn, Daniela. "Trauerrede für Christa Wolf." Held at the Akademie der Künste, 13 December 2011. *Wohin sind wir unterwegs? Zum Gedenken an Christa Wolf*. Sonderdruck Edition Suhrkamp. Frankfurt a.M.: Suhrkamp Verlag, 2012, pp. 43–47.

Deiritz, Karl, and Hannes Krauss. *Der deutsch-deutsche Literaturstreit oder Freunde, es spricht sich schlecht mit gebundener Zunge: Analysen und Materialien*. Hamburg: Luchterhand, 1991.

Eichhorn, Alfred, and Andreas Reinhardt, editors. *Nach langem Schweigen endlich sprechen: Briefe an Walter Janka*. Berlin: Aufbau-Verlag, 1990.

Firsching, Annette. *Kontinuität und Wandel im Werk von Christa Wolf*. Würzburg: Königshausen & Neumann, 1996.

Fries, Marilyn Sibley. "Christa Wolfs 'Ort' in Amerika." *Zwischen gestern und morgen: Schriftstellerinnen der DDR aus amerikanischer Sicht*, edited by Ute Brandes. Berlin: Peter Lang, 1992, pp. 169–82.
Gansel, Carsten, editor. *Christa Wolf: Im Strom der Erinnerung*. Göttingen: Vandenhoeck & Ruprecht, 2014.
Greiner, Ulrich. "Mangel an Feingefühl." *"Es geht nicht um Christa Wolf": Der Literaturstreit im vereinten Deutschland*, edited by Thomas Anz. Munich: Edition Spangenberg, 1991, pp. 66–76.
Grimm, Thomas, editor. *Christa Wolf: Umbrüche und Wendezeiten*. Berlin: Suhrkamp, 2019.
Gruner, Petra, editor. *Angepaßt oder mündig? Briefe an Christa Wolf im Herbst 1989*. Berlin: Volk und Wissen, 1990.
Hage, Volker. "Drüben bleiben? Die Schriftsteller in der DDR und ihr Staat." *Die Zeit*, 20 November 1987.
Hein, Christoph. "Die Freiheit, die ich meine." *Der Freitag*, 6 May 2009.
Hensel, Kerstin. *Auditorium panopticum*. Halle/Saale: Mitteldeutscher Verlag, 1991.
———. "Letter." *Gute Nacht, du Schöne: Autorinnen blicken zurück*, edited by Anna Mudry. Frankfurt a.M.: Luchterhand, 1991, pp. 119f.
Hilmes, Carola, and Ilse Nagelschmidt, editors. *Christa Wolf Handbuch: Leben – Werk – Wirkung*. Stuttgart: Metzler, 2016.
Hölderlin, Friedrich. "Andenken." *Sämtliche Werke, Briefe und Dokumente in zeitlicher Folge*, edited by. D.E. Sattler, Bremer Ausgabe, vol. XI. Munich: Luchterhand, 2004, pp. 121–23.
———. "Remembrance," translated by Richard Sieburth. *Hölderlin: Hyperion and Selected Poems*, edited by Eric L. Santner. The German Library, vol. 22. New York: Continuum, 1990, pp. 264–65.
Hörnigk, Therese. *Sich aussetzen. Das Wort ergreifen. Texte und Bilder zum 80. Geburtstag von Christa Wolf*. Göttingen: Wallstein, 2009.
Hörnigk, Therese, and Carsten Gansel, editors. *Zwischen Moskauer Novelle und Stadt der Engel: Neue Perspektiven auf das Lebenswerk von Christa Wolf*. Schriften der Christa Wolf Gesellschaft, vol. 1. Berlin: Verlag für Berlin-Brandenburg, 2015.
Horkheimer, Max, and Theodor W. Adorno. *Dialectic of Enlightenment*. Translated by Edmund Jephcott. Stanford, CA: Stanford University Press, 2002.
Janka, Walter. *Schwierigkeiten mit der Wahrheit*. rororo aktuell no. 12731. Reinbek bei Hamburg: Rowohlt, 1989.
Kirsch, Sarah. *Allerlei-Rauh*. Stuttgart: Deutsche Verlags-Anstalt, 1988.
Klausnitzer, Ralf. *Literatur und Wissen: Zugänge – Modelle – Analysen*. Berlin: De Gruyter, 2008.
Klocke, Sonja E., and Jennifer R. Hosek, editors. *Christa Wolf: A Companion*. Berlin: De Gruyter, 2018.
Köhler, Astrid. *Brückenschläge: DDR-Autoren vor und nach der Wiedervereinigung*. Göttingen: Vandenhoeck & Ruprecht, 2007.

Kuhrig, Herta, and Wulfram Speigner. "Gleichberechtigung der Frau: Aufgaben und ihre Realisierung in der DDR." *Zur gesellschaftlichen Stellung der Frau in der DDR*, edited by Herta Kuhrig. Leipzig: Verlag für die Frau, 1978, pp. 11–85.

Lenin, Wladimir Iljitsch: "Parteiorganisation und Parteiliteratur." *Werke*, vol. 10, edited by the Institut für Marxismus-Leninismus beim ZK der KPdSU. Berlin, 1970, pp. 29–34.

Ludwig, Janine. *Heiner Müller, Ikone West: Das dramatische Werk Heiner Müllers in der Bundesrepublik—Rezeption und Wirkung*. Frankfurt a.M.: Peter Lang, 2009.

———. "Die Utopie vom richtigen Leben: Schriftstellerinnen in der DDR." *Fiktionen und Realitäten: Schriftstellerinnen im deutschsprachigen Literaturbetrieb*, edited by Brigitte E. Jirku and Marion Schulz. Frankfurt a.M.: Peter Lang, 2013, pp. 235–59.

Lukács, Georg. "Ein Briefwechsel zwischen Anna Seghers und Georg Lukács." *Werke IV: Essays über den Realismus*. Berlin: Hermann Luchterhand Verlag, 1971.

Lukoschat, Helga. "VILs Very Important Ladies: Die hundert 'einflußreichsten' Frauen in Deutschland." *taz (die tageszeitung)*, 8 September 1990.

Magenau, Jörg. *Christa Wolf: Eine Biographie*. Revised and enlarged edition. Reinbek bei Hamburg: Rowohlt, 2013.

Meuser, Mirjam, and Janine Ludwig, editors. *Literatur ohne Land? Vol. 2: Schreibstrategien einer DDR-Literatur im vereinten Deutschland*. Freiburg: FWPF, 2014.

Morgner, Irmtraud. *Leben und Abenteuer der Trobadora Beatriz nach Zeugnissen ihrer Spielfrau Laura*. Berlin: Aufbau Verlag, 1974.

Müller, Heiner. "Der Schrecken die erste Erscheinung des Neuen: Zu einer Diskussion über Postmodernismus in New York." *Schriften. Werke 8*, edited by Frank Hörnigk. Frankfurt a.M.: Suhrkamp, 2005, pp. 208–12.

Pinkerneil, Beate, and Günter de Bruyn. "Gespräche über Christa Wolf. I. Gespräch über Günter de Bruyn." *Text + Kritik. Christa Wolf*, no. 46, 4th edition, edited by Heinz Ludwig. Arnold, 1994, pp. 9–14.

Raddatz, Fritz J. *Traditionen und Tendenzen: Materialien zur Literatur der DDR*. Frankfurt a.M.: Suhrkamp, 1972.

Reimann, Brigitte. *Franziska Linkerhand*. Berlin: Verlag Neues Leben, 1974.

——— and Christa Wolf. *Sei gegrüßt und lebe: Eine Freundschaft in Briefen 1964-1973*. Edited by Angela Drescher. Berlin: Aufbau Taschenbuch, 1997.

Schirrmacher, Frank. "Dem Druck des härteren, strengeren Lebens standhalten." *"Es geht nicht um Christa Wolf": Der Literaturstreit im vereinten Deutschland*, edited by Thomas Anz. Munich: Edition Spangenberg, 1991, pp. 77–89.

Schubbe, Elimar, editor. *Dokumente zur Kunst-, Literatur- und Kulturpolitik der SED (1946–1970)*. Stuttgart: Seewald Verlag, 1972.

Seghers, Anna. "Ein Briefwechsel zwischen Anna Seghers und Georg Lukács." *Werke IV: Essays über den Realismus*. Berlin: Hermann Luchterhand Verlag, 1971.

Skare, Roswitha. *Christa Wolfs* Was bleibt: *Kontext—Paratext—Text. Avhandling levert for graden doctor artium.* University of Tromsø, Det humanistiske fakultet Institutt for kultur og litteratur, December 2007. http://munin.uit.no/bitstream/handle/10037/1412/thesis_Skare.pdf?sequence=1 (accessed 21 September 2012).

Tetzner, Gerti. *Karen W.* Halle/Saale: Mitteldeutscher Verlag, 1974.

Ulbricht, Walter. "Kampf um ein realistisches Kunstschaffen" (Referat Walter Ulbrichts auf der II. Parteikonferenz der SED, 9. bis 12. Juli 1952, excerpt). *Dokumente zur Kunst-, Literatur- und Kulturpolitik der SED (1946–1970),* edited by Elimar Schubbe. Stuttgart: Seewald Verlag, 1972, pp. 239–40.

Waldstein, Edith. "Marxismus? Feminismus? Utopie? *Kein Ort. Nirgends* in American Classrooms." *Zwischen gestern und morgen: Schriftstellerinnen der DDR aus amerikanischer Sicht,* edited by Ute Brandes. Berlin: Peter Lang, 1992.

Wander, Maxie. *Guten Morgen, du Schöne: Protokolle nach Tonband.* Berlin: Buchverlag Der Morgen, 1977/Darmstadt and Neuwied: Luchterhand, 1978.

Wolf, Christa. "Achtung, Rauschgifthandel!" *Neuere deutsche Literatur,* vol. 2, 1955, pp. 136–40.

———. *Akteneinsicht Christa Wolf: Zerrspiegel und Dialog,* edited by Hermann Vinke. Hamburg: Luchterhand, 1993.

———. *The Author's Dimension: Selected Essays.* Edited by Alexander Stephan, translated by Jan van Heurck. New York: Farrar, Straus and Giroux, 1993.

———. "Berührung." Foreword to *Guten Morgen, du Schöne: Protokolle nach Tonband,* by Maxie Wander. Berlin: Buchverlag Der Morgen, 1977/Darmstadt and Neuwied: Luchterhand, 1978, pp. 9–29.

———. "Das haben wir nicht gelernt." *Wochenpost* 43, October 1989. Also in Gruner 9–11.

———. *Ein Tag im Jahr: 1960–2000.* Munich: Luchterhand, 2003.

———. "Heine, die Zensur und wir: Rede auf dem Außergewöhnlichen Schriftstellerkongress der DDR." 3 March 1990. *Im Dialog: Aktuelle Texte.* Darmstadt: Luchterhand, 1990, pp. 163–68.

———. "In Touch," translated by Jeanette Clausen. *German Feminism: Readings in Politics and Literature,* edited by Edith Hoshino Altbach et al. Albany, NY: State University of New York Press, 1984, pp. 161–69.

———. *Kassandra.* Darmstadt: Luchterhand, 1983.

———. *Kein Ort. Nirgends.* Berlin-East: Aufbau, 1979.

———. "Lesen und Schreiben." *Die Dimension des Autors: Essays und Aufsätze, Reden und Gespräche 1959–1985.* Darmstadt: Luchterhand, 1971, pp. 463–503.

———. *Medea. Stimmen.* Munich: Luchterhand, 1996.

———. "Momentary Interruption." *Parting from Phantoms: Selected Writings, 1990–1994,* translated by Jan van Heurck. Chicago: University of Chicago Press, 1997, pp. 9–13.

———. *Moskauer Novelle.* Halle (Saale): Mitteldeutscher Verlag, 1961.

———. *Nachdenken über Christa T.* Halle/Saale: Mitteldeutscher Verlag, 1968.

——— . "The Reader and the Writer." *The Author's Dimension: Selected Essays*, edited by Alexander Stephan, translated by Jan van Heurck. New York: Farrar, Straus and Giroux, 1993, pp. 20–57.

——— . "Schreiben als Lebensäußerung." (Gespräch mit Herlinde Koelbl, März, 1998). *Reden im Herbst*. In: *Werke 12. Essays/Gespräche/Reden/Briefe 1987–2000*, edited by Sonja Hilzinger. Munich: Luchterhand, 2001.

——— . "Schreiben im Zeitbezug. Gespräch mit Aafke Steenhuis." *Werke 12. Essays/Gespräche/Reden/Briefe 1987–2000*, edited by Sonja Hilzinger. Munich: Luchterhand, 2001, pp. 196–226.

——— . "Selbstversuch: Traktat zu einem Protokoll." *Blitz aus heiterm Himmel*, edited by Edith Anderson. Rostock: Hinstorff, 1975, pp. 47–82.

——— . "Self-Experiment," translated by Jeanette Clausen. *New German Critique*, vol. 13, Winter 1978, pp. 109–31.

——— . *Sommerstück*. Berlin: Aufbau Verlag, 1989.

——— . *The Quest for Christa T.* Translated by Christopher Middleton. New York: Farrar, Straus and Giroux, 1968.

——— . *Was bleibt. Erzählung*. Munich: Luchterhand, 1999 (1990?).

——— . "We Don't Know How." *The Author's Dimension: Selected Essays*, edited by Alexander Stephan, translated by Jan van Heurck. New York: Farrar, Straus and Giroux, 1993, pp. 299–302.

——— . "What Remains." *What Remains and Other Stories*, translated by Heike Schwarzbauer and Rick Takvorian. New York: Farrar, Straus and Giroux, 1993, pp. 231–95.

——— . "Zwischenrede." Rede zur Verleihung der Ehrendoktorwürde der Universität Hildesheim. *Auf dem Weg nach Tabou: Texte 1990–1994*. Cologne: Kiepenheuer & Witsch, 1994, pp. 17–22.

——— and Gerhard Wolf. *Ins Ungebundene geht eine Sehnsucht: Gesprächsraum [Projektionsraum] Romantik*. Berlin: Aufbau Verlag, 1985.

Wolf, Gerhard, editor. *Ein Text für C.W.* Berlin: Janus press, 1994.

Wolf, Sabine, editor. *Christa Wolf: Man steht sehr bequem zwischen allen Fronten—Briefe 1952–2011*. Berlin: Suhrkamp, 2016.

——— . *Sarah Kirsch, Christa Wolf. "Wir haben uns wirklich an allerhand gewöhnt." Der Briefwechsel*. Berlin: Suhrkamp, 2019.

Zantop, Susanne M., and Daniel Wilson, together with 172 signees: "Das Kind mit dem Bade." *Die Zeit*, no. 25, 18 June 1993.

Zentralkomitee der SED. "Der Kampf gegen den Formalismus in Kunst und Literatur, für eine fortschrittliche deutsche Kultur: Entschließung des Zentralkomitees der Sozialistischen Einheitspartei Deutschlands, angenommen auf der V. Tagung vom 15. bis 17. März 1951." *Dokumente zur Kunst-, Literatur- und Kulturpolitik der SED (1946–1970)*, edited by Elimar Schubbe. Stuttgart: Seewald Verlag, 1972, pp. 178–86.

CHAPTER 10

"This Is No Longer My World"
The Multiple Alienations of Christa Wolf

DANIELA COLOMBO

Christa Wolf's work, shaped by her own biography, entails constant re-examination of history and its failures. Her childhood and adolescence under National Socialism led her to critically examine the structures, the damage caused, and the legacy of fascism. While her later life in the GDR was marked by ongoing tension between conformity and resistance, events of the collapse of the GDR and the years after 1989 again led her to confront her own complicity and personal responsibility in this history.

Were one to map out the key phases of Wolf's biography, one would be struck by the intensity of her experiences of this history. Her biography could, in fact, be read in one way as a chronicle of endings and new beginnings. She was born into the Weimar Republic, lived her childhood and teen years during the Nazi period, and spent most of her adult life in the GDR, only to be forced to live out her late years in post-1989 unified Germany. These experiences found their way into Wolf's writing, so that many of her texts over the years deal with her attempt to come to terms with this history in introspective reflections about her own past life and roles in changing times. Entwined with these issues are several recurring motifs, including her struggle against a destructive desire for conformity, for "going-along," while simultaneously dissenting against many aspects of precisely that to which she seeks to conform. The struggle between these tendencies lies at the heart of many of Wolf's works.

In her oeuvre, at least since *The Quest for Christa T.* (*Nachdenken* über *Christa T.*, 1969), Wolf is not interested in merely describing historical events, but in coming to terms with the continuous effect of the past on the present. Citing Bertolt Brecht in her important 1973 interview with Hans Kaufmann, she described this way of regarding history as a constant in her work: "As Brecht wrote in 1953: 'We have been all too keen to turn our backs on the immediate past and, hungry with curiosity, look to the future.

But the future will depend on whether we can come to terms with the past'" ("Subjective Authenticity" 31).

Like Wolf, historian Klaus Bergmann emphasizes the role of one's life experiences in shaping the way one sees the past and faces the future:

> History is always a reflection on the past, which takes place in the present and is influenced by expectations for the future. With the forward movement of time, with increasing life experience and new challenges, the objects of memory and memories themselves change. Memories are constructed in accord with the situation of the person who is remembering. (Bergmann 91, "my translation")

In comparing Wolf's novels and novellas written after 1989 with those written prior to the collapse of the GDR, one can readily distinguish breaks, but also significant continuities. The essential themes of these works continue to reflect concern with various experiences of alienation. Thus, not only *Patterns of Childhood* (*Kindheitsmuster*, 1976), but also *City of Angels or, The Overcoat of Dr. Freud* (*Stadt der Engel oder The Overcoat of Dr. Freud*, 2010) question the individual's experience of alienation, which is not only made evident in the content, but also manifested formally in the split use of the personal pronouns used by the narrator to refer to herself as "I," "you," "she."

Similarly, *Sommerstück* (*Summer Scenes*, 1989), like *No Place on Earth* (*Kein Ort. Nirgends*, 1979) or *What Remains* (*Was bleibt*, 1990), describes the involuntary condition of being an outsider in society, whereas *Parting from Phantoms* (*Auf dem Weg nach Tabou*, 1994), a collection of texts written in the wake of German unification, formulates the nature of alienation in a "new" country, that is, reunited Germany.

The title figure of *Medea* (1996), a self-determined woman who is a foreigner in Corinth, is doubly an alien, and the novel explores in detail the treatment of both foreigners in general and this female foreigner in particular. What follows should shed light on these varying experiences of alienation, offered here as a kind of *tour d'horizon*.

A Stranger to Myself: *Patterns of Childhood* and *City of Angels*

"The past is never dead; It is not even past." Wolf borrows this epigraph to William Faulkner's 1951 novel *Requiem for a Nun* to introduce *Patterns of Childhood*. However, she adds a significant second sentence: "We detach ourselves from it and act as if it were alien" (11).[1]

Behind this statement lies the insight that the period of National Socialism still weighed heavily on the German present of the 1970s.[2] The behavior and responses of Germans of the author's generation were closely linked to their own childhood under fascism. Thus, this recognition that the past is not dead is coupled with a profound sense of alienation in relation to her own childhood ("A Model of Experience" 45; "Erfahrungsmuster" 814) In order to function, one had to forget and suppress, which, in time, inevitably triggered alienation and emotional numbness.

Patterns of Childhood is a complex, many-layered book. It is not only a tale about a childhood under fascism, but also about a National Socialist childhood in which the parents' life strategy was based on conformity and where they were defined *by what they were not* (149). The parents of the narrator had neither Jewish nor Communist friends and relatives, no hereditary illnesses in their family, no connections abroad, no knowledge of foreign languages, nor any predisposition to subversive thinking or "decadent" forms of art (149).[3] Lothar Baier calls attention to "how deeply the agency of an 'inner commanding authority' is implanted in the individuals, where it functions through a complex interplay of self-censorship, self-denial, and the distortion of reality accompanied by simultaneous accommodation of constraining facts" (64, my translation).

Such a well-rehearsed interplay cannot be undone from one day to the next. *Patterns of Childhood* reflects several kinds of alienations. Of her own childhood, Wolf said:

> There is, and this is perhaps one of the peculiarities of my life story … a sense of alienation from this period. From a definite moment, which one cannot trace to the exact day but certainly to the exact period, one is no longer the same person. I no longer feel that it was I who had thought, said or done these things. ("A Model of Experience" 45)

Even the child Nelly grows estranged from herself, both in terms of her feelings overall and of those toward her own body. As Wolf stated, it was her objective to overcome this estrangement in relation to her own childhood and, in the process, also to herself. This is best expressed through her use of the three personal pronouns: I, you, she. The novel culminates in the collapse of these "persons," as the third person "Nelly" comes together with the second person, "you," to form *one* person, which can ultimately be denoted as the "I" ("A Model of Experience" 45).[4] Based on the experience that one tries to barricade oneself from a burdening past and to seek distance, the beginning of *Patterns of Childhood* depicts the resulting self-estrangement: "to remain speechless, or else to live in the third person. The first is impossible, the second strange" (3).

City of Angels or, The Overcoat of Dr. Freud, published in 2010, which was to be the last novel to appear in Wolf's lifetime (she died in 2011), describes retrospectively, with a distance of some fifteen years, its narrator's stay of several months in Los Angeles in 1992–93 during which she deals with her personal history, as well as that of the GDR, which in 1990 had ceased to exist. Writing later in Germany, this first-person narrator recalls the time of her fellowship at the Getty Center and, on a third level, connects the biography of the protagonist addressed as "du" with important cultural events in the GDR during an even earlier time. Autobiographical in nature, the novel comprises a complex interplay of facts, travel reports, dreams, stories, and allusions to various periods of time.

Even a cursory glance at *City of Angels* elicits a comparison with *Patterns of Childhood*. Also in this novel, written thirty years later, one encounters the same central theme: "TO LOOK INTO MY OWN OTHERNESS was something I had avoided for a long time, until now" (88). Here, too, Wolf operates with a splitting of the personal form, whereby she emphasizes the difference between the first-person narrator writing in Los Angeles at the time of the story and the "Du" (you) remembering the past. This past begins in 1945 with the trek of refugees from the formerly German East, including the narrator and her family, and encompasses the entire history of the GDR and the aftermath of reunification, including both the fierce German literary dispute about Wolf's belated publication of *What Remains* (*Was bleibt*, 1990) and the subsequent debate about her early involvement with the GDR secret police (Stasi). However, the very core, the hot magma, in *City of Angels* concerns the question of how the narrator could have forgotten that she had been recruited as an informer (IM) by the Stasi from 1959 to 1962.

In Wolf's so-called perpetrator file ("Täterakten") of 1959, a report in her own handwriting, under her code name Margarete, had been found. The discovery of this file overwhelms her and leads to the question asked so many times: how could she have forgotten *that* fact? As in *Patterns of Childhood*, the narrator comes to understand that she has become an alien to herself. "Looking into these files completely undermined and defiled the past ... and poisoned the present along with it" (136).

With memory wanting, self-certainty falls apart. "Who is this reporting 'I' supposed to be? It's not just how much I've forgotten. What is maybe more troubling is that I'm not sure who's doing the remembering" (160–61). Or: "THE OTHERNESS IN YOU. I was convinced on the spot; it fit. Or, I thought, maybe the foreign in me too: a foreign body I had felt the way you can feel a growth in your body" (196). Here is the unknown as a pathological metaphor.

In California, a place unfamiliar to her, the first-person narrator tries to get closer to the "Du" by remembering her past. And as we have seen in *Patterns of Childhood*, this process of approaching the past takes place, as it were, through her encounter with the world of fixed objects—including the house, the playground, school, and synagogue—during the visit to the town of her birth. In *City of Angels*, Los Angeles becomes the excavation site for the narrator's own memories and a part of her process of nearing the "Du." A well-known quotation from Walter Benjamin that serves as an epigraph to the novel refers to this as well: "So for authentic memories, it is far less important that the investigator report on them than that he mark, quite precisely, the site where he gained possession of them" (Benjamin 576). For the first-person narrator, this place lies in the topography of the California metropolis with her own personal preferences: her lodging in the eccentric "Ms Victoria," Second and Third Streets, the center of the city, and time and again the Ocean Park promenade with its benches, as well as Pacific Palisades (which bore the nickname "Weimar on the Pacific"): all were meeting points for German exiles who had fled National Socialism.

In an American review, *City of Angels* was called a "stranger-in-a-strange-land-novel."[5] Far away in a strange land the narrator focuses on her own history, her own country. In the California sun she finds herself in a dazzling "cabinet of mirrors." Wherever she looks, she only sees and seeks herself and her life in and after the GDR. Heiner Müller's verses from *Vampire* (1995) could apply to Wolf's protagonist: "Statt Mauern stehen Spiegel um mich her" (317; Instead of walls, I am surrounded by mirrors [my translation]).

Whereas in *Patterns of Childhood* one had to forget and repress things in order to function, in *City of Angels* another justification for forgetting is proffered. Associations with the Stasi could be forgotten because they are not seen to have played an important part in the young protagonist's life. Finally, the feeling of alienation disappears and what remains is a hard-won insistence on "oneself," which consciously forgoes having to make an effective public or tactical apology. The true errors made, according to the first-person narrator in *City of Angels*, were not the visible ones, such as the signature on a Stasi document, but those that were caused by being silent: the neglect of her dying mother, because at the time the global political crisis of the "Prague Spring" and its suppression seemed more important; or the fact that she was never allowed to mourn her grandmother, who died of starvation while fleeing around 1945.

Alien within Society

Individuals or small groups of outsiders, who out of necessity live on the periphery of society, are expressly thematized in *No Place on Earth* and *Sommerstück*. Both texts were written—in part even at the same time—in the second half of the 1970s, but were reworked and published at different times.[6] Even though *What Remains* does not concern itself with a marginal group, it, too, depicts a female protagonist who, against her will, finds herself in the position of being an outsider.

All three texts were produced under similar sociopolitical conditions, which triggered consequent feelings of alienation within that society. *No Place on Earth* shows the constrained possibilities of life in a pre-industrialized society for the early Romantic writers Heinrich von Kleist and Karoline von Günderrode, while *Sommerstück* describes a contemporary retreat to the countryside of a circle of friends, who had been excluded from any constructive opportunities for participation in GDR society. Kleist and Günderrode experience outsiderdom in a society that is unable to offer them any viable alternative for constructing a meaningful existence for themselves. This alienation from the world around them finally drives both poets to their deaths. The title *No Place on Earth* itself reflects their feelings of rootlessness and alienation. In this story, Christa Wolf depicts the divergence between the needs of the individual and those of society, and, in conjunction with this, the marginalization of literature—and thus of the writer, excluded from societal self-realization. Through her textual practice of temporal and perspectival shifts in the text, the "temporal distance" between early Romanticism and the writer's present is erased in an "associative narrative flow": the problematic issues gain present relevance (Hörnigk 196).

In *No Place on Earth*, Christa Wolf portrays Kleist's and Günderrode's ultimately failed search for an interrelated, communal way of life, while *Sommerstück* depicts its (at least temporary) realization. Where Günderrode and Kleist in the end each fail at life, *Sommerstück* renders a contemporary attempt at countering the sociopolitical lack of alternatives with a fragile rural happiness among a circle of family and friends. This change in perspective is already hinted at in the title. The "no-place" of Kleist and Günderrode is followed in *Sommerstück* by an elegiac invocation of a limited and bright season in the countryside, a place where life is shaped by the rhythms of nature and times of day. Amid threats and exclusion from society, the protagonists celebrate their simple happiness among friends, children, grandchildren, nature, and old familiar objects; here the main character cultivates her hope that her literary drafts will someday appear as books.

Ellen and Jan, who have retreated to a village in Mecklenburg, are soon surrounded by a circle of like-minded people, and in this setting, a new start on the periphery of society at least seems possible. Like both Cassandra celebrating "life itself" before the catastrophe in the community at Scamander, and Medea in the artists' community around Oistros before her banishment, the circle in *Sommerstück* also seeks to make their utopia linger a while longer. Despite the experience of sisterhood,[7] however, the narrator does not for a moment lose her sense of the fragility of this so longed-for rural idyll, or of how much the naive "...retreat to country life was a new illusion."[8] Like *No Place on Earth*, *Sommerstück* reflects the feeling of alienation in one's own society, caused by the painful experience of not having creative possibilities and not being needed. At the same time, the accusation that society cannot afford to renounce the critical potential of art is also evident.

No Place on Earth and Sommerstück can also be read as a reaction to disappointments stemming from failure to attain one's own social and artistic aspirations. The consequences for cultural policy after Wolf Biermann's expulsion from the GDR in 1976, as well as Christa Wolf's personal experience of social marginalization, loss, and the resulting existential crisis, also mark both texts as very private reactions to the "realpolitik" of the GDR. The international reception of both texts outside their geopolitical origin suggests that failure to realize positive alternatives in life and society was also experienced as problematic outside of the GDR.

Alien in One's Own New Country: Post-Reunification Experiences

The theme of alienation in one's own society took on a further dimension with the reunification of Germany and the process it entailed, leading to the experience of likewise being an alien in one's own "new" country. *Medea: A Modern Retelling* (*Medea: Stimmen*, 1996) can be read from this point of view; indeed, when the novel was published in 1996, many reviewers reduced it to this refrain in their criticism. In the politically charged years after the fall of the Berlin Wall, Christa Wolf in particular spoke out critically in essays, letters, and journal entries, many of which were published in English in 1997 under the title *Parting from Phantoms: Selected Writings 1990–1994* (*Auf dem Weg nach Tabou: Texte 1990–1994*, 1994). As Wolf saw it, the period of reunification generated expectations that "the fall of the old regime, achieved by the masses, would lead to the revolutionary revival of our country" ("Momentary Interruption" ["Zwischenrede"] 10). Alas, this measure of hope was only proportional to the measure of disappointment that ensued. This renewed political disillusionment left its mark on Wolf. The texts in *Parting from Phantoms* reflect on the experience of reunification from an East German perspective, as the initial euphoria of the fall of the Wall gave way to reciprocal feelings of alienation between Eastern and Western Germans. As the GDR was reduced in popular opinion to nothing other than a state of injustice, many East Germans experienced on a psychological level a retrospective devaluation of their biographies ("Whatever Happened to Your Smile? Wasteland Berlin 1990" ["Wo ist euer Lächeln geblieben? Brachland Berlin 1990"] 41–42). People in East and West talked about each other but not with each other.[9] The feeling of alienation experienced by many former GDR citizens in the new German Republic in the first years after reunification was a logical consequence.[10]

For Wolf, the dilemmas and conflicts she had formerly focused on seemed to have lost their resonance in the "new" Germany. The texts that appeared after reunification deal with the old themes of conflict in very revised form, as Christa Wolf stated in a conversation with her granddaughter Jana Simon in 2008 (141).[11] As an author she now wrote against the inexorable loss of self, of identity, a fact she admitted in her journal, *One Day a Year* (*Ein Tag im Jahr*), published in 2003. With increasing age, marked by illnesses and a round of periodic hospitalizations, at the age of eighty years in 2008, Christa Wolf noted that her interest in external affairs was dwindling. Despite the fact that she continued to follow political events, they had lost their relevance to her own life, as can be seen in entries in the posthumous publication of the sequel to *One Day a Year*: "If I were to try to put my feelings into words, I would probably have to say: None of this concerns me any longer. My time has passed. This is no longer my world" (*Ein Tag im Jahr im Neuen Jahrhundert* 128, my translation). Gone was the once ever-present sense of being responsible for whatever happens: "Ich fühle mich nicht mehr verantwortlich für das, was geschieht" (130) ("I no longer feel responsible for what happens", my translation).

As these events, in the main geopolitical, were followed in quick succession by globalization and the financial crisis that began in 2008, Christa Wolf seems to have experienced a personal "Schrumpfprozess" (process of personal diminishment; Simon 237). Struggling with illness, she invested her remaining energy in the *City of Angels* manuscript, which she referred to as "Schwerarbeit" (difficult work; *Ein Tag im Jahr im Neuen Jahrhundert* 129). The resulting virtuoso work examines, uncompromisingly, for the last time many of the highs and lows of her life. In the end, what remains is a questioning of her own existence, freed from the hope that utopias were possible.

In the two decades between reunification and her death, Christa Wolf increasingly shifted her attention to the private world. The new age remained alien to her; despite her continued interest in being informed, she felt "ein wenig ausrangiert" (pushed aside; Simon 244). Retreat into the familial provided her with comfort and, from the perspective of one who is old, there was a certain sense of liberation in no longer having to feel responsible for the ways of the world.

Alien in One's Own Language

One of the great hopes that Christa Wolf expressed in her controversial 1990 novel, *What Remains*, was that language would be freed from the shackles of fear and censorship. In the book, which sparked the German literary dispute, the first-person narrator searches for her own earlier form of language. Under the constant and visible eye of the state secret service, she reflects on the effects of such surveillance upon her public and private actions. She describes the crisis of writing as a consequence of, as well as a silent hope for, finding that liberating gap in the system: "Don't panic. One day I will even talk about it in that other language which, as of yet, is in my ear but not on my tongue. Today I knew would still be too soon ... Would I ever find my language?" (231). These burgeoning hopes culminated at the historic 4 November 1989 demonstration on Alexanderplatz in Berlin. There Wolf made a plea for a freed language but had to recognize only a few weeks later that such hopes would crumble in the face of political realities that were pointing clearly in the direction of German unification.

As early as the 1960s, in her poetological essay *The Reader and the Writer* (*Lesen und Schreiben*, 1972), Wolf had formulated the ideal of an uncorrupted und incorruptible language, which she sought to realize throughout her life, both under the conditions of the GDR's so-called "socialism in practice" ("real existierender Sozialismus"), as well as later in unified Germany. Her literary oeuvre can be seen to revolve around this concern and the inner struggle to find a form of writing in a language of utmost authenticity.

Conclusion

Through all the changes and upheavals of her times, the analysis of various experiences of alienation remained a consistent feature of Wolf's writing. As a committed witness to her times, she personally experienced multiple forms of alienation in the twentieth century, which had been so laden with ideology. Alienation, in in its many forms, was thus a fundamental feature of her life experiences, but it was difficult to endure such outsiderdom when one longed for harmony with others. Thus, she sought to overcome her own alienation through relentless and painful introspection. In his funeral eulogy at the Dorotheenstädtischer Friedhof in Berlin (on 13 December 2011), writer and friend Volker Braun acknowledged this struggle: "Wer sie ist, das wollte sie schon immer wissen" ("She was always trying to learn who she really is," my translation.

In Braun's poignant summary: "Sie ging bis an die Grenze, an der man sich selbst als Fremder entgegenkommt" ("She pushed to the limit where one encounters oneself as an alien," my translation.

Translated from German by Sandra Belau, Peter Prins, and Hanna Schurtenberger

Daniela Colombo trained as a teacher in her native Switzerland before studying German literature and history at the University of Zurich and at the Humboldt University in Berlin, where she earned her Ph.D. with a dissertation on *Das Drama der Geschichte bei Heiner Müller und Christa Wolf* (Würzburg, 2009). Since then, her publications on Christa Wolf include "Schreiben am Ende der Alternativen: *Kein Ort. Nirgends* und *Sommerstück*" and "'Die Zeitschichten, durch die ich gegangen bin': Christa Wolf in ihren autobiografischen Texten *Kindheitsmuster* und *Stadt der Engel oder The Overcoat of Dr. Freud*" (both 2012). She presently teaches German at the Kantonsschule Romanshorn.

Notes

This essay is a slightly revised and longer version of Daniela Colombo, "Fremdheitserfahrungen als Konstante." *German Studies Review* 36.2 (2013): 365–372, based on a talk delivered at the German Studies Association Annual Conference in Milwaukee, Wisconsin, October 2012.

1. Interesting, as a comparison, is the beginning of *Medea: Stimmen*: "Auch tote Götter regieren" ("Even dead gods reign," 53).
2. In "A Model of Experience" ("Erfahrungsmuster") as part of a 1975 discussion on the writing of *Patterns of Childhood*, Wolf said that the present is everything "that today … impels us to act or not to act, determines how we act or choose not to" (43f.). In the same discussion Wolf also asserted that as a person marked by the period of National Socialism, it was her duty to speak out (42–43).
3. "Cast in ill-fitting roles, they were required only to remain nobodies. And that seems to come easily to us. Ignore, overlook, neglect, deny, unlearn, obliterate, forget" (149).
4. My analysis thus contradicts those critics who see in this splitting of a character—I, you, she—merely a means of understanding the text not as autobiography, but as fiction, a novel. For them, this splitting emphasizes the work's fictive character. I believe, however, that this splitting into three persons emphasizes the inner alienation, whereby the text culminates in the coming together of the three into one, signifying the overcoming of the alienation.
5. This probably refers to an early review by M.A. Orthofer, who invoked the term in an online review published on 3 August 2010: "*Stadt der Engel* is also a stranger-in-a-strange-land novel—feeling oddly dated when, despite referencing contemporary times (such as the financial crisis of 2009), the day-to-day background noise includes everything from the Rodney King trial to the first Clinton election." *Beyond its biblical origin in the story of Exodus, Stranger in a Strange Land was the title of a 1961 science fiction novel by Robert Heinlein.*
6. *Kein Ort. Nirgends* appeared in 1979. The afterword to *Sommerstück* indicates that the author wrote parts of that work in parallel to *Kein Ort. Nirgends*. *Sommerstück* was reworked in 1987 and published in 1989. I also believe that *Was bleibt* belongs to this series of works. It was written in June and July 1979, revised in November 1989, and published the following year.

7. Wolf frequently termed these intervals of togetherness in *Sommerstück* times of "sisterhood" or "sisterliness," and used the unusual word *beschwestern* (to "sister" or "treat like a sister") to describe their behavior toward one another (215).
8. *Sommerstück* 55. These words are spoken by Irene, but the insight they express is clearly to be understood as generally true.
9. Already in a letter to Jürgen Habermas on 7 December 1991, Wolf pointed out that to achieve mutual understanding, it is necessary to tell one's story or stories ("The Leftover Baggage of German History" 122).
10. It should be noted that this insight changed over time for Wolf, and her later texts came to deal more with her identity as a German, rather than as an East German, something she found herself having to confront in conversations while in the U.S. Unification becomes a less central concern than the issue of emerging neo-Nazism. Several texts in *Hierzulande. Andernorts* (1999) take up this issue in significant ways.
11. Jana Simon's 2013 volume of interviews with her grandparents, *"Sei dennoch unverzagt"* ("Be not daunted"), references Paul Fleming's famous seventeenth-century poem "An sich" (To Himself). The poem is also quoted in *City of Angels* (116).

Bibliography

Andersch, Alfred. *Winterspelt*. Zürich: Diogenes Verlag, 1974.
Baier, Lothar. "Wo habt ihr bloß alle gelebt? Christa Wolfs *Kindheitsmuster*, 1994 wiedergelesen." *TEXT+KRITIK 46: Christa Wolf*, edited by Heinz Ludwig Arnold. Munich: Edition TEXT+KRITIK, 1994, pp. 59–67.
Benjamin, Walter. "Excavation and Memory." *Selected Writings*, vol. 2, part 2, edited by Marcus Paul Bullock et al. Cambridge, MA: Belknap Press of Harvard University Press, 2005.
Bergmann, Klaus. "Gegenwarts- und Zukunftsbezug," *Handbuch Methoden im Geschichtsunterricht*, edited by Ulrich Mayer, Hans-Jürgen Pandel, and Gerhard Schneider. Schwalbach: Wochenschau, 2004.
Braun, Volker. "Totenrede für Christa Wolf." *Berliner Zeitung*, no. 292, 14 December 2011.
Faulkner, William. *Requiem for a Nun*. Harmondsworth: Penguin Books, 1965.
Hörnigk, Therese. *Christa Wolf*. Göttingen: Steidl, 1989.
Müller, Heiner. "Vampir." *Vampir. Werke 1: Die Gedichte*, edited by Frank Hörnigk. Frankfurt a.M.: Suhrkamp, 1998.
Orthofer, Michael. "*City of Angels* by Christa Wolf." *The Complete Review*, 18 March 2016, http://www.complete-review.com/reviews/ddr/wolfc3.htm.
Simon, Jana. *"Sei dennoch unverzagt": Gespräche mit meinen Grosseltern Christa und Gerhard Wolf*. Berlin: Ullstein, 2013.
Wolf, Christa. *Auf dem Weg nach Tabou: Texte 1990–1994*. Cologne: Kiepenheuer & Witsch, 1994.
———. *City of Angels or, The Overcoat of Dr. Freud*. Translated by Damion Searls. New York: Farrar, Straus and Giroux, 2010.

———. "Erfahrungsmuster." *Die Dimension des Autors: Essays und Aufsätze, Reden und Gespräche, 1959–1985*. Darmstadt: Luchterhand, 1987.

———. *Hierzulande. Andernorts*. Munich: Luchterhand, 1999.

———. *Kein Ort. Nirgends*. Frankfurt a.M.: Luchterhand, 1979.

———. *Kindheitsmuster*. Darmstadt: Luchterhand, 1976.

———. *Lesen und Schreiben*. Darmstadt: Luchterhand, 1972.

———. "The Leftover Baggage of German History: Correspondence with Jürgen Habermas." *Parting from Phantoms*, translated by Jan van Heurck. Chicago: University of Chicago Press, 1997, pp. 109–23.

———. *Medea: A Modern Retelling*. Translated by John Cullen. New York: Doubleday, 1998.

———. *Medea: Stimmen*. Frankfurt a.M.: Luchterhand, 1996.

———. *Nachdenken über Christa T*. Frankfurt a.M.: Luchterhand, 1969.

———. "A Model of Experience." *The Fourth Dimension: Interviews with Christa Wolf*, translated by Hilary Pilkington. London: Verso, 1988, pp. 39–63.

———. "Momentary Interruption." *Parting from Phantoms*, translated by Jan van Heurck. Chicago: University of Chicago Press, 1997, pp. 9–13.

———. *Parting from Phantoms*. Translated by Jan van Heurck. Chicago: University of Chicago Press, 1997.

———. *Patterns of Childhood*. Translated by Ursule Molinaro and Hedwig Rappolt. New York: Farrar, Straus and Giroux, 1980.

———. *Sommerstück*. Frankfurt a.M.: Luchterhand, 1989.

———. *Stadt der Engel oder The Overcoat of Dr. Freud*. Berlin: Suhrkamp, 2010.

———. "Subjective Authenticity: A Conversation with Hans Kaufmann." *The Fourth Dimension: Interviews with Christa Wolf*, translated by Hilary Pilkington. London: Verso, 1988, pp. 17–38.

———. "Subjektive Authentizität: Ein Gespräch mit Hans Kaufmann." *Die Dimension des Autors: Aufsätze, Essays, Gespräche, Reden. 1959–1985*, vol. 2. Berlin: Aufbau-Verlag, 1987, pp. 317–49.

———. *Ein Tag im Jahr. 1960–2000*. Berlin: Suhrkamp, 2003.

———. *Ein Tag im Jahr im neuen Jahrhundert. 2001–2011*. Edited by Gerhard Wolf. Berlin: Suhrkamp, 2013.

———. *Was bleibt*. Frankfurt a.M.: Luchterhand, 1990.

———. "Whatever Happened to Your Smile? Wasteland Berlin 1990." *Parting from Phantoms*, translated by Jan van Heurck. Chicago: University of Chicago Press, 1997, pp. 25–41.

———. "Wo ist euer Lächeln geblieben? Brachland Berlin 1990." *Auf dem Weg nach Tabou: Texte 1990–1994*. Cologne: Kiepenheuer & Witsch, 1994, pp. 38–57.

———. "Zwischenrede." *Auf dem Weg nach Tabou: Texte 1990–1994*. Cologne: Kiepenheuer & Witsch, 1994, pp. 17–22.

PART IV

Illness, Anxiety, and Trauma

CHAPTER 11

"To Follow the Trail of Pain"
Coming to Terms with the Past in Christa Wolf's In the Flesh

DEBORAH JANSON

Throughout her life, Christa Wolf's approach to writing literature was driven by a profound interest in the interconnections between the past, present, and future.[1] She came to terms with traumatic events from her past by incorporating memories of them into her works of fiction. She also turned to past literary works for analogies that shed light on contemporary difficulties and provide models for the future. Indeed, this practice of remembering the past in order to posit an ideal future involved giving voice to literary predecessors whose unfulfilled longings she shared. In the 1970s, for example, Wolf was drawn to some of the German Romantics, including Heinrich von Kleist and Karoline von Günderrode, whose depiction of social alienation and expression of longing for a progressive, humanistic community mirrored her own.[2] As a result, she became a leading voice among those GDR writers who countered the politically orthodox view of the Romantics as unrealistic and irrational, and therefore inappropriate role models for socialist citizens.[3] Instead, she and other writers involved in the re-evaluation of Romanticism maintained that the Romantics' socially critical perspective and focus on subjective experience could do more to promote the development of socialist society than could adherence to the orthodoxies of Socialist Realism.[4] Despite conflicts with GDR authorities, however, Wolf's utopian hopes for achieving self-realization and a sense of solidarity with others were ultimately bound to her belief in socialist ideals. With the collapse of the GDR and the subsequent unification of the two Germanys, she came to see that she was no longer able to advance such a vision and instead shifted her focus to coming to terms with the then recent past. Recognizing that it was no longer possible to "turn back the clock" and reform what had been a flawed system, she began the process of reflecting on her own experiences as an engaged GDR writer and citizen—a process that she viewed as a necessary precondition for moving forward.[5]

Certainly *In the Flesh* (*Leibhaftig*, 2002) can be read as Wolf's attempt to address the inner conflict that she felt over the demise of the GDR. The novel traces the recovery process of an unnamed protagonist—a stand-in for Wolf—who lies critically ill in an East Berlin hospital just before the collapse of the state. Her feverish dreams re-enact scenes that reflect the disillusionment, guilt, embarrassment, and despair she suffered as a result of her involvement in Party politics, while lines from literature—especially works by Goethe—comfort her and help her to interpret the dream-induced memories. The protagonist's physical condition—a burst appendix followed by severe infection—corresponds to health problems that Wolf herself experienced in the late 1980s, just as her mental suffering reflects Wolf's anguish over the loss of the GDR and what she had regarded as its utopian potential. The physical and emotional trauma of the protagonist is accompanied by her determination to remember and come to terms with the past in the hope of healing both mind and body. The novel thus reflects an embodied memory process that corresponds to the feminist art of memory discussed by Michaela Grobbel in her 2004 comparative study *Enacting Past and Present: The Memory Theaters of Djuna Barnes, Ingeborg Bachmann, and Marguerite Duras*. Unlike the classic art of memory, this approach, which, according to Grobbel, was popular among certain modernist and post-modernist women writers of the twentieth century, stresses the importance of corporeality in the memory process and attempts to present life not "as it happened," but as it is remembered (182). In their works, a remembering subject sees images and creates scenes that reactivate the memory traces of formerly repressed knowledge resulting from a traumatic history. Bodily symptoms, dream images, and memory scenes, which often can be traced to instances of complicity with corrupt or cruel regimes, comprise self-critical enactments of the past in the (fictional) present, calling attention to the relationship between past and present, and to the materiality of the memory process. All of these features can be seen in *In the Flesh*, where the protagonist, as a remembering subject, hopes to achieve full recovery by following the memory traces hidden in the recesses of her body: her trail of pain.

In both style and content, *In the Flesh*, like Wolf's earlier works, draws analogies between past and present in an experimental and subjective way that merges author and protagonist, reality and fiction.[6] The connections she makes between nature and the poetic spirit recall her Romantic sensibility, as do her depictions of socially engaged intellectuals who fail to achieve the progressive goals they hold dear, especially in those instances when they lack the support of the state while simultaneously feeling the need to align themselves with it. Yet, while this novel exhibits many similarities to Wolf's earlier works, *In the Flesh* also reveals differences in her approach to the past that suggest a new and less ideological outlook. The choice of Goethe as the literary predecessor to whom the protagonist most often turns, for example, suggests a departure from Wolf's earlier practice of invoking primarily the Romantics. Likewise, the protagonist's use of analogies to uncover similarities with her literary predecessors rather than to establish identification with them—a topic discussed in greater detail later in this essay—suggests a less dogmatic and less appropriative approach to the past. Furthermore, although Wolf's earlier works have consistently highlighted body-mind connections, the role of the body here gains even greater significance. It not only allows the protagonist to confront her past, but is also central to the theory of memory that *In the Flesh* elucidates. An examination of relevant passages in the novel will demonstrate how Wolf deploys physical states of pain and delirium, spatially conceived memories, dream images, and lines from literature to reconstruct the past of her remembering subject, thereby producing a self-critical mode of performance that provides a deeper understanding of her life in the GDR. On the one hand, then, the protagonist is a stand-in for Wolf and what she endured as an important writer in the GDR, while, on the other, she is clearly not Wolf, but a construct created to shed light on the relevance of past events for coming to terms with the present and anticipating the future. In this regard, *In the Flesh* can be considered the first of Wolf's works that employ what Catherine Smale refers to as the author's "late style" in her discussion of *City of Angels or, The Overcoat of Dr. Freud* (*Stadt der Engel oder The Overcoat of Dr. Freud*, 2010) (Klocke and Hosek 27). In both works, the possibility of the protagonist's imminent death—due either to critical illness or advanced age—causes her to simultaneously focus "in on herself while examining the general historical circumstances that have determined the pattern of her life" (Smale 188). The self-scrutiny with which both protagonists approach the past results in a narrative that connects the personal with the historical, thereby sustaining "two opposing temporalities: one consist[ing] of a retrospective connection to the past, to what has been, while the other is an anticipation of what will be—or rather, will have been" at some point in the future (187).

Wolf's realistic rendering of the protagonist's hospital experience includes both an objective—or external—realm consisting of the many medical procedures the protagonist is obliged to endure as well as visits from her husband and members of the hospital staff. In addition, there is a subjective realm—her interior life—that consists of both extreme physical suffering and intense "talkativeness" (Kaute 50). Her mind is filled with words and images—involuntary memories, lines from literature and mythology, feverish dreams, and sudden realizations—that offer both the protagonist and the novel's readers the means to comprehend her situation. When, in her delirious states, she sees tall flames rising up against dark buildings and hears the sounds of people being tortured, she imagines the evil in the world to be hiding in her body, awaiting surgical removal. This imagery relates to the novel's original (and translated) title, since "*leibhaftig*" means, literally, "arrested," or "captured," in the body, and figuratively, "the em*bodi*ment" of an idea. The word "*leibhaftig*" also refers to the devil "in the flesh," or the devil "incarnate," trapped in the protagonist's body. As a child, she had imagined that her soul resided in her appendix, and now, with her appendix removed, she wonders if she has lost her soul to the devil (89). This concern is also revealed by an allusion to Goethe's *Faust* when she employs a reversal of the original lines to ponder her own situation: "Is there a devil that always wills good and always does evil?" (81). The question reflects the protagonist's embarrassment about having been led astray by political ideology, and her awareness that the ideals that have guided her life, and that she had believed would also improve humankind, have ultimately only made things worse. The guilt she feels about all that has gone wrong in her homeland during her lifetime—including not only socialism in the GDR but also National Socialism, a regime she had supported in her youth[7]—has made her critically ill. Furthermore, the extreme physical pain caused by the infection becomes associated with the torture resulting from crimes committed even before she was born—crimes that, like those in her own lifetime, were executed by the powerful against the powerless:

> I am tormented by the history of pain and torture. The soldiers of Herod who impale tiny children on the points of their swords ... The conquistadores, the crusaders, the princes after the peasants' revolt. The woman, battered, floating in the Landwehr Canal ...[8] The martyrdom and destruction of bodies, my body among them. (13)

These lines emphasize the role that the body plays in remembering past trauma and demonstrate the interconnections between the private and public realms by recalling the physical and emotional agony of individuals who are victims of political crimes.

Connections between body and mind, public and private are sometimes expressed through the use of double signifiers—words and phrases that refer to both the protagonist's physical condition and to her mental state as it relates to GDR political history. She realizes that she has been poisoned not only by the infection in her body, but also by state ideology, and that she is "wounded" both physically and emotionally (63). She thus associates her need to "build up" her immune system with the political *Aufbau*-program of the 1950s (62). When a nurse tells her that she is first in line for an operation the following morning, she realizes that this standing is not a privilege determined by her social worth, but by the "severity of the case" (42).[9] Although she does not look forward to the operation, she decides that she "doesn't want to complain about future things, only about what's already happened" (34). These and other ambiguous expressions illustrate the protagonist's preoccupation with her body as metaphor. Her initial blindness to her poor health corresponds to her inability to foresee her country's demise, her physical collapse parallels the dire state of her country and warns of its imminent collapse.[10] Recognizing the various analogies, she thinks to herself: "My runaway body. Metaphorically. All that's transitory is just a metaphor" (10).

This line from Goethe's *Faust* about the transitoriness of metaphors is repeated several times over the course of the novel, calling to mind a view of literary history reminiscent of Walter Benjamin's allegorical approach. In his 1931 essay "Literary History and the Study of Literature" ("Literaturgeschichte und Literaturwissenschaft"), Benjamin advocated approaching past works of literature in a way that uncovers the meaning they hold for the present, instead of using them to illuminate the context in which they were written.[11] As Marianne Henn explains, "the orientation and production of comparative, illuminative images that serve as a medium and form of perception are decisive for Benjamin's attempt to develop the past so that it becomes a portrayal of our own time, i.e., the present" (13, my translation). Benjamin's approach informs Wolf's use of past literature to depict the present, as is evident in many of her works, including those that re-evaluate Romanticism or rewrite ancient Greek myths. Yet, curiously, the protagonist of *In the Flesh* admits that previously she had not understood what Goethe meant with his famous line ("All that's transitory is just a metaphor"), that only now has its meaning become clear to her (10). This admission suggests that the protagonist—and Wolf—have gained new insights as a result of the healing process, and correspondingly, a new approach to earlier works, both her own and those written by others.

In her earlier novels, *Cassandra* (*Kassandra*, 1983) and *Medea: A Modern Retelling* (*Medea: Stimmen*, 1996), Wolf refashioned the myths about these ancient Greek figures to establish parallels between their stories and specific political situations that directly impacted her life. In *Cassandra*, for example, the Trojan War provides the novel with both its historical setting and its allegorical meaning. Wolf saw in that war the same self-destructive, patriarchal thinking that was inherent in the nuclear arms race of the 1980s, and she viewed herself as a social critic like Cassandra, whose warnings about the future went unheeded.[12] Similarly, in *Medea*, Wolf's version of the tale no longer focuses on the topoi of jealousy and revenge, but instead on patriarchy's universal need for scapegoats as a means to retain power while shirking responsibility. Wolf once again identifies with her protagonist—the Medea she has created—implying that the defamation Medea suffered in ancient Corinth and the media attacks Wolf endured in the 1990s reflect similar instances of patriarchal domination.[13] Marcus Winkler thus argues that

Wolf's use of the past in her mythical re-creations entails a repetition of history that overlooks differences: "The mythical past—even if it has been revised in the meantime—is used to explain what is amiss about the present, it lends it an appearance of order." In the invented scenarios that serve as analogies to the present, the characters Cassandra and Medea are doomed, their utopian hopes replaced by "resignation and preparation for death" (269, my translation). For Wolf, these and other myths fatalistically determine what happens in the present, relegating any hope of achieving the utopian dreams she shares with her mythic counterparts to a distant and unreliable future.

Wolf's invocation of the mythic past is not unlike her identification with literary predecessors from the Romantic era. In *No Place on Earth* (*Kein Ort. Nirgends*, 1979), for example, she sets up structures of identity via a present-day frame in which a first-person plural narrator—a "we"—connects with the German Romantic writers Karoline von Günderrode and Heinrich von Kleist. While the embedded narrative is set entirely in the past, the frame creates a sense of identity not only between past writers and Christa Wolf, but also between past writers and everyone who shares Wolf's longing to live in an ideal world of their own making—a world free from social domination, alienation, exploitation, and environmental degradation. But here again, the only hope for those who partake in this common dream lies in an uncertain future. This is aptly illustrated toward the end of *No Place on Earth* when Kleist asks Günderrode what would happen if the longed-for second Golden Age never materialized. Günderrode's response, "If we cease to hope, then that which we fear will surely come" (117), is not reassuring. In the wake of Wolf Biermann's expatriation in November 1976, this conversation between Kleist and Günderrode hints at Wolf's growing doubt about the GDR's utopian potential and her despair over real-existing socialism—over the gap between "ideal and reality"—thereby unwittingly anticipating the inevitable sense of disillusionment she will experience a decade later.

The setting of *In the Flesh* reflects the moment in history that utopian socialists had feared, when the imminent collapse of the GDR and of the entire Soviet Bloc would signify the triumph of capitalism over communism. With the dissipation of all hope that a socialist utopia could ever be achieved, both Wolf and her protagonist are left to discern what had gone wrong and how to continue living despite the loss of their cherished dream and ultimate life purpose. This new orientation is accompanied by a change in how Wolf depicts the role that the past plays in shaping the present. Her protagonist realizes that Goethe's idea, "All that's transitory is *just* a metaphor" (italics added), suggests that past literature and history provide analogies for the present, but are not identical to it. This shift in Wolf's approach to past works distinguishes *In the Flesh* from her earlier texts. She does not choose to set *this* story of illness and disillusionment in the past or to merge figures from the past with those from the present in order to express a common sense of despair and longing. Instead, she lets past works of literature and myth shed light on the protagonist's present situation so that she (and her readers) may learn from them.

The protagonist's new understanding of Goethe's famous line about metaphors is reflected in literary and mythological references that appear throughout the novel. In one instance, the fairy tale "Sleeping Beauty" and the Greek myth about Ariadne helping Theseus out of Daedelus's labyrinth serve to illustrate the process of disillusionment (or awakening) that she and other utopian socialists underwent when government crimes were incontrovertibly exposed. Like the fairy tale heroine behind her wall of thorns, socialist idealists had been sleeping behind a wall that effectively kept the truth out, until the reign of sleep, or of misperceptions, was over (*In the Flesh* 10). Theseus's eventual escape from the labyrinth corresponds to the protagonist's ability to finally see the truth that had been hidden by government deception and her own idealistic longings. Here Wolf employs myth and fairy tales metaphorically but does not establish a direct identification between characters in past works and the protagonist of *In the Flesh*, nor does she allow the present to be determined fatalistically by a negative situation in the past.

In this novel, labyrinths are not only associated with disillusionment but may also represent physical entrapment and the difficult road to recovery. In the labyrinthine journeys experienced during her feverish dreams, the protagonist travels to hidden recesses of her body. These journeys allow her to gather her healing powers and to direct them at the "killer cells" residing there (15/88). Sometimes in these dreams she hears poetry that provides a fitting literary accompaniment to her struggle. These include a line from Goethe's "To the Moon" ("An den Mond," 1789), "Now finally giveth / my soul release" (cited in *In the Flesh* 66)—a thought that carries her "over and down. Into the depths. Into the shaft" to the Romantic image of her body as a mine, itself a labyrinthine space: "And so he journeys with his light by night / down into the mine. My body as a mine" (66).[14] The intense healing energy that she and her caregivers direct toward the infection in her body further illustrates the new ways in which Wolf deploys analogies here. Rather than succumbing to the power of the novel's central metaphor, which associates her physical breakdown with the collapse of the GDR, the protagonist manages, in the end, to resist death's strong pull. Hence, as Winkler notes, Wolf's approach in this novel contrasts with her appropriation of myth and metaphor in *Cassandra* and *Medea*:

> As therapy, mythology expresses the "intense desire to disappear," but the images [in *Leibhaftig*] awaken a resistance that leads back toward life. The main topics of both preceding texts—sickness, the absence of political alter-

natives, repetition, the temptation offered by death—return once more, but only as stations within the healing process. (274, my translation)

Wolf now draws on literature and myth, as well as on restored memories of hidden truths, to heal the emotional and physical wounds resulting from situations that she regrets, including her brief stint as a "Stasi informant" (IM) from 1959 to 1962 and her failure to even remember this activity until she read her Stasi files in May 1992 ("Die ängstliche Margarete" 158).

The protagonist's recovery is aided not only by her ability to uncover and accept repressed and painful memories, but also by the care shown to her by her loving husband and concerned hospital staff: surgeons, an anesthesiologist, a pathologist, nurses, and a custodian. By presenting the hospital employees in a positive light—as caring, well-trained professionals who do everything they can to save their patient's life—Wolf chooses to depict GDR society in a multi-faceted way, showing that it did not consist only of corrupt government officials and guilt-ridden writers, but also of individuals who embodied humane values and socialist ideals. The novel thus produces an "interesting ambivalence" in its readers, as Brigitte Kaute has pointed out: "On the one hand, the book serves as the story of a final farewell to socialist utopia ... On the other, it serves as a GDR-book ... in the sense that it depicts a deep and lasting attachment to the GDR that does not in any way signify leave-taking" (55, my translation).[15] This ambivalence reflects two prominent features of the memory work undertaken by Wolf and other GDR citizens following unification: the desire to free oneself from ideological blind spots while coming to terms with individual and collective instances of guilt and complicity, and the desire to embrace the past despite its shortcomings and to acknowledge positive aspects of GDR society.

Included in Wolf's conscious staging of a memory theater that enacts multiple aspects of life in the GDR is her creation of Kora Bachmann, the protagonist's anesthesiologist. When the protagonist first hears the anesthesiologist's name, she remarks that it is "[a] name with many associations" (37), a comment that suggests to the reader Wolf's intent to have her novel function as both fiction and theory—as a self-critical and self-referencing memory performance. For not only is "Kora" the name of the mythological goddess of the underworld who had the power to bring individuals back from the dead, "Bachmann" is the last name of one of Wolf's favorite writers, Ingeborg Bachmann, whose use of a "theater of thoughts" ("Gedankenbühne") in her novel *Malina* (1971) resembles in numerous ways Wolf's approach in *In the Flesh*. Both works contain traumatic dream images, including some that conjure up Nazi oppression and torture; both thematize the dynamics of denial and the desire to overcome it; and both include dialogues that the remembering subject conducts with herself to work through painful memories.[16]

The significant role that Kora Bachmann plays in the protagonist's recovery once again exposes the close connection between the protagonist and Wolf since it serves as a pointed reminder to readers that Ingeborg Bachmann influenced Wolf's/the protagonist's approach to remembering the past.

Kora, who functions not only as the protagonist's anesthesiologist but also, in her dreams, as a kind of guardian angel, accompanies her on delirious memory journeys, where they hover above the streets of Berlin and descend into its underbelly, a kind of "underworld," visiting traumatic scenes from German history that the protagonist—the remembering subject—has repressed. These are scenes that she must confront in order to overcome her denial of them, but which, with Kora's help, she can then put behind her. They allow her to realize that she must relinquish her hope that the socialist society she had envisioned would ever become reality, since it had been based not only on ideals she still cherishes, but also on illusion and denial. Yet even though she eventually comes to terms with this new, more pragmatic world view, the renunciation of her socialist dream continues to cause her great sadness. She asks Kora Bachmann, "whether she knew that the pain one felt over a loss was the measure of the hope that one had had beforehand" (125). Moreover, she identifies with the sense of loss expressed in poems by Goethe and other writers, including another line from "To the Moon": "Yet I once possessed / that which is so precious ... And now, to my torment / never can forget" (cited on p. 67). Works of literature and mythology, as well as personal memories that have heretofore been hidden in the recesses of her mind/body, thus provide the protagonist with insights into her situation that give her strength to recover. Indeed, as the final lines of the novel reveal, the protagonist cannot separate her lived experiences from those rendered in poetry, nor can she separate poetry from the natural world it describes. Finally able to leave her bed, she converses with her husband as they gaze out the hospital window onto the idyllic scene that stretches before them:

> The panorama is made up of city and gardens and the lake, which stretches off toward the horizon, sparkling in the sun. The way a lake sparkles in the sun, there are whole poems about that. "It's beautiful in nature, too," you say. I say, "Yes, it's beautiful." "But you mustn't cry," you say. "That," I say, "is in a poem, too." (126)

These melancholy yet poignant lines at the novel's conclusion call to mind the Romantic approach to life and literature that characterized Wolf's work since the late 1960s. They convey a strong sense of love—for nature and poetry, between husband and wife, and for life generally. Yet the closing lines also reflect the protagonist's fear that literature, however it may expand our understanding of the world, cannot bring about the social transformation she desires, at least not within her lifetime. This can be seen in the sadness she feels as she beholds the idyllic nature scene laden with poetic associations, and again in her husband's gentle suggestion that she might be better off if she did not identify so closely with the ideals she sees reflected in literature. The reason for her tears can also be found buried in the poem "Enigma," from which the line, "But you mustn't cry," is taken. Written by Ingeborg Bachmann, the poem describes a futureless time in which "Nothing more will come"—no spring, no summer, nothing that could be called "summer-like" (171). The protagonist's reference to this poem suggests the intense sadness that she feels over the permanent loss of something precious to her—not only of the utopian socialism with which she has long identified, but also of her own life, anticipated by her age and the near-death experience she has just gone through.

Before *In the Flesh*, Wolf's work had been characterized by a vision for the future that was based on unmet needs and longings that she shared with her fellow GDR citizens, as well as with individuals from the literary or historical past.[17] Like the Romantics before her, Wolf looked to the past for inspiration in imagining a future Golden Age, thereby sharing their common "yearning to recreate a paradise" (Sayre and Löwy 113). Yet, as already suggested, even though her protagonists in *Cassandra*, *Medea*, and *No Place on Earth* believed in a future where a community of like-minded individuals would share their ideals, the attainability of such a utopia was never presented as a certainty. The character Günderrode in *No Place on Earth* anticipates that future generations will share her ideals—"to think that we may be understood by beings who have not yet been born" (110)—but she acknowledges that hope alone keeps her dream alive. The forward-thinking women in *Cassandra* also wonder about their counterparts of the future, "[w]hether they would repair our omissions, rectify our mistakes" (132). And in *Medea*, there is no one who could answer Medea's question: "Is it possible to imagine a world, a time, where I would have a place. There's no one I could ask. That's the answer" (180). Yet, if decades before unification, Wolf had already sensed the futility of pursuing utopian socialism, why did she persist in communicating such a vision in her literary works throughout the 1980s and 1990s? According to Charity Scribner, Wolf's refusal to critique some of the SED's most dictatorial practices points openly to a politics of memory that was based in denial. Had Wolf fully acknowledged and exposed the state's brutal and hypocritical policies, she would have had even more difficulty maintaining her hope that utopian socialism could one day be established in the German Democratic Republic. Although she clung to this hope, Wolf was nonetheless aware of her tendency to deny traumatic or irreconcilable events. As Scribner explains: "Denial allows the subject to split his or her attitude toward the lost object so that its loss is simultaneously accepted and rejected" (214, my translation). In the tension between the strength of Wolf's longing to better humankind and her desire to depict reality truthfully, denial became an important means of sustaining her utopian vision.

Scribner's understanding of denial corresponds to the ambivalence Wolf expresses in her earlier works, in which she constructs a utopian vision for the future that she simultaneously doubts can be realized. As a result, her characters appear conflicted about what they want to believe and what deep within themselves they know to be true. Thus, out of allegiance to her family and the state, Wolf's Cassandra often refuses to acknowledge consciously the truth about the political situation in which she is entrapped, although she is able to see and express it during her visionary trances. In *Medea*, the opposite occurs: Glauce, the king's daughter, succumbs to epileptic seizures to avoid remembering traumatic family secrets. Eventually, Medea is able to show her how to uncover repressed memories without losing consciousness, but when the pain of loss, revelations, and betrayals once again becomes too much for her, Glauce commits suicide. These works hint at Wolf's half-repressed awareness that accepting the truth about the impracticability of her socialist ideals would mean relinquishing them, and that this loss had once been too much for her to bear.

Like Glauce, the protagonist of *In the Flesh* had suffered from her attempts to "reconcile irreconcilable things" (114), yet unlike Glauce, she ultimately uses her flights into the realm of the unconscious to work through guilt and overcome denial and, hence, to heal. As a result, the protagonist emerges from feverish, tormented dreams ready to examine what *really* took place during her life as a GDR writer. "To abandon one's defenses and follow the trail of pain," she tells Kora Bachmann, "would be worth the trouble. Would be worth living for" (184). Once made sick by the difficulty of living under "false alternatives," she now wants to deal fully with the trauma of her earlier years before turning to the future. This corresponds to Wolf's realization, pointed out at the beginning of this essay, that she and other contemporary writers should not rush to put forth a "future vision," but should instead focus on providing an honest rendering of their own history. Already in 1993, she suggests that writers should play an important role in this endeavor: "'the truth' about this time and about our lives must come from literature" ("Berlin" 242). This new focus would allow for a more accurate and rich understanding of the GDR past, based not only on historical and political documents, but also on subjective truths derived from personal experience.

Wolf's belief that fiction can contribute to a deeper and more accurate understanding of history corresponds to Walter Benjamin's view that literature should serve as an organ of history, that is, as a means of recognizing and imparting historical truth. In narrating the past, literature can uncover authentic experiences that shaped the lives of real people and that influence present-day needs that still remain unmet. What the protagonist realizes she must do—"follow the trail of pain"—is precisely the task that Wolf undertook by writing *In the Flesh*, and that she continued to pursue in *City of Angels or, The Overcoat of Dr. Freud*, published eight years later. In the latter work, its protagonist, another stand-in for Wolf, is preoccupied with reviewing her GDR past and with coming to terms with the then emerging media revelations that decades earlier she had served as a Stasi informant. In the novel's opening pages the protagonist references *In the Flesh* by discussing the difficult and yet necessary task of uncovering painful memories she had previously repressed:

> If someone had showed me a picture of the world of today, I would not have believed it, although my visions of the future were certainly gloomy enough. Whatever residual innocence I must still have been endowed with then has left me. What remained was a resolution that is hard to carry out, that remains unaccomplished, and that therefore lives on, unchanged to this day: To follow the traces of pain and suffering. (7)[18]

By allowing the protagonist of *In the Flesh* to revisit distressing situations from the past, Wolf began to trace the many pain-filled memories that marked her own intellectually rich and socially engaged life. The novel thus serves as a farewell to the GDR only in so far as the protagonist accepts the loss of her socialist dream and her utopian vision for the future. Her focus on coming to terms with issues that contribute specifically to an understanding of GDR history allows her to accept the past, including all the disappointments and mistakes it encompasses. Hence, in writing this novel, Wolf resisted turning her back on forty important years of her life, preferring instead to help shape a sense of collective identity among former GDR citizens that is based on common experiences, including traumatic ones.

Deborah Janson is Associate Professor of German in West Virginia University's Department of World Languages, Literatures and Linguistics. Her scholarly work has concentrated on the theme of national and personal identity in literature by minority and East German writers, and on feminist, ecocritical, and social justice concerns in works from the German Enlightenment and Romantic periods through the post-Wall era.

Notes

1. This interest is evident in many works by Wolf, including *Patterns of Childhood* (*Kindheitsmuster*, 1976), *No Place on Earth* (*Kein Ort. Nirgends*, 1979), *Cassandra* (*Kassandra*, 1983), *Medea: A Modern Retelling* (*Medea: Stimmen*, 1996), *In the Flesh* (*Leibhaftig*, 2002), and *City of Angels or, The Overcoat of Dr. Freud* (*Stadt der Engel oder The Overcoat of Dr. Freud*, 2010). It is also the subject of scholarly attention, as in the

essay, "'Erinnerte Zukunft': Gedächtnisrekonstruktion und Subjektkonstitution im Werk Christa Wolfs," (Remembered Future: Memory Reconstruction and Subject Configuration in Christa Wolf's Works) by Ortrud Gutjahr, who writes: "With her prose Christa Wolf attempts to pursue, in an archaeological work of memory, that which transcends time—the unredeemed aspects of the past that point to later life, to a not yet existent future, via a surplus of life unlived" (53, my translation).
2. In a 1982 interview with Frauke Meyer-Gosau titled "Kultur ist, was gelebt wird," Wolf clearly articulates the parallels she perceives between the German Romantic era of the early nineteenth century and GDR society of the 1970s. This interview was reprinted as "Projektionsraum Romantik" three years later, and translated in 1988 as "Romanticism in Perspective: A Conversation with Frauke Meyer-Gosau."
3. Wolf's contributions to the re-evaluation of Romanticism in the GDR include the novel *No Place on Earth* and essays about Bettina von Arnim, Karoline von Günderrode, and Heinrich von Kleist. All of these can be found, along with the interview "Projektionsraum Romantik," in the 1985 volume *Ins Ungebundene gehet eine Sehnsucht* (Into the Unconfined a Yearning Leads), which also contains works by her husband, Gerhard Wolf. Other participants in the re-evaluation include Günter Kunert, Franz Fühmann, and Günter de Bruyn.
4. The controversy over which literary tradition was most conducive to the development of socialism harkens back to the Expressionist debate of the 1930s, when Marxists of all varieties agreed that socialist literature must provide a realistic depiction of life, but disagreed about what constituted realism in literature. On the one hand, Georg Lukács and other orthodox Marxists, including Alfred Kurella, Klaus Mann, and Fritz Erpenbeck, argued in favor of the Classical/Realist tradition as the foundation for Socialist Realism and denounced Romanticism and Modernism as irrational, claiming that the Romantic tradition contributed to the development of twentieth-century fascism. Utopian and avant-garde Marxists, such as Walter Benjamin, Anna Seghers, Ernst Bloch, Rudolf Leonhard, and Bertolt Brecht, on the other hand, favored experimental techniques and advocated tolerance for diverse writing styles, recognizing that different life experiences and artistic temperaments call for different modes of literary expression. In 1949, GDR cultural politicians adopted Lukács's position in the literary heritage debate, pronouncing Romanticism too critical, subjective, irrational, and experimental to promote the development of socialism. (See Hans-Jürgen Schmitt's volume on this debate.)
5. This view is evident, for example, in a September 2001 interview with Wolf conducted by Bodo Harenberg, which was published in *buchreport.magazin* and titled "Der Einfluß der Autoren ist marginaler geworden" (The Influence of Writers Has Become More Marginal): "I am still working on the inner conflict I have regarding 'the sunken world' in which I spent most of my life in a very socially engaged manner. I don't yet know where the path will take me and whether I will then be free for a new vision" (my translation, original cited in Cosentino 122).
6. These characteristics were already evident in Wolf's work in the late 1960s and early 1970s, when she developed her signature approach, which she called "subjective authenticity." Introduced in the essay "Selbstinterview" (An Interview with Myself) in 1966 and employed throughout her novel *The Quest for Christa T.* (*Nachdenken über Christa T.*, 1968), Wolf explained this approach in the 1974 interview, "Subjective Authenticity: A Conversation with Hans Kaufmann" ("Subjektive Authentizität: Ein Gespräch mit Hans Kaufmann").

7. Already in *The Quest for Christa T.*, Wolf had addressed links between the Third Reich and the GDR by associating instances of cruelty in the GDR's "real existing socialism" with crimes committed by the Nazis. In *Patterns of Childhood*, this association between the two regimes is much stronger and is central to the novel's message, which questions GDR citizens' ability to solve the problems of their society when they have not yet dealt with the problems of their past.
8. This is a reference to Rosa Luxemburg, the communist leader who, on 15 January 1919, was bludgeoned and then murdered by members of the Free Corps in Berlin. Her body was thrown into the Landwehr Canal and not found for approximately five months.
9. The double meaning of this phrase, which refers both to the protagonist's dire condition as well as to the collapse of her country, is clearer in the German version: "sondern ... nach der Schwere des Falles," since "Fall" can mean not only "case," but also "collapse" or "downfall" (*Leibhaftig* 62).
10. The relationship that Wolf draws between a (female) GDR citizen's poor health and the country's social ills is also addressed in Costabile-Heming, Klocke (*Inscription and Rebellion*), and Smale.
11. Benjamin writes: "What is at stake is not to portray literary works in the context of their age, but to represent the age that perceives them—our age—in the age in which they arose. It is this that makes literature into an organon of history; and to achieve this, and not to reduce literature to the material of history, is the task of the literary historian" ("Literary History" 464).
12. In the essays that accompany the publication of *Cassandra*, a sense of Wolf's identification with her protagonist can be gleaned from various reflections about her. For example, she writes: "I seem to know more about her than I can prove. She seems to look at me, to affect me, more keenly than I would wish" (*Cassandra* 148). Wolf also remarks that Cassandra experienced "the collapse of all her alternatives" (150), a dilemma with which Wolf herself was frequently confronted. She alludes to her own disappointment with the GDR when she writes, "This moment in Cassandra's life must have come when she realized that her warnings were senseless, because the Troy she wanted to save did not exist" (162).
13. Wolf herself suggests this interpretation in a 1997 speech: "Why do we need human sacrifices? Why do we need scapegoats? In recent years, after the so-called 'Wende' in Germany resulted in the disappearance of the GDR from the stage of history, I saw reason to contemplate these questions" ("Von Kassandra zu Medea" 165, my translation). Already in 1993, three years before publishing *Medea*, Wolf expresses her sense of identification with the protagonists she creates after finding herself envious of another author for having written "a completely invented story": "When will I—or will I ever again—be able to write a book about a distant, invented character? I myself am the protagonist, there is no other way, I am exposed, have exposed myself" ("Berlin" 244).
14. As Winkler points out, "And so he journeys with his light by night / down into the mine" is a slight variation on a line from "Tabaklied" (Tobacco Song)—("Damit so fahren wir ins Bergwerk ein"), a poem from Achim von Arnim and Clemens Brentano's collection *Des Knaben Wunderhorn: Alte Deutsche Lieder* (The Boy's Magic Horn: Old German Songs).
15. Klocke also questions whether *In the Flesh* should be viewed as a farewell to the GDR (*Inscription and Rebellion* 72).

16. See Grobbel's discussion of Bachmann's use of a "theater of thoughts" in *Malina* (74–77).
17. See articles by Joanna Jablkowska and Flemming Finn Hansen for more on Wolf's concepts of "future hope" and "remembered future" ("Zukunftshoffnung" and "erinnerte Zukunft").
18. The wording for the last line of this passage, translated here as "to follow the traces of pain and suffering" and in *In the Flesh* as "to follow the trail of pain," is the same in both German works: "Der Spur der Schmerzen nachgehen" (*Stadt der Engel* 14; *Leibhaftig* 184).

Bibliography

"Die ängstliche Margarete." *Der Spiegel*, no. 4, 1993, pp. 158–65.
Arnim, Achim von, and Clemens Brentano, editors. "Tabaklied." *Des Knaben Wunderhorn: Alte deutsche Lieder*, Kritische Ausgabe, vol. 1, edited by Heinz Rölleke. Stuttgart: Reclam, 1987, p. 104.
Bachmann, Ingeborg. "Enigma." *Werke*, vol. 1, edited by Christine Koschel, Inge von Weidenbaum, and Clemens Munster. Munich: Piper, 1978, p. 171.
———. *Malina*. Frankfurt a.M.: Suhrkamp, 1971.
Benjamin, Walter. "Literary History and the Study of Literature." *Selected Writings*, vol. 2, part 2, 1931–1934, edited by Michael W. Jennings, Howard Eiland, and Gary Smith, translated by Rodney Livingstone. Cambridge, MA: Belknap Press of Harvard University Press, 2005, pp. 459–65.
———. "Literaturgeschichte als Literaturwissenschaft." *Kritiken und Rezension*, vol. 3 of *Gesammelte Schriften*, edited by Hella Tiedemann-Bartels. Frankfurt a.M.: Suhrkamp, 1980, pp. 283–90.
Cosentino, Christine. "Christa Wolfs *Leibhaftig* und Wolfgang Hilbigs *Das Provisorium*: Zwei 'Krankenberichte' an der Jahrtausendwende." *Germanic Notes and Reviews*, vol. 14, no. 2, 2003, pp. 121–27.
Costabile-Heming, Carol Anne. "Illness as Metaphor: Christa Wolf, the GDR, and Beyond." *Symposium*, vol. 64, no. 3, 2010, pp. 202–19.
Finn Hansen, Flemming. "'Erinnerte Zukunft': Ein zentraler Begriff der Poetik und Geschichtsauffassung Christa Wolfs." *Orbis Litterarum*, vol. 44, 1989, pp. 128–60.
Grobbel, Michaela. *Enacting Past and Present: The Memory Theaters of Djuna Barnes, Ingeborg Bachmann, and Marguerite Duras*. Oxford: Lexington Books, 2004.
Gutjahr, Ortrud. "'Erinnerte Zukunft': Gedächtnisrekonstruktion und Subjektkonstitution im Werk Christa Wolfs." *Erinnerte Zukunft: 11 Studien zum Werk Christa Wolfs*, edited by Wolfram Mauser. Würzburg: Königshausen und Neumann, 1985, pp. 53–80.
Harenberg, Bodo. "Der Einfluß der Autoren ist marginaler geworden." *buchreport. magazin*, September 2001. Reprinted as "'Ich habe die Arbeit gebraucht, um zu leben': Zur Erinnerung an die verstorbene Christa Wolf: Ein Interview."

buchreport, 1 December 2011, https://www.buchreport.de/news/ich-habe-die-arbeit-gebraucht-um-zu-leben/.
Henn, Marianne. "Einleitung." *Geschichte(n)—Erzählen: Konstruktionen von Vergangenheit in literarischen Werken deutschsprachiger Autorinnen seit dem 18. Jahrhundert*, edited by Marianne Henn, Irmela von der Lühe, and Anita Runge. Göttingen: Wallstein, 2005, pp. 7–17.
Jablkowska, Joanna. "Zwischen Geist und Macht: Der historische Diskurs als erfüllter Augenblick in *Kein Ort. Nirgends* von Christa Wolf." *Geschichte(n)—Erzählen: Konstruktionen von Vergangenheit in literarischen Werken deutschsprachiger Autorinnen seit dem 18. Jahrhundert*, edited by Marianne Henn, Irmela von der Lühe, and Anita Runge. Göttingen: Wallstein, 2005, pp. 107–24.
Kaute, Brigitte. "Sprach-Reflexion in Christa Wolf: *Leibhaftig*." *Studia Neophilologica*, vol. 75, 2003, pp. 47–57.
Klocke, Sonja. *Inscription and Rebellion: Illness and the Symptomatic Body in East German Literature*. Rochester, NY: Camden House, 2015.
Klocke, Sonja, and Jennifer R. Hosek. "Introduction." *Christa Wolf: A Companion*, edited by Sonja E. Klocke and Jennifer R. Hosek. Berlin: De Gruyter, 2018, pp. 1–34.
Sayre, Robert, and Michael Löwy. "Romanticism as a Feminist Vision: The Quest of Christa Wolf." *New German Critique*, vol. 64, 1995, 105–34.
Schmitt, Hans-Jürgen, editor. *Expressionismusdebatte: Materialien zu einer marxistischen Realismuskonzeption*. Frankfurt a.M.: Suhrkamp, 1978.
Scribner, Charity. "Von '*Leibhaftig*' aus zurückblicken: Verleugnung als Trope in Christa Wolfs Schreiben." *Weimarer Beiträge*, vol. 50, no. 2, 2004, pp. 212–26.
Smale, Catherine. "Towards a Late Style? Christa Wolf on Old Age, Death and Creativity in *Stadt der Engel oder The Overcoat of Dr. Freud*." *Christa Wolf: A Companion*, edited by Sonja E. Klocke and Jennifer R. Hosek. Berlin: De Gruyter, 2018, pp. 181–99.
Winkler, Marcus. "'Kassandra,' 'Medea,' *Leibhaftig*: Tendenzen von Christa Wolfs mythologischem Erzählen vor und nach der 'Wende'." *Wende des Erinnerns? Geschichtskonstruktionen in der deutschen Literatur nach 1989*, edited by Barbara Besslich, Katharina Grätz, and Olaf Hildebrand. Berlin: E. Schmidt, 2006, pp. 259–74.
Wolf, Christa. "Berlin, Monday, September 27, 1993." *Parting from Phantoms: Selected Writings, 1990–1994*, translated by Jan van Heurck. Chicago: University of Chicago Press, 1997, pp. 231–45.
———. *Cassandra: A Novel and Four Essays*. Translated by Jan van Heurck. New York: Farrar, Straus and Giroux, 1984.
———. *City of Angels or, The Overcoat of Dr. Freud*. Translated by Damion Searls. New York: Farrar, Straus and Giroux, 2013.
———. *In the Flesh*. Translated by John S. Barrett. Boston: David R. Godine, 2005.
———. *Kassandra*. Darmstadt: Luchterhand, 1983.
———. *Kein Ort. Nirgends*. Darmstadt: Luchterhand, 1979.

———. *Kindheitsmuster*. Berlin: Aufbau-Verlag, 1976.
———. "Kultur ist, was gelebt wird." *Alternative 143/144*, April/June 1982, pp. 118–27.
———. *Leibhaftig*. Munich: Luchterhand, 2002.
———. *Medea: A Modern Retelling*. Translated by John Cullen. New York: Doubleday, 1998.
———. *Medea: Stimmen*. Munich: Luchterhand, 1996.
———. *Nachdenken über Christa T.* Halle: Mitteldeutscher Verlag, 1968..
———. *No Place on Earth*. Translated by Jan van Heurck. New York: Farrar, Straus and Giroux, 1982.
———. *Patterns of Childhood*. Translated by Jan van Heurck. New York: Farrar, Straus and Giroux, 1984.
———. *The Quest for Christa T.* Translated by Christopher Middleton. New York: Farrar, Straus and Giroux, 1970.
———. "Romanticism in Perspective: A Conversation with Frauke Meyer-Gosau." *The Fourth Dimension: Interviews with Christa Wolf*, translated by Hilary Pilkington. London: Verso, 1988, pp. 90–102.
———. "Selbstinterview." *Die Dimension des Autors: Aufsätze, Essays, Gespräche, Reden. 1959–1985*, vol. 1. Berlin: Aufbau-Verlag, 1986, pp. 31–35.
———. *Stadt der Engel oder The Overcoat of Dr. Freud*. Berlin: Suhrkamp, 2010.
———. "Subjective Authenticity: A Conversation with Hans Kaufmann." *The Fourth Dimension: Interviews with Christa Wolf*, translated by Hilary Pilkington. London: Verso, 1988, pp. 17–38.
———. "Subjektive Authentizität: Ein Gespräch mit Hans Kaufmann." *Die Dimension des Autors: Aufsätze, Essays, Gespräche, Reden. 1959–1985*, vol. 2. Berlin: Aufbau-Verlag, 1986, pp. 317–49.
———. "Von Kassandra zu Medea." *Hierzulande Andernorts*. Munich: Luchterhand, 1999, pp. 158–68. Originally published in *Christa Wolfs Medea—Voraussetzungen zu einem Text—Mythos und Bild*, edited by Marianne Hochgeschurz and Gerhard Wolf. Berlin: Janus Press, 1998.
Wolf, Christa, and Gerhard Wolf. "Projektionsraum Romantik: Ein Gespräch." *Ins Ungebundene gehet eine Sehnsucht*. Berlin: Aufbau-Verlag, 1985, pp. 376–93.

CHAPTER 12

Deliberating the "ängstliche Margarete"
Coping with Anxiety in Christa Wolf's *City of Angels or, The Overcoat of Dr. Freud*

IVETT RITA GUNTERSDORFER

Find, reflecting on hell, that it must be
Even more like Los Angeles.
—Bertolt Brecht, cited in *City of Angels* 154[1]

"Die richtige Sprache hat sie nicht gefunden" (She hasn't found the right language). This was the final verdict of the assessment of Christa Wolf, appearing in *Der Spiegel* under the mocking headline "Die ängstliche Margarete" (Fearful/Mousy Margarete) in 1993. The critique was more than belittling of Wolf, who was by that time one of the most important and respected contemporary authors in Germany.[2] Although she had briefly informed the public about her recently (re)discovered involvement as an informant (IM) for the Stasi (secret police) under the cover name "IM Margarete" between 1959 and 1962,[3] the article in *Der Spiegel* criticized her silence about her past. Up to this point Wolf had missed the opportunity to give an extensive and plausible explanation of why she kept silent for so long about this early period in her writing career, when she was not only still committed to socialism, but also optimistic that the GDR government was working toward the same ideals that she had cherished. With the title of this article, *Der Spiegel* also put its finger directly on the wound of Christa Wolf—a wound that breaks open time and time again in Wolf's writing: *angst*.

In *City of Angels or, The Overcoat of Dr. Freud*,[4] Wolf's last major work (2010), she fills the void caused by her silence in the early 1990s, which had been labeled with the word "anxiousness" by *Der Spiegel*. In the novel she offers an explanation for her hesitations by alluding to the existence of multiple possible realities and takes her critics into a maze of equally plausible interpretations. With this demonstration of the complexity of existential *angst*, Wolf's late response grows into a multi-layered and complex case study of this emotion.

Although fear[5] was already an important motive in most of Wolf's earlier books, in the years leading up to the dissolution of the GDR in the 1980s, it became one of the main themes in her writings.[6] In *Cassandra* (1983), her most popular novel of the time, Wolf explores many forms of anxiety. She highlights the inner struggle of her protagonist as she endeavors to counteract the overpowering affect of fear. Cassandra's anxiety, with its own story of emergence and liberation, follows recurring patterns and gender-specific roles and often is a cause for illness. As the protagonist explains her emotions:

> It occurs to me that secretly I am tracking the story of my fear. Or more precisely, the story of its unbridling: more precisely still, of its setting free. Yes, it's true, fear too can be set free, and that shows that it belongs with everything and everyone who is oppressed. The king's daughter is not afraid, for fear is weakness and weakness can be amended by iron discipline. The madwoman is afraid, she is mad with fear. The captive is supposed to be afraid. The free woman learns to lay aside her unimportant fears and not to fear the one big important fear because she is no longer proud to share it with others. (53)

More than twenty years had passed since Wolf formulated this passage, but its message continues to resonate in her "fear-fraught manuscript" *City of Angels or, The Overcoat of Dr. Freud* (2010).[7] Deliverance from existential *angst* is what the protagonist has to achieve, and like Cassandra, she stands before the Lion Gates of Mycenae,[8] awaiting the judgment of her readers. As she grew older, however, a new stage of emotional maturity brought about a fundamental cognitive shift. While Cassandra's fear emerged from complex gender relations in her childhood, the protagonist of *City of Angels* now experiences harassment regarding her past. Concurrently, she faces writer's anxiety and the fear of death, as she acknowledges her own mortality.[9]

But it is not just the cause of the protagonists' anxiety that differs in these two novels. As we analyze *angst* in Wolfs "farewell" work, it becomes clear that this heroine reacts to anxiety differently than the protagonist in *Cassandra*. Sexuality and sexual tension is no longer a primary concern. It is for this reason that—in contrast to the novel's suggestive title—we should take a side step and employ a different methodological framework in contrast to the Freudian psychoanalysis. Because cognitive psychology studies the dynamics of personal judgment, cognitive coping, and involves an active mastery of confronting, the major themes in *City of Angels*, it is a more suitable tool here than standard Freudian analysis. As the following analysis shows, the cognitive approach serves not as a replacement of the Freudian paradigm, but rather as a more comprehensive approach, suggesting that literature can be analyzed with the help of different models of psychology,[10] even those that are not among the most common methods of scholarship on Christa Wolf's oeuvre, although several of the essayists in this volume do just that.

Who's Afraid of What?

City of Angels or, The Overcoat of Dr. Freud is a fictional story based on the nine months in 1992–93 that Christa Wolf spent in Los Angeles as a visiting scholar at the Getty Research Institute in Santa Monica. For her these were critical times. After the publication of *What Remains* (*Was bleibt*, 1990), Germany experienced one of the most contentious literary disputes (*Literaturstreit*) among writers and journalists in recent memory; and Wolf especially was a target for criticism. Among her many detractors, mostly men, and from the west, were such well-known and respected German literary critics as Ulrich Greiner, Frank Schirrmacher, and the very famous Marcel Reich-Ranicki. They repeatedly derided Wolf's loyalty to the GDR and her political views with defamatory statements that put into question her credibility as a legitimate "GDR-author."[11] For her it could have been nothing but the workings of the "deus ex machina" when, in 1992, she received the invitation from the Getty Institute, which helped her to distance herself from the emotional pain caused by the criticism in the German media. As she notes in her journal entry for 27 September 1992, her stay in Los Angeles had a very specific nature: "Flight? That would be too easy ... I am on vacation from reality" (*One Day a Year* 490 and 497).

In the *City of Angels* there can be no holiday with happy sunshine and cheerful pictures of the California coast for a writer of Wolf's stature. As soon as her protagonist arrives, anxiety becomes a major topic. On one of the first nights, as she cannot fall asleep in her new apartment in the MS. VICTORIA, the narrator recalls a poem by Bertolt Brecht:

> We have now decided to fear
> Bad life more than death. (26)[12]

According to the programmatic announcement of this poem, the fear of death is not the initial focus of the protagonist's attention. Responding to the questions of an Italian fellow at the Center (Getty Institute), the narrator replies flippantly that the notion of death as the "end of everything" ... "doesn't bother" her (80). Although the issues of aging and death intensify as the novel progresses, the first half of *City of Angels* is not about the inner fears of an aging author who faces death. It is rather a reflection, on two different time levels, of the inner-existential *angst* of an individual. On the first level, the reader encounters a protagonist who recalls an anxiety experienced in the past of the former GDR, to whom the author speaks in the "you" form. On the second level, in a more personal "I" form, we read the thoughts of the same protagonist in the present, talking about the threatening aspects of her intercultural experience and her feelings in attempting to overcome her fear of writing.[13] As she starts to remember the past (first level), the protagonist speaks out loud: "You certainly were afraid, the November of 1976 which is under discussion here" (119).[14] She acknowledges in the same melancholic tone: "I'm scared, of course" (115), as she openly speaks about her work ethic and about the seemingly simple question regarding her German nationality and her point of view on historical events in Germany.[15]

"Anyway, I was scared" (152). The bold and outspoken declaration of this emotion is an undoubtedly risky confession by the protagonist, as her friend Sally warns her: "You can't let any of that show here … When they smell the scent of fear on you they pounce. Like wild animals" (152). At this point, the reader feels the direct tie-in to Christa Wolf, who had received the most painfully negative critique and sarcastic mockery of her "anxiousness" with the epithet "die ängstliche Margarete" in *Der Spiegel*, which had exposed her as an allegedly active Stasi collaborator. By differentiating anxiety as experienced in the past (first level) and as the emotion of writer's anxiety in the present (second level), Wolf's last major book explains that the reasons behind one's actions, once they are seen in their emotional interdependence, are more complex than the author of the *Der Spiegel* article understood. As a response to the critique of *Der Spiegel*, *City of Angels* is not only an important work for Wolf, it is also central for understanding the situation of writers from the former GDR, who were typically confronted with such questions about collaboration and/or artistic freedom.[16]

How Wolf herself struggled through the harassment of the media cannot be stated with certainty, but we can observe the emotions in *City of Angels*, where the effect of *angst* predominates. When the protagonist of the novel finds herself in a stressful situation, she describes it in terms of the most common, bodily reactions of anxiety and immediately thinks about escaping.[17]

> There it stood, "IM,"[18] I didn't want to believe it but my body believed it right away—my heart started pounding, I was soaked in sweat, emergency! emergency! alarm bells, flight reflexes, I would have been glad to run away all the way to the edge of the world. Is Santa Monica the edge of the world? (152)

The sudden shock almost instantly turns into fear of writing, as the protagonist starts an inner investigation of the consequences of publicity and discovers that writing—which ought to be there to rescue her[19]—now can only represent an immediate threat for her: "Every line I write from now on will be used against me" (174).

This catch-22 situation turns into an irresolvable conflict: "Facts lined up one after the other don't give you reality, you know. Facts are not enough. There are many layers and facets to reality and the naked facts are only its surface" (194). But the narrator not only struggles with the "Iceberg model"[20] of facts. As she confesses to the philosopher Peter Gutman, her closest friend in Santa Monica: Due to the distance from the pain, which is necessary for becoming objective and realistic during the writing process, the script loses its authenticity (216). The undependability of memory has an even deeper consequence for the narrator. In the chapter "To look into my own otherness," she refers to herself as a "stranger" (88).

Psychoanalyses and the *Overcoat of Dr. Freud*

With the title of her book, Wolf draws our attention to Freud's conception of *angst*. The interpretation of the title metaphor of Freud's overcoat appears prominently in the middle section of the book: Bob Rice, the architectural guide for her group, tells the story of how he owned and lost Freud's overcoat, claiming that "he would be able to handle any situation in life in this coat..." (115). The narrator, who can no longer avoid the harassment of the media, wishes to possess a safeguard like that and picks up the idea for the title of her new novel, "The Overcoat of Dr. Freud," immediately after the conversation with Rice. With this choice, Wolf turns her book into a symbol: it will be her protective shield against attacks from the media.[21]

The most obvious Freudian interpretation is voiced by Peter Gutman:

> It's really very simple. You wanted to be loved. You wanted the authorities to love you too. That very early childhood fear of the thick snake lying under your bed at night ... But what did that snake have to do with your fears and lies, or of being discovered, or of your mother ... [T]he lie to the mother, that was where horror was implanted within you, bad conscience, fears ("If I did anything wrong today / Then dear God please look away"), self-doubt as the breeding ground for new fears and new offshoots of fear, and also the longing or need to be whole and irreproachable and in harmony with those in charge. To be loved by them. To avoid the deepest fear, of losing the mother's love. (199)

Gutman's interpretation could not be more psychoanalytic. It emphasizes early childhood anxiety about the loss of authoritative love, the theory of *communis opinio* by Freud. This potential explanation for the protagonist's past seems credible, as it also mirrors and corresponds to Cassandra's anxiety and therefore fits into the concept of fear in Wolf's oeuvre (Guntersdorfer 199–257). For the past of the protagonist (first level), this analysis is adequate: at the time when she experienced profound *angst* in the aftermath of the Biermann expatriation in 1976, and—more importantly—during her early involvement with the Stasi. However, in the present (second level) the main character in Santa Monica—unlike Cassandra—is not concerned with authority, mother-love, father-love, or early childhood experiences.[22]

Although at the beginning of her book Wolf offers a glimpse that shows she thinks about writing as "Zerstörungslust" (death libido), she later in the novel distances herself from this Freudian expression. In *City of Angels*, writing becomes instead an active healing process as it helps to reduce anxiety and overcome its related stress (Taberner 122–28).

To demonstrate this shift toward a metacognitive paradigm, the narrator uses the symbol of Freud's overcoat again in a conversation with Sally. After the protagonist confesses that she wishes she had the protection of Dr. Freud's overcoat, Sally warns her against losing control over her feelings: "On the contrary, [the overcoat is there] to take your self-defense mechanism away from you" (152). Immediately after this short dialogue, the narrator receives a negative message in a dream, where she is endlessly unloading a truck until she finds it "totally empty," leaving her with the feeling of hopelessness, drawing her back to her starting point: "What am I doing here?" (152–53).

This dream and the following self-evaluation is the turning point of the novel. The author makes a clear break with the overcoat metaphor. In the second part of the book we read: "Now writing is just working your way toward the border ... Not self-destruction but self-redemption. Not being afraid of unavoidable suffering" (205). Writing, according to the protagonist's thinking, is an active process, cognitive mental work against fear, not avoidance caused by an unconscious death libido.

Cognitive Psychology and the *City of Angels*

With this cognitive turn, directly after the chapter on the metaphoric meaning of Freud's overcoat, the author seems to ally herself with the historical changes within the discipline of psychology.[23] Starting in the early 1950s, experimental cognitive psychology emerged and cemented its legitimacy with a focus on observable goal-oriented behavior. In the 1980s, literary scholars also turned their attention to processes of attention, perception, and reasoning, leading to the emergence of a complex field of cognitive literary studies[24] which focuses on empirical and experimental methodologies that aim to provide evidence for the practice of literary criticism. With this cognitive turn in literary studies we have come full circle, as the literary work is now once again seen as "a deliberately constructed expression," an active mental and emotional project of the author and the reader (Herring 238). In *City of Angels*, the author describes the process of writing with two significant words, which should lead us away from the psychodynamic approach toward a cognitive direction: "aufräumen" (straighten things up, 77) and "sich heranarbeiten" (cleaning up and working to "get through it," 154). These expressions point to a self-conscious and mindful author, whose behavior is clearly observable by the reader. In cognitive psychology these verbs are described with the words "coping" or "mastery." Richard Lazarus and Susan Folkman, pioneers of the cognitive school, first defined coping as "constantly changing mental and behavioral efforts to manage specific external and/or internal demands that are appraised as taxing or exceeding the resources of the person" (141). Coping thus functions in two important ways: by managing or altering the problem by managing or altering the environment that causes the distress (problem-focused coping), and regulating the emotional response to the problem (emotion-focused coping), which depends on the self-control of a person (Lazarus 114).

According to Lazarus's theory, people react to a stressful situation, based on their own judgment of their potential control over the situation, with *angst*, anger, or escape. If one is convinced that it is possible to manage a situation, and it is not beyond his or her power, the reaction is anger, aggression, or attack. If, however, the situation appears to be completely beyond control, one tries to escape. And, most importantly for our interpretation, if the misery appears to be beyond one's influence, and there seems to be no potential to have an impact, the result is *angst*.[25]

Through comprehensive documentation of her time in Los Angeles, Wolf makes public her struggle to cope through these habits of behavior. In many instances, she lets her narrator describe in a plangent tone how she tries the unsuccessful strategy of escaping, which leads no further than the streets of Santa Monica: "I couldn't stand to be alone anymore, I had to be around people, so I walked to the Third Street Promenade" (206–7). Although these sudden dashes into the streets of Santa Monica are frequent, escape is not her most common way of coping. When we think of her cursing outbursts and hysterical seizures, we can state with even greater certainty that it is also not anger, which had been one of the most obvious emotions of Cassandra.[26] Instead, *City of Angels* reveals an author-protagonist, constantly in a state of mental adjustment, trying to adapt to the seemingly uncontrollable harassment of the media and repressing her fear of writing. The reader encounters extensive explanations of the narrator's dreams and inner feelings, and thereby follows word for word the many conversations of the protagonist. In fact, we might say that Wolf's book offers vivid proof that the author did not escape to Santa Monica in order to flee from the truth, but to confront it actively. The mental efforts—"emotion-focused coping"—of the protagonist do not follow a clear strategy. We can identify many examples of self-initiated attempts, through which the protagonist seeks to find answers regarding her past, to protect the self from the others, and to relieve her writer's anxiety as when she recalls, for example, poems by Paul Fleming (116).[27]

Another argument speaking in favor of the narrator's attempt to confront her *angst* is that she reads the diary and journal entries of fellow German writers, who, in an earlier and rather different "exile," had also lived in the Los Angeles area during and after the era of National Socialism in Germany. She immersed herself, for instance, in the works of several of them, but especially those by Thomas Mann.[28] Following Sally's advice, the narrator also translates charismatic life lessons of a Buddhist nun with great curiosity. The nun turns her attention to the problem of *"getting comfortable"* by avoiding suffering and to the idea of *"precision"* and *"openness"* toward the self (37, Wolf's italics). Besides this conscious mental work, the reader encounters the main character as an outgoing, socially active individual, who has numerous conversations with the research fellows at the Getty Center, among them Peter Gutman, who provides the previously mentioned Freudian explanation. With all of these attempts to cope as she works through the problematic situation, with rigorous thinking and an intentional reactivation of her memory in her "exile," the author continually lays bare her inner stress and anxiety.

Turn to Cognitive Magical Mastery: The Free Woman Learns ... Not to Fear the One Big Important Fear

In the last part of the book, the tone begins to yield to a sedate, calm voice. Christa Wolf moves toward the conclusion slowly, preparing the reader for a melancholic farewell from Los Angeles. Parallel to the recurring topic of aging in the second half of the book, the coping style of the author-protagonist changes into what the cognitive psychologist David. L. Gutmann calls "magical mastery." According to Gutmann, people cope in a "magical mastery" modus when they start to believe in the potential of help from unreal agents, such as angels or uncontrollable natural forces (95–100). As he also points out, this type of coping tends to increase with age as active coping (aggressive action) declines. The turn to "magical mastery" is one of the key moments of *City of Angels:* after one of the most extreme and painful episodes of active emotional mastery, in which she sings German folk songs out loud for an entire night (188–89), the protagonist wakes up to this magical turn:

> A few hours later I was sitting at the narrow end of the big table at my machine, I could see a low ridge of the roof and there was a blue bird, big and beautiful, with shimmering feathers that I had never seen there and I never saw again. It came right up to my window, sat down on the ledge, tilted its glittering silver head to the side, and looked at me. I knew that it was a messenger, and I understood the message, which cannot be expressed in words. (189)

We are not told what that message was. Instead, just a few pages later, we encounter another supernatural element. The mystery that had occupied the protagonist in Santa Monica is unexpectedly solved: the person with the initial letter "L.," whose correspondence the narrator reads during her stay, receives by coincidence a name and an identity. The protagonist attaches immense relevance to this sudden "*Glück*" (providence; Wolf's italics): "The workings of chance are strange. I find it almost embarrassing that chance can change mood so drastically, so that it suddenly seems possible that things will get better" (226).[29] The motivational power of this magical element appears directly after this conclusion, as the protagonist describes a dream in which she hears a voice:

> I dreamed about an enormous dark body of water that I had to cross. A red full moon hung in the sky. ... I walked and walked through the knee-high water. I couldn't see the shore and it seemed impossible that I would ever reach it. Still, I didn't feel afraid or hopeless. When I woke up, a voice I didn't recognize said: CITY OF ANGELS. I took it as a challenge. (298)

The power of the supernatural is evident here: it reduces anxiety, and the author-protagonist receives new energy for activity, that is, for writing.

The presence of these magical elements does not have only an optimistic effect on the protagonist. As the most influential unreal creature, the black angel Angelina enters the story, and the protagonist receives a most negative message from her: "Angelina told me you don't have to explain everything, and by the way, I was sick" (254). A few lines later, the appearance of the angel prompts the narrator to a devastating realization: "What had mattered before had lost its importance. Now I knew that I had to die. I knew how fragile we are. Old age began" (255).[30] By placing Angelina in the context of aging, the author reveals—in accordance with the cognitive theory of the real-life David L. Gutmann—a strong connection between old age and the magical. And, coincidentally, the fictional character Peter Gutman, who is not only the closest companion of the protagonist in Los Angeles, but also shares his last name with the well-known cognitive psychologist, is the one who affirms the existence of the supernatural: "And it's certainly possible that the City of Angels is teeming with angels" (272).

Either *City of Angels* or *The Overcoat of Dr. Freud*

Does this all mark Christa Wolf as an adherent of the cognitive mindset? When we consider the title of the book—*City of Angels or, The Overcoat of Dr. Freud*—we have to acknowledge that the author did not choose between the cognitive symbolism of the magical in the picture of the angel and the power of Freud's interpretative hierarchies. We also need not try to answer this question. Unlike modern experimental psychology, which, due to the nature of experiments, "has a tendency to reduce complexity, differentiation and embeddedness" (my translation),[31] Christa Wolf emphasized with her last book that literature serves as a counterargument to observable and measurable scientific reality. As she writes at the beginning of *City of Angels*, "There are several strands of memory" (28). And, as she coped with her *angst*, Wolf repudiated her critics. Instead of being an "ängstliche Margarete," she courageously used her fear to write a complex fiction. In the end, she teaches her supposedly sophisticated critics an important lesson: remembering the past triggers a broad spectrum of emotions and impressions in us, and for these we continually create different and co-existing answers. In this conscious choice of freedom lies the main argument of cognitive psychology, which—rather than psychoanalyses—focuses on active re-mastery and coping.

Ivett Rita Guntersdorfer studied Transnational German Studies, Intercultural Communications, and Psychology at the Ludwig-Maximilians Universität (LMU) in Munich before earning her Ph.D. at the University of California, Los Angeles. She subsequently joined the Junior Year in Munich Study Abroad Program and the Institute of Intercultural Communication at the LMU, where she is currently pursuing her habilitation. She has presented and written on Elfriede Jelinek, Christa Wolf, Arthur Schnitzler, and topics in cognitive psychology. Her book *Angst aus der Perspektive der Psychologie bei Arthur Schnitzler und Christa Wolf* appeared in 2013. Before becoming the Director of the American Year Abroad Program of Bowling Green State Univesity and the University of Salzburg, Dr. Guntersdorfer was professor and interim chair of the Institute for Intercultural Communication at the LMU-Munich.

Notes

1. Original poem: Bertolt Brecht, "Nachdenken über die Hölle," in *Gedichte in einem Band* 830.
2. By 1993 Wolf had published more than ten books and dozens of essays, among them the bestsellers *The Quest for Christa T.* (*Nachdenken über Christa T.*, 1968), *Patterns of Childhood* (*Kindheitsmuster*, 1976), and *Cassandra* (1983). She was awarded the Heinrich Mann Prize (1963), the Georg Büchner Prize (1980), and the Geschwister Scholl Prize (1987).
3. The fact that Christa Wolf had given three rather innocuous reports to the Stasi early in her life surprised Wolf herself, as she was inspecting the extensive Stasi records (42 binders) written about her. It then took her a few months until she informed the German press. (See Wolf, "Eine Auskunft." See also Magenau 423–34.)
4. Three more works edited by Gerhard Wolf were published after Christa Wolf's death in 2011: *August. Eine Erzählung*, 2012 (a short story); *Ein Tag im Jahr in neuen Jahrhundert*, 2013 (a continuation of Wolf's journal); and a pre-story of *Kindheitsmuster* with the title *Nachruf auf Lebende. Die Flucht*, 2013.

5. In the following analysis I will use "fear" and "anxiety" as interchangeable categories. They denote, however, somewhat different emotions: the synonyms for anxiety, such as apprehension, unease, concern, and worry, suggest an experience quite different from fear. As an existential emotion, the core theme of anxiety is facing an uncertain, existential threat in the future.
6. For extensive analyses of fear in Wolf's work, see Kanz and Guntersdorfer.
7. Wolf, *Ein Tag* 95. In 2007 she notes again her "fear of the manuscript" (110).
8. Right after her arrival in Los Angeles, the narrator visits an installation exhibition, where she recalls Cassandra's arrival in Mycenae: "The dark rectangle of sky sucked me in, it reminded me of the square Lion Gate of Mycenae, behind which darkness lay in wait for the vanquished, the final darkness [that] my night-dark rectangle of sky gave me only a foretaste of ... the senses vanished" (22–23).
9. See an extensive interpretation of aging in Wolf's work in Taberner 92–140.
10. There are several introductory approaches to cognitive literary analyses. Among them is the overview by Isabel Jaén and Julien J. Simon.
11. See the articles about the controversy in the German media in Thomas Anz's edited volume.
12. Refrain from the poem "Resolution der Kommunarden" from Brecht's *Svendborger Gedichte* (1926–39).
13. In the novel, Wolf mentions many dates and historical events without following any historical chronology. She reflects on the end of World War II, the Holocaust, the Cold War, the "Wende" in 1989 (50–51), and the time she was under surveillance in 1976–77 (125). In her essay upon the occasion of receiving the Thomas Mann Prize, Wolf writes, "Zeitschollen [sind in Santa Monica] in Bewegung geraten" (Clumps of time have begun to move (stir?)), 18, my translation.)
14. Gallagher sees shame as the major emotion in the book. It is important to note that angst and shame are often mentioned as affections that are closely related to each other. See Guntersdorfer 120f.
15. Christa Wolf refers here to the so-called Biermann Affair in 1976–77. She was one of the protesters who signed a petition against the expatriation of the popular poet/musician, who was critical of the GDR political system. Wolf therefore became a suspicious person in the eyes of the SED.
16. "Then, at last, it came, the question I was waiting for and dreading: What about Germany?" (74). This question appears again, paired with the same emotion, when the protagonist meets Ruth, the Holocaust survivor (95).
17. This type of bodily reaction has been recognized in psychology ever since Charles Darwin described it at the end of the nineteenth century. See Darwin 267–68.
18. IM is the acronym for "Informeller Mitarbeiter," in English translation "civilian informer." IMs were unofficial collaborators of the former East German Intelligence Service ("Stasi").
19. "[S]torytellers too have to destroy the 'original condition' by boldly observing people and transferring whatever seems to go on between them onto paper ... Whatever was there before has to be wiped out" (29).
20. The "Iceberg mode," which is mostly used in psychology and cultural theory, refers to the fact that one can see only the top of the iceberg in emotional problems.
21. The present chapter suggests that there is an apparent merging of Wolf and the novel's protagonist. A further explanation of this topic would go beyond the scope of this study.

22. Cassandra refers to the family constellation of her childhood many times as she explains the emergence and development of her anxiety. In particular, her relationship with her father receives special attention in her memories, which suggests a Freudian interpretation of her fear (Guntersdorfer 222–40).
23. There is evidence of Christa Wolf's interest in psychology. We read in the published interviews with her granddaughter, Jana Simon, that Wolf had considered studying psychology. Gerhard Wolf also mentions her obsession with her psychologist (Simon 217 and 242).
24. Among the ground-breaking monographs are Reuven Tsur's *Toward a Theory of Cognitive Poetics* and Lisa Zunshine's *Why We Read Fiction: Theory of Mind and the Novel*. For a comprehensive overview see Abrantes.
25. See the model by Lazarus translated into a diagram by Lutz von Rosenstiel (93).
26. Cassandra recounts bear a strong resemblance to anger attacks (Guntersdorfer 201–22).
27. Paul Fleming, "An Sich." This often-quoted Baroque sonnet was published in 1642 in the anthology *Teütsche Poemata*.
28. Among those authors are some of the best-known exiles, such as Thomas and Heinrich Mann, Bertolt Brecht, and Erich Maria Remarque, but the narrator also mentions some lesser-known writers, among them Paul Merker and Vicki Baum.
29. See the previous quote from *Cassandra*, referenced in note 8.
30. Wolf wrote these lines in a different font, signifying that she was copying her typewritten notes from Santa Monica.
31. Ute Frevert, "Alles eine Frage des Gefühls." Interview by Elisabeth von Thadden, *Die Zeit*, no. 37.

Bibliography

Abrantes, Ana Margarida. *Meaning and Mind: A Cognitive Approach to Peter Weiss' Prose Work*. Frankfurt a.M.: Peter Lang, 2010.

"Die ängstliche Margarete." *Der Spiegel*, 25 January 1993.

Anz, Thomas, editor. "Es geht nicht um Christa Wolf." *Der Literaturstreit im Vereinten Deutschland*. Munich: edition spangenberg, 1991.

Brecht, Bertolt. *Gedichte in einem Band*. Frankfurt a.M.: Suhrkamp, 1981.

Darwin, Charles. *Der Ausdruck der Gemüthsbewegungen bei dem Menschen und den Thieren*. Translated by J. Victor Carus. Reprint of the volume of 1877. Bremen: Salzwasser-Verlag, 2010.

Gallagher, Kaleen. "The Problem of Shame in Christa Wolf's Stadt der Engel oder The Overcoat of Dr. Freud." *German Life and Letters*, vol. 65, no. 3, 2012, pp. 378–97.

Guntersdorfer, Ivett Rita. *Angst aus der Perspektive der Psychologie bei Arthur Schnitzler und Christa Wolf*. Würzburg: Königshausen & Neumann, 2013.

Gutmann, David L. "The Country of Old Men: Cross-cultural Studies in the Psychology of Later Life." *Culture and Personality*, edited by Robert A. LeVine. Chicago: Aldine Publishing Co., 1974, pp. 95–122.

Herring, Henry D. "Constructivist Interpretation: The Value of Cognitive Psychology for Literary Understanding." *Psychological Perspectives on Literature: Freudian Dissidents and Not-Freudians*, edited by Joseph Natoli. Hamden: The Shoe String Press, 1984, pp. 225–45.

Kanz, Christine. *Angst und Geschlechterdifferenzen: Ingeborg Bachmanns Todesarten-Projekt in Kontexten der Gegenwartsliteratur*. Ergebnisse der Frauenforschung vol. 52. Stuttgart/Weimar: Verlag J.B. Metzler, 1999.

Lazarus, Richard S. *Stress and Emotion: A New Synthesis*. New York: Springer, 2006.

Lazarus, Richard S., and Susan Folkman. *Stress, Appraisal and Coping*. New York: Springer, 1984.

Magenau, Jörg. *Christa Wolf: Eine Biographie*. 2nd edition. Berlin: Kindler, 2002.

Michelis, Angelica. "'To Learn to Live without Alternatives': Forgetting as Remembering in Christa Wolf's *The City of Angels; or, The Overcoat of Dr. Freud*." *Journal of Literature and Trauma Studies*, vol. 3, no. 1, 2014, pp. 63–80.

Rosenstiel, Lutz von. *Grundlagen der Organisationspsychologie*. Stuttgart: Schäffer-Poeschel, 2000.

Simon, Jana. *Sei dennoch unverzagt: Gespräche mit meinen Großeltern Christa und Gerhard Wolf*. Berlin: Ullstein, 2013.

Taberner, Stuart. *Aging and Old-Age Style in Günter Grass, Ruth Klüger, Christa Wolf, and Martin Walser: The Mannerism of a Late Period*. Rochester, NY: Camden House, 2013.

Thadden, Elisabeth von. "Alles eine Frage des Gefühls: Was interessiert den Geist heute so lebhaft an den Emotionen? Geht es uns nur ums Wohlfühlen? Ein Gespräch mit der Historikerin Ute Frevert und der Soziologin Eva Illouz." *Die Zeit*, no. 37, 7 September 2012.

Tsur, Reuven. *Toward a Theory of Cognitive Poetics*. Amsterdam: North Holland, 1991.

Wolf, Christa. "Eine Auskunft." *Berliner Zeitung*, 21 February 1993.

———. *Cassandra*. Translated by Jan van Heurck. London: Daunt Books, 2013.

———. *City of Angels or, The Overcoat of Dr. Freud*. Translated by Damion Searls. New York: Farrar, Straus and Giroux, 2013.

———. *One Day a Year 1960–2000*. Translated by Lowell A. Bangerter. New York: Europa Editions, 2007.

———. *Ein Tag im neuen Jahrhundert 2001–2011*. Edited by Gerhard Wolf. Frankfurt a.M.: Suhrkamp, 2013.

———. "Zu Thomas Mann." *Rede, daß ich dich sehe*. Frankfurt a.M: Suhrkamp, 2012, pp. 13–25.

Zunshine, Lisa. *Why We Read Fiction: Theory of Mind and the Novel*. Columbus: Ohio State University Press, 2006.

CHAPTER 13

Coming Full Circle
Trauma, Empathy, and Writing in "Change of Perspective" ("Blickwechsel," 1970) and "August" (2011)

FRIEDERIKE EIGLER

In a 2008 conversation with her granddaughter (and author) Jana Simon, Christa Wolf states that *City of Angels* (*Stadt der Engel*, 2010) was going to be her last work (141). *City of Angels* might have been her last major novel, but it turned out not to be her last piece of fiction. In 2011, a few months before her death, Wolf wrote the story "August." For a number of reasons this story is puzzling, especially for readers familiar with her work. First, it focuses on the character August—who made a short appearance in the 1976 novel *Patterns of Childhood* (*Kindheitsmuster*)—and on his memories of the immediate postwar period, a time that Wolf had not explored in any detail for many decades. Furthermore, the text seems to lack the narrative complexity of most of her previous fiction. Thirdly, there are few explicit self-referential comments on the processes of writing and remembering that were a trademark of Wolf's work ever since her *Quest for Christa T.* (*Nachdenken über Christa T.*, 1968). In fact, there is a marked contrast between the ease with which August remembers his past, including his childhood at the end of the war, and the arduous process of memory and self-investigation, often connected to psychological distress and illness, that marks the characters in Wolf's *City of Angels* as well as many of her other works.[1]

The story's surprising simplicity and the fact that it is Wolf's last creative work are likely to have contributed to the response in the media. Unlike the mixed reception of some of Wolf's earlier works (especially of those that appeared since unification), reviews of her posthumously published story "August" were generally positive and at times enthusiastic.[2] Echoing the author's moving dedication to Gerhard Wolf that is included in the first edition as facsimile of her handwritten note, most critics read "August" in highly personal terms. This is illustrated in the following excerpts from reviews in the *Frankfurter Allgemeine Zeitung* and *DIE ZEIT*, printed on the back cover of the 2014 edition.[3]

> One of the most beautiful stories Christa Wolf ever wrote. So loving and concise, at the same time understated and heartwarming. (*FAZ*)

> Half a year before her death, the important German writer presented a touching short story to her husband—a present also for the reader. (*DIE ZEIT*)[4]

These excerpts do not do justice to the full-length reviews that appeared in the feuilletons of major German newspapers. But these quotations, combined with the afterword by Gerhard Wolf for the 2014 edition, both exemplify and reinforce some of the main tenets of the reception. By highlighting the fact that Christa Wolf presented the story to her husband at their sixtieth wedding anniversary, a few months before her death, the paratexts place her work primarily in a biographical context.[5] Furthermore, words like "liebevoll" (loving), "warmherzig" (heartwarming), and "anrührend" (touching) foster the impression that "August" is a slightly sentimental story, written by the ailing author. Put differently, reading "August" primarily in personal terms has the effect of shifting the emphasis from the literary to the biographical realm and thus curtailing the reach and significance of Wolf's final creative work.[6]

Another way of approaching the story, one I would like to pursue here, is to place "August" in the context of Wolf's oeuvre—and in the context of (East) German literature more generally. Several reviews comment on the relationship between the story "August" and *Patterns of Childhood*, where the character August first appeared without receiving much narrative attention (less than twenty lines in a 500-page novel). While this is noteworthy, I suggest looking at "August" also in the context of Wolf's story "Change of Perspective"[7] ("Blickwechsel," 1970). This story, which Wolf later revised and incorporated into the novel *Patterns of Childhood*, is more comparable in length and genre than the comprehensive autobiographical novel. Furthermore, "Change of Perspective" establishes a narrative constellation—summarized in the story's title—that then also shapes the novel.

In many ways, Wolf's story "Change of Perspective" and her last story "August," written more than forty years later, complement one another. The early story illustrates how guilt, suffering, and trauma are intertwined in the unsettling historical moment at the end of the war. In "August," Wolf returns to the period immediately following the war. In contrast to most critics' focus on the uplifting storyline and character description, I argue that—even more so than "Change of Perspective"—this late story both references and veils traumatic experiences. Yet unlike "Change of Perspective," "August" also highlights the role of empathy in a particular historical context—the end of World War II—that East German writers of Wolf's generation had long approached in a highly critical manner, emphasizing German guilt and marginalizing German wartime suffering.

Both "Change of Perspective" and "August" allude to the flight and expulsion of ethnic Germans at the end of the war, historical events that could not be openly discussed in East Germany.[8] Public discourses focused instead on the successful integration of the expellees into the new Socialist homeland.[9] Until recently it was presumed that forced migration was therefore rarely addressed in East German literature. Yet Bill Niven shows in his 2014 monograph *Representations of Flight and Expulsion in East German Prose Works* that literature provided a semi-public arena where these events were indeed explored. His study provides ample evidence that East German authors included (post-)memories of flight and expulsion in their work throughout the four decades of the GDR's existence (19–24).[10] Wolf's novel *Patterns of Childhood* is one of the most prominent examples, but for many decades scholars in both East and West Germany rarely discussed it in this context.[11]

Wolf's story "Change of Perspective" predates *Patterns of Childhood* and addresses some of the events that make up the last part of the novel. The historical backdrop for the story are the final days of the war during which the main protagonist (and narrator), together with members of her family, flees westward, ahead of the approaching Soviet army. As suggested in the story's title, the narrator's view of the world around her changes dramatically with the beginning of the flight (47). With the hasty departure from Landsberg an der Warthe (today Gorzów Wielkopolski in Poland), the family's sheltered middle-class life is turned on its head (5). As the narrator explains, a "stranger" ("Fremdling") takes hold of her. She attributes her sudden awareness that this departure is final and that she will never see her hometown again to this "stranger in her" (9). It is in this context that she mentions a "horror" that defies description:

> It was on that cold January morning, when I was hurrying out of my town toward Küstrin on board a truck, greatly surprised at how gray indeed was that town in which I had always found all the light and all the colors I needed. The someone inside me said slowly and clearly, You'll never see this again.
>
> My horror was indescribable. (9)

The protagonist keeps this knowledge to herself, encloses it inside her. In the remainder of the story there is no further reference to the shock caused by flight and the loss of home. Rather, the "change of perspective" occasioned by the sudden flight turns the protagonist into an observer. The stranger that takes hold of her compels her: "Take a good look!" (6). This position of critical witness corresponds to a narrative voice that is thoroughly ironic and at times sarcastic. An example is the narrator's response to the imminent victory of the allied forces: "... the world stubbornly refused to end and we were not prepared to cope after a messed-up end of the world" (14). Replete with irony, the narrator references the shared belief that a defeat of Nazi Germany can only equal "the end of the world." The use of the first-person plural indicates that her inquisitive view does not only focus on other characters but also includes herself.

A more prominent example of implied self-criticism is the narrative rendering of an encounter with a group of former concentration camp prisoners and the ambivalent response of the narrator: "And I felt even less up to talk with the concentration-camp prisoner who sat with us by the fire ... And least of all did I feel like knowing about the sadness and the dismay which were in his voice when he asked us 'Where, then, have you lived all these years?'" (20). This comment, "least of all did I feel like knowing," is the penultimate in a series of negations that culminate in the defiant admission "I did not feel up to liberation" (20). As this quotation indicates, "Change of Perspective" complicates both the suggestion that there was genuine interest in the victims of Nazi Germany and the notion that the Allies liberated Germany from National Socialism not only politically but also mentally. Put differently, "Change of Perspective" challenges a view that was at the heart of the dominant anti-fascist narrative in East Germany by presenting a far more complex tale: "liberation" cannot be reduced to a historical event—the defeat of Nazi Germany—but is a long and difficult process that involves working through the continued and insidious influence of Nazi ideology on individuals, including the narrator herself (53). It is fitting that this arduous process itself is no longer the subject of the story but of the much longer novel *Patterns of Childhood*. The "change of perspective" that sets in with the flight separates the narrator from her earlier self. In *Patterns of Childhood* the narrator can approach the girl that came of age during National Socialism only in the third person, not in the first.

According to Niven, one of the main differences between East and West German literature is that GDR authors consistently combine attention to Germans as victims with the awareness of Germans as perpetrators. He employs the term "critical empathy" to describe this position of relative emotional distance that insists on the primacy of German guilt. "Change of Perspective" is a case in point. The story draws attention to the victims of Nazi Germany and the war (via the concentration camp prisoners) while portraying the plight of the German refugees dispassionately and frequently with irony or sarcasm. This narrative stance leaves little room for empathy. An exception is the representation of the violent death of one of the refugees who is killed in a US Air Force attack on civilians. But even this harrowing event is narrated from the perspective of a relatively detached observer.[12]

The void marked by a shock that is beyond description in "Change of Perspective"—and the corresponding lack of affect with which the narrator responds to the events associated with flight—can be read intradiegetically as a symptom of painful or traumatic experiences. Considering that the story was written in 1970, decades after the war, this void also points at a much deeper level to the dissociation from wartime experiences, a phenomenon Wolf considered symptomatic for the generation that came of age during the war and National Socialism.[13] At the same time, the event that remains "indescribable" in "Change of Perspective" also references the discursive limits of addressing the loss of home in the context of flight and expulsion in Socialist East Germany. In sum, "Change of Perspective" illustrates two significant aspects of East German literature: the historical circumstances of flight and expulsion are addressed but suffering and traumatic experiences are downplayed.

The constraints in the GDR regarding collective memory of National Socialism and the war were more pronounced than in the FRG, but it is important to note that a number of West German authors of Wolf's generation shared her reservations regarding the literary exploration of German wartime suffering.[14] The best example is Günter Grass, who addressed the flight of Germans from Danzig/Gdansk early on in his novel *The Tin Drum* (*Die Blechtrommel*, 1959), but without giving much attention to the plight of expellees. While Grass returned to this historical period in several of his works, only in his novel *Crabwalk* (*Im Krebsgang*, 2002) did he engage with German wartime suffering in more detail and with some degree of empathy. He did so both at the plot level (that is, in the context of the sinking of the ship Gustloff and the drowning of thousands of civilians in the winter of 1945) and at the level of metahistorical reflection (an unnamed character, alter ego of the author, comments self-critically on the failure of his generation to have addressed these events).

In his 2000 speech in Vilnius, Lithuania, titled "Ich erinnere mich..." (I remember...), Grass spoke about related issues with reference to collective memory and to his own biography. Reminiscent of W.G. Sebald, who just one year earlier had published his lectures *On the Natural History of Destruction* (*Literatur und Luftkrieg*, 1999), Grass is critical of dominant memory discourses in Germany. He notes that historically there were good reasons for focusing primarily on German wartime crimes and the Holocaust (31), but in a surprising shift he then turns to German victims of the war and states, "Das Schweigen der Opfer ist dennoch unüberhörbar" ("The silence of the victims is nevertheless audible [literally: cannot not be heard]," 33).[15] Grass, like Sebald before him, bemoans what Michael Rothberg has called a "competitive approach" to collective memory, one that sees memory as a zero-sum game and assumes that the memory of one group automatically displaces that of another. Overall, Grass's 2000 speech marks a shift in his own approach to the past by drawing attention to German wartime suffering, including his own loss of home in Danzig at the end of the war.

Toward the end of Wolf's last novel, *City of Angels*, there is a passage that reads like her response to Grass's comment on the "audible silence" of the victims. On a sleepless night during a visit to a Native American reservation, the narrator is haunted by the image of her grandmother, who starved to death during the flight at the end of the war. The narrator explains to her imaginary companion Angelina that she "never really mourned her" because "I refused to let myself think that she was an innocent victim ... I cut off my feelings because I needed to, and wanted to, see the loss of our home and our suffering as a just punishment for German crimes. I didn't let myself feel my pain. When she died, my grandmother was only a little older than I am now, Angelina. And now I see her face at night when I can't sleep. Why now? And why here?" (308–9).

In an analysis of the narrator's self-critical observation, Silke von der Emde explains that being "immersed in the antifascist ideology of the GDR ... prohibited her [the narrator] thinking about German suffering after the war as other than a just punishment" (this volume). Based on a politically informed competitive approach to collective memory, Wolf prioritized collective guilt over individual suffering, even when it came to the literary portrayal of her grandmother in *Patterns of Childhood*.[16] Von der Emde references this passage in *City of Angels* to show the extent to which Wolf's lifelong literary engagement with the complex processes of remembering evolved into a multi-directional network of memories (as conceptualized by Rothberg): "Empathy with others and their memories of trauma and abuse [that is, the encounter with Native Americans during her trip] create possibilities for a fresh understanding of one's own past."

The haunting memory of the grandmother and the narrator's regret, more than half a century later, about her response to her grandmother's death correspond with Grass's comment on the "audible silence" of the victims in his 2000 speech. Both exemplify the late realization by authors of the first generation, including Wolf and Grass, of their lack of engagement with German wartime suffering in general and the human toll of flight and expulsion in particular. In light of this central passage in *City of Angels*, it is even more significant that Wolf returned to the immediate postwar period in her last piece of fiction.

The story "August" focuses on a figure that, like the grandmother, also remained on the margins of Wolf's *Patterns of Childhood*. As the reader learns after a long opening passage that recalls the situation of an orphaned child at the end of the war, the story is narrated from the perspective of the aging character August who grew up in East Germany and who is now, long after unification, about to retire from his occupation as bus driver for a tourism agency. During a return bus trip from Prague to Berlin, he recalls with great clarity the time he spent in the sanatorium as a sickly eight-year-old child[17] who had lost his father in the war and his mother during the flight. The setting is familiar to readers of *Patterns of Childhood*, an old castle in the Soviet occupation zone, now turned half-sanatorium for tuberculosis patients, half orphanage for children who lost their parents in the war. August describes his infatuation with the sixteen-year-old Lilo, an early version of the character Nelly in *Patterns of Childhood*. Like Nelly, Lilo helps out in the sanatorium while recovering from the tuberculosis that she contracted after fleeing from the East. But in marked contrast to the slight disdain with which the little boy is treated in the novel (404–5), we now hear from the perspective of August himself. Most importantly, we learn that Lilo took an interest in the orphaned child and that August remembers her fondly even now, approximately sixty years later.

The act of remembering is addressed, but not problematized; rather, the entire story is framed by an afternoon in the life of the aging character, during which he reminisces about his life. The story's first line, "August is remembering..." (1), thus contrasts sharply with the opening of "Change of Perspective," "I've forgotten..." (3). August himself comments on his early memories several times in the narrative: "He realizes that he can flick through the old stories like through a picture book, nothing forgotten, no pictures faded" (71). This clarity corresponds with internal focalization at the narrative level; his memories are presented from the perspective of the child, and only occasionally mediated by the perspective of the 68-year-old character August.

Yet despite the semblance of simplicity and immediacy, "August" is a carefully crafted text with intertextual references and traces of subtle irony. Examples are allusions to the literary universe of the *Magic Mountain* and to "Tonio Kröger," among others. Aspects narrated with an ironic twist include the eight-year-old clinging to Lilo (14), and the jealousy with which he responds when Lilo attends to the needs of other children (29) or goes for walks with her friend Harry (39). Multi-voiced in the Bakhtinian sense of the term, the dominant narrative perspective of the young August is inflected by the voices of others. For example, when Lilo is asked to stay away from a young patient whose tuberculosis has worsened, the narrative shifts briefly from August's perspective to Lilo's voice: "But she could not just stay away from Little Hannelore now; what would she think? She would stand by the door, she wouldn't go close to Hannelore's bed ..." (33–34).

The "touching" tone of this story contrasts sharply with the self-critical bent and at times piercing sarcasm of "Change of Perspective." Yet, arguably, "August" both hides and exposes a traumatic core that recalls the "indescribable" loss in "Change of Perspective." For instance, August remembers his mother only in the vaguest possible terms. At one point in the narrative, he recalls that he could only remember her hands but not her face when she was reading a book to him (27). With reference to another orphaned child, this kind of "forgetting" is explicitly tied to traumatic experiences during the flight: when the five-year-old *Findling* (foundling), who survived the flight but cannot even remember his first name, acts up and is hard to control, Lilo challenges the nurse who insists, "He is not right in the head … he belongs somewhere else entirely" (29). Instead, Lilo maintains, "He'd been damaged by something he'd experienced, which was too much for him; that's why he'd forgotten everything" (29).[18] This explanation corresponds with a simple but powerful definition of trauma and one of its symptoms—forgetting or, perhaps more accurately, dissociation.

Overall, the narrative suggests that August's clinging to Lilo, his insatiable desire to be around her, is a response to the fact that she is the first person to ask for his name and to recognize him as an individual after the harrowing experience of flight and the loss of his mother (14). Adding a self-referential twist, the text draws attention to the role of stories and literature in screening—or perhaps processing—some of these traumatic experiences. An example is August's intense interest in a poem that ends with reference to a dead child (38).[19] For the reader familiar with Wolf's oeuvre, this image might recall a horrifying incident mentioned briefly in *Patterns of Childhood*, namely Nelly's encounter with a woman who realizes that her newborn baby froze to death during the flight.

The story "August" ends with Lilo's recovery and her departure from the sanatorium. Arguably, Lilo's departure re-enacts August's loss of parents and home. The narrative simply states, "August's heart clenched" (72). This second loss—combined with August's continued experience with state-run institutions during his youth and education (22)—might explain the marked change in his personality as indicated when the aging August recalls that his late wife Trude considered him a "genügsamer Mensch" (translated as: "he really didn't ask much") and muses that:

> He's had a good life, no one can tell him otherwise. August doesn't know if he has changed since he was a child, but he remembers very well that Lilo once said to him: You can't get enough, can you? (37)

In contrast to his insatiable desire to be around Lilo as a child, August's notion of a "good life" as an adult seems predicated on his giving up desire and any claim to agency that goes beyond his narrowly circumscribed personal sphere. This comparison of his adult life with his younger self at the sanatorium is the closest the narrative comes to alluding to the long-term effects of trauma and loss.

Even though the story "August" is narrated via internal focalization of its title figure, we learn very little about his inner life, especially when compared with almost all other principal characters in Wolf's work. What we do find out is that he leads a withdrawn life and that he felt secure and content in his long marriage. We learn, however, little more about his late wife than that she was the more educated and active of the two, and the one who proposed marriage, in part because she saw in August a reliable and good man. We find out that they enjoyed the small pleasures of everyday life in their East Berlin apartment and that they never had children. We do not learn about any passions, positive or negative, or about any inner conflicts or social or political issues that affected their lives or their thinking in the GDR or in unified Germany. In fact, the collapse of Socialist East Germany and the unification that followed are barely registered in the story.

In sum, "August" represents in many ways the complete opposite of the principal characters and central issues of Wolf's main oeuvre, starting with *They Divided the Sky* (*Der geteilte Himmel*, 1964), *The Quest for Christa T.*, and *Patterns of Childhood* and ending with *In the Flesh* (*Leibhaftig*, 2002) and *City of Angels*. In all of these works the female protagonists grapple with the individual's role in changing political systems (National Socialism, socialism, and later capitalism), with ethical dilemmas, and with the difficult processes of self-exploration via remembering and writing. By contrast, a voice that inserts itself in the first-person narrative of "August," refracting the internal focalization, comments at one point, "It has never occurred to him to think about himself" (55). This observation summarizes succinctly the main difference between August and almost all other principal characters in Wolf's work.

In a comparative analysis of "Change of Perspective," *City of Angels*, and "August," Katja Schubert addresses this major shift in Wolf's last story. According to Schubert, Wolf seems no longer interested in issues of larger historical or social significance and has abandoned any reference to utopian thinking. Overall, she reads "August" as a sign of Wolf's profound resignation at the end of her life, as her farewell to history and a farewell to storytelling (241–42). While I find Schubert's comments compelling, I suggest a different approach: instead of arguing that Wolf's last work cancels out her lifelong creative engagement with the roles and responsibilities of the individual in society, I read "August" as an attempt to revisit and reconsider aspects of her own literary and biographical universe, especially as it pertains to the aftermath of World War II. From this vantage point, "August" is neither a statement of resignation nor a testament that repeals her lifelong creative and intellectual efforts.[20] Rather, in "August" Wolf re-examines the complex constellation of trauma, empathy, and creative writing.

As a result, her final story begins to undo what the narrator in *Patterns of Childhood* aptly identifies as *Panzerung* or emotional armor,[21] a lack of empathy that characterizes both the character Nelly at the end of the war and the narrator at the time of writing in the early to mid-1970s.[22] The story does so at a number of different levels: intradiegetically, in the attention and affection Lilo extends not only to August but also to the other children and fellow patients. Significantly, as we learn from August's perspective, it is the shared grief for the loss of one of the youngest patients (Hannelörchen) that marks a moment of deep emotional connection with Lilo. This suggests that "August" is also a story of Lilo: through the filter of August's lens, the reader witnesses her care for fellow patients in the sanatorium and her response to the loss of many, including the death of young patients and friends.

Extradiegetically, the "emotional fortification" is challenged by Wolf's decision to revisit a minor and rather unsympathetically portrayed character from her 1976 novel *Patterns of Childhood* and to put him at the center of her last piece of fiction. Both the intra- and extradiegetic dimensions overlap in a self-referential passage at the end of the story. When Lilo has recovered and leaves August behind in the sanatorium, she promises that she will remember him (40). And here, as with virtually all of Wolf's writing, fiction is closely intertwined with the author's life, an approach to creative writing that Wolf termed "subjective authenticity" early on in her career. As we find out from her husband's afterword to the 2014 edition (81–82), the character August is not only based on a real person, but this boy wrote many letters to Christa Ihlenfeld after she left the sanatorium (a detail that is also mentioned in *Patterns of Childhood*). Wolf kept these letters throughout her life. With the story "August," the author Christa Wolf fulfills the promise of Lilo, her fictionalized alter ego: Wolf remembers him not just privately (via his letters) but publicly by writing a story and finding a language that the character August himself lacks.[23] With her final story, she gives August a voice and a biography.

Yet even in a story that gives August a voice of his own, his early traumatic experiences at the end of the war are merely referenced but not explored. Rather, the story focuses on August's memories of "his good life"[24] and only alludes to the lasting effects of severe loss. While in many of Wolf's other works the narrator seeks to access painful memories, making straightforward narration impossible,[25] August remembers selectively but with ease. Having the character August tell his story facilitates a recovery of his agency vis-à-vis major biographical ruptures and the experience of loss. From this vantage point, Wolf's final work is not only a story about empathy but also one about the power of literature.

As this contribution has illustrated, there are important East German and German dimensions to both "Change of Perspective" and "August." Yet the strikingly different ways in which these "minor works"[26] grapple with the relationship between collective and individual memory, and the need for both critical distance and empathy, also have relevance in a range of cultural and transnational contexts today.

Friederike Eigler is George M. Roth Professor of German at Georgetown University and has widely published on twentieth- and twenty-first-century German literature and culture with a special focus on memory, space/place, and gender. Major publications include *Gedächtnis und Geschichte in Generationenromane seit der Wende* (Schmidt, 2005); *Narratives of Place, Space, and Belonging: Toward a Transnational Approach to Flight and Expulsion* (Camden, 2014); and a special issue of *Colloquia Germanica* on "Contemporary German Literature and Europe," co-edited with Anke Biendarra (2020). Her current research looks at literary contributions to European memory and representations of forced labor and at the response of literary organizations to displaced writers. Eigler is also editor of *Gegenwartsliteratur: A German Studies Yearbook*.

Notes

1. On the processes of remembering and writing as Wolf's response to conflicts or "Störungen" ("disturbances"), see Carsten Gansel's 2010 interview with the author (353–66) and his contribution (15–41) to the 2014 volume *Christa Wolf—Im Strom der Erinnerung*.
2. See the reviews of "August" in *FAZ* (18 November 2012; 21 December 2012), *DIE ZEIT* (3 January 2012, *Süddeutsche Zeitung* (3 December 2012), *Tagesspiegel* (12 October 2012), *Frankfurter Rundschau* (31 October 2012), *Mitteldeutsche Zeitung* (10 October 2012), and *Freitag* (25 October 2012), among others.
3. *August. Erzählungen* (2014) includes three stories, "August," "Change of Perspective," and "Zu einem Datum" (Regarding a Date)—and a brief afterword by Gerhard Wolf, who comments on the autobiographical dimension of all three stories.
4. Unless otherwise indicated, translations from German are my own. The review in *DIE ZEIT*, written by Iris Radisch, appeared on 3 January 2013; the review in the *FAZ*, signed with the initials "VW," appeared on 18 November 2012.
5. The photo of a young Christa Ihlenfeld on the cover of the 2014 edition reinforces an autobiographical reading of the texts.
6. This shift from Wolf's creative work to the biographical realm also marked the public responses to her death. For a compelling critique of the political implications, see Klocke.
7. The English translation referenced in the bibliography uses the title "Exchanging Glances." In my discussion I will instead use the title "Change of Perspective" because it captures the second and arguably more significant meaning of the original German title.
8. These events involved the Soviet Union and its instrumental role in changing the postwar borders of Germany, Poland, and the USSR—changes that resulted in the expansion of the Soviet Union at the price of displacing millions of Poles and

Germans. In Socialist East Germany, public as well as scholarly discourse about these events was thus tightly controlled, if not censored.

9. In the GDR, the term "Vertriebene" (expellees) was replaced with the euphemistic "Umsiedler" (resettler), a term that obscures the fact that in many cases people were forced to leave their homeland.
10. According to Niven, representations of flight and expulsion in Wolf's work from "Moskauer Novelle" (1961) to "August" evolve through the same stages that he identifies in East German literature in general: "literature of reconstruction, literature of retrospection, literature of revisiting, literature questioning official silences, and, finally, literature reassessing the trope of integration" (191).
11. One of the first scholars to discuss the novel in this context was Louis Ferdinand Helbig (136–38). For more recent scholarship, see Björn Schaal, Angelika Bammer, and Niven. For an overview of the scholarship on flight and expulsion, see Eigler 60–63.
12. See Helbig for a critical discussion of some contradictory historical details in "Change of Perspective" (240).
13. Wolf explores this constellation in depth in *Patterns of Childhood*. The novel's narrative structure and the use of the second and third person instead of the first are literary means to articulate this split between past and present selves. The "stranger" in "Change of Perspective" prefigures this split and explains the difficulties of using the first person in the novel.
14. At times, Niven overemphasizes the differences between East and West German literature. Considering Germany's responsibility for the war and the Holocaust, a number of West German authors, including Günter Grass, Siegfried Lenz, and Horst Bienek, were also reluctant to engage with Germans as victims in their writings.
15. While there was never complete silence (or even a taboo) regarding the representations of German wartime suffering, in the new millennium collective memory discourses have become broader and more varied.
16. In conversations with her granddaughter, Wolf makes similar remarks about the loss of home, confirming the autobiographical dimension of her creative work (Simon 214).
17. There are slight variances between the information provided in the novel and the story. For instance, August is ten years old in the novel and only eight in the story.
18. At one point in the story, when the boy threatens to commit suicide, Lilo rescues him by assuring him of her affection (60–62).
19. The line quoted in "August" reveals that it is Goethe's famous "Erlkönig" ("King of the Elves").
20. See Jana Hensel, who rejects the idea that "August" constitutes Wolf's "testament."
21. This short paragraph is left out of the English translation. In *Kindheitsmuster*, the image of *Panzerung* is evoked in the context of a dream toward the end of the novel, when the narrator realizes that her efforts to gain access to Nelly, her former self, might be failing (517). Significantly, the dream follows right after the short description of August, a passage that lacks empathy for the orphaned child (*Patterns* 404–5).
22. As mentioned, this position is characteristic for a generation that grew up during National Socialism and was then shaped by the selective view of the past in the GDR.

23. The story draws attention to the fact that August is not a good writer (64) and that he frequently has trouble finding the right words (74).
24. The final words of "August" read: "Immer noch nicht ist er imstande in Worte zu fassen, was er fühlt. Er fühlt etwas wie Dankbarkeit dafür, daß es in seinem Leben etwas gegeben hat, was er, wenn er es ausdrücken könnte, Glück nennen würde" (40). ("He is still not capable of putting what he feels into words. He feels something like gratitude that there was something in his life that, if he could express it, he'd call happiness," 74). This passage echoes Wolf's dedication of the story to her husband, "Große Worte sind zwischen uns nicht üblich. Nur so viel: Ich habe Glück gehabt" (83). The German phrase "Glück haben" (to be lucky) also evokes the other meaning of "Glück" (happiness), a final example for the intricate network of the author's fiction and life. (This connection is not quite captured in the English translation: "We are not ones for great statements. Only this much—I have been lucky.")
25. According to Pierre Janet, traumatic memory resists the human meaning-making capacity for narration. The goal of therapy is thus to turn "traumatic memory" into "narrative memory" (quoted in Leys 105).
26. These shorter prose works by Wolf (in either the German original and/or in translation) lend themselves to teaching in educational contexts outside of Germany.

Bibliography

Bammer, Angelika. "When Poland Was Home: Nostalgic Returns in Grass and Wolf." *Germany, Poland, and Postmemorial Relations: In Search of a Livable Past*, edited by Kristin Kopp and Joanna Niżyńska. New York: Palgrave Macmillan, 2012, pp. 109–30.

Eigler, Friederike. *Heimat, Space, Narrative: Toward a Transnational Approach to Flight and Expulsion*. Rochester, NY: Camden House, 2014.

Gansel, Carsten. "Erinnerung, Aufstörung und 'blinde Flecken' im Werk von Christa Wolf." *Christa Wolf–Im Strom Der Erinnerung*, edited by Carsten Gansel. Göttingen: V&R Unipress, 2014, pp. 15–41.

———. "'Zum Schreiben haben mich Konflikte getrieben': Gespräch mit Christa Wolf." *Christa Wolf–Im Strom Der Erinnerung*, edited by Carsten Gansel. Göttingen: V&R Unipress, 2014, pp. 353–66.

Grass, Günter. "Ich erinnere mich..." *Die Zukunft der Erinnerung*, edited by Martin Wälde. Göttingen: Steidl, 2001.

Helbig, Louis Ferdinand. *Der ungeheure Verlust: Flucht und Vertreibung in der deutschsprachigen Bellestristik der Nachkriegszeit*. 2nd edition. Wiesbaden: Harrassowitz, 1989.

Hensel, Jana. "Christa Wolfs 'August'." *Freitag*, 25 October 2012.

Klocke, Sonja. "The Triumph of the Obituary: Constructing Christa Wolf for the Berlin Republic." *German Studies Review*, vol. 36, no. 5, 2014, pp. 317–36.

Leys, Ruth. *Trauma: A Genealogy*. Chicago: University of Chicago Press, 2000.

Niven, Bill. *Representations of Flight and Expulsion in East German Prose Works*. Rochester, NY: Camden House, 2014.
Schaal, Björn. *Jenseits von Oder und Lethe: Flucht, Vertreibung und Heimatverlust in Erzähltexten nach 1945*. Trier: Wissenschaftlicher Verlag, 2006.
Schubert, Katja. "Fuite et expulsion des Allemands après la Seconde Guerre mondiale dans l'œuvre tardive de Christa Wolf." *Fuite et expulsions des Allemands: Transnationalé et représentations 19e-21e siècle*, edited by Carola Hähnel-Mesnard and Dominque Herbet. Villeneuve d'Ascq: Presses Universitaires du Septentrion, 2016, pp. 231–42.
Sebald, W. G. *On the Natural History of Destruction* (*Literatur und Luftkrieg*, 1999). Translated by Anthea Bell. New York: Random House, 2003.
Simon, Jana. *Sei dennoch unverzagt: Gespräche mit meinen Großeltern Christa und Gerhard Wolf*. Berlin: Ullstein, 2013.
Rothberg, Michael. *Multidirectional Memory: Remembering the Holocaust in the Age of Decolonization*. Stanford, CA: Stanford University Press, 2009.
Wolf, Christa. *August. Erzählungen* [includes "Blickwechsel"]. Berlin: Suhrkamp, 2014.
———. "August." Translated by Katy Derbyshire. Berlin: Suhrkamp, 2012.
———. *City of Angels or, The Overcoat of Dr. Freud*. Translated by Damion Searls. New York: Farrar, Straus and Giroux, 2014.
———. "Exchanging Glances" [translated in the present article as "Change of Perspective"]. *What Remains and Other Stories*, translated by Heike Schwarzbauer and Rick Takvorian. New York: Farrar, Straus and Giroux, 1993, pp. 3–20.
———. *Kindheitsmuster. Roman* (1976). Munich: dtv, 1999.
———. *Patterns of Childhood*. Translated by Ursule Molinaro and Hedwig Rappolt. New York: Farrar, Straus and Giroux, 1980.

PART V

Christa Wolf and the Visual Arts

CHAPTER 14

A Woman's Voice on Screen
Christa Wolf and the Cinema

BARTON BYG

Throughout her career, cinema was important to Christa Wolf: as a producer of work for films in various forms, as one who responded to cinema both formally and substantively in her writings, and as a "public intellectual" who sought to use film and media, along with other aspects of the author's public role, as a means to engage with cultural and social issues in her country. A brief overview of the numerous points at which Wolf's biography and career intersected with the cinema will help us to understand her legacy in the realm of film. Against this background, I will then explore the post-1989 voice of Christa Wolf, compellingly recorded in the 1990 film *Zeitschleifen* (Time Loops) by Karlheinz Mund and Daniela Dahn and again powerfully evoked in the 2014 film *Der Fluch der Medea* (The Curse of Medea) by Branwen Okpako. The cinema plays a central role in *Zeitschleifen*, as the dialog between Dahn and Wolf circles around the meaning of art and the legacy of the recently defunct GDR. Okpako's film, on the other hand, uses the means of cinema to explore the basic elements of Christa Wolf's cultural presence in 2010 and after. If Wolf tells Dahn in the 1990 film that she really "has given up hope" that Europeans will see the destruction that their history is leading to, Okpako's version of Wolf's own voice, juxtaposed with texts from her *Medea: A Modern Retelling* (*Medea: Stimmen*, 1996), places the earlier elegiac, modernist tone in another context, beyond the end of the GDR, and in a visual dialog with the Greece of antiquity and the Africa of today.

At the outset, however, it may be instructive to also note some parallels between two landmark works of European literature and film of the Cold War period: in East Germany, Christa Wolf's novel *They Divided the Sky* (*Der geteilte Himmel*, 1963) and, with her close involvement in the screenplay, the 1964 film adaptation by Konrad Wolf (no relation); and, in France, Marguerite Duras's script for the film *Hiroshima mon amour* (dir. Alain Resnais, 1959). Although not directly or biographically connected, the works of Christa Wolf and Marguerite Duras in this period are aesthetically and critically parallel. Uniting them is a positioning of the female voice in narrative that has a melancholy yet modernist aspect, a consistent and crucial characteristic of both authors' prose. Various critics have underscored that *Hiroshima mon amour* and *They Divided the Sky* were important turning points in the careers of their authors: Julia Kristeva, for example, has maintained that "all of Marguerite Duras's oeuvre may be found in the text of *Hiroshima mon amour*" (143). Writing of the film *Der geteilte Himmel* after a retrospective in 1986, Peter W. Jansen found it "surprisingly modern, or rather already even post-modern ... [It] is years ahead of many films that were made later. Konrad Wolf himself was never able to surpass it."

Among the influences on Christa Wolf's prose are the "filmic" techniques of flashback and montage, which became central to her writing, at least since *The Quest for Christa T. (Nachdenken über Christa T.,* 1968). Nor should it be forgotten that Christa Wolf and Gerhard Wolf, her husband and occasional collaborator, worked together on screenplays with Konrad Wolf and other directors throughout the "times of tumult," as Therese Hörnigk has called the early 1960s in the GDR (107). Konrad Wolf had proposed making a film of Christa Wolf's literary debut, *Moskauer Novelle (Moscow Novella,* 1961), even before the work had appeared in book form; the screenplay was only abandoned due to Soviet objections. This was followed by their collaboration on the script for the film *Divided Heaven*, which Christa Wolf called "a very intensive collaboration" (Hörnigk 30). The author said she had to rethink the whole novel anew to produce the screenplay for the film, after weeks and weeks of work with Gerhard Wolf, Konrad Wolf, Willi Brückner, and Kurt Barthel (later to be the director in 1966 of *Fräulein Schmetterling* [Miss Butterfly], another banned film).[1] Among other changes, ten characters were dropped, while ten new ones were added, with the result that even Wolf herself could no longer keep the two works separate in her mind (*Progress-Dienst* 1964).[2] After the film was completed, she noted improvement over the book: "I now see many strands of the plot much more clearly than in the novel" (Konrad Wolf, "Zuschauer als Mitgestalter"). By 1989 she held a more critical view of the film, but as she told Therese Hörnigk in their interview, "Between the images and also outside the dialogs, our utopian thinking is apparent, our visions light up..." (30). *Divided Heaven* was followed by another unrealized project with Konrad Wolf called "Ein Mann kehrt heim" (A Man Returns Home); the partly finished film *Fräulein Schmetterling* (Miss Butterfly), which fell victim to the 11th Plenum in 1965–66;[3] the adaptation of Anna Seghers's *Die Toten bleiben jung* (The Dead Stay Young; dir. Joachim Kunert, 1968); and the film based on her version of the folktale *Till Eulenspiegel* (dir. Rainer Simon, 1973), also with Gerhard Wolf.[4]

Film occupied a prominent place in Wolf's life in other ways as well. Her husband and literary collaborator Gerhard Wolf not only worked with her on projects for which she was author/scriptwriter, he was also active as a dramaturg in his own right with the DEFA studios, such as in his work on Konrad Wolf's 1968 landmark film *I Was 19* (*Ich war 19*). The Wolfs' former son-in-law Rainer Simon, who directed the couple's *Till Eulenspiegel*, represented another connection to the world of film. The work on Seghers's *The Dead Stay Young* (*Die Toten bleiben jung*, 1968) as well as *Till Eulenspiegel* (1973) could in itself serve as a microcosm in which to see the interwoven threads of GDR culture at the time and Christa Wolf's involvement with it. Anna Seghers was a friend and mentor, but also a stalwart Communist exile. After *Divided Heaven*, Wolf undertook a biography of Seghers, which was never completed, but which contributed to the anti-fascist film *Die Toten bleiben jung*. Walter Janka, a Spanish Civil War veteran, but also a victim of Stalinist repression leading to his imprisonment in 1956, was another kind of Communist role model. His trial had led to his removal as head of the prestigious Aufbau-Verlag, where Gerhard Wolf later worked. Janka's "rehabilitation" after prison began with work as dramaturg at the DEFA studios, beginning with Konrad Wolf's *Goya*. From that time on, he was involved with film projects that both Gerhard and Christa Wolf worked on and was also their literary and political interlocutor and confidant. It is poignant that the breakthrough for Janka's influence in the GDR did not come until just before the fall of the Berlin Wall, with the publication of his autobiography, *Schwierigkeiten mit der Wahrheit* (Difficulties with the Truth, 1990), in West Germany. The public presentation of this confrontation with Stalinist corruption in the very foundations of GDR socialism included an introduction written by Christa Wolf but read by actor Ulrich Mühe, best known in the US for his role as the Stasi surveillance officer in the film *The Lives of Others* (*Das Leben der Anderen*, dir. Florian Henckel von Donnersmarck, 2006). Wolf also read this piece on the same evening in the famous gathering in the East Berlin Erlöserkirche ("Wider den Schlaf der Vernunft" [Against the Sleep of Reason]).

Thus, by the mid-1960s, Christa Wolf had joined quite a number of GDR literary figures whose work also included writing for the screen; other prominent examples include Ulrich Plenzdorf, Jurek Becker, and Günter Rücker. On the basis of her several film projects, then, it was not surprising that she was one of the "film authors" who responded to a controversial questionnaire published by the GDR film journal *Filmwissenschaftliche Mitteilungen* in 1965. Its lists of the most significant films of the preceding twenty years, from the GDR and internationally, featured prominently films from capitalist countries: the French New Wave, as well as works by Fellini and Antonioni. This was precisely the direction of modernist formal innovation that *Divided Heaven* had represented, along with the dozen films banned in the turmoil of the 11th Plenum. In the survey, *Hiroshima mon amour* is one of the films most often mentioned by the East German film artists, including Konrad Wolf. Christa Wolf did not refer to it, however, but instead mentioned Luchino Visconti's *Rocco and His Brothers* (1960) and Federico Fellini's *La dolce vita* (1960), 8 ½ (1963), and *La strada* (1954), among others.

That Wolf was occupied with questions of modern film aesthetics and their relationship to the traumas of history is also apparent in her critical juxtaposition of Ingmar Bergman's film *The Silence* (1963) and the West German Auschwitz trials in 1964 (Christa Wolf, *The Author's Dimension* 6). As we shall see, this film and its evocative title remained in the discourse employed by Gerhard and Christa Wolf to reflect on the vicissitudes of GDR cinema even after 1989, for instance in *Zeitschleifen*. In addition to formal questions of film, memory, and montage, the question of national identity and historical memory played a significant role in the productive collaboration between Christa Wolf and Konrad Wolf. As she recalled in a 1989 interview, the theme of her *Moskauer Novelle*, the love between a German woman and a Russian man, was very close to Konrad Wolf's own divided affinities, since he had grown up in exile in the Soviet Union (Hörnigk 30). *Divided Heaven* was also not the first of Konrad Wolf's films to treat an impossible love (as does *Hiroshima mon amour*): his prizewinning film *Sterne* (*Stars*, 1959), written by Angel Wagenstein, depicts a non-commissioned officer of the German Wehrmacht who falls in love with a Jewish Greek woman who is part of a transport bound for Auschwitz.[5] There is much biographical and other evidence of the great artistic and personal influence that Christa Wolf and Konrad Wolf had on each other, particularly in their early collaborations in the 1960s, in the context of the 11th Plenum, and in their reactions to the expatriation of Wolf Biermann in 1976.[6] Scriptwriter Wolfgang Kohlhaase had interviewed her on their relationship in preparation for the film *Die Zeit, die bleibt* (The Time that Remains, dir. Lew Hohmann, 1985) several years after Konrad Wolf's death. She never published these reflections and, in the 1980s, commented on the difficulty of engaging with the topic: "He was for many years an important person to me; our relationship was too complicated for me to even remotely describe here" (Hörnigk 30). To my knowledge, Christa Wolf never did write extensively on her relationship with Konrad Wolf.

Although a discussion of the importance of the film *Der geteilte Himmel* for the development of the novel *Nachdenken über Christa T.* is beyond the scope of the present overview, Alexander Stephan has asserted as much on the basis of the debate over the film's formal innovations: "Precisely the debate about the formal techniques of the film demonstrates that it was no longer such a long way to Christa Wolf's next novel, *The Quest for Christa T.* (*Nachdenken über Christa T.*)" (Stephan 58). Although Stephan does not elaborate, this seems to confirm the influence on Wolf of the modifications of the earlier novel undertaken by the film adaptation. For the moment, one connection should be recalled: Christa Wolf received the news of the death of her friend Christa Tabbert in 1963, that is, at the time *They Divided the Sky* appeared and during the preparation of the film adaptation. If Heinrich Mohr is also correct in stating that a first draft of *The Quest for Christa T.* was finished in 1965, this would also make it likely that Christa Wolf had concerned herself with both works at the same time (Mohr 226n8). The common denominator between *They Divided the Sky* and *Christa T.*, which was both a breakthrough in narrative technique and a provocation for a socialist cultural policy of optimism, was precisely the element of mourning and its necessity for the construction of subjectivity.

The gender dynamics in Duras's film *Hiroshima mon amour* have been made explicit even in the conscious choice by a male director of a woman's perspective and a female voice (Morin 27). Both *Hiroshima mon amour* and *Divided Heaven* are now recognized as modernist breakthroughs—by male directors—partly because they use female protagonists to explore narrative subjectivity and traumatic cultural memory. The intervention of several men in cultural policy positions in support of the modernism of Christa Wolf's book and the film was important as well. In her long interview with Wolf, Therese Hörnigk noted "that not unimportant people from the cultural sector decided at some point to mitigate the intensity of the debate and protect you from the most outrageous attacks" (34). Such support from part of the GDR cultural establishment included the award of both the Heinrich-Mann-Preis (for the novel) and the National-Preis II. Klasse (for the film), as well as publications documenting the discussion of both works (see Reso). The film was more easily accepted, according to the author, because it was directed by Konrad Wolf (Hörnigk 31). Wolf even attributed her own position of increasing authority partly to the fact that, as a woman, she was an exception (Hörnigk 25). Her success contributed to the new and more modern image of socialism that SED social policies and the New Economic Program (1963–68) had hoped to create. As Therese Hörnigk puts it:

> Christa Wolf was presumably not in demand as a speaker at conferences and forums just because of her critical, yet supportive engagement. It was also because she was the prototype of an emancipated and good-looking young woman who was able to demonstrate women's equal rights, which had been secured in law but not everywhere put into practice. (97)

Divided Heaven and *Hiroshima mon amour* each represented a modernist turning point in their respective national cinemas. The new waves that began to make themselves felt in Europe in 1959 and after were the expression of a new generation finding its own subjectivity in contrast to the old. Yet the basic shared experience of this generation was still World War II or, for the younger ones, the memory of their parents' shock and "inability to mourn"[7] in the immediate postwar years. Christa Wolf illustrated this sense for the older generation's bankruptcy in Manfred's monolog about his family history in *They Divided the Sky* (43)—his father's opportunistic transition from wearing a Nazi uniform to a Party badge in the GDR. But in the years between the construction of the Berlin Wall and the 11th Plenum, Wolf explained, "We believed that we had earned for ourselves a certain space of freedom. We authors, of our generation above all, even the younger ones … We had to find our own courage, developing ourselves as subjects, which was very difficult at that time" (Hörnigk 30). The closing of the GDR border with the Berlin Wall in 1961 had led to exaggerated optimism that it would quickly lead to socialism with democracy, and thereby to "finding a national subjectivity." But why is "modernism" a necessary ingredient in this reconstruction of subjectivity, and why is "female subjectivity" such an integral part of this modernism? The answer lies in the alienation, break, or doubling that is required for the self to come into existence and say "I"—and particularly to say "I" from a female point of view. Alienation and a traumatic break are found for both Wolf and Duras in the memory of the "grand fantasms" (to use Julia Kristeva's term) of fascism and the atomic bomb. And as Kristeva also explains, this process leads to an interweaving of the political, the autobiographical, and the authorial:

> Durassian melancholy, however, also explores history. Within the psychic microcosm of the subject, private pain absorbs political horror. This French woman in Hiroshima may be Stendhalian, perhaps eternal, but she nonetheless exists because of the war, the Nazis, and the bomb. And yet, through its integration in private life, political life loses the autonomy that our conscience religiously wants to reserve for it. (143)

While the fantasm in *Hiroshima mon amour* was the memory of the lover's death (and the woman's inability to differentiate it from her own), in *They Divided the Sky* it is Rita Seidel's memory of her own collapse or attempted suicide. In the novel, however, the moment where she falls in front of two approaching railway cars at the factory where she works is embedded in a narrative of her progressing recovery. As she lies in a hospital bed, she can see the cars rolling toward her, but she still cannot differentiate between herself as subject and object: "And where they meet, that's where she is. That's where I am" (5). Three paragraphs later, however, the narration intervenes to predict that this fantasm can be overcome: "What she needs to struggle against now is this insistent feeling: they're coming right at me" (6).

The film has removed this fantasm further from any time and place in the narrative of Rita's recovery and leaves the impression that it remains a constitutive part of her identity. Her collapse and the approaching railway car are seen once at the beginning of the film and once at the end, and in identical form. Her memory of it, however, is not located in the hospital, which she leaves in order to continue her recuperation at a sanatorium. Instead, in the film the hospital and sanatorium are absent altogether, replaced by what is supposedly her childhood home, a small house under an incredibly high, arched highway bridge, which recurs as a leitmotif—another signifier of a divided sky. The traumatic memory itself remains separate from this location, and is also not clearly placed in a temporal progression. A doubling is provided by the repetition of the scene, while Rita's sensation, "They're coming right at me," is conveyed by the shot composition. Instead of two cars (which are to meet as they strike Rita), there is only one. Rather than being at the intersection of two tracks, Rita is shown at far left of the wide screen, while the converging lines of perspective reflect the car's threatening movement from right to left. This asymmetry stands in stark contrast to the otherwise carefully balanced composition, which often divides the screen in half. Rita's confrontation with death is presented not with the sensation, "They're coming right at me," but rather by an extreme close-up of her eyes, turning toward the sky as she falls.

At its conclusion, the film thus juxtaposes two images of female subjectivity in the GDR and vis-à-vis German history: the eyes turned up as one falls into unconsciousness and the eyes straight ahead as the modern young woman walks confidently down the street and toward the camera. Both the confident, engaged citizen and the mourning self are still also present in the post-1989 view of Wolf's film work presented in the documentary *Zeitschleifen* by Karlheinz Mund and the writer Daniela Dahn. The title of the film is taken from Christa Wolf's comments at the time Bertolt Brecht's grave had been smeared with anti-Semitic graffiti after the opening of the Berlin Wall, as if time were repeating itself in a loop of film or tape. Her words at the time, anticipating the importance of voices later in her work and in Branwen Okpako's *The Curse of Medea*, were: "That, even that, we had not been able to prevent."

It is instructive that in 1990–91, *Zeitschleifen*, in its look back on Christa Wolf's films, focuses mainly on the 11th Plenum that banned *Fräulein Schmetterling*, along with most feature films made in 1965 and the then recent television adaptation of *Selbstversuch* (Self-Experiment, dir. Peter Vogel, 1990), not *They Divided the Sky*. Since *Fräulein Schmetterling* is an irreverent satire and *Selbstversuch* a futuristic fantasy, the most elegiac tone in *Zeitschleifen*, I would argue, is instead present in the voice-over of Christa Wolf reading from *The Quest for Christa T.*, while on the screen we see images tracing the events of fall 1989 leading to the opening of the Berlin Wall:

> Our words, not even false ones—how easy it would be if they were!—but the person speaking them has become a different person. Does that change

anything? [pause in the reading; paragraph in the novel] Christa T. began, very early on, when one thinks about it, to ask herself what change means. (56)

While the text from *The Quest for Christa T.* involves female subjectivity turning inward on itself, on the more engaged side is a long discussion of the dynamics around the 11th Plenum in 1965 among Christa Wolf, Gerhard Wolf, and Klaus Wischnewski, former head dramaturg at DEFA, who had been removed from his post at the time. Here Wolf makes it clear that she felt compelled to speak out in defense of culture at the party plenary, in response to the attacks on her film in production, attacks that echoed language used in threats of punishment for counter-revolutionaries in Hungary in 1956.

The transition to the discussion of film in *Zeitschleifen* underscores the importance of film in Wolf's career, as well as in the history of the GDR. The first images from the banned *Fräulein Schmetterling* appear immediately after Christa Wolf describes the change in her position toward the Party: instead of attempting to reconcile her disagreement by insisting to officials, "I want the same thing as you," she observes that she had begun to realize, "I want something different." And here Dahn and Mund cut to the first image of Berlin from *Fräulein Schmetterling*. As Wischnewski and the Wolfs look at clips of the film on a monitor, they also discuss what could not be tolerated in the atmosphere of the mid-1960s: hidden camera observations of how GDR citizens really look, on the street or while shopping, "showing the social tensions, the loneliness, isolation and alienation." The importance of the 11th Plenum to the three of them once the Wall came down reflects the importance of the films banned that year for many other GDR cultural producers as well.[8] But this emphasis on the caesura in GDR film history represented by the banning of films in 1965–66 obscures the fact that Christa and Gerhard Wolf were active immediately after the 11th Plenum in an attempt to revive the stunned GDR film industry. Filmmakers returned to anti-fascist themes and World War II, but now with a continuation of modernist, formal experimentation: Konrad Wolf was convinced to exploit his own autobiography for *I Was 19* (*Ich war 19*, 1967), for which Gerhard Wolf served as dramaturg. At the same time, Christa Wolf, with a team of writers, adapted Anna Seghers's novel *The Dead Stay Young*, which was filmed in a starkly stylized manner by Joachim Kunert. Simultaneously, yet another radical film was produced and banned: Heiner Carow's *Die Russen kommen* (*The Russians Are Coming*, 1968, which had been intended as a counterpart to *I Was 19*.

In *Zeitschleifen* the subject of gender comes up in the clip from *Selbstversuch*, Wolf's story of an experiment in which a female scientist turns herself into a man. In the story, a man's tendency to see events in a detached way, as opportunities for manipulation, is connected with the film medium itself. In their introduction to the English publication of the story in 1978, Helen Fehervary and Sara Lennox write:

What is it that Wolf's heroine finds so essential in her female mode of existence? Wolf gives us only hints to go on, but the feminine psychology she presents seems to involve an alternative mode of appropriating the world. The male mode corresponds to what one might term positivistic, or scientific in its worst sense: the external world is taken to exist independently, unaffected by the subject's interaction with it—"Like at the movies." (110–11)

In the clip from *Zeitschleifen*, we hear a male scientist ask the central character, played by Johanna Schall: "How do you feel, Fräulein Anders?" "Like at the movies," she replies. To which the man says, "You, too?" As she states in her discussion with Daniela Dahn in *Zeitschleifen*, Wolf regarded the assertion that a career of accomplishment could not coexist with a private life as a purely male way of looking at the world.

Two key aspects of Christa Wolf's film career would be underappreciated if we stopped with *Zeitschleifen*: first, satire and wit in regard to everyday life, from a woman's point of view; and second, Christa Wolf's use of film, among many other tools, in her role as a public intellectual. As Fehervary and Lennox wrote of Wolf and "Self-Experiment" in 1978: "Like other GDR writers, she views her works as performing a specific social function within their society, both criticizing existing conditions and encouraging change" (109). In this context, it is significant that in 1989, just before the collapse of the GDR, Wolf participated in a taboo-breaking film by Roland Steiner, *Unsere Kinder* (Our Children, 1989), on the phenomenon of right-wing skinheads in the GDR. In this film, author Stefan Heym also makes an appearance, asserting that his generation has failed the world by bringing it to the brink of catastrophe, an even more dangerous situation than the years 1930–33; he even predicts that irreversible environmental damage will result in the political discrediting of his own generation. Christa Wolf, too, is present in the film, not, however, making pronouncements, but in conversation with two young skinheads, asking them about their motivations and about their view of Germany and its history. She tries to explain the feelings of guilt and shame, still not dealt with, with which the older generation thus burdens the younger ones, who see no reason to support the society before them. Empathy with victims is beyond the understanding of her young interlocutors, but she listens attentively to their assertion of the need to believe in something strong and positive.

Because *Zeitschleifen*, too, offers such eloquent testimony about the engagement with society in Wolf's works, from literature to film, I see Daniela Dahn's subsequent engagement as a public intellectual as a continuation of the collaboration between Dahn and Wolf represented in the film. Dahn is, after all, currently vice-president of the Willy-Brandt-Kreis,[9] an organization of intellectuals and public figures from East and West that seeks to engage in productive dialog on the issues facing Germany today. Christa Wolf was also a member.

The stress on *Fräulein Schmetterling*, as opposed to the more history-laden works such as *They Divided the Sky*, emphasizes, even in the fraught period of 1990, the culturally engaged and even humorous, playful, and impertinent aspect of Wolf's film work. For example, even the title "Miss Butterfly" evokes the playful fantasy that challenges everyday life: the protagonist Helene Raupe (the German word for caterpillar, not yet a butterfly), orphaned and not yet eighteen, is confronted by social welfare officials named Herr Himmelblau and Frau Fertig (as the German names mean "Sky Blue" and "Finished," suggesting both vacuous and judgmental personalities, the latter had to be changed to "Fenster" [window] to gain script approval). Helene tries on various roles, from clerk in a lingerie shop to bus conductor, but her inability to hold a job is contrasted with a shocking range of fantasy images: flying over the city, distributing flowers to passers-by with a mime from the circus, blowing soap bubbles in a lecture hall while a man explains human reproduction, dancing a floor exercise that is transformed to the rooftops and towers of the city, and romancing a glamorous boxer. Many images of women's fashion are contrasted with the ruins and construction sites and everyday drudgery of Berlin. A fairy-tale frog appears on a birthday cake, and Helene even dances alone in her apartment to the U.S. pop song "Wooly Bully" by Sam the Sham and the Pharaohs.[10]

Melancholy modernism is certainly one of the principal aspects of Wolf's protagonists' position in contemporary society, and it was a major aspect of her narrative innovations. But in such public works as the film projects, even starting with the confident strides of Rita Seidel at the end of *Divided Heaven*, Wolf's female characters represent a challenge to the status quo based on fantasy and humor as well.

Branwen Okpako uses the medium of film to bring the image of Christa Wolf up to the present. Her film *The Curse of Medea* (2014) is an innovative construction based on interviews with Wolf in 2010, excerpts from the novel *Medea: A Modern Retelling*, and documentary material, mainly from 1989, related to the subsequent revelations of Wolf's early cooperation with the Stasi. As Okpako put it:

> Medea's experiences are similar to those of an immigrant in Germany, whose culture is viewed with skepticism and disinterest and who is encouraged by her host country to integrate and to adapt to the actual culture, just as Medea's Colchians are asked by the Corinthians to bow down before the superiority of their culture. I wanted to translate this text into a film, and the special circumstances, the way the book came to be, played an important role for me.[11]

The discussion proceeds from Wolf's initial refusal to agree that *Medea* was in some way a reaction to 1989 and the way she was subsequently treated in the media to an admission that "I have always written on the basis of conflicts," although "the content determines the form." Wolf confirms to Okpako that the Medea project had gone back to the fundamental themes of *Cassandra*, "An interweaving—if you wish, that is feminine...." Wolf finally does allow that the novel began with her reaction to the public attacks but soon went beyond them, as she needed to "generalize" ("verallgemeinern") the story and thus looked for other levels, for multiple voices. She no longer needed the personal motivation.

Here, Okpako takes her at her word and places the novel not only in the linear progression from 1989 to 1996, or even in the metaphorical world of Medea between two powers, being made a scapegoat by the leaders of Corinth because she knows the crime on which their state was based. As Okpako's Medea says, "Either I am mad or your state is founded on a crime." Here, Okpako also goes beyond critic Holly Case's East/West summary of the novel:

> In *Medea: A Modern Retelling* (1996), she [Wolf] rewrote the legend of Jason and Medea as a story about a society in the West (Corinth) that, because it cannot come to terms with its past, chooses a scapegoat for its own crime of infanticide: Medea, a woman from the East (Colchis). "They wanted to save Corinth. We wanted to save Colchis .... On this disc we call Earth there is nothing but victors and victims."

This is all present, to be sure, but Okpako connects the power of the myth and the beauty of the German language to Africa as well. The tree where Jason finds the fleece is an African tree. The gardens on screen while Medea's healing powers are described are African gardens. And in the despair of political and even mythical failures, the endurance of the work attests to it as a source of hope in spite of the incompatibility of truth and experience. While the Wolf interview and the documentary materials belong to the past, the words and the faces belong to the present, or even the future.

Here the film builds on two of Okpako's earlier works, *The Pilot and the Passenger* (2007), on the poet Christopher Okigbo, and the more recent video installation entitled *Christa / Christopher* (2013). Through projections on facing walls, Wolf and Okigbo enter into a dialog—a construction for the audience of "engaged" authors meeting though times and spaces that never intersected in reality.

Thus, Okpako's film allows us a new way of asking who Christa Wolf is now. Is she the author whose voice we hear over a blank black screen in the cinema, being interviewed in 2010 by the filmmaker? Is she the public figure we see in the video excerpts, reading the text "Für unser Land" (For Our Country, a co-authored appeal, pleading for GDR citizens to remain committed to East Germany as a socialist state while insisting on reform in 1989[12])? Okpako has reframed the video clips to emphasize the hands and faces of the speakers from the GDR documentary clips as well as the hands of Jason and the faces of Medea and the women around her. Or is Wolf the subject of journalism and the *Literaturstreit* (literary critics' controversy)[13] indicated here by words on the screen, newspaper clippings, and a close-up pan across Christa Wolf's face in newsprint? The film opens, after all, with Wolf's voice over a dark screen saying, "But you need images." Or is she to be found most powerfully in her literary figures, in the voices she created? Here, too, there is both melancholy and feminist engagement, words delving into both the everyday and the immense historical burdens placed on the everyday. In the imageless interview with Okpako, one can hear Christa Wolf's labored breath, suggesting exhaustion or even mortality. But she is also the voice of Medea, lent by the actor Sheri Hagen in Branwen Okpako's film.

The construction of the film's conclusion is revealing. The interview with Wolf concludes with an irreconcilability: she admits that she did not really expect "Für unser Land" to have an impact, but she accepted both that fact and her being chosen as the one to read it publicly as historically inevitable. People don't want constant revolution, she says, they also want freedom to travel, and of course, "Konsum." Consumerism is thus Wolf's last word, and the last "documentary" image is the West German 100 DM note held aloft, as *Begrüssungsgeld*, the "welcome money" that was given to East Germans arriving in the West in the days after the fall of the Berlin Wall. But after that, there is no place on earth for Christa Wolf's voice. Medea is only a voice, a text, and the face, in extreme close-up, of Sheri Hagen speaking the words: "Where can I go? Is it possible to imagine a world, a time, where I would have a place? There's no one I could ask. That's the answer."

But there *is* someone there: as with the earlier characters from *Medea: A Modern Retelling*, Okpako has the actor speak most lines directed to a microphone within the frame, or at a slight angle off camera. But at decisive moments, as here in conclusion, the actor looks directly at the camera. There is someone there. That is the answer.

Barton Byg is Professor Emeritus at the University of Massachusetts Amherst. Based in the faculty of German and Scandinavian Studies, he founded the DEFA Film library and served as associate faculty in Comparative Literature and Communication, and as a founding faculty member of the UMass International Program in Film Studies. Principal areas of research and teaching include the work of filmmakers Danièle Huillet and Jean-Marie Straub, GDR cinema and culture, documentary film, culture of the Cold War, memory culture, landscape and film, and color and film. The DEFA Film Library at UMass Amherst is the only archive and study center outside Europe devoted to the cinema of the German Democratic Republic.

Notes

1. These remarks are from an undated clipping from *Freie Presse Zwickau*, in the materials on the film consulted before 1990 at the Staatliches Filmarchiv der DDR.
2. The streamlining of characters was no doubt seen as necessary to make the film comprehensible, since the number of locations and roles makes its fragmentary structure challenging to viewers, even after decades of experiments with film narrative.
3. The 11th Plenum of the Socialist Unity Party of the GDR was a low point in GDR cultural history. Initially a party meeting intended to discuss economic matters, the focus vehemently turned to artistic endeavors across a wide spectrum. These were attacked as too "negative," presumably Western-influenced, and destructive of socialism. Most of the feature films of that year were banned and never screened until after the Berlin Wall fell. In 1989–90, the films were quickly brought out, if screenable versions could be found at all, and presented at the 1990 Berlin International Film Festival.
4. In his essay, *"Fräulein Schmetterling* – Probleme der Rekonstruktion," to accompany the film's partial restoration in 2005, Ralf Schenk gives an even fuller overview of Christa Wolf's film-related adaptation projects. (See p. 32 of the DEFA-Stiftung/Bundesfilmarchiv brochure.)
5. It is also worth investigating whether the unrealized idea for this film, or *Moskauer Novelle* itself, had any influence on Iris Gusner or her film *Were the Earth Not Round* (*Wäre die Erde nicht rund*, 1982) which had a similar theme and was criticized by authorities for similar reasons as the film scenario for *Moskauer Novelle*.
6. See Magenau, e.g., 288, 316. Notes on their relationship are also found in Christa Wolf's *Ein Tag im Jahr* (*One Day a Year*, 2003). As the Konrad Wolf biography describes it, their connection soured after the expatriation of Wolf Biermann in 1976, another break of trust between cultural figures and the state. As president of the GDR's Academy of Arts, Konrad Wolf did not voice opposition to the move to expel Biermann, unlike Christa and Gerhard Wolf and many other prominent artists and intellectuals. (See Jacobsen and Aurich 464–65 and 467–68.)
7. See Mitscherlich and Mitscherlich. This psychological interpretation of postwar (West) German society in regard to the Nazi past became a touchstone for many analyses of "coming to terms with the past" (*Vergangenheitsbewältigung*) in Germany.
8. *Fräulein Schmetterling* was not shown along with the others in 1990, since it was in such a fragmentary state that the director chose not to attempt a screenable version. Only in 2005 did the DEFA Foundation in Berlin produce almost two hours of rough footage, edited together on the basis of Christa Wolf's script.
9. See http://www.willy-brandt-kreis.de/.
10. See Lacosta. Sam the Sham was actually Domingo "Sam" Samudio.
11. Branwen Okpako, Filmmaker's Statement in Berlinale Forum film catalog 2014: https://www.berlinale.de/en/archive/jahresarchive/2014/02_programm_2014/02_filmdatenblatt_2014_20147520.html#tab=filmStills.
12. See http://www.ddr89.de/texte/land.html.
13. Georgina Paul places *Medea* in the context of the *Literaturstreit* (64).

Bibliography

Barthel, Kurt, dir. *Fräulein Schmetterling* (Miss Butterfly). GDR, 1966 (Reconstructions 2005 and 2019–20).
Case, Holly. "Blind Spot: On Christa Wolf." *The Nation*, 4 June 2012, pp. 11–19, http://www.thenation.com/article/167925/blind-spot-christa-wolf.
Duras, Marguerite. *Hiroshima mon amour*. Paris: Gallimard, 1960.
Fehervary, Helen, and Sara Lennox. "Introduction to Christa Wolf's *Self-Experiment*." *New German Critique*, vol. 13, Winter 1978, pp. 109–12.
Fräulein Schmetterling. DEFA-Studio für Spielfilme 1965–66. Schnittfassung im Auftrag des Bundesarchiv–Filmarchivs und der DEFA-Stiftung, 2005. Brochure.
Henckel von Donnersmarck, Florian, dir. *Das Leben der Anderen* (The Lives of Others). Germany, 2006.
Hohmann, Lew, dir., and Wolfgang Kohlhaase. *Die Zeit, die bleibt: Ein Film über Konrad Wolf* (The Time that Remains: A Film about Konrad Wolf). GDR, 1985.
Hörnigk, Therese. *Christa Wolf*. Berlin: Volk und Wissen, 1989/2005.
Jakobsen, Wolfgang, and Rolf Aurich. *Der Sonnensucher: Konrad Wolf*. Berlin: Aufbau, 2005.
Janka, Walter. *Schwierigkeiten mit der Wahrheit*. Reinbek bei Hamburg: Rowohlt, 1990.
Jansen, Peter. "Die Geometrie der Trennung: Erinnerungen an Konrad Wolfs Film *Der geteilte Himmel*." *Süddeutsche Zeitung*, 15 January 1986.
Kristeva, Julia. "The Pain of Sorrow in the Modern World: The Works of Marguerite Duras." *PMLA*, vol. 102, no. 2, 1987, pp. 138–52.
Kunert, Joachim, dir. *Die Toten bleiben jung. Nach dem Roman von Anna Seghers* (The Dead Stay Young). GDR, 1968.
Lacosta, Teresa Palomo. "Sam the Sham and the Pharaohs." *Handbook of Texas Music*, edited by Laurie E. Jasinsky. Denton, TX: Texas State Historical Association, n.p.
Magenau, Jörg. *Christa Wolf: Eine Biographie*. Berlin: Kindler, 2009.
Mitscherlich, Alexander, and Margarete Mitscherlich. *The Inability to Mourn: Principles of Collective Behavior*. New York: Grove Press, 1975.
Mohr, Heinrich. "Productive Longing: Structure, Theme, and Political Relevance in Christa Wolf's *The Quest for Christa T*." *Responses to Christa Wolf: Critical Essays*, edited by Marilyn Sibley Fries. Detroit: Wayne State University Press, 1989.
Morin, Edgar. "Aspects sociologiques de la genèse du film." *Tu n'as rien vu à Hiroshima! un grand film, hiroshima, mon amour*, edited by Pierre Vermeylen. Brussels: Université libre, Institut de Sociologie. Séminaire du Film et du Cinéma, 1962, pp. 25–30.
Mund, Karlheinz, dir., and Daniela Dahn. *Zeitschleifen—im Dialog mit Christa Wolf* (Time Loops). Germany, 1990.

Okpako, Branwen. *Christa / Christopher*, video installation at The Space Between Us. Berlin: IFA Galleries, 2013.
———, dir. *Der Fluch der Medea* (The Curse of Medea). Germany, 2014.
———, dir. *The Pilot and the Passenger*. Germany, 2007.
Paul, Georgina. "Christa Wolf's *Medea: Stimmen* (*Medea: A Modern Retelling*)." *The Novel in German since 1990*, edited by Stuart Taberner. Cambridge: Cambridge University Press, 2011, pp. 64–78.
Progress-Dienst, 40/64. Brochure, 1964. n.p.
Resnais, Alain, dir. *Hiroshima mon amour*. France, 1959.
Reso, Martin. *Der geteilte Himmel und seine Kritiker: Dokumentation*. Halle (Saale): Mitteldeutscher Verlag, 1965.
Simon, Rainer, dir. *Till Eulenspiegel*. GDR, 1973.
Steiner, Roland, dir. *Unsere Kinder* (Our Children). GDR, 1989
Stephan, Alexander, ed. *Edition Text + Kritik 46: Christa Wolf*. Munich: Beck, 1976.
Wolf, Christa. *The Author's Dimension: Selected Essays*. New York: Farrar, Straus and Giroux, 1993.
———. *Cassandra: A Novel and Four Essays*. New York: Farrar, Straus and Giroux, 1984.
———. *Ein Tag im Jahr: 1960–2000*. Munich: Luchterhand, 2003.
———. *Medea: A Modern Retelling*. New York: Nan A. Talese, 1998.
———. *Moskauer Novelle*. Halle (Saale): Mitteldeutscher Verlag, 1961.
———. *The Quest for Christa T*. New York: Farrar, Straus and Giroux, 1970.
———. "Self-Experiment." *New German Critique*, vol. 13, Winter 1978, pp. 109–31.
———. *They Divided the Sky: A Novel*. Ottawa: University of Ottawa Press, 2013 [database online].
———. "Wider den Schlaf der Vernunft." *Christa Wolf im Dialog: Aktuelle Texte*. Frankfurt a.M.: Luchterhand, 1990, pp. 98–100.
Wolf, Konrad, dir. *Der geteilte Himmel* (*Divided Heaven*). GDR, 1964.
———, dir. *Ich war 19* (I Was 19). GDR, 1967.
———, dir. *Goya*. GDR/USSR, 1971.
———, dir. *Sterne / Zwezdy* (*Stars*). GDR/Bulgaria, 1959.
———, "Zuschauer als Mitgestalter." *BZ am Abend*, 26 August 1964.

CHAPTER 15

Women at the Edge of a Nervous Breakdown
The Berlin Wall and the Collapse of Female Consciousness in Divided Heaven *and* Good Bye, Lenin!

SUSANNE RINNER

The image of a woman "breaking down" is ubiquitous in the arts. In German literature, it has a rich history, with the best-known example perhaps being the Marquise of O. in Heinrich von Kleist's 1808 novella of the same title. In the twentieth century, two successful works dealing with the by now long-gone German Democratic Republic (GDR) are connected through the image of women who lose consciousness temporarily—namely Christa Wolf's 1963 *Divided Heaven* (*Der geteilte Himmel*) and Wolfgang Becker's hit film *Good Bye, Lenin!* (2003). Even though these two works were written/produced forty years apart, a time span as long as the existence of the GDR itself, they are connected by a remarkable similarity: both feature female protagonists who decide to give up the love of their lives, who become socialists, and who collapse when confronted with the Berlin Wall, the first when it was built, the second after it had been torn down.[1]

Divided Heaven and *Good Bye, Lenin!* have been studied within their historical context and their aesthetic traditions. Reading *Divided Heaven* through the lens of *Good Bye, Lenin!* and its appropriation of the central element of Wolf's novel, namely the figure of the unconscious woman, places Wolf's early text in the context of cultural production in Germany after 1989. This context allows the reader to revisit *Divided Heaven* as a mediated response to the fall of the Berlin Wall and the end of the GDR. This interpretative approach also emphasizes the continued relevance of Wolf's project of "subjective authenticity" as a way to analyze and reflect upon female identity and its representation in and contribution to the text. Challenging the assumed distance between the author and her text and between language and the world, Wolf's approach suggests that the process of writing is important for the self as a process of self-actualization. The image of the unconscious woman in *Divided Heaven* captures one moment of this search for female agency which is reflected upon forty years later in *Good Bye, Lenin!*

Recent scholarship focuses on the representation of illness in Christa Wolf's oeuvre. Carol Anne Costabile-Heming suggests reading Wolf's 2002 narrative *Leibhaftig* as a commentary on contexts that extend beyond the boundaries of both individual and GDR reality. In her monograph on the representation of illness, the health sciences, and the health care system in the GDR, Sonja Klocke studies the convergence of illness, gender, representations of the body, and the (socialist) state. Her reading of novels published before and after the fall of the Wall oscillate between an analysis of illness and the health care system in the GDR in its rhetorical, discursive, and aesthetic complexities and the assertation that the novels serve as a memory archive of lived experience in the GDR. Focusing on the representation of female bodies, Klocke suggests that a character's health, or lack thereof, turns into a seismograph of the political and social conditions of the state: "A character's physical breakdown might challenge the ideology at the core of a portrayed state; a patient's survival, in turn, can signal victory and possibly confirm an ideology" (9). Klocke's astute observation supports the reading of the unconscious women in *Divided Heaven* and *Good Bye, Lenin!*, one surviving and the other succumbing.

Inspired by Elisabeth Bronfen's work on visual culture, we can explore how images of the unconscious woman in literary texts and films reference each other, how these images move from one text to another, and how, in this process, their significance is juxtaposed, transferred, and superimposed. Both *Divided Heaven* and *Good Bye, Lenin!* represent their female protagonists during times of significant personal and historical upheaval. Wolf's character Rita Seidel faces the construction of the Berlin Wall and the loss of her fiancé, while Becker's character Christiane Kerner is uprooted by the fall of the Berlin Wall and the realization that her children might not be as strong supporters of the socialist state as she is. I suggest reading Becker's construction of the unconscious female as an attempt to revisit and adapt the historical matter that is at stake, namely the aftermath of the GDR, by using the same image that Wolf originally used to make sense of the political situation in 1961. As an approach to reading images as metaphors, allegories, or signs that transcend their immediate aesthetic context and connotation, Bronfen's notion of "crossmapping" provides a critical framework for understanding the importance of the image of the unconscious woman in the continuing debates that shape the cultural memory of the GDR and the Cold War.

Feminist criticism also leads us to ask why female protagonists collapse when confronted with the Berlin Wall. In her 1992 study, *Over Her Dead Body: Death, Femininity, and the Aesthetic*, Bronfen argues that "femininity and death cause a disorder to stability, mark moments of ambivalence, disruption or duplicity, and their eradication produces a recuperation of order, a return to stability" (xiii). Neither Wolf nor Becker chose to represent death, but rather employ physiological breakdowns as a means for their characters to represent, respond to, and grapple with their personal situations as well as with larger historical and political questions. Since the characters are merely unconscious, they are able to recover and to reinsert themselves into the text and into history. What, then, does the image of physical collapse and the time of convalescence as a time of reflection, remembering, and narration (in Rita's case), and as a time of stubborn melancholy before a final reconciliation (in Christiane's case) contribute to a gendered representation of storytelling and to female agency in the historical process? The collapse of the female characters challenges the notion of women as the weaker sex and instead embeds the collapse in a narrative of recovery. As a medium of subjectivity and authenticity, the body breaks down without breaking completely, thereby allowing the characters to use the time of convalescence for a critical analysis, a process of soul searching, and an opportunity to question and self-question in order to take charge of their own narratives.

Bronfen suggests that images that are preserved, formalized, and passed on are able to transform sustainable affects into effective signs:

> Whenever a strong subjective response encounters conventional representations of affects in the sphere of the cultural imagination, one needs to approach this rather messy encounter theoretically. Therefore, I understand my *Crossmapping* as a way of reading in which theoretical and aesthetic approaches toward our cultural memory determine each other. (*Crossmapping* 8f)

Insight into the connection between these otherwise very different texts via the image of the unconscious woman triggered my strong emotional response to the role and function of women as represented in the arts and as subjects in the historical process. Specifically, I wonder whether Becker's appropriation could be read as an attempt to follow in Wolf's footsteps in order to emphasize specifically female traits which, as Sara Lennox suggests, Wolf considers not only different, but also more valuable than some specifically male traits. Although Lennox ultimately cautions against essentialist understandings of female and male characteristics in Wolf's writing, the representation of physical collapse, pain, and illness as symptoms of emotional and psychological confrontations with personal as well as historical challenges should not be misunderstood as female weakness or loss of agency.

What do these gendered representations tell us about memory of the GDR? In the case of *Divided Heaven*, why does Rita repress her memory of the Berlin Wall during her recovery? If her collapse represents a traumatic experience, then it is worth questioning whether there is a critical potential in this representation. Or does Rita's physical collapse enable her to undergo the kind of socialist re-education that encourages and motivates her to stay in the GDR, even though she would have had the opportunity to leave in order to join her fiancé, Manfred, in West Berlin?

In the case of *Good Bye, Lenin!* we have to ask why the female protagonist continues to believe in the socialist state, even in the face of its obvious demise. Furthermore, this film points to important tropes in the field of German memory studies, such as the representation of silence as a way of dealing with guilt and the creation and transmission of memories from one generation to the next. The loss of consciousness leads to a loss of activity, a loss of speech, and a loss of linear time. While this moment of unconsciousness entails an ethical dilemma, namely the characters' inability to bear witness to their times, the subsequent process of recovery opens up a self-reflective and self-reflexive space that allows them to ponder the difficulty, "Ich zu sagen," (of saying "I," Kaufmann 95), a lifelong concern that is present in much of Wolf's work.

In *Divided Heaven*, Christa Wolf avoids any direct reference to the beginning of the construction of the Berlin Wall in August 1961. Forty years after the building of the Wall and more than two decades after its dismantling, it would be easy to cite Wolf's blind spot in order to dismiss her work. Yet to do so would foreclose her unique perspective on the politics of memory that has, to a great extent and in many important ways, informed the current discourse on memory in German Studies. Charity Scribner describes the relationship between the text and the historical event in the following way: "Although Wolf circumvents the barricading of the German-German frontier, this event haunts every page of *Der geteilte Himmel*, and provides a framework for the narrative through its conspicuous absence" (61). *Divided Heaven* reaches its climax in the summer of 1961 when Rita must decide whether or not to join Manfred, who had defected to West Berlin. Thus, she experiences the loss that is caused by Germany's division even before the Wall has been built. In her 2008 study *Film and Memory*, Anke Pinkert suggests that Rita's physical and mental collapse serves as a narrative motivation for the complex flashback structure of the text. Because of this narrative structure, *Divided Heaven* functions as a prime example for fiction as memory text. These flashbacks dramatize Rita's memories, her mourning, and her gradual convalescence. Instead of reading the film as yet another example of the genre of socialist women's film that replaces psychological interiority, subjectivity, and the private with collective political participation, Pinkert argues that past experiences of war, imprisonment, and death hover in the stories of the postwar daughters, pervading the phantasmatic fullness of the socialist imaginary embodied by or projected onto young female protagonists. Scribner describes Rita as undergoing a journey from the "blurred margins of girlhood into the centre of history" (62).

I would like to focus on one specific moment of this journey, namely when Rita's body serves as the site of transformation by allowing her time to work through her options in order to find her place in society. The literary and visual representations focus specifically on the physical breakdown of the body and its unconscious state as an image of emotional and psychological despair, of a loss that extends beyond Rita's loss of her fiancé. In her essay on Wolf's 2002 narrative *In the Flesh* (*Leibhaftig*), Therese Hörnigk asserts that: "Ever since the publication of *Divided Heaven*, illness as metaphor—Susan Sontag's definition has been quoted frequently—is a theme that has taken on the significance of a leitmotif in Christa Wolf's oeuvre. In nearly all of her texts, illnesses are indicative of unresolved conflicts" (70, my translation). I wish to examine this image of the female body as one that embodies the response to a seminal historical event in a physical breakdown, beginning with Scribner's striking formulation:

> Since Rita's blackout happens precisely when the Berlin Wall goes up, it allows her to exit conveniently from the political crisis. By the time she regains consciousness, the Wall has completely redefined the Berlin cityscape, and instilled itself into the minds of all Germans as the symbol of a divided nation, a divided Europe, and a divided memory. (62)

By taking another look at this constellation I want to interrogate the effect of this representation on our understanding of women as agents in society and in historical processes.

Daniela Berghahn engages with the 1964 film version of *Divided Heaven* and suggests that the film provides a critical message because of its representation of human suffering in the face of the Berlin Wall. She points out that

> film-makers in both the East and the West have argued that one of the reasons for choosing female protagonists in the first place was that the depiction of women frequently went hand in hand with a high degree of female subjectivity. In politicized, state-controlled film cultures the depiction of female subjectivity was a strategy that enabled film-makers to subtly voice dissent or broach taboos. (563)

In her discussion of the official response to the film, Berghahn asks whether "the skillful construction of the female allegory of nation, combined with female subjectivity ... enabled Wolf to critique official historiography and remain unscathed?" (564–65).

Nineteen-year-old Rita Seidel is portrayed as an idealistic young woman who firmly believes in the GDR, which, in her mind, is clearly the "better" Germany. At work in a railway carriage factory and at the teacher training college, she learns to reconcile her ideals of socialism with the less than perfect reality. In spite of the manifold problems she encounters, she becomes increasingly engaged in the collective-minded culture of East Germany. Her fiancé Manfred, however, ten years older and an ambitious doctoral student of chemistry, is ambivalent about the attempt to build a new society. He is depicted as a cynical individualist who feels disenfranchised when one of his inventions is not adopted for industrial production. In the representation of these two characters, it is implied that they belong to different generations, with Manfred's life overshadowed by the Nazi past, whereas Rita is too young to have her own memories of the Nazi past. This generational divide has important repercussions. When Manfred defects to the West in the hope that Rita will join him, she is faced with the dilemma of thousands of East Germans who contemplated leaving the GDR while this was still possible. Shortly before the erection of the Berlin Wall, Rita visits Manfred in West Berlin. In stark contrast to East Berlin, West Berlin is represented as a bourgeois consumer paradise. Rita and Manfred enjoy a meal at a nice restaurant with white tablecloths and cloth napkins, impeccable service, and a choice of select dishes. However, the opportunity to participate in this consumer society cannot obscure the Nazi past. Manfred rents a room in a dark and gloomy apartment owned by an old lady who appears to be suspicious of Rita. The atmosphere is so oppressive that the couple leave the apartment immediately and spend their whole day exploring West Berlin. However, they cannot escape the numerous reminders of the legacy of the Third Reich, in particular the allusions to issues of guilt and ongoing responsibility for the Holocaust. A camera shot that places the couple in front of a billboard for the detergent Persil, evoking the so-called "Persilscheine," certificates of denazification after 1945, is a particularly powerful reminder of the aftermath of National Socialism. Against this backdrop, Rita now has to make a choice between her love for Manfred and her commitment to socialism. This billboard, and not so much the actual Wall, seems to represent the division between the two characters. When Rita realizes that the ideological differences between Manfred and herself have also caused an emotional distance, she returns to the GDR. But her decision is not presented as an unambiguous affirmation of the GDR. Following the break-up, Rita suffers a nervous breakdown. The generational rift between Manfred and Rita seems to be mirrored in the gender divide: Rita represses her memory of the Berlin Wall and finds an albeit uncomfortable home in the collective, whereas Manfred continues to fight for the implementation of his discoveries within the structures of a western liberal, capitalist society.

In the film made forty years later, *Good Bye, Lenin!*, Christiane Kerner, a devout socialist and single mother of two, actually experiences two physical and emotional breakdowns. The first occurs after she is questioned by Stasi officers about the whereabouts of her husband, who is on his third business trip to West Germany. While she is being questioned in the kitchen, her two children watch the televised launch of the Russian space ship Soyuz 31 on 26 August 1978. This event was celebrated as a victory of the Socialist East, as proclaimed by headlines in the Party newspaper *Neues Deutschland*: "The first German in Space: The East German Sigmund Jähn!" (depicted in *Good Bye, Lenin!*). The children experience the excitement of one of the most celebrated achievements of the twentieth century, namely manned space flight. Christiane's son Alex particularly identifies with the astronaut and dreams of following in his footsteps. For the nightly children's TV program, his hero sends home images of the marriage in space between the East German Sandmännchen (little sandman) and the Russian Matryoshka doll Masha. This marriage, a match made in space, serves not only as a symbol of discovery and adventure and of the (alleged) political friendship between the Soviet Union and the GDR, but also as a symbol for a happy family life. In contrast, witnessing the interrogation of his mother through the open door, Alex infers that his father has left them for a girlfriend in the capitalist West. The day of great triumph for East Germany coincides with the day when Christiane Kerner is faced with the fact that her husband has defected to the West, a situation similar to what Rita experienced just seventeen years earlier, but with one important difference: whereas Rita was able to visit Manfred in West Berlin and to decide whether to join him or to return to East Germany, in 1978 the Berlin Wall prevents Christiane and her children from simply taking a train to the West in order to reunite their family, had they wished to do so. At this point in the narrative, we do not learn more about the situation, since Christiane cuts short the Stasi officer's questioning by screaming, "Leave me alone!" The next scene shows her locked in a mental institution, unwilling or unable to speak or engage with her children. Upon her eventual return home, she appears transformed and is now a staunch, albeit critical, supporter of East Germany and a doting mother to her children, who encourages her son to live his dream of becoming a space traveler.

The motive of space travel provides another opportunity for crossmapping between *Divided Heaven* and *Good Bye, Lenin!* In *Divided Heaven*, the test drive of a new and improved train built in East Germany coincides with the news of the first manned space flight conducted by the Russians in April 1961. This groundbreaking technological success took place just four months before the Berlin Wall was built. The Russian success further fueled the Cold War and led to a space race that changed the configuration of the East-West divide by adding an upward dimension that turned the metaphysics of heaven into a sky that could be measured, explored, and owned. Henning Wrage asserts that "a man leaving earth, ascending toward heaven, and returning alive was not just the catalyst for a propaganda offensive but became a core metaphor for the redemptive vision of a new socialist society" (73). However, I would caution that the crossmapping of this metaphor can only be understood as a critical and self-critical intervention into the discourse of progress, be it historical or technological or both and regardless of its ideological orientation. Already in *Divided Heaven* and certainly in *Good Bye, Lenin!* the news of manned space flight is overshadowed by less than ideal conditions on earth.

In 1989 Christiane Kerner is invited to a Party function celebrating the fortieth anniversary of the GDR. On her way there, she encounters a demonstration calling for basic civil rights such as freedom of the press and the right to travel. As the police forcefully break up the demonstration, Christiane attempts to stop them, but the officers ignore her and ask her to leave. Relegated to the role of helpless bystander, she recognizes Alex among those who are being arrested and collapses. She suffers a heart attack and remains in a coma during the events surrounding the fall of the Berlin Wall. When she awakes, she does not know that the whole world has changed and does not remember that she had collapsed when she saw her son among the peaceful protesters. Since she remains a staunch supporter of the old GDR after she awakens, it is also not clear whether her collapse was caused by seeing her son among those who were demanding radical change or whether it was caused by the insight, however temporary, that the state she supports uses violence against its own citizens and that freedom does not exist.

This scene is one more example of the crossmapping that occurs between *Divided Heaven* and *Good Bye, Lenin!* In her journal *One Day a Year (Ein Tag im Jahr: 1960–2000*, 2003), Wolf remembers her daughter's participation at the demonstrations in East Berlin on 7 October 1989, on the eve of the fortieth anniversary celebrations of the GDR. In her entry from 27 September 1990, just a year later, Wolf reflects on her involvement in the committee that investigated GDR brutality against the participants in one of the last demonstrations that took place before the fall of the Berlin Wall.[2] Like the fictitious Christiane Kerner, Wolf is belatedly confronted with the realization that the state she lived in mistreated those who peacefully asked for their civil rights, including her own daughter. Wolf's journal juxtaposes her search for her daughter after her arrest with the healing process that her participation in the committee offers. Reading these images of police brutality against citizens in the comic rendering of *Good Bye, Lenin!* against Wolf's journal entry adds to the complexity of representing personal and historical responsibility in the aftermath of the fall of the Wall.

It is noteworthy that Christiane Kerner's son feels guilty and thus tries to compensate by recreating the GDR for his mother. After all, the doctor had cautioned that she needed rest and that any excitement could cause another, this time fatal, heart attack. He does not, however, suggest going so far as to recreate the GDR. Thus, the son, as a representative of the next generation, perpetuates another trope that haunts the representation of German history in the twentieth century: the silence that covers guilt, whether real or perceived, and that burdens the individual, society, and the relationship between generations. Alex attempts to maintain the illusion of the continued existence of the GDR and thus, one could argue, is nonetheless responsible for the second heart attack that leads to his mother's death. This breakdown occurs when she is able to free herself from the constraints of her bedroom and leaves her apartment, only to realize that the world has changed in incomprehensible ways. She is hospitalized again, and Alex once more attempts to maintain the illusion of the GDR. Only his girlfriend Lara, a Russian immigrant and his mother's nurse, breaks the silence and tells her the truth about the historical events. Her character alludes to the increasing importance of non-ethnic Germans, for example Germans with a hyphenated identity or migrants who move to Germany, as participants in a seemingly national discourse about German identity. In the end, as Jennifer Kapczynski notes, Christiane and her son Alex are each convinced of the truths of their own versions of the family history:

> As the attentive viewer will notice, Alex's narration is inaccurate: Alex claims that his mother died without ever knowing the truth about her beloved country. He speaks of her as a true believer, even as the film suggests that her reasons for state loyalty were largely personal: before her death, she confesses that she stayed not out of ideological devotion, but rather for fear that she would lose her children if she applied for an exit visa. Alex's errors suggest a disconnect between history and memory: neither his mother nor his mother's country existed quite as he remembers them. Becker presents us with a final sequence that is at once nostalgic for a time and place of lost promise and that calls into question the validity of that nostalgia, based as it is on faulty recollections. (85)

Clearly, the past is multi-layered and consists of the complex interactions of individuals being swept up by historical forces as can be observed in seminal historical events of the twentieth century, for example two world wars, the Holocaust, the division of Germany, the fall of the Berlin Wall, and the end of the Cold War. While the narrator Alex attempts to establish the truth, the audience realizes that it is only his truth and that, as in previous generational conflicts, the truth depends on the perspective of each protagonist, their knowledge, and their ability and willingness to communicate with others. Christiane's two breakdowns significantly shape the events and the different perspectives that emerge as truths about their family history; they also add to the importance of gender as a critical category in these memory debates.

Bronfen's theory of "crossmapping" allows me to trace images of women on the edge of a nervous breakdown in two texts that are separated by a time span of the forty years that were shaped first by the construction and then the fall of the Berlin Wall. In both texts, the Wall serves as a starting point for telling stories. The individual's physical breakdown is mirrored first in the construction and then in the collapse of the Berlin Wall. The legacy of the actual physicality of the Wall and its significance during the Cold War and up to the present in the twenty-first century are at stake in my re-reading of the images of the unconscious woman, images that tie these two very different works together. Bronfen's approach is particularly helpful since *Divided Heaven* also exists as a film made by Konrad Wolf in 1964 that enables us to trace the image in visual media. Bronfen describes her comparative reading of texts of different medialities as an attempt

> to juxtapose the visual quality of narrative texts and critical discourse with the narrative quality of images. ... A *Crossmapping*, so my argument, creates a critical space for thinking which intervenes, just like art itself, with the cultural imagination. ... Therefore, *Crossmapping* constitutes a method of reading in which theoretical and aesthetic approaches to our cultural memory rely on each other. Whereas theory responds to demands that were already formalized in the context of aesthetic representation, critical metaphors draw our attention to their ongoing relevance in the contemporary context. (*Crossmappings* 8f. in German original; my translation)

As an approach to reading images as metaphors that transcend their immediate aesthetic context and connotation, crossmapping provides a critical framework for understanding the image of the unconscious woman as an important figure in the debates that have shaped the cultural memory of the Cold War. The image also serves as an invitation to reconsider women's roles in the public sphere and to engage in discussions of gender differences, gender equality, and feminism.

The crossmapping that occurs in *Divided Heaven* and *Good Bye, Lenin!* challenges our understanding and potentially our self-understanding of/as women in the historical process. If we view, as Anke Pinkert suggests, "the antifascist DEFA films as archives and sites of collective memory in the context of a post-unification public" (11), then what happens when we engage with Bronfen's crossmapping and examine one image as a transformation, appropriation, and superimposition of the other and place it within a broader historical context? In addition to the Berlin Wall as a symbol of the Cold War, the twentieth century was marked by the emergence of social movements in the 1970s, in particular the feminist movement. This broader historical context would enable the question of how the representation of the female character shapes the perception of the audience of women as agents in the historical process. These memory contests point to the privileged space of crossmapped images in exploring the ambiguity of historical processes and the relation between the personal and the political. These images propel women from the margin to the center of history, even as female agency is temporarily limited by the physical collapse of the protagonists and framed by the Berlin Wall.

Susanne Rinner is a teacher-scholar and the author of *The German Student Movement and the Literary Imagination: Transnational Memories of Protest and Dissent* (2013). In 2012, she edited a special issue of *International Poetry Review* with a focus on poetry written in German by multilingual authors. From 2007–2019, Susanne worked at the University of North Carolina at Greensboro as an Associate Professor of German Studies. Currently, she teaches at Western Washington University and works as the Program Director for SPARK for German, a joint project of the American Association of Teachers of German (AATG) and the Goethe-Institut. In 2018 and 2019, Susanne served as AATG President. She volunteers as a translator for the project *Migrants of the Mediterranean.*

Notes

1. For a variety of approaches to the legacy of the Berlin Wall in a global context, see Gerstenberger and Evans. For a variety of disciplinary approaches to the multifaceted implications of borders and boundaries, see Silberman.
2. I would like to thank Kaleen M. Gallagher, University of Cambridge, England, for the reference.

Bibliography

Arndt, Stefan, Bernd Lichtenberg, Wolfgang Becker, et al. *Good Bye, Lenin!* Culver City, CA: Columbia TriStar Home Entertainment, 2003.
Berghahn, Daniela. "Do the Right Thing? Female Allegories of Nation in Aleksandr Askoldov's *Komissar* (USSR 1967/1987) and Konrad Wolf's *Der geteilte Himmel* (GDR 1964)." *Historical Journal of Film, Radio and Television*, vol. 26, no. 4, 2006, pp. 561–77.
Bronfen, Elisabeth. *Crossmappings: Essays zur visuellen Kultur.* Zürich: Scheidegger & Spiess, 2009.
———. *Over Her Dead Body: Death, Femininity, and the Aesthetic.* New York: Routledge, 1992.
Costabile-Heming, Carol Anne. "Illness as Metaphor: Christa Wolf, the GDR, and Beyond." *Symposium*, vol. 64, no. 3, 2010, pp. 202–19.
Gerstenberger, Katharina, and Jana Evans Braziel. *After the Berlin Wall: Germany and Beyond.* New York: Palgrave Macmillan, 2011.
Hörnigk, Therese. "Der Körper als Seismograph allgemeinen Zusammenbruchs: Christa Wolfs Erzählung *Leibhaftig*." *20 Jahre Mauerfall: Diskurse, Rückbauten, Perspektiven*, edited by Marta Fernández Bueno and Torben Lohmüller. Bern: Peter Lang, 2012, pp. 65–73.

Kapczynski, Jennifer M. "Negotiating Nostalgia: The GDR Past in *Berlin Is in Germany* and *Good Bye, Lenin!*" *The Germanic Review*, vol. 82, no. 1, 2007, pp. 78–100.

Kaufmann, Hans. "Gespräch mit Christa Wolf." *Weimarer Beiträge*, vol. 20, no. 6, 1974, pp. 90–112.

Klocke, Sonja E. *Inscription and Rebellion: Illness and the Symptomatic Body in East German Literature*. Rochester, NY: Camden House, 2015.

Lennox, Sara. "'Der Versuch, man selbst zu sein': Christa Wolf und der Feminismus." *Die Frau als Heldin und Autorin: Neue kritische Ansätze zur deutschen Literatur*, edited by Wolfgang Paulsen. Bern: Francke, 1979, pp. 217–22.

Pinkert, Anke. *Film and Memory in East Germany*. Bloomington: Indiana University Press, 2008.

Scribner, Charity. "August 1961: Christa Wolf and the Politics of Disavowal." *German Life and Letters*, vol. 55, no. 1, 2002, pp. 61–74.

Silberman, Marc. *The German Wall: Fallout in Europe*. New York: Palgrave Macmillan, 2011.

Wolf, Christa. *Der geteilte Himmel*. Halle: Mitteldeutscher Verlag, 1963.

———. *Divided Heaven*. Translated by Joan Becker. New York: Adler's Foreign Books, 1965.

———. *Ein Tag im Jahr: 1960–2000*. Munich: Luchterhand Literaturverlag, 2003.

———. *Leibhaftig*. Munich: Luchterhand Verlag, 2002.

———. *One Day a Year: 1960–2000*. Translated by Lowell A. Bangerter. New York: Europa Editions, 2007.

Wrage, Henning. "Politics, Culture, and Media Before and After the Berlin Wall." *The German Wall: Fallout in Europe*, edited by Marc Silberman. New York: Palgrave Macmillan, 2011, pp. 59–76.

CHAPTER 16

The Impact of Christa Wolf's *Cassandra* on Women Artists in East Germany

APRIL A. EISMAN

In November 2012, an art exhibition opened at the Galerie Forum Amalienpark in Berlin Pankow to mark the one-year anniversary of Christa Wolf's passing (Ruthe).[1] Titled *Wortwelten Bildwelten: Malerfreunde zum Gedenken an Christa Wolf* (Word Worlds, Picture Worlds: Painter Friends in Memory of Christa Wolf), the exhibition celebrated the important role that Wolf had played for artists, especially in East Germany, both as a collector (with her husband, Gerhard Wolf) and as a source of inspiration and support.[2] Many of the works included by the twelve artists in the exhibition made reference to Wolf herself or to specific texts she had written, including *Patterns of Childhood* (*Kindheitsmuster*, 1976), *No Place on Earth* (*Kein Ort. Nirgends*, 1979), and especially *Cassandra* (*Kassandra*, 1984).[3] Two of the artists, Nuria Quevedo and Angela Hampel, included works on the latter, a book that had led to their lasting friendships with the Wolfs. They were not alone. Published in 1983–84, *Cassandra* sparked a major chord among artists, and especially women, throughout German-speaking Europe, inspiring them to create prints, drawings, and paintings on the topic.[4] Some wrote letters to Wolf, while others gave her images they had created. The response among artists in East Germany alone was so great that in 1987 the Staatliche Galerie Moritzburg Halle organized an exhibition on the topic, *Kassandra—Studioausstellung* (Cassandra—Studio Exhibition), the posters for which were designed by Hampel (Wieg).[5]

One of Christa Wolf's best-known and most popular books, *Cassandra* retells the story of the Trojan War from a woman's perspective, that of the previously minor character, Cassandra, a woman who can see into the future, but whose warnings about it are doomed to be ignored. Whereas in the original stories from antiquity, this fate was the result of Cassandra having rejected Apollo's advances after he had given her the gift of prophecy, in Wolf's book, it is the result of power relations and the fact that those without power—in this case women—have no impact on events. The book itself is a criticism of war, which it blames not on imperialism, as was the official doctrine in East Germany, but rather on patriarchy. As the literary scholar Lorna Martens explained it, "Cassandra's account of the Trojan War revokes Homer's: in her interior monologue the story of the *Iliad* becomes a dark story of slaughter, rape, treachery, perversion, abuse of power, and sheer bloodthirstiness. Achilles is not a hero but simply a beast..." (105). This aligning of patriarchy with war and brutality, and the concomitant praise of matriarchal inclusiveness and pacifism, made *Cassandra* at once controversial for the East German government and inspirational for many women on both sides of the Berlin Wall.[6]

This chapter looks at the considerable impact that *Cassandra* had on women artists in East Germany. In particular, it focuses on work by Nuria Quevedo (b. 1938) and Angela Hampel (b. 1956), artists from two generations who created some of the best-known artworks in response to the book. Already well established within the East German art scene when the book was published, Quevedo created a series of prints and drawings, some of which were later included in an illustrated edition of the novel. These works emphasize the timeless quality of human relationships as found in Wolf's novel. Hampel, on the other hand, focused on a modern-day reinterpretation in her prints and paintings, creating punk-inspired images of Cassandra and her "crew," including Penthesilea. Ultimately, we shall see the much greater impact that *Cassandra* had on Hampel, the result in part of the latter's young age: *Cassandra* not only affected her art, it also awakened a "feminist" consciousness that led Hampel to try to effect change in conditions for women artists in East Germany in ways that can still be seen in Germany today in the various exhibitions and events held by the Dresdner Sezession 89. This examination will also show the strong connection between Christa Wolf and these artists.

Wolf's *Cassandra* in Context

Before turning to the impact of *Cassandra* on Quevedo and Hampel, it is important to first look at the context in which Christa Wolf wrote her novel, both because she was not the only artist to turn to the classical woman prophet at this critical point in time and because her book would change how this figure was portrayed in art. Indeed, it is the timing of the book's publication, coming as it did at the height of the 1983 crisis surrounding the stationing of Pershing II cruise missiles in Europe—together with its focus on a strong female character and the importance of the female perspective—that contributed to its success.

One of the first visual artists in East Germany to engage with the topic of Cassandra was Rolf Kuhrt, a printmaker from Leipzig. In 1979, a year before Wolf began to write her novel, Kuhrt created the first of what would become more than 100 drawings, prints, and paintings of Cassandra. These images, which often show her shrinking away from the viewer or covering her face, as if the world she sees is too horrific to look at any further, were created in response to an escalation in Cold War tensions at the time: 1979 marked the beginning of the war in Afghanistan as well as the Iranian Revolution. It was also the year when NATO decided to station Pershing II cruise missiles in Europe, a decision protested by people around the world, including Germans on both sides of the Wall.

Another artist who responded with images of Cassandra was Heidrun Hegewald (b. 1936), a painter and printmaker active in Berlin. In *Cassandra Sees a Serpent's Egg* (1981 Figure 16.1), which was inspired by Ingmar Bergman's recent film, *The Serpents Egg* (1979), a young mother holds a baby to her chest while calling out a warning. She faces the opposite direction of everyone else in the image, who appear to be mesmerized by something in the distance behind her. Striding toward this unseen thing is a figure in a hat and mask whose demeanor and clothes suggest a Nazi brownshirt. He or she carries an egg that contains a snake within it, a symbol of evil and the always-existent threat of fascism.

Both Kuhrt and Hegewald were drawing upon an image of Cassandra that had emerged in Germany during the Third Reich, when visual artists like Karl Hofer identified with her plight, calling out against the dangers around them without being heard. Before this time, Cassandra had been portrayed most frequently in the visual arts as a femme fatale, especially by the Pre-Raphaelites, or as a victim of violence, most often in scenes of Ajax grabbing her by the hair and pulling her away from the statue of Athena.[7] After World War II, Cassandra largely disappeared as a theme in German art until she re-emerged in East Germany in the late 1970s as someone warning in vain about the horrors to come, an alter ego for artists worried by the escalation of the Cold War and its implications for the future. Wolf picked up a variation of this view for her book, creating a feminist icon in the process.

Nuria Quevedo's Cassandra: The Timelessness of Human Relations

One of the first artists in East Germany to respond to Wolf's version of Cassandra was Nuria Quevedo. Born in Barcelona in 1938, Quevedo and her family fled Franco's Spain, settling in East Berlin in 1952. She later studied art at the Berlin Academy in Weißensee (1958–63) and at the Academy of Arts in Berlin (1969–72). By the time Christa Wolf was working on *Cassandra*, Quevedo was an established artist in East Germany, known in particular for her black and white literary illustrations and quiet, often melancholic portrait paintings. She also knew Christa Wolf, having met her through mutual friends a few years earlier.[8] Indeed, Quevedo visited the Wolfs at their home in Mecklenburg several times in the early 1980s while Wolf was writing *Cassandra*.

In a postcard that Quevedo sent to Christa Wolf on 31 August 1982, several months before the book was published, the artist mentions having received Wolf's text from the publisher, who wanted her to create illustrations for it. She also mentioned having "already made a small series of drawings ... that I would like to show you in the fall before I begin working on the printing plates" (Wolf and Wolf, *Unsere Freunde* 42).[9]

Figure 16.1. Heidrun Hegewald, *Cassandra Sees a Serpent's Egg* (*Kassandra sieht ein Schlangenei*), 1981, acrylic on canvas, 134 × 154 cm. Photo: Kunstarchiv Beeskow © 2021 Artists Rights Society (ARS), New York / VG Bild-Kunst, Bonn.

Quevedo made at least twelve drawings based on *Cassandra*. The images focus on stocky, simplified nude figures that suggest a timeless quality also found in the engravings. Wolf later stated that these works, which "were not illustrations, showed me a deep archaic level of the figure" ("Ein Ring für Nuria Quevedo" 134). In one, a woman is giving birth (Figure 16.2); in another, a mother crouches protectively over her child; in a third, we see Cassandra standing quietly with death, who wears a cloak (Figure 16.3).

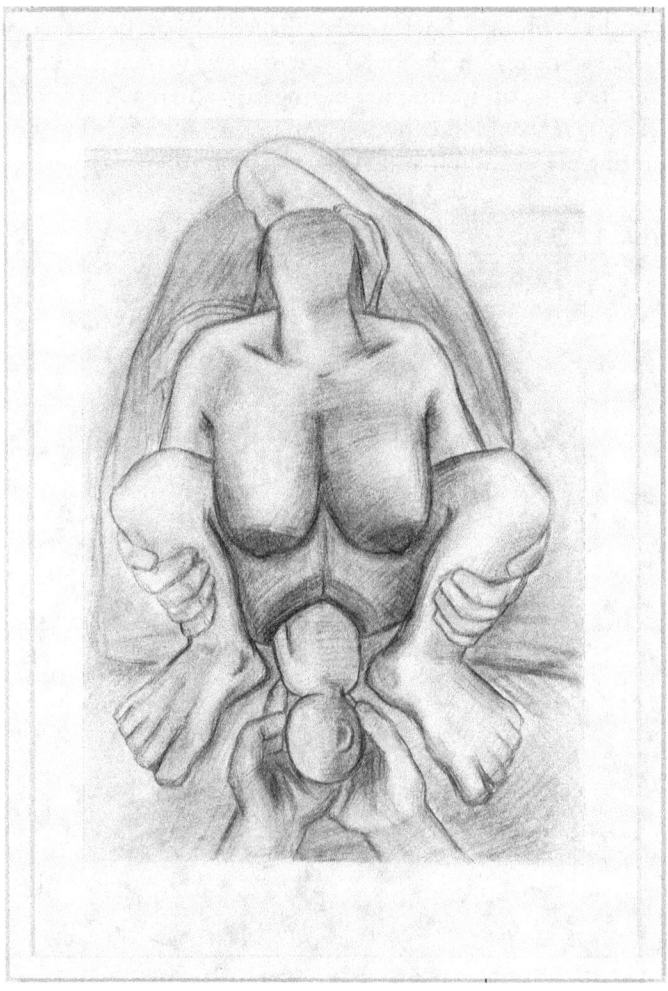

Figure 16.2. Nuria Quevedo, Study for *Cassandra (Kassandra)* by Christa Wolf, 1982, charcoal, 87.6 × 60.3 cm. Photo: Paetzold 1986/Deutsche Fotothek © 2021 Artists Rights Society (ARS), New York / VG Bild-Kunst, Bonn.

Whereas the drawings, like the novel, emphasize the woman's perspective in their choice of subject matter, the prints focus on the timeless nature of human relations and include images of a man and woman fighting (Figure 16.4), two men fighting, and of two women finding solace in each other, in addition to images of Cassandra standing confident and alone or with the quiet figure of death.

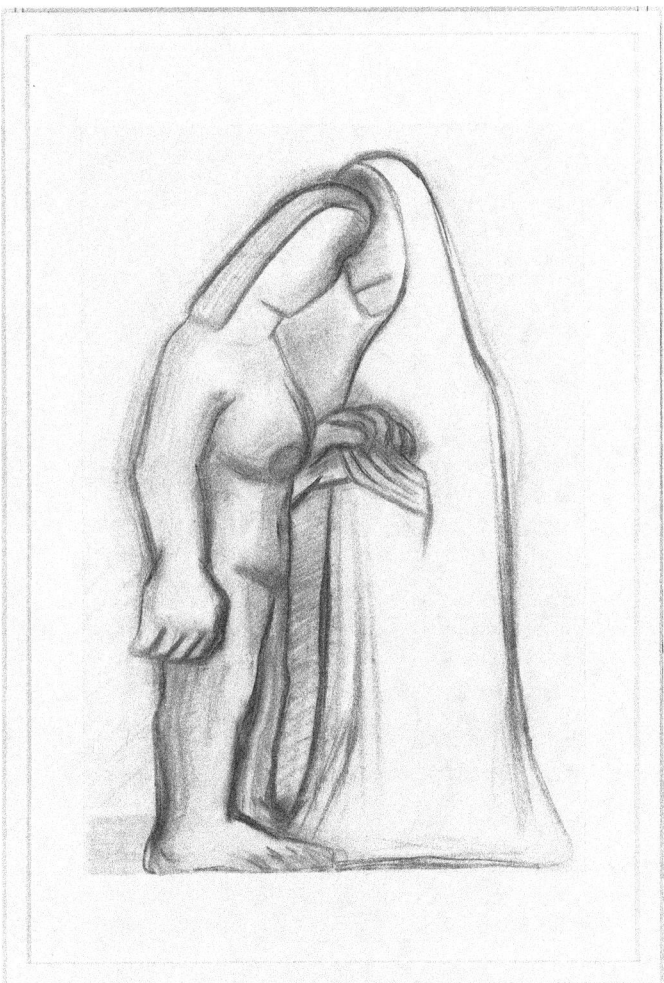

Figure 16.3. Nuria Quevedo, Study for *Cassandra (Kassandra)* by Christa Wolf, 1982, charcoal, 87.6 × 60.3 cm. Photo: Paetzold 1986/Deutsche Fotothek © 2021 Artists Rights Society (ARS), New York / VG Bild-Kunst, Bonn.

In 1984, eleven of these engravings were included in an illustrated edition of the book.[10] A year later, nine appeared as part of a limited-edition art portfolio, *Grafik zu Kassandra von Christa Wolf: mit Tagebuchnotizen der Autorin / Nuria Quevedo* (Prints for Christa Wolf's *Cassandra*: With Journal Entries by the Author, Nuria Quevedo).[11] The prints are thus well known and perhaps the first that come to mind when one talks about the impact of Wolf's *Cassandra* on women artists in East Germany. For Quevedo, however,

Figure 16.4. Nuria Quevedo, Study for *Cassandra (Kassandra)* by Christa Wolf, 1982, charcoal, 87.6 × 60 cm. Photo: Paetzold 1986/Deutsche Fotothek © 2021 Artists Rights Society (ARS), New York / VG Bild-Kunst, Bonn.

the impact of the novel can primarily be measured in terms of the emergence of the subject in her art. Her style, for example, did not change as a result of the encounter, nor did she really engage with the feminist aspect of the book for which *Cassandra* is best known. Indeed, her images emphasize a timeless, human struggle rather than a battle between the sexes. The impact of this novel on Angela Hampel, by comparison, was more significant, affecting both her artwork and her thinking, especially coming as it did early in her career.

Angela Hampel's Cassandra: Mythological Women for the Contemporary World

Hampel first read *Cassandra* in 1984, shortly after its publication in the GDR. At this time, she was twenty-eight years old and part way through her *Kandidatenzeit*, the three-year period—funded by the government—that many visual artists were given after graduating from an East German art academy to help them transition into their new role as professional artists. She spent these years reading widely and creating art, and it was during this time that she found her artistic voice: large Neo-Expressionist works in bright colors that focus on people, often women, who are most frequently shown alone or in pairs. The women usually appear confident, even aggressive, and sport punk hairstyles, such as mohawks in a variety of vivid colors. Not coincidentally, these works emerged in her oeuvre in the same year that she first read *Cassandra*. Hampel later explained her encounter with the book:

> When Christa Wolf's *Cassandra* came into the bookstores, it was for me—and not only for me—a kind of revelation. It was a possibility for identification, as a woman, as a woman artist. It was encouragement and confirmation. And it was for me the beginning of a persistent search for feminine roots, for my roots in this world, that continues to the present. (Hampel and Trende 16)

Indeed, *Cassandra* can be seen as the catalyst for Hampel's feminist engagement with the East German art world, which ultimately led to positive changes for women artists that can still be felt in unified Germany today.

The impact of *Cassandra* on Hampel's art and thinking was immediate, not only on her style, but also on the content of her work. In 1984, she created five paintings on the topic. Three show a couple struggling with each other. The other two each focus on a single figure. In one, a woman with a mohawk sits alone, holding one hand to her face in despair. Is it Cassandra when she is locked away in a wicker-lined basket in the grave of heroes? The other (Figure 16.5) shows a red figure with yellow spots against a blue background. The figure tumbles through the air, perhaps Cassandra in the grip of one of her prophetic seizures?

Figure 16.5. Angela Hampel, print from the series on *Cassandra (Kassandra)* by Christa Wolf, 1984–85, gouache and acrylic on paper, 110.5 × 85 cm. Kulturstiftung Sachsen-Anhalt, Kunstmuseum Moritzburg Halle (Saale). Photo: Punctum/Bertram Kober © 2021 Artists Rights Society (ARS), New York / VG Bild-Kunst, Bonn.

These paintings were included in the *Expressivität heute* (Expressiveness Today) exhibition held in Berlin in 1985. This exhibition marked the emergence of the youngest generation of East German artists—in this case, all from Dresden—onto the national stage. Praised for their new, "aggressive" style and thematic focus on the present, these artists included Hubertus Giebe, Johannes Heisig, Lutz Fleischer, Walter Libuda, and Trak Wendisch, in addition to Hampel, who was the only woman of the six. They ranged in age from twenty-six to thirty-four. This exhibition—and these paintings of Cassandra—generated some of the earliest mentions of Hampel in the East German press. According to one reviewer, Hampel was the real discovery in the exhibition:

> [Her] crude, unsparing Cassandra-pages based on Christa Wolf's narrative are the most manifest of the "new expressionism." The strong emotionality of her color pages in acrylic and latex consists of the figurative, gestural evocation of human situations of angst, loneliness, desire and violence ... [that are] intended to be wholly aggressive, wholly [focused] on the uncomfortable truth. (Sülflohn 4)

Figure 16.6. Angela Hampel, *Come, Cassandra…* (*Komm, Kassandra…*), from the seven-print series *Kassandra*, 1984, lithograph, 52 × 70 cm. Kulturstiftung Sachsen-Anhalt, Kunstmuseum Moritzburg Halle (Saale). Photo: Kulturstiftung Sachsen-Anhalt © 2021 Artists Rights Society (ARS), New York / VG Bild-Kunst, Bonn.

Another reviewer also highlighted Hampel's Cassandra paintings: "in an ecstatic paint application, a furious explosion of color [*Farbfeuerwerk*] she identifies with the classical seer and warns against the sinister imperialist striving for war in the world and lets her embattled figures grow into a single existential cry of humanity" (Rüth).

In addition to paintings, Hampel also created a series of prints. In perhaps the best known of these (Figure 16.6), a woman crosses her arms in front of herself and pulls her long black hair away from her head in both directions. The hair on one side appears to end in a thick dread, while that on top of her head appears short and spiky. She meets our gaze with piercing eyes. Her right breast is exposed but largely disappears in the echo of triangular shapes. In some copies of the print, a short text appears in the bottom left quadrant of the image that gives the woman voice, an invitation that at the same time carries threatening undertones: "Come into the house… yes, you." In another print (Figure 16.7), Cassandra stares defiantly out of the picture frame at us, the viewers, while adjusting the end of her long ponytail. For Hampel, hair is a symbol of strength that often plays an important role in her art. When asked about it in a recent interview, she pointed out how women are often disempowered—from Rapunzel to those who slept with German soldiers during World War II—by having their hair cut off.[12]

Hampel later showed these prints to Christa Wolf, who promptly bought them for her collection (Interview). Wolf mentions the encounter in *One Day a Year* (*Ein Tag im Jahr*, 2008) for the year 1984, stating that she spread the seven prints across the floor to look at them and was pleased with "the Cassandra motif entirely contemporary. I am happy" (368). Wolf later expressed in greater detail her surprise and delight upon first seeing the young

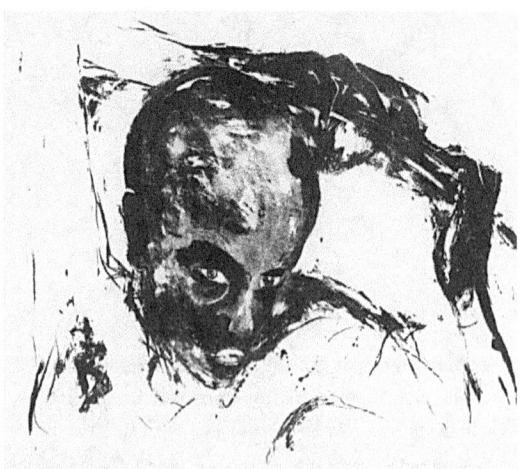

Figure 16.7. Angela Hampel, from the series *Cassandra (Kassandra)/Penthesilea*, 1984/85, lithograph, 52 × 60 cm. Kunstfonds Dresden © 2021 Artists Rights Society (ARS), New York / VG Bild-Kunst, Bonn.

punk-inspired figures, which were quite different from her own portrayal: "Angela's images gave me a push: yes, this is how a young Cassandra could be today: anticlassical, challenging, cheeky, angry, everything but resigned. But not without fate…" (Wolf and Wolf, *Malerfreunde* 179). Wolf saw in these images reflections of the young Hampel herself. These prints, rather than the paintings, are Hampel's best-known works on the topic today.

In another series of lithographs, Hampel focused on Penthesilea, the Amazon warrior queen who figures in *Cassandra* as an example of a woman who has adapted to masculine culture. In the novel, Cassandra describes Penthesilea as "sharp-eyed and sharp-tongued, she was a shade too strident for my taste. Her every appearance, her every sentence was a challenge to someone" (117); "Penthesilea with her wild black hair that stood out from her head in all directions" (115). Hampel brings these descriptions to life in her print series, *Zu Christa Wolfs Kassandra (From Christa Wolf's Cassandra)*. In one of the images (Figure 16.8), Penthesilea makes eye contact with the viewer while stroking the end of a blade. She sports a short, spiky mohawk and seems to be covered in the spots of a wild cat. The text on the left side of the image quotes a conversation between her and another woman that takes place in the novel. Arisbe asks, "And us? Will we also become butchers?" to which Penthesilea responds, "We will do what we must…" As in the other

Figure 16.8. Angela Hampel, *And us? (Und wir?)*, from the seven-print series *Cassandra (Kassandra)*, 1984, lithograph, 47.7 × 75.8 cm. Kulturstiftung Sachsen-Anhalt, Kunstmuseum Moritzburg Halle (Saale). Photo: Kulturstiftung Sachsen-Anhalt © 2021 Artists Rights Society (ARS), New York / VG Bild-Kunst, Bonn.

two images, the woman appears strong, if threatening, and in control. She makes eye contact with the viewer. And her punk-inspired hair suggests that she is part of the underground, a rebel.

From images inspired directly by the book, Hampel expanded into an exploration of women in myth more generally. As she stated in 2005, "Inevitably I came across Penthesilea, Medea ... and their mutilation within an almost exclusively male-defined world" (Hampel and Trende 16). In 1985–86, Hampel created three paintings focusing on Medea, a great sorceress from antiquity on whom Wolf would also focus in a book published ten years later, *Medea: A Modern Retelling* (*Medea: Stimmen*, 1996). She also looked at women's portrayal in the Bible, including Judith and Salome. Both of these women are frequent figures in the history of art. In sharp contrast to their usual portrayal as femme fatales, however, Hampel shows them as fierce, yet vulnerable individuals. They do not seduce us, the viewer. Rather, they appear as tragic figures, with the heavy use of blue in the canvases emphasizing melancholia.

Although inspired by Christa Wolf's *Cassandra*, Hampel's investigation of mythological figures from antiquity and the Bible also fits within a larger turn toward mythological subjects in East German art of the 1970s and 1980s. This trend resulted in part from the relaxation of cultural policy in the wake of Erich Honecker becoming head of the East German state in 1971 and in part from a desire to address current events through the guise of allegory. According to the (East) German art historian Peter Arlt, Cassandra first emerged in the visual arts of East Germany in the 1970s, with representations of her increasing in the early 1980s. In comparison to her male counterparts, like Icarus, however, there were relatively few images of Cassandra and even fewer artists creating them (Arlt 116). Other female figures such as Medea, Salome, and Judith do not appear on his list. Hampel's focus on strong female mythological figures in her work thus points to—and begins to address—a significant absence in the mythological subjects being created by visual artists in East Germany in the 1980s, an absence that reflects upon an issue that Wolf had addressed in *Cassandra*: the marginalization of the female perspective in patriarchal society.

With these Neo-Expressionist paintings of powerful women, Hampel gained both national and international prominence. Already in September 1986, just two years after first reading *Cassandra*, one of her paintings appeared on the cover of *Bildende Kunst*, the most important journal for the visual arts in the GDR. She also began exhibiting work in the West in these years, including at the prestigious Venice Biennale in 1988.[13] For several of these exhibitions, she was allowed to travel to West Germany, where she spoke with women about her work and about women's issues, and often brought back literature to read and share with her colleagues in the East.

These exchanges helped to radicalize her stance on equality, a stance that had first begun to take shape with her reading of *Cassandra*.

Like many women in East Germany, Hampel had taken employment and equality as givens. Over time, however, she began to realize that the rhetoric of equality did not match her own experiences. At the Dresden Academy of Fine Arts, for example, where she had studied painting, women were outnumbered by men as both students and teachers. She also had to face unwanted sexual advances and the assumption at art openings that she was the wife or girlfriend of an artist in the exhibition (Interview). Increasingly, she came to believe that women saw and experienced the world differently than men, a difference that was validated by her reading of Wolf's *Cassandra* with its criticism of patriarchy and emphasis on the value of a feminine perspective.

Reading *Cassandra* not only contributed to Hampel finding her artistic voice, it also helped to lay the foundation for feminist consciousness in East Germany, a development in which Hampel played an important role. In November 1988, for example, she gave a now-famous speech at the Tenth Congress of the Association of Visual Artists (Verband Bildender Künstler der DDR) in which she pointed out the absence of women in leadership positions within the organization. After citing a number of problems with current policies, she ended the speech by stating—in a sentence that could have been written by Christa Wolf—"The cause of our worldwide misery is the thousands of years of male dominance in politics, economics, culture, and religion... Without a compensating feminization of society, humanity will not have a future" (Hampel, Speech for the X. Kongreß des Verbandes 43).

In addition to giving speeches, Hampel began organizing meetings that brought women together on a regular basis to discuss their work and to suggest and read books together. These meetings led to the organization and implementation of the first Pleinair for Women Artists with Children in the GDR, which took place in May 1988. With the Artists' Association paying for childcare, the women in attendance were able to work together and exchange ideas for several days in a supportive, communal environment.

A year later, just shortly after the Berlin Wall fell, Hampel and twenty-two other women met at the Galerie Mitte in Dresden, where they decided to found their own association, the Dresdner Sezession 89. They held their founding exhibition six months later and have been together now for more than twenty-five years, enduring the radical changes of the post-Wall period, which included having to move three times, a fact reflected in the name of their current gallery, *galerie drei*. Committed to and run by women artists, the gallery regularly holds events and lectures—including one by Christa Wolf in 1991—as well as exhibitions of work by women artists on a six-week rotation.

Conclusion

Christa Wolf's *Cassandra* had a demonstrable impact on women artists in East Germany. As Susanne Altmann noted after interviewing many artists for the 2011 exhibition, *Entdeckt! Rebellische Künstlerinnen in der DDR* (Discovered! Rebellious Women Artists in the GDR), "most of the women interviewed had devoured [this book] immediately and attest today to the enormous meaning it had for them in the formation of a feminine understanding..." (5). Not everyone expressed its importance as explicitly in their art as did Quevedo and Hampel. Some simply established contact with Christa Wolf, writing letters to her about how much the book meant to them (Wolf and Wolf, *Unsere Freunde* 58–61). Nor were the results limited to iconographic ones. In the case of Hampel, *Cassandra* helped create an outspoken proponent for women's issues and thus led to concrete events that improved the quality of life for a number of women artists in East Germany, such as the Pleinair for Women Artists with Children in 1988 and the founding of the Dresdner Sezession 89. The latter, in particular, shows the enduring impact that *Cassandra* has had—and continues to have—on women artists, offering women in Dresden an organization for exhibiting artwork and discussing issues important to women up to the present day.[14]

Cassandra also led to strong relationships between the Wolfs and a number of artists, including Quevedo and Hampel. In 1993, Wolf wrote a text about Quevedo, describing a visit to her studio in Berlin and their discussion of a new painting in which they compared interpretations of the work (Wolf, "Die Zeichen der Nuria Quevedo" 123). She also told of how she looked at a painting of Quevedo's every evening as she sat down to dinner, an image painted from a spot in Barcelona where she herself had once stood and taken a photograph, thus emphasizing the commonalities they shared. Seven years later, in the opening speech at an exhibition of Quevedo's work, Wolf described the deepening of their relationship: "In the 1980s, we began to exchange short letters and cards about Quevedo's works for *Cassandra*, which, like all of her many works inspired by literary texts, are not illustrations. They showed me a deep, archaic layer of the figure" ("Ein Ring für Nuria Quevedo" 135). In the same speech, Wolf also spoke of how they shared the same birthday (18 March)—Wolf was nine years older—and how "every year I receive from her a drawn flower" on this day.

Cassandra also led to a close friendship and lasting working relationship between the Wolfs and Hampel. According to Wolf, who was twenty-seven years older than the artist, "Angela Hampel is close to me, although, no: because she is so different from me. And because then suddenly points of contact flare up" ("Gestalten im Spannungsfeld" 179). One senses the admiration Wolf had for Hampel, perhaps seeing her as a younger version of

Figure 16.9. Angela Hampel, painting on the cover of Christa Wolf's novel *Cassandra (Kassandra)*, dtv series © 2021 Artists Rights Society (ARS), New York / VG Bild-Kunst, Bonn.

herself, one not limited by the generational loyalties she herself faced as someone who had grown up during the Third Reich and lived in the GDR since its founding. In 1991, Wolf gave a speech for the Dresdner Sezession 89, where she spoke about the scandal surrounding *What Remains* (*Was bleibt?* 1990) with regard to the nature of her own relationship to the East German government. In the following year, 1992, Gerhard Wolf's Janus Press published the largest and most important catalog of Hampel's work to date, *Angela Hampel, 1982 bis 1992: Eine Künstlerin in Dresden* (An Artist in Dresden). He also published a calendar of original graphic work by her each year from 1994 to 1999. Hampel's work was used as well on the covers of at least seven of Christa Wolf's books in the Deutscher Taschenbuch Verlag (dtv) paperback series. According to Hampel, the three of them selected the

Figure 16.10. Angela Hampel, *Hope Dies Last* (*Die Hoffnung stirbt zuletzt*), 2012, mixed media, 100 × 70 cm. Photo: Angela Hampel. © 2021 Artists Rights Society (ARS), New York / VG Bild-Kunst, Bonn.

cover images from prints and drawings she had already created. For the cover of *Cassandra* (Figure 16.9), they chose an image—painted loosely in black, white, and red washes—of a young woman with dark hair holding an animal, perhaps a dog, while cautiously meeting the viewer's gaze.

At the memorial exhibition in 2012, Quevedo showed some of the prints she had created for *Cassandra* in the early 1980s. Hampel, too, showed work related to *Cassandra*, but they were drawings she had created in 2012. In one, *Hope Dies Last* (Figure 16.10), which makes reference to a statement Christa Wolf made in an interview in 2008 about the Prague Spring forty years earlier in which she spoke about hope being the last thing to die, Hampel shows a naked woman holding a white dove in her hand. The images are dark—black and white drawings covered in messy washes of brown ink. The figure looks sad, almost hopeless but for the bird, a reflection, perhaps in part, on the sadness of having lost a friend as well as a literary great. And yet the bird signals that hope has not died: Wolf's writings and the artwork they inspired live on.

April A. Eisman (MA Courtauld Institute of Art, Ph.D. University of Pittsburgh) is Associate Professor of Art History at Iowa State University. Her research focuses on contemporary art and theory with an emphasis on East German art and its reception. Publications include *Bernhard Heisig and the Fight for Modern Art in East Germany* (Camden House, 2018) and *Kunst in der DDR: 30 Jahre danach* (co-edited with Gisela Schirmer, Guernica Gesellschaft, 2020). Currently she is completing a monograph on Angela Hampel and co-curating an exhibition of Hampel's work at the Städtische Galerie Dresden that will open in May 2022.

Notes

The research for this text was funded by an American Association of University Women Postdoctoral Research Leave Fellowship and a grant from the Center for Excellence in the Arts and Humanities at Iowa State University. I would like to thank Grant Arndt, Gerald Fetz, Paula Hanssen, Sebastian Heiduschke, Patricia Herminghouse, and Thomas Maulucci for their feedback on earlier drafts of this text as well as Mathilde Arnoux at the Centre Allemand D'Histoire de l'Art in Paris where this text was first presented. I am also grateful to Angela Hampel and Nuria Quevedo for meeting with me to discuss their work.

1. The exhibition ran from 3 November to 2 December 2012.
2. In 1995 and 2010, Gerhard Wolf organized two art exhibitions from their personal collection, each with a substantial catalog that details their relationship to the artists. Gerhard Wolf was also involved with the 2012 exhibition.

3. The twelve artists were Ellen Fuhr, Annette Gundermann, Hartwig Hamer, Angela Hampel, Martin Hoffmann, Dorothee Helena Jacobs, Liz Mields-Kratochwil, Helge Leiberg, Gerda Lepke, Thomas K. Müller, Nuria Quevedo, and Günter Uecker. Nine of these artists grew up in East Germany.
4. *Cassandra* was published in 1983 in West Germany and 1984 in East Germany. According to Gerhard Wolf, they own so many works inspired by Cassandra that they could mount an exhibition of just those images alone (Wolf and Wolf, *Unsere Freunde* 63).
5. This exhibition explored the topic of Cassandra in German art since the nineteenth century.
6. There was a multi-issue discussion of *Cassandra* in *Sinn und Form* after one of its editors, Wilhelm Girnus, criticized Wolf for suggesting that "history is not at base a struggle between exploiter and exploited, but between men and women, or even more grotesquely, between 'male' and 'female' thinking" (Martens 102). *Sinn und Form* had published some excerpts of Wolf's "Frankfurter Vorlesungen" (Heft 1, 1983). Editor Girnus published his criticism of Wolf's contribution in the next issue, followed by Wolf's response in Heft 4. The next issue included comments from three readers and Girnus had the final word in Heft 5.
7. This is a common portrayal of Cassandra on Classical pottery.
8. Wolf states that she first encountered Quevedo's work at the latter's exhibition in Schwerin in 1981, and that they first met at a birthday party for Kurt Stern (Wolf, "Ein Ring für Nuria" 129).
9. Except where otherwise noted, all translations from German are mine.
10. A second edition appeared in 1987.
11. There were 120 numbered and signed copies of this portfolio.
12. Angela Hampel, interview by April A. Eisman, 4 March 2013, Dresden. Audio recording. Hereafter cited as "Interview."
13. Exhibitions in the West included Junge Künstler der DDR (1984), DDR Künstlerinnen (1985), Dresden Heute (1985), and Zeitvergleich '88.
14. According to co-founder Sigrun Hellmich, the Dresdner Sezession 89 has faced many struggles over the past two decades, but Angela Hampel was one of the members who always "persisted [even] when some in the group wanted to give up" (Hellmich 69).

Bibliography

Altmann, Susanne. *Entdeckt! Rebellische Künstlerinnen in der DDR*. Mannheim: Kunsthalle Mannheim, 2011.

Arlt, Peter. "Mythos—Phantasie—Wirklichkeit." *Bildende Kunst*, no. 3. 1985, pp. 115–17.

Emmerich, Wolfgang. "Autobiographical Writing in Three Generations of a GDR Family: Christa Wolf—Annette Simon—Jana Simon." *Twenty Years On: Competing Memories of the GDR in Postunification Germany*, edited by Renate Rechtien and Dennis Tate. New York: Camden House, 2011, pp. 141–57.

Engelmann, Gebhard, et al. "Zuschriften an Wilhelm Girnus." *Sinn und Form*, vol. 44, no. 5, September/October 1983, pp. 1087–96.

Girnus, Wilhelm. "Kein 'Wenn und Aber' und das poetische Licht Sapphos: Noch einmal zu Christa Wolf." *Sinn und Form*, vol. 44, no. 5, September/October 1983, pp. 1096–105.

———. "Wer baute das siebentorige Theben?" *Sinn und Form*, vol. 44, no. 2, March/April 1983, pp. 439–47.

Hampel, Angela. Speech for the X. Kongreß des Verbandes. *X. Kongress des Verbandes Bildender Künstler der Deutschen Demokratischen Republik, Berlin, 22–24.11.1988, Dokumenation I, Plenum*. Berlin: VBKD-ZV, 1988, pp. 41–43.

Hampel, Angela, and Klaus Trende. "'Das Herstellen von Schönheit—ein ungeheurer Akt': Angela Hampel—Klaus Trende—Ein Gespräch." *Frauensachen I: Angela Hampel. Malerei, Zeichnungen, Grafik*. Cottbus: Druckzone, 2005, pp. 15–21.

Hellmich, Sigrun. "Die Dresdner Sezession 89: Eine Künstlerinnengruppe zwischen Anspruch und Realität." *Dresdner Heft*, vol. 18, no. 2, 2000, p. 69.

Martens, Lorna. "Wolf on Matriarchy: Cassandra." *The Promised Land? Feminist Writing in the GDR*, edited by Lorna Martens. Albany: SUNY Press, 2007, pp. 99–108.

Quevedo, Nuria. *Grafik zu Kassandra von Christa Wolf: mit Tagebuchnotizen der Autorin / Nuria Quevedo*. Leipzig: Reclam, 1985.

Rüth, Barbara. "Innere Bewegtheit kraftvoller Bilder: 40. Studioausstellung im Berliner Alten Museum." *National Zeitung*, 23 July 1985.

Ruthe, Ingeborg. "Ausstellung Christa Wolf: Ihre Freunde, die Maler." *Berliner Zeitung*, 7 November 2012.

Sülflohn, Sabine. "Expressivität heute. Kabinettausstellung fünf [sic] junger Maler im Berliner Alten Museum." *Neue Zeit*, 8 July 1985, p. 4.

Wieg, Cornelia, editor. *Kassandra—Studioausstellung*. Halle: Staatliche Galerie Moritzburg, 1987.

Wolf, Christa. "Aus den 'Frankfurter Vorlesungen': Ein Brief über Eindeutigkeit und Mehrdeutigkeit, Bestimmtheit und Unbestimmtheit; Über sehr alte Zustände und neue Seh-Raster; Über Objektivität." *Sinn und Form*, vol. 44, no. 1, January/February 1983, pp. 38–62.

———. *Cassandra. A Novel and Four Essays*. Translated by Jan van Heurck. New York: Farrar, Straus & Giroux, 1984.

———. "Die Zeichen der Nuria Quevedo" (1993). *Malerfreunde Christa Wolf Gerhard Wolf—Leben mit Bildern*, by Christa Wolf and Gerhard Wolf. Halle: Projekte, 2010, pp. 123–27.

———. "Gestalten im Spannungsfeld—Angela Hampel" (2000). *Malerfreunde Christa Wolf Gerhard Wolf—Leben mit Bildern*, by Christa Wolf and Gerhard Wolf. Halle: Projekte, 2010, pp. 179–80.

———. *Medea: Stimmen*. Munich: Luchterhand Literaturverlag, 1996.

———. "Ein Ring für Nuria" (2000). *Malerfreunde Christa Wolf Gerhard Wolf—Leben mit Bildern*. Halle: Projekte, 2010, pp. 129–32.

———. "Ein Ring für Nuria Quevedo" (2000). *Rede, daß ich dich sehe*, by Christa Wolf. Berlin: Suhrkamp, 2012, pp. 134–39.
———. *Ein Tag im Jahr:1960–2000*. Frankfurt a.M.: Suhrkamp, 2008.
———. "Zur Information." *Sinn und Form*, vol. 44, no. 4, July/August 1983, pp. 863–66.
Wolf, Christa, and Gerhard Wolf. *Malerfreunde Christa Wolf Gerhard Wolf—Leben mit Bildern*. Halle: Projekte, 2010.
———. *Unsere Freunde, die Maler: Bilder, Essays, Dokumente*. Berlin: Gerhard Wolf Janus Press, 1995.

INDEX

Academy of Arts, Berlin, 92, 247
Achilles, 13, 245
Adelson, Leslie, 24
Adorno, Theodor, 7, 67, 115, 140
Alexander Platz, Berlin (4. November 1989), 143–144
"A Model of Experience," 78, 82, 159
alienations, 153, 161, 163, 222
Anasazi, 29–30
anxiety, 34, 46–48, 52, 188
anti-Fascism, 29, 67, 205–206
Anz, Thomas, 128, 130, 134
Applegate, Celia, 75
Arbeits- und Forschungsstelle Privatbibliothek C. und W. Wolf, 16
Aristotle/Aristotelian, 47, 57
Arnim, Achim von, 184
Arnim, Bettina von, 183
Arlt, Peter, 256
Assmann, Jan and Aleida, 23, 85, 87–90, 92, 100. See also Jan Assmann, 38, 57
Auf dem Weg nach Tabou/Parting for Phantoms, 158–163
"August," 11, 201–202, 207, 209–210
Auschwitz Trials, 220
author, authorship, authorial, authority, 35–36, 47–48, 51, 55
"Author's Dimension, The," 220
autobiography/autobiographical, 36, 39, 47, 49, 51–52, 55, 87
Autoritätsgläubige, 125

Bachmann, Ingeborg, 172, 178–180, 184
Bahr, Erhard, 52, 57, 163
Baier, Lothar, 159
Bartel, Kurt and Willi Bruckner, 218
Bathrick, David, 1, 4, 51–52, 57, 60, 69, 181
Becker, Wolfgang, "Good-Bye, Lenin," 232, 237–239

"Begrüssungsgeld" (Welcome Money), 228
Benjamin, Walter, 27, 34, 38–40, 113–115, 117, 161, 165, 175, 179, 181, 183–185
Benn, Gottfried, 1, 54
Berghahn, Daniela, 236
Bergman, Ingmar, 219, 249
Bergmann, 158, 162
Berlin, 10, 43, 49, 54, 56, 58, 181. *See also* Berlin Wall, 20, 22, 223, 232–233, 236–331, 245, 258
Berlin Academy in Weissensee, 247
Berliner Zeitung, 52, 59, 64, 129, 131
Bielefeld Conference, 1959/1964, 91
Biermann, Wolf, 163, 167, 176, 196. *See also* Wolf Biermann Affäre, 15
Birmele, Jutta, 73
Bitsburg, 66
Blickle, Peter, 75
"Blickwechsel" ("Change of Perspective"), 11, 201–202, 204–208, 210
"Blitz aus heiterem Himmel" (C. Wolf), 142
Bloch, Benjamin, 7
Bloch, Ernst, 81, 113–114, 119, 125
Böll, Heinrich, 73
Brandt Kreis, 225
Braun, Volker, 142, 149, 165, 169
Brecht, Bertolt, 22, 35, 67, 91, 113, 153, 188, 190, 194, 223
Bredel, Willi, 67–70
Bronfen, Elisabeth, 233–234, 237–238, 240, 244–245
Bund deutscher Mädel (League of German Girls), 1, 80
Burmeister, Brigitte, 142

California, 35–36, 38, 41, 43, 49, 52, 165, etc.
Carr, David, 104, 106
Carrow, Heiner, "Die Russen kommen," 224, 223–225

Central Committee of the SED "11th Plenary Session, 5
Chaplin, Charlie, 28
Charlioni, Anna, 69–70
Chernobyl, 7
Christa Wolf and the Cinema, 217
Christa Wolf: A Companion (Sonja E. Klocke and Jennifer Hosek), 16, 173, 184
Christa Wolf Handbuch: Leben—Werk—Wirkung (Carla Hilms and Ilse Nagelschmidt), 16
Christa Wolf Society, 147
City of Angels or, The Overcoat of Dr. Freud (*Stadt der Engel oder: The Overcoat of Dr. Freud*), 1, 6, 8–10, 21–22, 25–28, 34–39, 41–44, 46–49, 60, 65–68, 85, 89, 93–95, 104, 112–113, 117–118, 126, 129–130, 158–160, 161, 163–165, 173, 182, 185, 188–193, 196, 201, 206, 209
coat/overcoat, 34–59
cognitive psychology, 193
Cold War, 233, 238, 240–241
Critical Realism, 116
cross-reference, cross-mapping, 27, 234, 238, 240–241, 244

Dahn, Daniela, 141–143, 146–147, 222–225, 227, 229. *See also* Karlheinz Mund, 223–225
Damm, Sigrid, 142
death/dying, 39, 41–43, 45, 48–49, 53, 55–56
"depth," 102–103
DEFA Studios, 219, 223, 228, 235, 241
Der geteilte Himmel (*Divided Heaven/Divided Sky*), 4, 12, 22–23, 73, 118, 209, 217–218, 219–222, 226, 235–236
Deutschlandfunk, 67, 69
Die Zeit, 206
Dialogue, 35, 37, 45, 52, 58
Doctorow, Edgar L., 39
Döblin, Alfred, 67
Dream, 36, 42, 48, 57
Dresden Academy of Fine Arts, 257, 261
Dresdener Sezession, 91, 245, 258
Duras, Margaret, 10, 217–218, 221–224
Dwyer, Anna, 111

East German Feminism, 139. *See also* Brigitte Reumann and Gerti Tetzner, 140–141
East German Literature, 203
East German Ministry for State Security, 94, 96
Eigler, Friederike, 24
"Ein Gespräch," 112, 114
Ein Tag im Jahr, 1960–2000 (One Day a Year), 6, 21, 85, 88, 103, 105, 129, 131, 148, 164, 168, 205–215, 255, 258
Ein Tag im Jahr im Neuen Jahrhundert (One Day a Year in the New Century), 164, 168
Eleventh (11th) Plenary 93, 96, 139
empathy, 204, 209–210
environmentalism, 225
exile/exilic, 34–40, 43, 48–50, 52, 55–58
Expressionist Debate, 113, 137
Expressivität Heute (Exhibit Berlin 1985), 253

fear, 35–36, 42, 45, 48
Fehervary, Helen, 113–114, 116. *See also* Fehervary, Helen and Sara Lennox, 224–225
Feminist Modernism, 140
fetish, fetishism, fetishistic, 35–37, 43–45, 49–51, 53, 56–57
Feuchtwanger, Lion, 67
fiction/fictional/fictionality, 35–36, 39–41, 43, 46–47, 49–52, 56
Fleischer, Lutz, 253
Fleming, Paul, 45, 54
Fourth Dimension, (Christa Wolf), 45, 54, 102, 104
Frankfurt Poetics Lectures, 114, 116, 200
Frankfurter Allgemeine Zeitung, 202, 206
Freud, Sigmund, "Freudian Model, 10, 65–68. *See also* disturbance and memory, 49
Open Letter to Romain Foland, 49
overcoat, 34–37, 40–42, 44, 56, 193
paradigm, 193
psychoanalysis, 189, 192
remembering, 46
"Für unser Land" (Christa Wolf), 143, 145, 227, 231–232

Galerie Forum Amalienpark, Berlin Pankow, 244
Ganger, Carmen, "La Ciudad de Los Angeles o El abrigo dei Dr. Freud," 37
Gauck Behörde, 55, 64, 66
GDR Writers' Conference 1959, 90
GDR Socialism, 219
Gegenwartsliteratur, 100
Gelbart, Larry, 37
Genette, Gerard, 101, 103
Gensel, Carsten, 22, 57–58
German-Jewish emigration, 27, 35, 40, 54, 56
German reunification, 143, 161, 164, 209
(German) Romanticism, 75, 172–173, 175–177, 179
Gerstenberger, Katharina and Patricia Herminghouse, 24
Getty Research Institute (Center), 4, 8, 11, 60, 65, 89, 92, 94, 130, 132, 146–147, 160, 190, 194–195
Giebe, Hubertus, 253
Goethe, Johann von, *Faust*, 172, 174–176, 181
Gogol, Nikolai, 39–40, 42, 45
"Good Bye, Lenin," 12
Grass, Günter, 13–15, 125, 127, 132, 134, 205–206, 209–210, 236–237, 239, 242. See also Grass, *Im Krebsgang/Crabswalk*, 205 and *Die Blechtrommel/The Tin Drum*, 205
Greiner, Ulrich, 128, 130, 190
Grobbel, Miochael, 172, 185

Günderrode, Karoline von, 128, 161–162, 166, 171, 175–176, 179
Gusdorf, Georges, 86
Gusner, Iris, 229

Hall, Barnaby, 54
Halbwachs, Maurice, 87, 89
Hampel, Angela, 13, 244–245, 251–258
Harich, Wolfgang, 28
Hegewald, Heidrun, 246, 251
Heimat, 5, 73–74, 76–82. See also Heimatkunde, 73 and Heimatrecht, 74
Heisig, Johannes, 253
Henckel von Donnersmark, Florian, 219

Henn, Marianne, 175
Hermlin, Stephan, 125
heterochronicity, 99–112
Hetzkampagne (smear campaign), 128
Heym, Stefan, 225, 229
"Hiroshima mon amour," 12
Historians' Debate, 28, 66
Hofer, Karl, 246
Hofmannsthal, Hugo von, "Chandos Brief", 48–49
Hölderlin, Friedrich, 13, 94, 147
holocaust, 27–28, 67, 205, 237, 240
Honecker, Erich, 91, 256
Hoover, Edgar J. (FBI), 28
Horkheimer, Max, 22–23, 140
Hörnigk, Therese, 68, 147, 161, 218, 220–222, 224–226, 236, 240
Humboldt Universität Berlin, 16
humor, 230, 225–226
Husserl, Edmund, 104
Huyssen, Andreas, 26–27, 113, 125

IM/Inoffizieller Mitarbeiter, 3, 64, 66, 96, 125, 127–131, 133, 160, 178, 191–192
"inability to mourn", 3. See also "inability to write," 48
intertextuality, 23, 39, 40, 42

Jablkowska, Joanne, 185
Jameson, Frederic, 113
Janka, Walter, 28, 142, 144, 219, 223

Kapczynski, Jennifer, 240, 244
Kassandra/Cassandra, 12, 21, 23, 126–127, 138, 140–141, 148, 161, 175–177, 180–722, 184, 189, 192, 194, 244–258
Kaufmann, Hans, 6, 88, 91–92, 115, 153, 161, 196, 235
Kaute, Brigitte, 173, 178
Kein Ort Nirgends/No Place on Earth, 21, 23, 113, 118, 148, 158, 161–162, 176, 180, 244
Kindheitsmuster/Pattern of Childhood, 2–3, 5, 8–9, 11, 15, 21, 23, 28, 34, 36, 42–43, 45, 49, 65, 74, 76, 78, 80–82, 85, 89, 92–96, 103–104, 113, 118, 158–520, 201, 203–204, 206–210, 244

Kirsch, Sarah, 23, 141, 143
Kleist, Heinrich, 161–162, 171, 176, 232, 236
Klocke, Sonja, 233
Kohlhaase, Wolfgang, 220
Kollwitz, Käthe, 13
Königsdorf, Helga, 244
Körpersprache, 25
Kristeva, Julia, 222, 226
Kuhn, Anna, 21, 27, 48, 51, 53, 56, 58
Kuhrt, Rolf, 246
Kunert, Günter, 67, 69
Kunert, Joachim, 218

Lance, Alain and Renate Lance, *Villes des Anges: Ou The Overcoat of Dr. Freud*, 37, 59
Landsberg an der Warthe/Gorzow (L. now called G), 73, 76, 78–82, 203, 207
language/linguistic, 34, 37–95, 46–48, 52
Lazarus, Richard and "Susan Folkmart, "Late Style," 43, 49, 52, 55, 58
Leeder, Karen, 15
Leibhaft/In the Flesh, 10, 21, 24–25, 126, 130, 172–175, 76, 180–182, 184–185, 233, 236
Lejeune, Philippe, 86
Lennox, Sara, 234, 238
Lentz, Michael, 56, 58
Lenz, Jakob Michael Reinhold, 113
Levy, Daniel, 3. *See also* Levy, Daniel and Natan Snaider, 26–27
Libuda, Walter, 253
Literaturstreit/Literature Debate, 13, 24, 63, 136, 138, 144, 146, 148, 194, 232, 228
London, 35, 40, 43–44, 50, 52, 55, 57–58
London Freud Museum, 4, 43
London *Independent*, 15
Los Alamos, 30
Los Angeles, 25–27, 35, 37, 40, 43, 49, 52, 55–57, 59, 195–196
Lubjanka, 68
Lukács, Georg, 7, 89, 110–112, 114–129, 137–139
Luxemburg, Rosa, 139, 180, 184

Magenau, Jörg, 22, 112, 118, 144–145, 199

Mann, Heinrich, 67, 199
Mann, Thomas, 35, 67, 195, 205
"Margarete," 49, 60, 64, 126, 160, 178, 188. *See also* "ängstliche Margarete", 182, 188, 191–192, 197, 201
Maron, Monika, 125, 127
Martens, Lorna, 245, 249
Marxist aesthetics, 112–114
Massey, Doreen, 101, 103, 105
Mayer, Hans, 112, 114
Maiziere, Lothar de, 146
McGrane, Sally, 14
Medea, Stimmen, 21, 23–24, 126, 130, 146, 158, 163, 175–177, 180–182, 184, 217
memory, 1, 60, 65, 158, 201, 207, 209–211, 220–223. *See also* multi-directional memory, 206
memory amnesia, 125
memory pattern, 87
memory process, 172
memory scenes, 172
metafiction(al)/metanarrative, 50
sense memory, 89
metonymy/metonymic, 43, 50, 53, 55, 56
Michelis, Angelica, 51–52
Minden, Michael, 53, 58
mnenomic, 34, 37, 40, 42–44, 47, 49, 54
Mohr, Heinrich, 221
Molinaro, Ursule, 53, 59
Molnar, Michael, 40, 43, 53, 55, 56
Morgner, Irmtraud, 133, 140, 142
Moskauer Novelle, 4, 7, 147, 218
mourning, 221–223
Mühe, Ulrich, 219
Müller, Heiner, 120, 165, 172

Nachdenken über Christa T./The Quest for Christa T., 4, 8, 10, 64, 85, 91, 126, 129, 139, 148, 153, 201, 209, 218, 220, 223–224
naturalism, 118
Narrative Fetishism, 3, 66
National Socialism, 21, 23, 35, 66, 73–76, 79, 82, 158, 161, 174, 178, 195, 205–209, 213
Nazi/Nazi propaganda/Nazi ideology, 5, 67, 75, 79–81, 103, 204, 237

Neruda, Pablo, "Book of Questions," 39
Neues Deutschland, 238, 242
Neutra, Richard, 4, 35, 40–41, 65
New Subjectivity, 127, 129
Niven, Bill, 203
Nunan, Anna, 85–86, 47

Oder-Neisse River, 39, 76–77
Oedipus of Thebes, 39, 51
Okpako, Branwen, *Der Flucht Medea* (The Curse of Medea), 217, 221, 223, 226–228, 230–231
"Otherness" or "Words of an Other", 38–43, 46, 55–56

Pacific Palisades, 63, 161
Pain and Trail of Pain, 171, 173–174
perpetrator's file (Täterakte), 52, 160
Peterson, Tracie, "City of Angels," 37
Phantasmagoria/Phantassmagoric/Phantom, 44, 50, 55
Pinkert, Anke (Film and Memory), 235, 241
pleasure principle, 53, 66
Plenary, 11th, Assembly of the Central Committee, 93, 137, 139, 218, 220, 222–224, 228
Plenzdorf, Ulrich, 219
Poetic License, 47
Politbüro, 89
Pormeister, Eve, 51–52, 58
Pound, Ezra ("Exile's Letter"), 48, 58
Prague Spring, 161
presence/present, 35–36, 38–39, 42–43, 45–46, 48–51, 55–56
pronoun/person(a), 35, 38–40, 43, 45–48, 50–52, 54, 56
psychanalysis/psychoanalytic (association), 34, 36, 38, 40, 45–46, 49–52, 54–47

Quevedo, Nuria, 13, 244–250, 258

Rappolt, Hedwig, 53, 59
Reader and Writer (Lesen und Schreiben), 90, 101, 104, 115–118, 120, 138, 140, 165, 169
Real Existing Socialism, 60, 165
Reich-Ranicki, Marcel, 190

repression, 36, 40, 52, 54
Resch, Margit, 14, 111
resistance, 44–48
Resnais, Alain, 12
Reumann, Brigitte, 141
Ricour, Paul, 101, 103
Romanticism/Romantics, 138, 171, 175–176, 179–180, 183
Rosenberg, Robert, *Stadt der Engel*, 37, 58
Rothberg, Michael, 3, 27–30, 205–206

Said, Edward, 55, 58
"Sand and Pines," 73
Santa Monica, 22, 26–27, 191–192, 194–195
Santner, Eric, 3, 66, 68
Schirrmacher, Frank, 145, 147, 190
Schneider, Peter, 125, 127
"Schreiben im Zeitbezug" (Christa Wolf), 67, 142
Schubert, Helga, 143
Schubert, Katja, 209
Schutz, Helga, 142
Schwarzbauer, Heike, 59
Scribner, Charity, 180–181, 184, 239–240, 140
Searls, Damion, CITY OF ANGELS OR, THE OVERCOAT OF DR. FREUD, 37
Sebald, W.G., 205, 209. See also Sebald's *Luftkrieg und Literatur/On the National History of Destruction*, 205
SED, 9, 137, 180
Seghers, Anna, 86, 112, 114, 116, 118, 137–138, 140, 218–219, 223–224
"Selbstversuch" (Christa Wolf), 140, 223–225
Shakespeare, William, 42, 50, 54, 58
Shoah (the), 23
Silberling, Brad, 37, 58
Simon, Annette, 54
Simon, Jana, 112, 114, 168
Simon, Rainer, 218–219
sincerity, 125–126
Smale, Catherine, 173, 177, 184
Smith, Sidone, 87, 89–90

Socialist Realism, 116, 138, 171, 183. *See also* Zhdenovian Socialist Realism, 116
Sommerstück (Christa Wolf), 23, 137
Sozialistische Menschengemeinschaft, 136, 158, 162
Spaßkultur, 24, 131
Spiegel, Der, 134, 188–191, 192–195
Staatliche Galerie Moritzberg, Halle, 244
Staatsdichter, 24
Stalin, Stalinism, 3
Stasi/Stasi file, 3–4, 8–9, 15, 64–66, 94, 105, 110, 160, 178, 192, 219, 238. *See also* IM, 94, 160
  Stasi informer, 129, 182
  Stasi victim, 125
Steiner, Roland, 224–225
Stephan, Alexander, 220
Stiftung Archiv der Akademie der Künste Berlin, 16
Stillhalte Literatur, 127
Stobart, Craig, 58
Störfall: Nachrichten eines Tages/Accident: A Day's News, 7
subjective authenticity, 4, 6, 7, 86–87, 88–89, 91, 93, 110–111, 115–118, 137, 162, 210
Sündenbock (scape goat), 130
Sznaider, Nathan, 3, 26–27

Tetzner, Gerti, 141
therapy/therapeutic/therapist, 34–35, 45–47, 50, 54, 56
Third Reich, 2, 26, 78, 103, 237
Till Eulenspiegel, 218–219
time/times/and time and narration, 8, 101, 104–105
Trail of Pain, 17
transference/transferential, 37, 40, 42, 46–53, 58
transnational memory, 21–22, 26, 27
trauma, 207–209
Trauerarbeit, 4, 66

Ulbricht, Walter, 89, 137, 139
uncanny, 34–37, 42–43, 53, 57
unconscious(ness), 34, 37, 46, 48
"Unsere Freunde," Galerie Mitte, 258

Vaihinger, Hans, 46
Verband Bildender Künstler der DDR, 257
Vergangenheitsbewältigung, 2, 21, 54
Vergegenwärtigung, 2, 21, 95
Vinke, Hermann, 52, 58
Volksgemeinschaft, 79
von der Emde, Silke, 206

Walser, Martin, 73, 129
Wander, Maxi, 23, 25, 139, 141
Was bleibt (What Remains?), 8–9, 23–24, 99, 106, 110, 126–128, 130–131, 144–145, 161, 164
Weigel, Sigrid, 25
Weimar under the Palms (or: Weimar am Pazifik), 35, 161
Weinert, Erich, 67
Wenders, Wim, 63
Wendish, Trak, 253
Werfel, Franz, 67
"Wider den Schlaf der Vernunft", 129
Wiederspiegelungs Theorie (Reflexion theory), 115, 138
Winkler, Marcus, 175, 177, 179, 184
Winnicot, Donald W., 47, 50
Wischniewski, Klaus, 224
Wisniewski, Roswitha, 80
Wittgenstein, Ludwig, 54, 58
Wolf, Gerhard, 144, 146, 148, 201–202, 206, 210, 218–220, 224, 244, 248. *See also* Wolf und Wolf, *Malerfreunde*, 247–255
Wolf, Konrad, 12, 217–220, 221–222, 224, 245. *See also* "Der Schmetterling," 218, 223, 226
women artists in East Germany, 244
World War I, 75
World War II, 203, 209
"Wortwelten Bildwelder: Malenfreunde zum Gedenken von Christa Wolf, 244
Wrage, Henning, 238, 6, 99, 100, 106

"Zeitgenossenschaft", 6, 99–100, 106, 108
"Zeitschleifen" (time loops), 217
Zeplin, Rosemarie, 142
"Zerstörungslust" (death libido), 193

www.ingramcontent.com/pod-product-compliance
Lightning Source LLC
Chambersburg PA
CBHW071152070526
44584CB00019B/2755